T0199211

Cultivating an Ecological Conscience

CULTIVATING
— AN —
ECOLOGICAL
CONSCIENCE

*Essays from a
Farmer Philosopher*

FREDERICK L. KIRSCHENMANN

Edited by Constance L. Falk

COUNTERPOINT

BERKELEY

Copyright © 2010 by The University Press of Kentucky.
All rights reserved under International and
Pan-American Copyright Conventions.

Library of Congress Cataloging-in-Publication Data is available.

ISBN: 978-1-58243-752-1

Cover photo by Constance L. Falk

Printed in the United States of America

COUNTERPOINT
2560 Ninth Street, Suite 318
Berkeley, CA 94710
www.counterpointpress.com

For my mother, whose profound respect for all of God's creation planted in me the first seeds of appreciation for reverence; and for my father, who first instilled a land ethic into my conscience. This book is also for David Vetter, who showed me the way to appreciate and practice both of these principles on a real farm.

A land ethic, then, reflects the existence of an ecological conscience, and this in turn reflects a conviction of individual responsibility for the health of the land. Health is the capacity of the land for self-renewal. Conservation is our effort to understand and preserve this capacity.
—Aldo Leopold, *A Sand County Almanac*

Let ours be a time remembered for the awakening of a new reverence for life, the firm resolve to achieve sustainability, the quickening of the struggle for justice and peace, and the joyful celebration of life.
—Last paragraph of the Earth Charter, available at
   www.earthcharter.org

Contents

Contents

Contents

Acknowledgments

All of my friends and colleagues have, of course, been a vital and integral part of my journey, and without them I doubt I would ever have recognized the richness of my own experience. With respect to this particular collection of essays, I owe a special debt of gratitude to one friend and colleague, without whom the essays would have continued to be separate moments in the journey without any order or symmetry. Dr. Constance Falk, New Mexico State University, took an interest in my work a few years ago and encouraged me to publish it. I remarked that I did not have the time, interest, or skill to perform the monumental task of preparing these essays for publication. Without her enormous contribution of time, this book would never have seen the light of day. Without her skillful editing and arrangement, these essays would have remained disjointed. Readers interested in learning more about unpublished materials referenced in the text can contact me at leopold1@iastate.edu.

Family members, naturally, are always part of one's life and work. I have had the special good fortune to receive consistent inspiration and insight from my daughter, Annie, and my son, Damon, who have always loved the farm and have taken deep personal interest in developing philosophical and practical ideas to improve the ecological soundness of our food and agriculture systems. My wife, Carolyn, has similarly enriched my understanding of ecological health and has contributed immensely to my understanding of ecological eating. She taught me that it is important to first ask how we can maintain the health of the ecosystem in which we live and *then* ask how to eat healthily from it.

—F. L. K.

The editor expresses her appreciation to Sylvia Beuhler, administrative assistant at New Mexico State University, for scanning documents and keeping me on track; Norman Wirzba, Candace Chaney, and Stephen Wrinn at the University Press of Kentucky, whose gentle, patient guidance made this process as painless as possible; Brent Winter, for his expert copyediting; Joanie Quinn, marketing director of the New Mexico Organic Commodity Commission, for inviting Fred Kirschenmann to be the keynote speaker at the 2006 New Mexico Organic Conference, for reading an early draft of the introduction, and for being a great friend; Ethel Heinle, office coordinator at International Certification Services in Medina, North Dakota, for forwarding copies of Kirschenmann's papers from the 1990s; and Julie Moore for providing expert help in tracking down reference material. My greatest heartfelt thanks go to Fred Kirschenmann for giving me the opportunity to edit this volume.

—C. L. F.

Editor's Introduction

In the mid-1970s, Fred Kirschenmann told a class of graduating seniors that education is like a baseball mitt. You might think mitts are to protect your hand and education is to help you get a good job, he said, but the true purpose of baseball mitts is to extend your reach so you can catch balls you would otherwise miss. Likewise, education helps you extend your imagination to catch opportunities otherwise beyond your grasp (see Kirschenmann's essay in this volume, "What's an Education For?"). Three decades later, Kirschenmann continues unveiling basic principles to help us grasp the challenges we face.

In the 1970s, energy shortages, hunger, poverty, and pollution appeared to be humankind's main problems. It seemed we could solve them if we just deployed the right technologies. We now know these crises were early warnings of the human-induced, planetary-scale degradation of all life. Fundamentally, our predicament can be traced to the gradual shift in our self-image from being part of nature to being separate from and conquerors of the natural world. According to Kirschenmann, our fascination with technologies now distracts us from recognizing two important human shortcomings: our belief that we can solve problems without nature, and our habit of ignoring the consequences of our technologies in the complex natural world.

This volume of selected works spans his career, a career marked above all by a concern for ecological priorities and a conviction that people can and will make a difference if they understand the relevant issues and pertinent choices. Kirschenmann's themes are grounded in his experience on his North Dakota farm, where he grappled with the sometimes harsh rhythms of nature and inherited his father's legacy of independent thinking and deep appreciation for the value of healthy soil.

Kirschenmann sometimes spoke of an early memory in which he and his father were in the car returning from church services. In their church, parishioners had the practice of standing up and talking openly about their faith. On the way home, his father railed about the hypocrisy and false piety of the people spouting off in church when he knew they could not be trusted on Monday morning in the business world. From that early lesson, Fred Kirschenmann began his career of exploring ethical choices, challenging authority and doctrines, and poking holes in bad policies, poor logic, and official practice.

Like the other two pillars of agrarian philosophy of his generation, Wendell Berry and Wes Jackson, Kirschenmann has been one of the most respected critics of the industrial food and farming paradigm of the late twentieth century. Along with Berry and Jackson, Kirschenmann has looked to the wisdom of Aldo Leopold and Sir Albert Howard for inspiration and guidance. Another, less-known influence was Liberty Hyde Bailey, who also guided Leopold's thinking. A common thread in the works of these writers is their awareness of the deleterious effects of the industrial system, not only on how we grow food but also on human consciousness. Industrialism, powered by fossil fuels and reductionist scientific methods, has enabled us to think we have mastered nature and can take from it what we need and excrete back into it without consequences.

All three of these agrarian leaders have emphasized systems thinking and the importance of caring for the soil, land, and community. Like Jackson, Kirschenmann embraces technologies when he thinks they can enhance the regenerative capacities of ecosystems; Berry, on the other hand, has been much more suspicious of technology. Jackson has perhaps been less sanguine than Kirschenmann about humanity's ability to embrace planetary survival as a primary concern. Berry's gifts have been his prodigious literary output and his deep philosophical exploration of agrarianism. Jackson has reconceptualized midwestern agriculture, applying science to create a perennial polyculture system that mimics the prairie—a completely original paradigm for farming.

Kirschenmann's gift has been his relentless organizing and public speaking. In 1986, he was invited to testify before a congressional committee about the U.S. Department of Agriculture's (USDA) Low-Input Sustainable Agriculture program, a forerunner of the current Sustainable Agriculture Research and Education grant program. Since giving that impassioned talk, Kirschenmann's calendar has been filled with requests by groups across the country to talk about organic and sustainable agriculture. More than twenty years later, he was invited to testify before a congressional committee about the threat that transgenic crops pose to organic farmers (see "Is the USDA Accounting for the Costs to Farmers from Contamination Caused by Genetically Engineered Plants?").

Also like Berry and Jackson, Kirschenmann's work is based on a lifetime attachment to a specific farm and ecosystem, "becoming native" to a place, in Jackson's oft-quoted words. Even as Kirschenmann plies his trade as national extension agent and public intellectual, he maintains close ties to his family farm in North Dakota, helping with advice about combine maintenance, marketing strategies, cattle watering, harvest schedules, and general morale. He returns to the farm every summer for "tractor therapy." In the article "A Journey toward Sustainability," written for this volume, he provides an update on the family farm situation, which was profiled in Miranda Productions's award-winning 1996 film, *My Father's Garden.*

Kirschenmann has long argued that industrial methods cannot "feed the world." His response goes beyond directly challenging the science (or lack of it) behind the claim that production should be intensified to increase yields. He now is much more concerned about the paradigm that gives rise to such flawed reasoning. Quoting the work of entomologist Joe Lewis, Kirschenmann said this paradigm uses a "single-tactic therapeutic intervention" approach to solving problems. Unfortunately, reductionist therapeutic interventions usually aggravate problems because we use them without understanding systems dynamics ("Questioning Biotechnology's Claims and Imagining Alternatives"). This same issue plagues our efforts in medicine, agriculture, criminal justice, and social work.

Because reductionist, linear, and Cartesian control efforts have failed to create just, fair, humane, and healthy societies, nongovernmental organizations have proliferated. Paul Hawken has characterized nongovernmental organizations as the Earth's immune-system response to humanity's ecocide.[1] However, this response has centuries of globalized pillaging to catch up with.

Kirschenmann's efforts as part of the immune system are evident in the many organizations for which he has provided leadership. For example, he helped create the Northern Plains Sustainable Agricultural Society in 1979 ("A Transcendent Vision"). In 1980, he helped found Farm Verified

Organic, an international organic certification company and the first U.S. certification organization to obtain accreditation by the International Federation of Organic Agriculture Movements.

He was also instrumental in the creation of the USDA's National Organic Program, having served on the National Organic Standards Board during the critical years in which the USDA considered genetic engineering, sewage sludge, and irradiation to be potentially acceptable parts of an organic standard. Two recent instances where Kirschenmann provided institutional leadership by creating connections are the Agriculture of the Middle project and the Stone Barns Center for Food and Agriculture. The Ag of the Middle effort focuses on the plight of midsize family farms, whose disappearance from the landscape are of great concern ("A Pig's Tale: Marketing Stories for New Value Chains" and "A Bright Future for 'Farmers of the Middle'"). Kirschenmann's contribution to the direction and management at Stone Barns is elucidated in the article "Rethinking Food," which he wrote exclusively for this volume.

The essence of prayer is paying close attention, according to poet W. H. Auden, who struggled with faith and religious belief.[2] If prayer means paying such close attention to someone or something outside yourself that you forget your own ego, then Kirschenmann has been praying his whole life—not an inappropriate activity for an ordained minister with a Ph.D. in historical theology. His body of work is the prayer of someone focusing on the problems of farming, the soil, the planet, and humanity.

Kirschenmann demonstrated that his ego is secondary after he was unceremoniously removed from the directorship of the Leopold Center for Sustainable Agriculture in 2005. His reaction was to focus on the job at hand, not on his title or the opportunity for justifiable self-pity. Complaining about things is not his style, a legacy of the Russian-German immigrant culture in North Dakota that disparaged a picky eater as "schnagich" ("The Pleasure of Good Eating").

The fame garnered recently by other writers addressing the topics of food and agriculture is immaterial to him. He celebrates their success, incorporates their thinking into his own, and recommends their works in his talks. His generosity to other writers shows up in the many forewords and introductions he has written ("Foreword to *Farming with the Wild: Enhancing Biodiversity on Farms and Ranches*").

Paying close attention was a necessity if Kirschenmann was to convert his father's 3,100-acre farm in North Dakota to a farm that was not only certified organic but biodynamic, and this in 1977, when few people knew what those terms meant. He embraced the challenge after his student, David Vetter, explained organic farming principles to him ("A Transcendent Vision"). Put yourself in Kirschenmann's shoes: You are a college dean, destined to ascend the ranks of academic administration, definitely presidential material for a major university. Your father, a North Dakota farmer who had urged you to get an education so you could leave the farm, is in declining health. What do you do?

If you are paying attention, you listen to a student with ideas about enhancing the soil. You seize the opportunity to participate in the last years of your parents' lives and experiment with a new type of agriculture, even though virtually every person in the community you left behind—and in the one you returned to—thinks you must be daft ("Pilgrimage to a Barnyard"). Paying close attention involves continuity and dedication, enabling Kirschenmann to accumulate long-term relationships like pollen on a honeybee. Because of his seemingly effortless cultivation of lifelong friends, we can catch up with David Vetter in these essays. In 2002, Vetter had developed a line of organic open-pollinated corn, but his corn was being contaminated by a nearby crop of genetically engineered corn. Kirschenmann used this story to illustrate the dangers of biotechnology in his 2002 article "Questioning Biotechnology's Claims and Imagining Alternatives."

Kirschenmann's message is now informed not only by his faith and farming experiences but also by advances in scientific understanding. His basic themes of systems thinking, care for the soil, and an ecological perspective are now buttressed by the latest findings in science and other fields. He has explored relevant topics in soil science, energy and thermodynamics, history, philosophy, ecological economics, climate change, sustainable design, effective management, agro-ecology, and emergence as the primary quality of biological systems. Thus, he no longer talks about saving the planet as he did three decades ago; he now recognizes that we cannot save the planet in terms of preserving "things as they are" because biotic systems are a "web of relationships full of emergent properties." At best, we can "engage the biotic community in ways that enhance its capacity for renewal" ("What Constitutes Sound Science?"). This really is our best hope for averting the ecological crises that threaten biotic life (ours included) on the planet, if in fact we still have time to do so.

Although Kirschenmann has kept pace with scientific advances, this book is mainly meant to be a story of a journey. The book is structured thematically but also chronologically within three sections, so that the journey's evolution can be appreciated. Kirschenmann's farming philosophy, experience, and practices are grouped in the section "Working at Home: Lessons from Kirschenmann Family Farms." The development of his critique of industrial farming and food production is presented in the second section, "Cracks in the Bridges: Inspecting the Industrial Food System." Kirschenmann's efforts to create and lead new organizations are presented in the third part, "Envisioning an Alternative Food and Farming System."

Organizing essays written over time provides an interesting window into the evolution of someone's thinking, the evolving body of literature being read, and the impact of life experiences. In Kirschenmann's case, it is a journey that I think others will find valuable, particularly beginning writers who may labor under the notion that writers emerge fully polished. The earlier essays were written at the beginning of his career as a farmer, and they are mostly devoted to the production strategies involved in making the transition from conventional agriculture to a sustainable system. As he continued to farm, write, teach, and think, he developed more comprehensive and inclusive ideas about agriculture and ecology, and the later essays reflect this shift. Even some of Kirschenmann's most recent thinking continues to evolve. For example, throughout much of his writing he contrasts "maximum" production with "optimum" production. More recently, however, he abandons "optimum" production in favor of "resilient" production, a shift inspired by the resilient-thinking literature and further observations on his farm ("Redefining Sustainability: From 'Greening' to Enhancing Capacity for Self-Renewal" and "A Journey toward Sustainability").

In the late 1970s, the nation was reeling from the first set of geopolitical peak-oil crises. In a commencement address to high-school seniors in 1977, Kirschenmann said the reason people need to extend their wisdom and imagination was to "save the planet for ourselves and our children." He told the graduates to analyze the big ideas that shape our lives because there is "not much time left to rethink our basic relationship with the environment and the people in it." He urged those seniors to find a career that is gratifying at a deep level, not just financially remunerative, advice that has not grown stale with time. By the end of the first decade of the twenty-first century, those high-school students will be approaching their fiftieth birthday. I am curious to know if they took Kirschenmann's message to heart and found careers that help support the inner connectedness of all life. Certainly his work has done so. The final essay in this volume, "Using What We Know to Make a Difference," is his recent effort to provide helpful guidance on how to respond to the challenges we face.

In 2009, Kirschenmann still bristles with the same sense of urgency that characterized his early work, but he always takes the time to engage people in honest conversation, because he believes people make the best choices when they explore problems together. He answers all e-mails and phone calls he receives, because he says that if people take the time to contact him, he should respond. He notes that

> in a conversation there is never any single right or wrong response. This is where creativity comes in. The alternatives that exist depend in large part on the alternatives we encourage. Good science is inventive. . . .
>
> . . . Conversation always takes place in the particular. We cannot have a conversation with an abstraction. We can only have conversations with particular individuals. . . .
>
> Conversation is a useful metaphor for describing good science and good soil management, although the science of the industrial world has been a monologue rather than a dialogue. ["What Constitutes Sound Science?"]

I invite readers of this volume to engage neighbors, families, friends, and colleagues in creative conversations about the interconnectedness of all life and how we might enhance the capacity for renewal in our soils, farms, and communities.

Preface

I have never written anything with the intent that it be published as a collection of essays. Most of what I have written over the years has been in response to requests for papers that were given as speeches or published as articles in magazines or journals, or to address issues that concerned me. Accordingly, this collection may appear disjointed.

When I reflect upon my writing, however, I see that it represents a personal journey in the evolution of an ecological conscience. This was not something I set out to do at any point in my life. Like most journeys, it was more of an unanticipated adventure than a premeditated course of action.

It all started with my father. My parents began farming in North Dakota right after they got married, in 1930, and the Dust Bowl hit shortly thereafter, so their early years in farming were extremely stressful. Somehow my father understood intuitively that the Dust Bowl was not just about the weather but about the way farmers farmed. Consequently, he decided that this "would never ever happen to his farm again," and he became a radical conservationist. While he didn't always agree with the newly formed Soil Conservation Service about how the land should be cared for, caring for the land became his top priority.

I can remember him admonishing me with a pointed finger, even when I was four or five years old, that "taking care of the land" was our most important requirement. Without my being aware of it, those lectures instilled in me a kind of land ethic that determined the course of my life.

This early inoculation of a deeply felt principle created an early curiosity about values. Why did people choose to do what they did? Why did they prefer one course of action rather than another? That curiosity drew me into the fields of philosophy and theology during my educational journey. I majored in religion at Yankton College in Yankton, South Dakota, a liberal arts college that challenged its students to think critically. It was the faculty at Yankton College who taught me that it was not only appropriate but necessary to question values openly and to think independently.

I was a junior in college when I first read Aldo Leopold's *A Sand County Almanac*. I remember being immensely inspired by it. Leopold's writing about the land ethic confirmed the importance of my father's early admonitions. Still, the importance of Leopold's ecological thinking did not register with me at the time, and his use of the phrase "ecological conscience" slipped by me unnoticed. An awareness of the importance of ecological thinking came much later in my life.

Inspired by a faculty member at Yankton College, I decided to attend the Hartford Theological Seminary in Hartford, Connecticut, and then went on to the Divinity School at the University of Chicago to acquire more discipline with respect to values. Upon finishing graduate school, I entered a career in higher education, teaching in the fields of religion and philosophy. The opportunity to engage students with respect to their own values turned out to be another great inspiration for me. Traditional teacher/student roles tended to dissipate rather quickly as we entered a dialogue concerning values. One student in particular changed the course of my life and led me down a path that helped me recognize the ecological conscience that had been evolving in my own life since those early days of instruction by my father.

I encountered that student, David Vetter, in the late 1960s. As director of the Consortium for Higher Education Religion Studies in Dayton, Ohio, I became interested in working with students who wanted careers that transcended the ordinary job market. David had completed his undergraduate work at the University of Nebraska and had worked as a research assistant in a project examining the impact of organic field management on soil quality. When I arrived in Dayton, David was a student at United Theological Seminary and was interested in developing a career that nurtured a land ethic. I was immediately drawn to him.

David shared with me results of his Nebraska research, which demonstrated that well-managed organic practices significantly enriched the biological health of soil. Immediately, my mind flew back to the image of my father, with his finger pointed at me, admonishing me to take care of the land. At this point, my intense interest in values and continuing interest in agriculture began to merge in a new way that has stayed with me for the rest of my life.

In 1976 my father had a mild heart attack, so I decided to leave higher education and return to our North Dakota farm to manage it for my father and to convert our three-thousand-acre grain and livestock operation to an organic farm. It was my first opportunity to apply my newly merged interests in agriculture and values on a real farm.

Although the learning curve on the farm was steep, David Vetter continued to be an important mentor. I began to read everything I thought relevant to this new way of farming and this ethical imperative. The writings of Sir Albert Howard, J. I. Rodale, and F. H. King were particularly instructive. Later the insightful work of Wendell Berry and Wes Jackson provided additional inspiration.

Equally important was the formation of an association of farmers in the northern plains who were also interested in this new path in agriculture. In 1979 we formally launched the North Dakota Natural Farmers Association, later to be renamed the Northern Plains Sustainable Agriculture Society. We openly shared with each other what we learned on our own farms, a learning society like no other in my experience.

Eventually I was drawn back to Leopold, and I began reading all of his essays. Given the profound appreciation of the interrelationship and interdependence of everything in nature that had evolved in me, I was now able to read Leopold with new eyes. His deep understanding of ecological thinking became clear to me, and this time his phrase "ecological conscience" stood out like a bright light in a dark room. Suddenly I became aware that an ecological conscience had been struggling to be born in me ever since my father's early lectures to me. Leopold's description of our ethical mandate has since become the summation of all that is important to me and my work: "A land ethic, then, reflects the existence of an ecological conscience, and this in turn reflects a conviction of individual responsibility for the health of the land. Health is the capacity of the land for self-renewal. Conservation is our effort to understand and preserve this capacity."[1]

From my perspective, these essays are all part of a whole and are tightly woven together in this incredible journey that has been my privilege to experience. Since joining the Leopold Center for Sustainable Agriculture at Iowa State University, and recently also the Stone Barns Center for Food and Agriculture in New York, I have had the opportunity to read and confer with a diverse group of colleagues on these issues. My thinking has been enriched by the writings of others, especially ecologists like C. S. Holling. His perceptive analysis of how dynamic systems (such as farming) function has been especially helpful in addressing some of today's agricultural challenges.

As I continue to read and write about these issues, I am reminded daily that my own educational journey is far from over. Recently I have come across the work of the newly formed Resilience Alliance, a group of scholars examining how landscapes and communities can absorb disturbances and maintain functions. Their insights have proved especially useful to those of us wrestling with the task of envisioning a new agriculture that can adapt itself to the shocks of rapidly depleting energy and water resources and increasing climate instability.[2]

PART 1

Working at Home
Lessons from Kirschenmann Family Farms

Theological Reflections while Castrating Calves

I am indebted to Gene Logsdon, who reviewed this volume of essays, for suggesting that I write one additional paper on the subject of "Theological Reflections while Castrating Calves." He was suggesting, I think, that he would like to know more about what transcendent thoughts go through my mind while I am doing mundane things like castrating calves on my farm. Needless to say, that was an invitation too intriguing for a farmer/philosopher to ignore. Simultaneously it occurred to me that a brief introductory essay of this kind might prepare the reader for the diverse writings that follow, which were written over a span of more than thirty years.

In our industrial culture it might seem weird to suggest that anyone would be engaged in "theological reflections" while castrating calves. Ever since the seventeenth century, our industrial culture has taught us to specialize, separate facts from values, and simplify our management tasks in the interest of efficiency.

Reductionist thinking, which separates thoughts and actions into silos, never seemed to work well for me as a farmer. Multitasking comes with farming, even though it may be distracting and decrease efficiency and effectiveness. I don't just concentrate on the levers to be manipulated as I operate the combine. I also pay attention to the sounds of the machine as clues to whether things are operating properly. I have to anticipate changes in the flow of grain into the combine so as not to overload the machine as I move down the field. While I am working out in my head what the yield of a particular wheat field might be as I amble down the field, I also try to avoid jumping frogs whose lives I'd rather not end by running them through the combine.

The multitasking involved in operating farm equipment reminds me of Michael Polanyi's description of the ways in which we know. Our industrial culture has taught us to detach ourselves from what we want to know, in order to be objective. On the farm, I know things best by immersing myself in the things I wish to know. As Polanyi put it, "It brings home to us that it is not by *looking* at things, but by *dwelling in them,* that we understand their joint meaning."[1] Thus, contemplating a host of ethical and values issues while castrating a calf is the only way to "know" about it; it is a way of "dwelling" in the fullness of the act.

In fact, values are to be contemplated in almost everything done on the farm. I could never castrate a calf without thinking about the values issues involved—the pain to the calf versus the demands in the marketplace for a particular quality of meat that cannot be achieved without castration. The choice is either to turn bull calves into steers so they can hang out together in the same pasture, or to leave the male calves as bulls and segregate them from female calves so they don't breed prematurely or inbreed. Nor could I ever castrate a calf without agonizing over the most "humane" way to do it.

I remember a mid-1990s meeting in Washington, D.C., called by Michael Fox, who was the director of the farm animal division of the Humane Society of the United States. Michael had arranged for a group of us to gather for the better part of two days at the Humane Society and work with him to develop a set of humane animal standards that he hoped could be incorporated into the organic standards of the U.S. Department of Agriculture (USDA). Michael had invited farmers, ranchers, animal scientists, and activists to review the draft standards he had created.

When we got to the section dealing with castration, his proposed standard called for ranchers to use local anesthesia before initiating castration. I remember sitting across the table from Mel Coleman Sr., a well-known cattle rancher from Colorado, and we smiled at each other as we contemplated this seemingly rational requirement.

I told Michael that I fully supported his intent to reduce the calf's pain, but in my humble opinion, the greatest discomfort to the calf (provided the procedure was done professionally) was not the quick incision necessary to perform the castration but being confined in a squeeze chute to perform the procedure. I reminded him that using a local anesthesia meant that the calf would have to be confined in an extremely uncomfortable position for at least fifteen or twenty minutes while waiting for the anesthetic to take effect, rather than the normal two to three minutes it takes to castrate a calf professionally. The latter seemed to me to be much more humane to the calf, not less. He agreed and dropped the requirement from his proposed standard.

I tell this story to remind us that making value judgments about farming is not always as simple as it seems, especially if you are not "dwelling" in the business of farming. Is it better to occasionally use a mold-board plow on a field to get more effective weed control, leaving the field temporarily more vulnerable to erosion? Or should you use an herbicide to control the weeds, eliminating the need for the plow but introducing other risks to the environment? Is it better to have cattle on your farm or not? Cattle emit methane gas, but they also create manure that can be composted to restore the biological health of the soil. Without cattle, synthetic fertilizers are needed to maintain appropriate nutrient levels in the soil, but they contribute to nitrate leaching, which ends up adding to the size of the dead zone in the Gulf of Mexico. The manufacture and delivery of synthetic fertilizers, of course, adds its own ecological footprint.

But to me there are deeper reflections embedded in this discussion—reflections that go to the heart of how we live our lives on planet Earth and whether we can find a truly meaningful quality of life along the way.

One Sunday morning, years ago, my lawyer/wife and I were prevented from going to church that day by requirements on the farm. We were riding across the prairie that morning, among our cattle, when my wife asked me where, if anyplace, I saw "god" in our farm. I pointed to some Canadian thistles in a fence line and to the calves surrounding us and said, "in every thistle in our fields and every calf humping another calf in our pasture." I did not say this to be cute or disrespectful of her question but to convey the fact that in my theology, the divine always meets us in the flesh—*all* flesh—*all* relationships, not just our relationship with humans or relationships we like. This seems to me to be at the heart of the concept of the incarnation.

Unfortunately, in Christian religions we have too often reduced the doctrine of the incarnation to a one-time event—the time on that first Christmas Eve when God decided, on just that one occasion, to participate in our world by meeting us in the flesh, in the form of Jesus of Nazareth.

That is unfortunate. In the first place, this rather narrow interpretation of the doctrine of incarnation makes Christianity an exclusivist religion that quickly reaches the conclusion that only those who become Christians can experience the divine in their lives, and they can do so only by submitting to a particular interpretation of Christian religion. All of this despite the fact that, as Garry Wills reminds us, both Jesus and St. Paul were opposed to "religion" and were, in fact both "killed by it."[2]

There is a deeper meaning to the concept of incarnation that I think we miss with this limited religious interpretation. This deeper meaning is beautifully expressed in the familiar parable of the Good Samaritan (Luke 10:25–37). I think we sometimes miss the profound insight of this story because we have come to regard it as a moral tale, a kind of admonition telling us what we *must* do to be a good neighbor. But that was not the point of the parable.

The parable is a response to a question posed by a lawyer (not unlike my wife): "What must I do to inherit eternal life?" In other words, the parable is part of the question we all harbor: How do we discover the kind of life that has eternal qualities to it? In the midst of all of life's experiences, how do we identify and incorporate those that truly have lasting meaning and significance for our lives and make life a joy to live?

Jesus's response to the lawyer's question was much more precocious than mine to my wife's question. Jesus responded by saying, "You are a lawyer—tell me, what does the law say?" The lawyer quickly replies, "Love the Lord your God with all your heart and all your soul and all your strength and all your mind, and your neighbor as yourself." And Jesus responds, "You are right, do that and you will live."

But the lawyer, determined to "justify himself," asks the next question: "And who is my neighbor?" Apparently the lawyer knew here what the law stated—what was necessary to truly experience an eternal quality of life—namely that it required him to enter into relationships with the "neighbor," in the flesh, in love. And he was apparently not ready to open himself to that requirement, so he tried to push it aside by asking an academic question: "Who is my neighbor?" In other words, let's have an academic discussion about who is a neighbor, so I don't have to face the fact that I'm not ready to enter into a relationship of love.

Jesus then responds to the lawyer's question by telling a story.

Once upon a time, he said, there was a Jew on his way from Jerusalem to Jericho, and he fell in among thieves who beat him up, robbed him, and left him on the side of the road for dead. Now, by chance, a Jewish priest came by and saw the Jew lying in the ditch near death, but he did not want to get involved and apparently had religious duties to attend to in Jerusalem, so he passed by on the other side of the road. Similarly, a Levite Jew came by, and he too decided he did not want to become involved and apparently had legal issues to attend to in Jerusalem, so he also passed by on the other side. But then a Samaritan—remember that Jews and Samaritans were mortal enemies and detested each other—came by, stopped, got down off his donkey, attended to the man's wounds, put him on his own donkey, took him to the nearest hotel, and nursed him back to life. When he had to leave to attend to his business, he asked the innkeeper to take care of the man, and if there was any additional cost he would reimburse him on his way back.

Then Jesus turns to the lawyer and asks, "Now which of these was a neighbor to the man in the ditch?" The lawyer responds, "The one who showed mercy." And Jesus replies, "Go and do likewise and you will live."

So the parable is not a moral tale instructing us how to be a good neighbor, but a story designed to answer the lawyer's question—"What must I do to inherit eternal life?" The story tells us that we can only experience the divine qualities of life through love—through flesh-and-blood *relationships,* even relationships with those who may happen to be our enemies.

Now if one combines this profound insight with other stories in the Judeo-Christian tradition (or other spiritual texts, for that matter), one is impressed by the fact that such flesh and blood relationships are not limited to humans but can include other species as well. The biblical Garden of Eden story (Genesis 3) is particularly intriguing in this connection. The story reminds us that we are placed in the garden of creation to "service it and to care for it" and that while we are invited to eat of the "tree of life," we are to avoid the "tree of knowledge." The tree of life, it seems quite clear, is the garden of creation itself; we are invited to relate openly and freely to all life in the garden. As long as we do, we are promised a fulfilling quality of life. It is when we decide to eat of the tree of knowledge—when we start to think we know better, consider ourselves separate, believing that we are in control—it is then that life becomes "cursed": the soil, farming, interpersonal relationships—indeed, *all* relationships—become cursed.

All members of the biotic community represent an opportunity for relationships that have the potential to enrich our lives. Unpleasant relationships, like trying to deal with Canadian thistle or saving the life of someone we detest, have as much (or more) potential for enriching our lives as relationships we crave. The point is to relate in love—with care, respect, and humility.

As mentioned in another essay in this volume ("On Being an 'Objective Farmer'"), Barry Lopez, one of the great naturalists of our time, reminds us that even in the midst of some of the "shrinking and eviscerated habitats" in our world, there are incredible opportunities for experiencing the eternal qualities of life if we are willing to "dwell in" these relationships. As Lopez puts it, they teach us "humility and fallibility" and therefore represent for us "the antithesis to progress." I can attest to the fact that Canadian thistle on a farm can do that for a farmer.

In his recent book, *The Myth of Progress,* Tom Wessels[3] points out that in simple engagement with fellow members of the biotic community we learn the source of true quality of life. He warns us that our current "march toward progress," focused on industrial consumerism and materialistic aspirations, destroys our world and *prevents* us from experiencing the simple, eternal qualities of life that await us in ordinary communal relationships with our fellow creatures in the biotic community.

This brings us back to our need to develop an "ecological conscience," that awareness that *all* of the members of the biotic community of which we are a part are our "neighbors" and that eternal qualities of life await us in those relationships. A first step, as Aldo Leopold reminded us, is to recognize that we are but "plain members and citizens" of that community and not its "conquerors."

I have been extremely fortunate in my life—and grateful—that I have so often been humiliated by all that I have not known as I encounter the divine in the flesh-and-blood experiences of daily life on a farm, including the simple act of castrating calves. This is a mystery that constantly unfolds in the web of life that exists in the soil, in the community of insects and birds that occupy our prairie, in my attempt to keep Canadian thistle at bay, in the simple observation that because it is all still evolving, replete with emergent properties, I will never be able to understand, let alone predict, how it will all evolve. And for that very reason it may be important for us to proceed, as Kevin McCann advised us, as "if each species is sacred."[4]

This does not mean that all life is produced by a divine force separate from nature or that rocks and trees have "souls," as the animist religions proposed. It is rather that the deeper meanings in our own lives are revealed to us in loving flesh-and-blood relationships with all the "plain members and citizens" of the biotic community that surrounds us every day. It is all part of the evolution of an ecological conscience.

On Behalf of American Farmers

A little less than two years ago, I left a career in higher education and returned to my birthplace in North Dakota to manage our family's farm. My decision was motivated by the conviction that the field of agriculture poses some of the most formidable challenges in today's world. While worldwide food shortages and global population explosion present staggering challenges to agriculture, there are other issues that intrigue me on a food-producing farm. Among them are the challenges of rebuilding the soil to produce food that is more nutritious, adopting styles of farming that will consume less energy, farming without using toxic chemicals, and developing effective conservation practices to protect the soil against wind and water erosion.

Since returning to the farm I have become keenly aware of the economic issues that have given rise to recent farmer protests. This problem is best illustrated by making a trip to a farm equipment store to compare the cost of essential parts with the current price of grain. This past summer, for example, I had to pay $21.00 for three steel-hardened bolts ¾ inch in diameter and ten inches long. At current local wheat prices ($2.80 per bushel) it takes 7½ bushels of wheat to pay for the three bolts. Farm economists tell us that it now costs $4.33 to produce a bushel of wheat. That means that it cost me $32.48 to produce the $21.00 worth of wheat to buy the bolts. It should be noted, too, that I had no choice. I either had to pay the $21.00 for the bolts or abandon a $30,000 piece of equipment.

That incident serves to illustrate how, in the past five years, costs of essential expenditures in a farming operation, such as farm equipment, parts,

This is an edited version of a paper presented at one of the first U.S. gatherings of organic farmers, in Bismarck, North Dakota, in December 1978.

and energy, have exploded, while grain prices are down 30 percent (even with the slight price improvement in 1978). It was something of an economic shock for me to remember that when I was a boy, in the 1940s, our farm sold wheat for well over $2.00 per bushel, but now in the late 1970s we're still selling wheat for less than $3.00 per bushel.

Farmers are, in fact, caught in a three-way economic squeeze that is wholly dictated to them. They are told what prices they will receive for the products they produce. They are told what prices they will pay for the products and services they have to buy. And they are told how much freight they will pay to ship their grain to the mills and their equipment from the factories. Farmers are the only American businessmen who are forced to buy retail, sell wholesale, and pay the freight both ways. Farmers have no way of influencing prices in relation to the actual costs of production or of passing their increased costs along to consumers. Farmers interpret these realities as subsidizing the rest of the nation with cheap food so that an inflation-ridden populace can escape some of the consequences of a shrinking dollar.

Farmers have no one to champion their cause in this squeeze. Laborers have their unions, businesses have their conglomerates, and professionals have their associations. Each has the muscle to demand some annual increments to offset some of the inflationary pinch. Farmers have no political clout (they constitute less than 4 percent of the voting population), powerful lobbies, corporate structure, nor organization to effectively promote their interests in the political process or marketplace.

Even the cabinet officer appointed to represent farmers, the Secretary of Agriculture, seems to find it hard to support farmers in their economic struggle for survival. Farmers are particularly disheartened by Secretary Berglund's assumption that the protests of American farmers are motivated by selfish interests and that farmers are in trouble largely because of bad management decisions, which has led to a supply-demand imbalance. This is an extremely narrow view of the matter.

When it comes to food production, our nation simply *must* begin thinking in global terms. Anyone who views food surpluses and mismanagement in terms of oversupply can only have in mind a narrow and privileged enclave of mankind. They must assume that the privileged few can maintain their favored position against the rising tide of undernourished peoples who are demanding equity with increasing determination. Under the present circumstances of global overpopulation and starvation, we ought to be developing a policy of producing and stockpiling as much grain as we can, as Stephen Schneider argues so persuasively in his book *The Genesis Strategy.*[1] Farmers sense the wisdom of this policy intuitively.

Nevertheless, farmers are aware that even under existing policies, they are likely to reap large financial gains in the not-too-distant future if they can only hang on through the present economic depression. That future is inevitable in the face of increasing world food demands and decreasing acres of soil that are suitable for food production. But farmers detest this bust-boom economy because they realize that in the long run it is not good for them, the consumer, or the country.

The movement toward absentee ownership of farmland will likely increase without changes in the economics of farming. Vast acreages will change hands during the next decade because most farm operators in the major farm belts are now in their late sixties. Given the present economics of farming, it is virtually impossible for young would-be farmers to buy land. Even sons and daughters of owner-operators often can't take over the family farm because they have to sell too much land to pay estate taxes.

Absentee corporate ownership will further increase the cost of food production because such farms are much less efficient than owner-operator units. Farms that are individually owned by traditional families are incredibly efficient, partly because owner-operators are very conscious of avoiding waste and partly because they operate with very low labor costs.

Labor costs of traditional farms are low because family members on owner-operator farms work as a unit and are willing to put in long hours of hard work for *their* farm. My own working day, for example, usually begins around 4:30 A.M. and ends around 10:00 P.M. A seven-day work week is normal. These are not exceptional hours for most farmers I know. Having worked in educational bureaucracies and corporate businesses, I know that no farm worker in an absentee corporate structure would produce at this level. Consequently, the increase in labor costs alone, in such a corporate structure, would increase the cost of producing food. Most farmers have not read E. F. Schumacher's *Small Is Beautiful,* but their practical sense of sound economics led them to operate on Schumacher's principles long before he published his book.[2]

When farmers express disdain for corporate farming, they aren't mouthing nostalgic platitudes about preserving their grandfather's style of

24

farming. Farmers are largely progressive, always on the lookout for innovative ways of doing things. However, corporate farms, managed by absentee owners whose primary motive is short-term profit, will not protect the soil, and a new era of bonanza farming and another Dust Bowl could result. This fear is well-founded. Lockeretz noted at least four major causes of the 1930s Dust Bowl. They were:

- Single-crop farming
- Failure to return organic matter to the soil
- Choosing cropping systems for maximum return under best weather conditions rather than protecting the soil during unfavorable conditions
- Large-scale mechanization that led to the cultivation of larger fields[3]

With the transfer of land into the hands of absentee corporate landlords in North Dakota, all four of these features are being reintroduced into the state's cropping systems.

Anyone who knows farmers also knows that most farm operators detest direct government subsidies. Farmers are used to working for their returns and have never liked receiving money from the government for something they didn't do. Farmers are, at the same time, acutely aware of the slander directed against them when they are accused of getting "handouts" when they receive subsidies, while large corporations, such as airplane manufacturers, transportation systems, and railroads, are told that subsidies in *their* cases constitute necessary economic stimulation and are in the national interest.

One way to approach the issue might be through William Albrecht's old proposal of establishing a soil-depletion allowance for farmers.[4] If it makes good economic sense for the government to recognize that oil companies bear unusual costs because they need to drill new wells in order to supply the country with oil, it makes just as much sense to recognize the same principle for farmers, who must replace nutrients to the soil taken from it by crops in order to supply the country with food. A soil-depletion allowance, consequently, makes as much sense as an oil-depletion allowance. Such a policy could accomplish a dual objective: putting farmers on an economic par with other industries, and conserving the productive capacity of our soils to help protect the nation against future famine.

It is very clear to me that farmers are only asking for two things. They are asking to be placed on an economic par with the rest of the entrepreneurs of this country, and they are asking that they be allowed to continue doing what they do so well—produce food on fertile, healthy soil and preserve the means by which that productivity can be protected for the future.

These seem like reasonable requests.

Pilgrimage to a Barnyard

The invitation said, "Write about your spiritual struggle. Tell us how you see Christ and the world differently now." I was overcome with gratitude and terror—gratitude for the fact someone thought my struggle worth sharing, but terror that this was uncharted water.

A Hard, Weird Decision

It's hard to be sure now, and it was hard to be sure then. Part of the struggle has always been not being sure. The beginning was lonely. No one else was doing what I was doing. No neighbor had left a budding career in higher education to undertake the task of managing a farm in an isolated area under difficult economic conditions. Converting a farm from accepted, conventional, chemical, agribusiness management practices to an organic farm was unheard of in the area. Organic agriculture was derided by ag experts, frowned upon by the United States Department of Agriculture, and ridiculed by many farmers. While something compelled me to believe it was the right thing to do, there was no one with whom to check my perceptions or to confirm the weird, new, compelling interpretation of the gospel that began to push its way into my life.

Was I crazy? Was I off on an insane journey, deluded by boyhood fantasies of playing in my old sand pit? Was I running home to Daddy's farm to escape the challenge of urban life? Or was I responding to an unknown and unrecognized ministry that even I didn't understand? There was no way to know the answers and no one with whom to share the questions.

Part of the struggle had to do with letting go. Letting go of other

---

This is an edited version of a paper that originally was published in the Spring 1989 issue of *Peniel,* a local newspaper serving both South and North Dakota.

people's expectations (especially people I cared about) was probably the most unsettling. The dean of my graduate studies, who was also my thesis advisor, had let it be known to a friend that he expected me to become one of the leading thinkers in American theology. Was I letting him down? Was I running away from a responsibility that had been thrust upon me? My colleagues at the university expected me to continue my intellectual pursuits and were concerned that I'd atrophy on a farm in North Dakota. Were they right? My family never said so, but I couldn't help wondering if they had expected to grow up in a culturally creative urban environment instead of the isolation and economic hardships of a North Dakota farm. Was I letting them down?

I had to also let go of fear. That was perhaps the most difficult. There was the fear of the unknown and the fear of failure. Where would all this end? Would I join the ranks of bankrupt farmers, too old to pursue meaningful alternative careers, too broke to start over, too poor to provide basic health care for themselves in their senior years?

Second, there was the fear of being discredited. Surely leaving the academic world to manage a farm would not enhance my professional résumé. But would I also be considered inept in the rural community, especially because I was going against the orthodox way of doing things? Was my decision too bizarre to expect anyone to accept it at face value? Colleagues at the university wondered what the "real" reason was. Folks around the farm were certain there had to be "more to it." Even relatives wondered why I couldn't hold down a job.

From Hard, Lonely Work to Shared Passion

Then came the long night of nothing. We made the move and started farming. We made mistakes. We were isolated. We started settling into mundane routines shared by most of our neighbors. We got up early in the morning, worked hard all day, and went to bed tired late at night. Yet, nothing was happening. What kind of calling was this?

Slowly, out of night's loneliness, boredom, and fear, a small light began to shine. We discovered other farmers in the state with a similar passion for caring for the earth. We met farmers who saw "vocation" in their work, a calling to be responsible stewards of the land by providing uncontaminated, nutritious food for the human community. We started a group—sharing our successes and our failures. We shared our pain and our joy. We shielded each other from the ridicule of those who didn't understand what we were doing. We celebrated together and our bond grew.

Today requests pour in from many corners of the world. People want us to share our vision and experience. We are hearing from farmers who share our theology of food production and agriculture. Requests come from merchants, universities, politicians, conservationists, and foundations. These requests open opportunities for ministry that far exceed available energy.

New Understanding

Through it all, Christ and the world have remained the same for me, but my relationship to both has changed. For the first time, I understand the quote attributed to Søren Kierkegaard, who said that faith was casting oneself on fifty thousand fathoms of water and being joyful. I understand now that there is no way of knowing in advance if one is called or deluded. The only way to find out is to jump in and see what happens.

I've learned too that when the gospel says, over and over again, "Don't be afraid," it means it. There is always new life waiting to push its way into our lives, and we really don't need to be afraid; if we let in new life, no matter how painful or strange it may seem, everything we were afraid of doesn't matter. I now know more fully what it means to seek first the kingdom, and what once was worrisome is no more.

I've also come to appreciate the insistence of the biblical witness that God usually chooses those we reject and chooses to be made known in unorthodox ways and places. I've always admired that intellectually, but I now experience it existentially. I have experienced Martin Luther's Christmas sermon, in which he reminds us that on Christmas Eve, God was in a cold, smelly barn where a couple of frightened teenagers were having their first baby without so much as a pail of warm water.

An Unexpected Peace

Finally, there is the peace. A sense of centeredness has crept upon us almost unnoticed. It is a silent part of the prairie that surrounds us. It truly doesn't matter anymore if we fail, if we don't meet others' expectations, if others think us weird, or even if pain and disillusionment fill our days and nights. The peace passes understanding. It's just there. The world, even with its injustice and violence, is gentle and good and is a garden of sustenance, hope, and quietude.

Low-Input Farming in Practice

Putting a System Together and Making It Work

A practicing farm is always different from a theoretical farm or a research farm. A theoretical farm represents the manner in which a farm might work or ideally should work. On a research farm, a piece of the farm is isolated, reduced to its simplest form, and analyzed under controlled circumstances. A practicing farm may be shaped by ideals and guided by research, but it also includes the variables that are removed in research for the sake of reliable analysis, and that are removed in theoretical designs for the sake of purity. In fact, real life always includes these variables. They are what E. F. Schumacher called "the messiness of growth."[1] It is the presence of this "messiness" that makes it difficult to describe a practicing farm in a uniform manner.

This doesn't mean that we should refrain from speaking about farms in practice, any more than it means that we should stop doing controlled research just because we can't apply it exactly. It probably does mean that we need to look at both kinds of data with a bit more humility than is common.

At the outset, I admit to a preference for the word "sustainable" over "low-input." The term "low-input" emphasizes the wrong end of the input-output equation. Reducing certain inputs may increase short-term efficiencies on a practicing farm; if the right inputs are reduced, environmental degradation can be decreased. But "low-input" lends itself too easily to the notion of "mining." Low-input suggests we can obtain efficiencies through "getting by with less" rather than "restoring what we use in order to keep

Presented at the Institute for Alternative Agriculture Symposium on Sustainable Agriculture, February 28, 1989, Washington, D.C., and published in *American Journal of Alternative Agriculture* 4 (1989): 106–10.

going." It is the latter notion, integral to the word "sustainable," that we need to attend to if we are going to solve some of the problems confronting agriculture. Simply cutting back on inputs will work for only a brief period of time, if at all.

The agriculture community has not yet agreed on a precise definition for the word "sustainable," but that should not immobilize us. There are a number of working definitions that can serve us well while we wait for a universally acceptable definition to emerge. Wendell Berry has referred to sustainable agriculture as an agriculture that "depletes neither soil nor people."[2] William Lockeretz has referred to it as an agriculture that "is capable of enduring."[3] And Canadian entomologist Stuart Hill has referred to it as a system that is based, as much as possible, on "renewable resources and the recycling of nonrenewable resources and minimally impacting the environment."[4] All of these ways of referring to sustainable agriculture are broad goal statements, not descriptions of specific agricultural practices. Identifying those practices that are truly sustainable will take time, experience, and research.

Putting a System Together

Numerous approaches are available to develop a practicing sustainable system. The task is somewhat similar to that of a medical doctor who prescribes rules of conduct that enable a patient to take better care of his body. While such prescriptions involve a good bit of science, they also involve art. Much depends on the personality of the patient, the personality of the doctor, how the two get on together, and how skillful the doctor is in anticipating the patient's responses to certain suggestions. Similarly, in putting a sustainable system together for a practicing farm, much depends on the farmer, the farm, how they get on together, and how skillful the farmer is in anticipating how his farm will respond to his stewardship.

Furthermore, there is probably more than one way to start. Farmer Jim Bender has suggested, for example, that one should begin "one method at a time."[5] Bender proposes that a farmer first become comfortable with some kind of rotation and diversified system before attempting to reduce inputs.

In my experience, a "whole systems" approach provides a more attractive starting point. A rotation that works with substantial amounts of nonrenewable inputs, for example, may not work without them. In a whole-systems approach, one would take a small piece of the whole farm and experimentally introduce a complete sustainable system on that acre-age. This portion would incorporate all of the components of a potentially sustainable system. Based on the disclosures from this small part of the farm, one would then begin to apply the process to the rest of the farm. On our farm, the latter approach made more sense. Regardless how one begins, sustainable systems involve common elements, including pitfalls to avoid, practices to incorporate, and problems to anticipate.

Pitfalls to Avoid

The first pitfall to avoid is the notion that successful farming is a matter of following the right recipe. In modern, conventional agriculture, progressive farming is largely a matter of following the right prescription. A successful farmer uses soil tests to match up yield expectations with a standard set of inputs. He reads labels carefully and applies standard recommendations for controlling weeds and insects and ensuring proper soil fertility. The func-tion of research, in this view, is to develop a standard model that anyone with some management cleverness can transplant to any farm operation.

Traditional farming, learned through apprenticeship, proceeds differ-ently. In the past, young farmers spent decades studying the subtleties of signs in nature and individual fields and animals to help them anticipate how certain practices affected natural systems. Embedded in this learning process was the notion that no two fields or animals would respond to the farmer's husbandry in exactly the same way.

Putting a successful sustainable system together requires that we re-kindle this notion of cooperating with nature and discard our intrigue with "managing" the earth. This will take time, because, as E. F. Schumacher pointed out, with "standardized farming" we have lost the traditional knowledge of how "to cooperate with the soil."[6]

A return to such principles may also be attractive to research scientists. At a recent conference on sustainable agriculture, some farmers described how they were controlling weeds by trying to understand how different weeds behaved in different environments and were then applying strate-gies accordingly. Afterward, a weed specialist from one of the land-grant universities expressed his excitement about this approach because it enabled him "to be a weed scientist again, instead of a label reader."

A second pitfall to avoid is the temptation to apply a potentially sustainable system immediately. Several key facets of sustainable systems reveal the hazards of such wholesale conversion.

A sustainable system is a living system, not a set of mechanical connections. Living systems always behave differently under different circumstances, because they always try to adapt themselves to their environments. This means that even if the experimental acreage on one's own farm (let alone the sustainable system on a neighbor's farm) is very successful, one courts disaster by simply transferring it intact to the rest of the farm. When dealing with a living system, there is no substitute for using one's imagination to anticipate how a working model will adapt to a new field.

Adopting a sustainable system is a process, not a technique. The *process* used on experimental acreage—for example, selecting a starting point for a viable rotation, developing soil-conserving practices, and introducing greater diversity—has to be applied to the rest of the farm. What is transferred to new acreage is the process of moving from one management strategy to another, not an intact set of practices and crops.

Moreover, the task of developing a sustainable system is never done. Sustainable practices require constant attention to new ways of responding to the same problems as well as a lifelong commitment to nurturing the system.

A third pitfall to avoid is the temptation to change techniques without changing systems. Some farmers may construe new approaches to farming as simply adapting new techniques to what they have always done. That will not work in developing a sustainable system. Putting a sustainable system into practice involves a complex set of interconnections. A sustainable system of annual crop production, for example, will not work apart from an appropriate crop rotation. Attempting to switch to a sustainable system by withdrawing inputs without simultaneously developing a soil-building program and an appropriate crop-rotation scheme would be disastrous.

Practices to Incorporate

Three management practices key to any sustainable farm are an appropriate crop-rotation scheme, a regenerative soil-conserving strategy, and a system of interactive diversification. Orchards, vineyards, and perennial polycultures aside, crop rotations are one of the most effective tools for controlling insects, disease, and weeds, for maintaining acceptable nitrogen and moisture levels in the soil, for improving soil tilth and structure, and for reducing soil erosion. For example, William Ball, extension agronomist at North Dakota State University, noted that fifteen of the most common crop-attacking insects in North Dakota can be partially or entirely controlled through crop rotations.[7]

One of the most challenging tasks in putting a sustainable system together on a practicing farm is developing a crop rotation that is sustainable and that meets the needs of the farm. Farm needs include markets for the crops in the rotation, soil type, moisture and climate conditions, equipment requirements, and on-farm feed and cash-flow needs. Thus, sustainability requires a crop rotation that accomplishes several objectives. Crop rotation should provide effective weed control and should include:

- cool-season and warm-season plants that are rotated
- plants with allelopathic properties
- legumes or grasses that choke out weeds
- crops that lend themselves well to mechanical weed control
- crops with fibrous root systems that improve soil structure and create a more favorable environment for the crops while robbing weeds of space to thrive in
- rotation adjustments that attack target perennial weeds
- a range of crops to help maintain a balance of nutrients in the soil, giving a competitive advantage to the growing crop

These strategies help reduce weed competition with growing crops. Toxic herbicides made from nonrenewable sources of energy can therefore be eliminated from the practicing farmer's weed-control arsenal.

A crop rotation should also provide effective insect and disease control. This can be accomplished by sufficiently isolating crops that are susceptible to the same insects and diseases. Physically isolating similar crops in the rotation, as well as similar crops seeded in previous years, is crucial to this strategy.

A crop rotation should also improve soil conditions. Soil tilth and soil structure can be improved by including deep-rooted plants and plants with fibrous root systems in the rotation. These root systems can increase soil aggregate stability. Studies have shown that monocropping and black-fallow practices pulverize soil. The smaller soil crumbs increase evaporability and compaction and cause soil to puddle and crust. Increasing soil aggregate stability, however, increases water infiltration and retention and thereby not only improves the soil's ability to sustain plants during drought conditions but also helps to reduce soil erosion by both wind and water. Furthermore, improved soil structure increases biological activity in the soil and enables plants to utilize soil moisture and soil nutrients more readily.[8]

Crop rotation also contributes to regenerating and conserving soils. Legumes are particularly essential to maintaining soil nitrogen levels. Other soil nutrients and trace elements are released or enhanced by certain crops in the rotation. Buckwheat, for example, absorbs phosphorus very efficiently; it helps release fixed soil phosphorus by building up a store of organic phosphorus. Combining buckwheat with a legume provides a further benefit because the deep-rooted legume brings up phosphorus from deeper soil, something buckwheat cannot accomplish with its shallow roots.

Green-manure crops are also important in regenerative soil-conserving strategies. Green manure adds organic matter to the soil, assists in dissolving insoluble nutrients, brings up nutrients from the subsoil, and improves the soil's water-holding capacity, thereby enhancing soil productive capacity and reducing erosion.

Livestock manure is another key to a regenerative soil-conserving system. Although handling costs make livestock manure less efficient than green manure, it is still a desirable soil amendment.[9] Composting manure increases its value. In the composting process, high temperatures destroy most weed seeds, and the raw material is reduced to about one-fourth its original volume, decreasing the cost of spreading. Composting stabilizes the nutrients, reducing the risk of pollution. Composting also provides more stable humus, which improves soil aeration, water infiltration, and water-holding capacity.[10] Additionally, a good regenerative soil-conserving system should include traditional soil-conservation techniques such as wind barriers, grassed waterways, strip cropping, conserving tillage, and cover crops.

The third essential practice of sustainable farms is an interactive diversification system. The requirements of a good crop rotation and soil-building strategy, noted above, have already established the necessity for diversity. These diverse components should form an interactive system that takes advantage of symbiotic relationships. Such interaction increases farm efficiency and survivability.

An integrated crop and livestock system creates mutual support between the two components. Crop residue is an excellent feed source for livestock, and manure can be composted and returned to the fields as a fertility source for crops. Integrated crop and livestock systems minimize the effects of weather-related adversities. Crops hit by untimely rains can be fed to livestock, mitigating the loss. When cash crops are damaged by hail, they can still be grazed to recoup some of the loss, because the farm still has the cash livestock receipts to fall back on. Such strategies can be crucial to farm survival.

Problems to Anticipate

In any new venture, it is important to anticipate problems. The first difficulty faced in transitioning to a self-renewing and self-regulating system is the problem of input withdrawal. One cannot withdraw the inputs all at once. Until pest cycles are broken with a good crop rotation, pesticides may still be needed. Until soil is restored through regenerative practices, synthetic fertilizers may be necessary.

Additional facilities may also be needed to change systems. A diverse crop rotation requires additional storage space to accommodate new crop varieties. If livestock are added to the farm, facilities for housing and handling them will be required.

A third problem to anticipate is matching equipment needs with the new management practices. Livestock manure requires equipment for composting and spreading. Green manure requires equipment to properly incorporate vegetation. Soil-conserving tillage and mechanical weed control require equipment that kills weeds and properly prepares seedbeds. Blade plows, rodweeders, harrows, no-till seeders, and rotary hoes may need to be purchased. Because labor requirements may increase in the transition, labor needs must be assessed and built into the farm's economic plan.

Finally, until the weed-control strategies outlined are fully implemented, weed control without herbicides may be difficult. Effective weed management is one of the most challenging problems facing growers who eliminate their herbicide input, especially when a farm has had a long history of monocropping.

Making It Work

If a sustainable system is assembled using these strategies, then making it work is primarily a matter of exercising practical wisdom and craftsmanship. No standard recipe exists for organizing or managing a farm to make this system work, but some clues from an unlikely source may be helpful.

One of the classical architects of management strategies for making things work was Niccolo Machiavelli, a sixteenth-century Italian statesman. Machiavelli may be an unorthodox source of clues for how to make a sustainable farm work, especially because he was an advocate of unbridled power who believed that the ends always justify the means. Sustainable agriculture, on the other hand, focuses on submitting to the power of nature and employing tools of gentle adjustment. Nevertheless, even though Machiavelli's political philosophy may be disagreeable, he provides some pearls of wisdom on how to make things work.

As translated by Bull, Machiavelli noted that a wise king always lives in the province he rules, because that is the only way to recognize problems in a timely manner: "As the doctors say of a wasting disease, to start with it is easy to cure but difficult to diagnose; after a time, unless it has been diagnosed and treated at the outset, it becomes easy to diagnose but difficult to cure."[11] Thus, if a ruler lacks close, personal knowledge of his realm, evils "are allowed to grow so that everyone can recognize them, there is no longer any remedy to be found."[12]

Recognizing problems in a timely manner through close, personal observations is crucial to making a sustainable system work. If one allows a weed problem to grow so that everyone in the neighborhood can recognize it, it is probably too late to find a remedy. Weed and insect problems can only be solved without pesticides by utilizing preventive management strategies. Consequently, if a farmer wants to reduce or eliminate reliance on fertilizers and pesticides, it will be necessary to walk the fields, scrutinize weed problems, carefully analyze growing plants, and give close attention to the entire soil profile. That means the farmer has to live on the farm. Absentee sustainable farming will not work. Sustainable practices probably also will not work on farms too large to be personally managed by the owner-operator.

Second, Machiavelli suggests that enterprises need to develop in accordance with natural growth patterns. "States quickly founded, like all other things of rapid beginnings and growth, can't have deep roots . . . so that the first storm destroys them."[13]

The pace of transitioning to sustainable systems is important. It takes time for soil to regenerate itself and to break insect, weed, and disease cycles.

Farmers need time to discover the right combination of sustainable strategies for a particular farm. On the other hand, Machiavelli recognized the importance of a certain degree of impetuousness. He suggested that, if one were to wait until all arrangements were made and everything was settled, one would never succeed. "It is better to be impetuous than circumspect," he said.[14] While it is important to allow a sustainable system to develop according to its own principles of growth, it is also important not to be too cautious. One can always find good reasons to delay. Without a certain degree of impetuousness, one would probably never start.

Finally, Machiavelli recognizes the importance of embracing ambiguity: "Then, no government should ever imagine that it can always adopt a safe course; rather, it should regard all possible courses of action as risky. This is the way things are: whenever one tries to escape one danger one runs into another. Prudence consists in being able to assess the nature of a particular threat and in accepting the lesser evil."[15] Any farmer who has put a sustainable system together and tried to make it work can probably relate to that statement. Often one tries to avoid one problem only to run into another. Clearly, there are no absolutely right or wrong answers. Most farmers recognize the need to develop an ability to judge among the lesser of several difficulties. In sustainable practices, one discovers, for example, that not all weeds are bad and that practices that appear good in the short term may be destructive in the long term.

Beyond Machiavelli's clues, two other suggestions may help make a sustainable farm system work. A farmer contemplating transitioning to a sustainable system needs to make a firm commitment to the philosophy and practice of sustainable agriculture. Cooperating with a living system always brings surprises and disappointments; without a steady commitment, a farmer might become disenchanted and abandon the project.

Luck, imagination, and a sense of humor play a large role in making sustainable farming systems work. On our own farm, some of the most successful practices we use were discovered largely through luck. We are continually reminded of the importance of using our imaginations as we try to cooperate with nature's ecosystems. Refusing to become locked into standard ways of doing things and continually imagining new possibilities is crucial. A sense of humor is indispensable. Farming has enormous potential for exposing one's capacity for stupidity. Sustainable farming probably increases that potential because it requires more thought, imagination, and management.

Finally, being part of a support group is important. Gathering and sharing information with other farmers who are trying to make similar systems work on their own farms is extremely valuable. Recently, such sustainable agriculture groups have also begun to interact with university researchers; the results appear to be very positive for everyone involved. The information and imagination generated by such groups can be an indispensable source of inspiration to farmers involved in sustainable agriculture.

A Transcendent Vision

I'm a third-generation Russian German farmer; my ancestors have deep ties to the land. In the eighteenth century, following the Seven Years' War, the Russian czar recruited a group of German farmers to immigrate to the Volga River region of Russia, promising virgin, fertile farmland. This was true, but he failed to tell them the land was inhabited by outlaws that the local authorities couldn't control. Our family history includes stories of forebears going out with teams of oxen and keeping weapons at their sides to protect themselves.

In the late nineteenth century, faced with forced conscription into the Russian army or jail, many Russian Germans immigrated to the United States instead. A settlement headquarters in Lincoln, Nebraska, operated by the German department of the Congregational Church, helped Russian Germans resettle on land available for homesteading. My dad remembered the land where his father first homesteaded as a beautiful quarter section so flat you could see from corner to corner, with nary a rock in sight, and he never forgave his father's decision to move to North Dakota to farm this hilly, rock-infested land. The reason for the move, so I'm told, is that my grandfather didn't want his offspring to marry any of those "heathen German Lutherans" in Nebraska. Russian Germans were determined to always remain German and true to the faith they inherited. So my grandfather decided to move his family to a Russian German colony in south-central North Dakota.

My father, who is 81, has this fierce determination characteristic of

This is an edited version of an essay by Frederick and Janet Kirschenmann, "A Transcendent Vision," in *Caretakers of Creation: Farmers Reflect on Their Faith and Work,* ed. Patrick Slattery, 27–38 (Minneapolis: ACTA, 1991).

Russian Germans. His lifelong goal has always been to be the best wheat farmer in Stutsman County, no matter what it takes. Two factors have always pushed him: to improve the farm every year, transforming prairie sod into farmland that can yield fifty bushels of wheat to the acre; and to care for the land, leaving it in better condition every season.

These two visions have clashed at times, but my father has come to understand and fully support the concepts behind sustainable agriculture. He takes great delight in seeing the earthworm population return and in the noticeably improved soil structure. His desire for progress also has been satisfied by having our grain receive a small premium from the specialized markets we've tapped.

From Soil Mining to Synthetic Fertilizer

Some mistakenly romanticize farming of the past and believe the land was better cared for then. However, my grandfather's style of farming was to break sod and grow wheat for about six years until the soil's fertility was depleted. Then he broke new ground. Livestock manure was spread on the closest fields simply to get it out of the barns without much thought to restoring the health of the soil.

By the 1940s, this prairie-busting style of farming was running out of new land to "mine." Following the war, petroleum companies sought new markets and found one in farmers looking to boost slumping yields. They seized upon the nineteenth-century theories of German scientist Justus von Liebig, who maintained that plants needed only nitrogen, phosphorus, and potash to stimulate growth. Nitrogen can be made from petroleum processes; the other two elements are mined and processed.

Farms saw these new inputs as their salvation. County extension agents and top farmers assured others that the synthetic products wouldn't hurt the land, and many farmers saw positive proof in their own fields. In the early years, the mechanical technology to apply fertilizers wasn't too advanced, and the fertilizer wasn't well granulated. Often the drive belt would slip or the fertilizer applicator would plug up, resulting in part of the field not being treated. Visually, it was obvious which part of a field wasn't fertilized, convincing my father he could never again farm without fertilizer.

Shifting from mining new soil to making existing acres more productive by purchasing outside inputs was an easy transition. Use of synthetic fertilizer encouraged farmers to raise specialized crops and abandon crop rotation. Farmers began to raise continuous crops of whatever produced the best returns in the marketplace. To attain ever-higher yields, they needed to buy more fertilizer. Because monoculture also invites weed, insect, and fungus problems, new markets for chemical companies were created.

Growing Up Close to the Soil

I appreciated the personal space growing up on the farm, and I always enjoyed the solitude of getting on a tractor and being close to the earth. The richness of the soil, especially when worked in the spring, had a profound influence on me. My dad's near-obsession with preventing our land from eroding was ingrained into me as a child. As I grew older, he passed on to me his sense of wonder for the miracle of the soil's productivity, and a profound sense of responsibility to care for it.

Traditional farmers have been role models for me. They still subscribe to an older ethic and never bought into the high-tech, quick-fix approach to agriculture. These farmers also have been role models of religious faith for me. Like the old Testament prophet Amos, they radiate a profound sense of place and a consuming passion for caring for the land.

Wendell Berry, one of the leading philosophers of the sustainable agriculture movement, has noted how a sense of place is tied to the biblical admonition that a people who possess no vision will perish. This vision is not a transcendent, disconnected flash of insight; rather, it's a vision of being rooted in one's own place and the sense of responsibility to care for that place. It's the just vision of the Hebrews, the vision of a people having their own vineyard or sitting under their own fig tree.

Challenging the Church Elders

The German Congregation Reformed Church played a major role in my upbringing. My religious experiences in church were of a pietistic nature. A lot of lip service was paid to connecting one's Sunday experience in church to our business dealings in everyday life, but in terms of actual behavior this was not always the case. The church was the receptacle of our Russian German culture, a place where tradition was to be preserved at all costs. I was one of the young radicals who fought hard for church services to be conducted in English rather than German. English had long replaced German as the primary language spoken in the marketplace. Why not in the church? We viewed the elders who took the opposite position as intransigent, maintaining a tradition that no longer was valid. Looking back, I suspect that I wasn't sensitive enough to the cultural context of this issue.

Following high school and throughout my ten years of higher education, I did not intend to return home to farm full-time. I never really planned out my life. Instead I seemed to stumble onto new possibilities, often late in each school year.

I went to Yankton College in Yankton, South Dakota, and majored in religion, graduating in 1957. Following the example of a faculty member whom I admired, I went from Yankton to Hartford Seminary Foundation in Hartford, Connecticut, where I received a bachelor's degree in divinity. I did postgraduate master's degree work and obtained a Ph.D. in historical theology from the University of Chicago.

I enjoyed academic life but realized it lacked the immediate satisfaction inherent in farming. When you plant seeds and see them emerge ten days later, there's a tangible sense of satisfaction. You don't get the same sort of experience when you teach introductory philosophy. Even though you do your best to convey the material in as enlightening and interesting way as possible, you're always left wondering whether or not you've made a difference in anyone's life.

Ministry to the Soil

It was a student who changed my life and redirected my thinking, making it possible for me to return to the land. In the early 1970s I was the director of the Consortium for Higher Education in Religious Studies at Dayton, Ohio. David Vetter, fresh out of the University of Nebraska with a bachelor's degree in soil science, enrolled in the school. He came to Dayton United Theological Seminary primarily to obtain skills in ministry so he could return to his home farm near Marquette, Nebraska, and develop what he described as "ministry to the soil."

Having a farm background, I was immediately drawn to David. He shared with me his intense conviction that conventional agriculture was detrimental to the soil and that soils could be managed without synthetic inputs. I was intrigued by his ideas. I bounced them off my father, and he concurred with many of them.

At age sixty-nine, my father felt it was no longer possible for him to switch to an altogether new style of farm management. This situation bothered me. We had 3,100 acres entrusted to us, and we were not caring for this land in the best way possible. In 1977, after twenty-five years away, I returned to our North Dakota farm home with my family. It wasn't really a difficult transition. For many years we had come home one month during the summer to help bring in the wheat harvest.

The disadvantages of rural living are those associated with culture. To hear the symphony, you have to plan a special trip to Minneapolis or Winnipeg. However, in contrast, urban people don't experience a culture tied to the community of life that is drawn from the soil. The greatest danger of the demise of rural communities is the disappearance of local land wisdom. This presents the strongest argument I know for maintaining family farm life.

Learning from Mistakes

We returned to the farm fully committed to farming without synthetic inputs, but at the time there wasn't much practical information available on how to do so. Mostly we relied on David Vetter's advice. He advised us to plant companion fields, using synthetic inputs on one field and organic alternatives on the other. The first year we went organic on about one-third of our acres. We saw virtually no difference in yields, and weed control wasn't a serious problem. The weather cooperated, and a warm spring helped free up soil nitrogen. It was an ideal growing season.

Buoyed by our success in 1977, we decided to quit chemicals on the entire farm the following year. It was a disaster. The residual fertility in the fields had been played out, and the resulting low fertility resulted in depressed yields. Weed competition was fierce, and green foxtail (pigeongrass) was rampant. Our durum wheat averaged only seventeen bushels to the acre, and we were docked badly when we sold the grain because of high weed-seed levels in the grain.

Looking back, it's obvious we went too fast. The soil responds to inputs, and it takes time for it to adjust when you stop using them. We also didn't understand the importance of a well-thought-out rotation. Instead, we simply continued my father's wheat-oats-fallow rotation.

Our experience should warn others to devise a good transition plan for going from one farming system to another. It's best to begin with a limited number of acres, no more than a farmer can afford to risk. Oats with an underseeded legume crop are a good beginning because if the oats don't turn out well, the crop can always be mowed and harvested for hay.

On our farm we subsequently established a five-year rotation. Hard red spring wheat, a cool-weather crop planted early, puts high nutrient demands on the soil. We follow wheat with winter rye, which has an allopathic (weed-suppressing) effect on the soil. The next crop we grow in rotation is sunflowers, which is a warm-weather crop planted later. Their deep roots go far down to tap soil nutrients. We follow sunflowers with buckwheat, underseeded with clover. Buckwheat is planted late, so tillage beforehand allows us to kill several flushes of germinating weeds. Buckwheat emerges quickly and produces a canopy that smothers weeds. In the fifth year, we grow clover in our soil-building year. The clover, of course, fixes nitrogen and builds up soil organic matter, the opposite effect of regular black fallow. In addition to our standard rotation we'll occasionally grow crops of millet, flax, soybeans, and barley.

Alternating warm-season and cool-season crops is a lot like boxing: If you don't get the weeds with the right, you can get them with the left. Spring wheat planted early will germinate at a soil temperature of 40° F, while pigeon grass germinates at 50°. Therefore, the crop can suppress the weeds if it is planted early. Waiting to plant warm-season crops such as sunflowers, buckwheat, or millet provides a chance to kill many weeds with tillage. Our standard fall tillage tools are a chisel plow or Noble blade (V-plow). In the spring, we use a field cultivator or harrow to stimulate weed-seed germination. A rod weeder is a handy spring tillage tool to destroy weeds and volunteer sunflowers. We also rotary hoe fields planted to sunflowers until the plants are two or three inches high.

Premium Price for Grain

The grain produced on our farm is sold to the Mercantile Food Company, an organic grain exporter in Georgetown, Connecticut. We receive about a 15 percent premium for our certified organic grain above the extra handling and marketing costs. At present there's a big demand in the specialty market for organically certified grain.

Our 100-head beef herd fits in nicely with our overall farming operation. Manure from the cattle helps maintain soil fertility levels. We make about 1,200 tons of compost a year, enough to cover 400 acres at our usual application rate of three tons an acre. In our feedlot we stack the manure in windrows four to five feet high and leave it for about eight to ten weeks, allowing decomposition, before we spread it. We aerate the stacks with a front-end loader.

We've seen the difference compost can make. I recall one field where we spread compost only two-thirds of the way across a three-quarter-mile field. The oats were ten inches taller where there was compost, and they yielded at least 20 percent to 30 percent better.

The great majority of the feed consumed by our livestock during winter months is crop residue: oat and millet straw plus alfalfa. During the summer, the livestock graze on 900 acres of perennial native prairie grasses. Several years ago we changed from spring to fall calving. Spring calving in a dry lot meant a lot of disease and high veterinary bills. Since the switch, scouring problems[1] have been eliminated.

The Advantage of Diversity

Diversity and flexibility can be powerful tools put to the farmer's advantage. Monoculture agriculture forces a grower to rely on purchased inputs to support plant growth and control pests and weeds. This inevitably involves a substantial cash outlay in the spring to buy all the inputs. The diversified farmer, in contrast, rarely needs to borrow money to finance input purchases for spring planting. Diversity also reduces crop loss from hail or other natural disasters.

Rotation reduces the risk of too much or too little moisture. For example, between September 1987 and August 1988 we received just 1.3 inches of rain. We still harvested half a crop of wheat, about seventeen bushels to the acre. Barley yielded nine bushels an acre, and sunflower and millet yields were down 20 percent, while oats and rye were a total loss. In comparison, some of my monocropping neighbors never pulled their combines out of the shed. If you have four crops and one fails, that is a 25 percent loss. If you have one crop and it fails, you have a 100 percent loss.

We've seen a change in our soil structure over the past fourteen years. Fuel consumption has dropped because our soil's tilth has improved. Continuous monocropping and aggressive tillage break down soil particles and cause compaction so that water and air can't readily infiltrate the soil. Deep-rooted crops such as sunflowers and legumes help improve soil structure.

Sustainable farming is probably easier on the plains than in the Corn Belt, largely because of farm government programs. For example, Iowa farmers derive 80 percent of their net income from government programs, according to a recent study. Participation in these government programs virtually locks farmers into corn monocropping.

Another advantage plains farmers have is cold weather, which kills insects. Farmers in warmer climates must pay more attention to insect control. Each region has its own ecology and unique set of problems; there are no recipe-book solutions.

Eleven years ago we organized the Northern Plains Sustainable Agricultural Society. We met for the first time, twenty-three of us, in 1979 in Bismarck, North Dakota, to form this informal association. Our purpose was to meet annually to share information on our farming systems. Without any vigorous promotion, our association has grown to 200 farmers from the Dakotas, Montana, Minnesota, and the Canadian provinces of Manitoba and Saskatchewan. I served two three-year terms as president. All of us involved in the organization seem to share the same values. Our beliefs can be summed up in a line our organization borrowed from Wendell Berry: "A sustainable agriculture depletes neither soil nor people."

The philosophy of sustainable agriculture is underpinned by a theological understanding that the resource base and environment must be protected. Consider the Genesis account of Creation and the Garden of Eden story. Both of these make it clear that man and woman are placed in the garden to service and take care of it. The very notion of sustainability strikes me as a transcendent concept. It defies easy definition and finite language, as does any transcendent concept. A universally acceptable definition simply is impossible. It is a goal, a vision, a journey.

Expanding the Vision of Sustainable Agriculture

Sustainable agriculture is often presented as an alternative to conventional agriculture. Framing the issue in that fashion leads to the conclusion that sustainable agriculture is simply another way to farm, or another way to produce food. However, sustainable agriculture may be part of a much more comprehensive change in society. Some have referred to this more inclusive shift as an "ecological revolution."[1] From this perspective, sustainable agriculture may be part of a conceptual revolution that could be as mind-bending as the Copernican revolution that began in the sixteenth century.

Stepping Out and Stepping Back In

In *Dominion: Can Nature and Culture Co-Exist?* Niles Eldredge evaluates changes we might anticipate in our short- and long-term future based on our evolutionary past. He explores who we have become as a human species and how we relate to nature. Such an evolutionary perspective sheds light on the prospect of an ecological revolution and agriculture's role in it.

Agriculture has played a key role in shaping the way we see ourselves and our relationship to the earth. Agriculture, introduced some 10,000 years ago, started us down the path of believing that we could "step out of" our local ecosystems.[2] The practice of domesticating plants and animals for food led us to believe that we could survive and solve all of our problems through human cleverness. For the first time, we believed ourselves

A condensed version of this essay was delivered as a speech at the Northeast Organic Farming Association New Jersey Annual Conference, March 6, 1996. This is an edited version of an essay that first appeared in *For All Generations: Making World Agriculture More Sustainable,* edited by J. Patrick Madden and Scott G. Chaplowe, 38–57 (Glendale, Calif.: OM Publishing, 1997).

capable of escaping our dependence on local ecosystems: "As here and there we plucked local populations of a few plant and animal species from their natural surroundings, domesticating them, we of course transformed ourselves. We removed ourselves from the fundamental position in nature that we had heretofore shared with absolutely all other species since life began. We abruptly stepped out of the local ecosystem. We told Mother Nature we didn't need her anymore, that we could take care of ourselves."[3]

This sense of having stepped out of our local ecosystems fostered two perceptions that have now brought us to the brink of disaster. First, believing that we were no longer dependent on our local ecosystems, we fancied we could control or manipulate those systems with impunity. Second, we concluded that we could solve all our problems on a global scale. This dual belief was repeatedly vindicated by our ingenious ability to seemingly "technofix" most of our problems.

But we have now reached a point where we need to make some radical course corrections if we want to survive beyond the next century with any kind of quality of life. No doubt we will continue to come up with many additional technological fixes, but such fixes are no longer adequate. Furthermore, our fixes sometimes create their own set of problems, often the very problems the fixes were designed to solve. As Eldredge puts it: "No doubt we will go on thinking up neat things. That's what we are good at, and what has brought us to our present state—a state that has many wonderful things to commend it. But it is a state also marked by out-of-control human population growth and its direct consequences: rapidly escalating degradation of the physical state of the planet's surface, mushrooming destruction of the Earth's terrestrial and aquatic ecosystems, loss of thousands of species every year, loss of less technologically advanced human societies— all of which lead to some grim prognostications of our own midterm ecological survival."[4] Moreover, if we are to restore the planetary system to ecological health, we cannot do it on a global scale because there is no global ecosystem, only *local* ecosystems. The only way we can have a healthy global environment is by restoring the health of a lot of local environments.[5]

This raises a number of interesting propositions for agriculture in the next century. The obvious task is to bring the human population into equilibrium with other species and then to design an agriculture that keeps the human population fed while maintaining that equilibrium. More importantly, agriculture may play a key role in unfurling the ecological revolution ahead.

First, if agriculture played a key role in fostering the belief that we could step out of our local ecosystems, could it also play a role in helping us step back in? Eldredge argues that one of the reasons it is difficult for modern humans to recognize their dependence on local ecosystems is that we are so disconnected from the natural world, "we don't even know the most basic details of our own food production."[6] Such alienation separates us from fundamental cycles of life and death, birth and decay, production, and waste recycling. We are deprived of the opportunity to experience the drama of species connectedness. Hence it is "small wonder people have a hard time getting concerned that a particular species of pine tree in the Pacific Northwest or a particular seabird species, let alone some, as yet, undiscovered species of beetle in the depths of the Amazonian rain forest, is under imminent threat of extinction. How can the demise of any of those species possibly have an impact on us?"[7] If we redesign agriculture to make us more aware of the "most basic details of our own food production," then agriculture might help us become more aware of our dependence on local ecosystems and thereby motivate us to restore and maintain them.

Second, agriculture could be designed to restore the health of local ecologies and support local economies, rather than to support global economies at the expense of local ecologies. A new production ethic could evolve that combines the need to produce with the need to sustain the means of production. Such an ethic would likely modify the goals of agriculture and end our tendency to reduce agriculture to a production system driven solely by economic forces. An agriculture designed to help us step back into our local ecosystems will foster a new food system with new economic relationships. A diversified, ecologically grounded agriculture will give birth to a more diversified, local food system and a more vibrant local economy. Such a new food and farming system will become part of a healthier ecological neighborhood.

Accordingly, sustainable agriculture is more than an alternative farming system. It is part of the ecological revolution that many now believe is essential to our survival. If agriculture is to be truly sustainable, it must encompass this larger vision.

Agriculture vs. Agribusiness

If the mission of sustainable agriculture is to facilitate a comprehensive ecological revolution, then farming is much more than a business. However, during the past several decades we have succeeded in reducing agri*culture* to agri*business*. It may now be necessary to transform agribusiness into agriculture, steeped in agroecology.

It may be useful here to explore the root meanings of the terms. The term "agriculture" is made up of two words, *ager* from the Greek (meaning "field" or "land") and *colere* from the Latin (meaning "to cultivate"). *Colere*, however, is multifaceted; both "cult" and "culture" are derived from *colere*. Embedded in its meaning is the notion of a community caring for its own refinement. *Colere* presumes a transcendent ethic guiding the community in its efforts to enhance its quality of life. We may therefore assume that to ancient people the word agri*culture* meant cultivation of plants and domestication of animals in the context of a caring community committed to the sacred obligation of caring for the land.

The word agroecology came into our vocabulary around 1970 and refers to a way of practicing agriculture that attempts to balance environmental and economic risks of farming while maintaining productivity over the long term.[8,9] Agroecology refers to farming practices that "have the general effect of making the agro ecosystem more like the natural ecosystem and less like the urban-industrial system, and hence a less disorderly and a more harmonious component of our total landscape."[10] Agroecology also refers to an alternative food system that supports ecologically sound farming practices. In fact, it is reasonable to believe that without alternative food system infrastructures, it may not be possible to farm in an ecologically sound manner: "When agricultural products become valued more as market commodities to be sold to the highest bidder rather than as food to nourish us, and when short-term yields are maximized at the expense of long-term sustainable production, then the agro ecosystem becomes more of a drain than a contribution to the life-support environment."[11]

Our word "business" comes from the Old English *bisig,* meaning to be constantly occupied. In the sixteenth and seventeenth centuries, it also carried the connotation of impertinence and mischievousness. The word *agribusiness* was presumably introduced as a way of urging farmers to think about farming as a business "like any other" and *not* as a way of life. Since the 1970s, agribusiness propaganda has been warning farmers that if they want to survive, they had better get on the agribusiness bandwagon.

While the etymological roots of these terms are instructive, perhaps even more illuminating is the connotation they carry in the agricultural community. "Agri*culture*" is now generally shunned because it refers to old-fashioned and ineffective farming practices of the past. Agri*culture* is considered synonymous with poor management and nostalgic adherence to farming methods that do not meet the challenges of modern market realities. Land-grant universities, consequently, have distanced themselves from agri*culture*. Farm magazines almost universally prefer the word agri*business*. In mainstream agricultural circles, agri*business* is synonymous with high-tech, modern, efficient farming that uses best management practices, while agri*culture* is a vestige of the past. The barely recognized agro*ecology* is hardly ever used in farm magazines.

This suggests that the shift from agriculture to agribusiness was more than an appeal to farmers to become more skilled in business management. It was, in fact, designed to legitimize the industrial agriculture paradigm. That paradigm included a productionist ethic that made maximum production the single goal of farming, and it introduced a global food and agriculture infrastructure based on specialization, uniformity, and centralized control.

But industrial agriculture is experiencing at least three sets of problems: agronomic, social, and biospheric. While it is not in the scope of this essay to fully delineate each of these sets of problems, it is important to recognize them.

- Agronomic problems include unprecedented soil loss, depleting groundwater, pesticide resistance, and deterioration of soil and water quality.
- Social problems include deteriorating rural communities, the loss of family farms, increased health risks, the concentration of wealth and power in agribusiness corporations (with a concomitant diminishing of free and open markets), and community distress over factory farms.
- Biospheric problems include depletion of fossil fuel energy resources, global warming, wildlife destruction, reduced biodiversity, and ecological imbalances.

Solving these problems will likely hinge on the evolution of a new production ethic that combines restoring the health of local ecosystems with maintaining optimum production.[12] It will recognize the seamless connections between healthy soil, healthy ecological neighborhoods, and vibrant human communities. Agriculture will be designed to fit into local ecologies. We can only manage local ecosystems in an ecologically sensitive manner when local people live in local ecosystems long enough and intimately enough to know how to manage them in an ecologically sound manner.[13]

Local Economies vs. Globalization

A vibrant local economy is essential to an agriculture designed to maintain the health of local ecosystems. David Korten asserts that "healthy societies depend on healthy, empowered local communities that build caring relationships among people and help us connect to a particular piece of the living earth with which our lives are intertwined."[14] That can only happen when local people have control of local economies and can hold each other accountable for local actions. However, the most pervasive trend in business since the end of World War II has been globalization. In terms of wealth, "global companies have overtaken numerous national economies."[15] When the wealth of transnational corporations exceeds that of national economies, they exercise enormous power over the way local citizens live in local ecosystems. "The decisions of global corporations affect not only the business and markets in which they function, but also the lives and environments of the people in whose communities they operate."[16]

Transnationals could help improve local economies, because increased employment contributes to social stability and quality of life. But global corporate power can also destroy local economies because it can extract local raw materials, dump hazardous waste, disrupt ecologies, exploit labor, deprive citizens of the opportunity to produce their own food, and force communities to become dependent on expensive, imported, value-added products that (in the absence of local production and processing) become essential for survival. As Wendell Berry has pointed out, such an economy is extractive, colonial, and based on the principle "that it is permissible to ruin one place or culture for the sake of another."[17]

Transnational corporations, which by definition have no loyalty to place, unavoidably become extractive economies that disable people. As David Korten describes the situation, global *corporations cooperate* to force *people to compete.* That inevitably leads to local competition for scarce resources and the willingness to destroy local capital for the sake of individual gain. As a result, local ecosystem health always suffers. Local agriculture participates in this destruction of the local environment for the sake of economic survival. Korten suggests it is essential that we change our economic infrastructures to force *corporations to compete* so that *people can cooperate.* That requires a political process designed to protect the rights of local citizens and to foster local communities driven by vibrant local economies.

In the late eighteenth century, Adam Smith recognized that apart from "community" and a framework of justice, competition becomes destructive. Smith's ideal market economy consists of four components:

- The community comprises small farmers, artisans, buyers, and sellers.
- Entrepreneurs function within a set of commercial rules, sanctioned and protected by the state, that prevent business monopolies.
- Capital is locally rooted, with the owners living in the communities in which they do business.
- Free and open markets are available.[18]

Today's global markets hardly subscribe to Adam Smith's free-market principles.[19–21] In fact, they resemble the mercantilism that he despised. In today's globalized, top-down, vertically integrated agribusiness system, free and open markets are rapidly disappearing, monopolies are increasingly protected and supported by government, and local communities are routinely decimated.

The current factory-farm hog industry is a good case in point. In North Carolina, Smithfield Foods entered into preferred contract arrangements with a few large hog producers, each producing in excess of 100,000 hogs. All independent hog producers were relegated to what economists call "residual suppliers." Because Smithfield Foods is the only market for hogs in North Carolina, this arrangement put more than half of the independent hog producers in North Carolina out of business within a few years. Such oligopolistic scenarios are being played out in all sectors of the global agricultural economy. Almost 90 percent of fed steers and heifers are now packed by just four companies. The rest of the meat industry is similarly concentrated.[22, 23]

Genetically engineered and patented seed, designed to meet definite end-use specifications, will likely force grain farmers into similar business straitjackets. Corn farmers, for example, will have to decide whether they want to raise corn for fructose, milling, chips, or feed, and then will have to contract with the company that owns the seed patent for the seed designed to meet those specific end uses. In most cases, the company that owns the seed will also own the market or will be affiliated with a company that does. There will be no market for ordinary corn!

Such companies, of course, prefer to do business with the largest producers and will issue them preferred contracts. Smaller producers are forced out of business. As "residual suppliers," smaller producers have a less favored status in these closed markets, and no alternative markets exist. If the broiler industry is a harbinger of the future, large producers also become subservient to the monopoly corporation. In 1992, *Time* magazine referred to farmers who sign contracts to produce chickens for Tyson as "serfs on their own land."[24]

In such a globalized, controlled market, it is difficult to imagine how a local agriculture, supported by a local economy and designed to nurture healthy local ecosystems, can survive. Global economies don't care about local ecosystems. Global economies are designed to maximize returns to investors, the vast majority of whom live far removed from the local ecosystems where the farming is done. Consequently, if we are going to redesign agriculture to participate in the ecological revolution, local market infrastructures are needed. Only in this way can agriculture contribute to the life-support systems in which we live.

Feeding the World vs. Well-Fed Villages

Demographers now predict that global human population growth will "stabilize" at around 10 or 12 billion people in the next century. One can't help but wonder what "stabilization" means in this context. The planet will not only be crowded with humans, but culture and community will be strained, creating great potential for chaos and disease. Local, sustainable agriculture has to grapple with this problem.

Some contend the population problem can be addressed by simply producing more food. Dennis Avery, for example, has suggested that population predictions make it imperative that we accelerate input-intensive, global, industrial agriculture to increase yields. Avery argues that an ecologically oriented agriculture would consign billions of people to starvation, degrade the environment, and destroy millions of acres of wildlife habitat.[25] He assumes that ecological agriculture would yield far less protein per acre than chemical-intensive agriculture (an assumption not backed up by independent research). Thus, in his argument, additional huge quantities of wilderness and fragile lands for food production would be cultivated. Scenarios like Avery's assume that expanding human populations simply require increased food production.

Ervin Laszlo, prominent member of the Club of Rome and advisor to the director-general of UNESCO, sees the problem quite differently. According to Laszlo, the global community is moving into a "fifth wave" that he characterizes as an era of "global stress."[26] He says, "The late-twentieth-century world is overpopulated, overpolluted, overarmed, and extremely energy- and resource-hungry. It is also increasingly polarized, with a small minority of well-off industrialized countries surrounded by a rising sea of poor, underdeveloped states."[27] In other words, the problems of the next century cannot be neatly reduced to population growth and the need for more food. Producing sufficient food will only be one small part of a much more complex set of problems: "Problems of population, poverty, militarization, waste and environmental degradation, climate change, and food and energy shortages are the principal causes of intensifying stress in the global system."[28]

Given Laszlo's perspective, the challenge facing agriculture may be quite different from the one Avery suggests. We know, of course, that millions of people are already starving to death on our planet, with a present population of 5.7 billion. Malnutrition is not due to lack of food production; it is a political, social, and economic problem. Simply intensifying the use of chemical input to increase the yields of corn and soybeans won't change that. As Korten points out, "There is scarcely a country in the world that does not have the resources and technology needed to provide its people with their basic needs for food, clothing, shelter, education and health care."[29] But even if the population problem *could* be solved by producing more food, intensifying industrial agriculture may not actually increase food production, because further increases in yield may depend more on improving soil quality and moisture conservation than on intensified use of manufactured inputs.

Furthermore, the increased use of toxic inputs to increase yields may result in a net *decrease* of available food. For example, 60 percent of the world's population today depends on fish and seafood for 40 percent of its annual protein. There is ample evidence to confirm that land-based industrial agriculture's environmental impact on aquatic and marine habitats is seriously diminishing the food supply from this critical source.[30] Increasing the yields of land-based agriculture (assuming it can be done) at the expense of aquatic agriculture is, therefore, hardly the way to feed more people.

Given the complex set of problems Laszlo describes, adequate food production must accompany a system of people/food/land equilibrium. The best way to achieve such an equilibrium is through local community-based agriculture, tied to ecologically responsible local land use, rooted in local culture. In her enlightening book on the culture of the Ladakh people of the western Himalayas, Helena Norberg-Hodge points out that despite the very scarce resources and extreme climates in the desert highlands where they live, the Ladakh are well nourished, unusually healthy, and free of social and environmental stresses.[31] This balance of environmental, social, and physical health is attributed to their sense of being part of their local ecosystem. Population stabilization, adequate nourishment, environmental and human health, and social harmony are part of the fabric of local culture and woven into their sense of ecological integration: "That population control is an important factor in maintaining balance with the environment is clear. The link with 'social harmony' is perhaps less so. Nevertheless, it seems that social friction is likely to be reduced if the number of people depending on a fixed quantity of resources remains the same from generation to generation. Under those circumstances, the need for scrambling and fighting to survive is clearly minimized."[32]

It may be, then, that the best way to "stabilize" future populations is to redesign agriculture to meet the needs of local communities within local ecosystems, and thereby begin to develop a sense of equilibrium between people and the land. Of course, this requires that local people in local communities have access to the land and tools required to feed themselves.

Keeping local villages fed would be the first priority of agriculture. Exporting surpluses would become a second priority. Localized agriculture cannot be achieved in a globalized system designed to maximize returns to a handful of transnational corporations. In many parts of the world, global industrial agriculture usurps local resources of poor countries to produce and export exotic foods, so their governments can pay off national debts to the industrialized world. In that scenario, additional production will not feed the world, regardless of how input-intensive it is.

Consumers or Customers

The web of local culture and local agriculture, designed to fit the needs of local ecologies in local ecosystems, also suggests that a sound ecological agriculture may not be possible without a new consumption ethic. The industrial ethic has turned us all into voracious *consumers.*

Consumerism grew out of the industrial era. Erich Fromm suggests that it was the industrial era's illusion that we could fully control nature and create our own "second world" that led us to believe in "unlimited production and, hence, unlimited consumption."[33] This fostered a new Trinitarian religion: "unlimited production, absolute freedom and unrestricted happiness."[34] This new industrial religion transformed us into consumers, turned inward, intent on usurping nature to satisfy our own individual desires, even at the expense of our neighbors. As consumers we became individual siphons on society, instead of cooperating members of a local neighborhood.

Fromm, incidentally, asserted that this consumption ethic was destined to fail because it was based on two faulty psychological premises: that the chief aim of life is maximum pleasure and that greed can lead to harmony and peace.[35]

We can never achieve a people/food/land equilibrium without both a new consumption ethic and a new production ethic. The new consumption ethic must be based on satisfying the needs of local communities within the constraints of local ecosystems, rather than on the desires of individuals driven by illusions of unlimited resources. In other words, commercial transactions must be driven by community *custom* designed to enrich the fabric of the entire community, rather than individual satisfaction driven by whatever subjective need we may feel. Such an ethic would transform us from *consumers* into *customers.*

In the summer of 1995 our family had the opportunity to function as customers instead of consumers in our local community. The incident may serve as an example of how we could begin to evolve a new consumption ethic within local communities.

My father became ill with a debilitating stroke early in 1995. He wanted to stay at home, on the farm, where he could be with family members in familiar surroundings. In order to comply with that wish, we needed a part-time caretaker on the farm. In consumer fashion we contacted the bureaucratic agencies, both public and private, to see if we could find someone for the job.

We followed every lead. No one was willing to take the job, mostly because no one was willing to come out to a farm to take care of an old, debilitated man. In desperation, we called a neighbor to see if she could recommend anyone. She called back later that day and offered to take the job herself.

The weeks that followed were remarkable. My father knew the neighbor and was delighted by her care. She not only provided professional care but a level of love and compassion that nurtured my father throughout his final months of life. Providing care for him in his home was far less expensive than a care facility would have been, and the income our neighbor earned was much needed by her family.

After my father's death, our neighbor remarked how satisfying the caregiving had been for her and that she would have loved to become a nurse if she had the education. We encouraged her to consider going back to school. There were the usual barriers—cost and fear were paramount. We helped with the application process at a local college. The college put together a financial aid package that considerably reduced her cost. Then our family established a scholarship fund in memory of my father, which raised enough additional money from the community to fund her first year of college. The money our family put into the scholarship fund was a fraction of what the additional cost of putting my father into a care facility would have been.

Our neighbor is now in school to become a nurse. Her family is well-rooted in the community and not likely to move once she graduates. Therefore, when she graduates she will practice nursing in our community, a remote rural area where local health care is inadequate at best. These were all commercial transactions that took place within the fabric of community custom, an example of individuals contracting with one another to fulfill mutual needs that end up enriching the local community. Everyone benefits from such customer relationships.

How might food and agriculture transactions be transformed to enable people to become customers of local economies serving human interests, instead of consumers of global economies serving corporate interests?

Foodsheds vs. Global Markets

Designing food systems to meet the needs of local sustainable agriculture, within local communities, and suited to the ecologies of local ecosystems will not be easy. To describe this reality, the concept of a "foodshed" works well. A foodshed is a region (similar to a watershed) defined by biological, social, and economic boundaries. The first priority of the foodshed would be to produce all of the nutrient requirements *for* people living in the food-shed, *by* people in the foodshed. The second priority would be to produce food for export.

Such a food system would bring many benefits to local communities. Trade would truly be "free." As John Cobb points out, trade is only free when people are free *not to trade*.[36] People living in self-sufficient foodsheds would be free to import certain foods if they wished, but they would also be free to avoid imports. Foodsheds would shorten supply lines and avoid many problems with transportation, packaging, shelf life, and energy consumption. Nutritious food would be produced to feed the community, not to withstand commercial shipping and make profits for distant corporations.

Foodsheds would give people more control over the quality of their food. Because food would be locally produced, foodshed citizens would have a more direct voice in determining the way food is produced and processed, helping to limit related environmental impacts. Foodsheds would diversify the local food system and markets and provide the opportunity to redesign agriculture to fit into local ecologies instead of global economies.

Such foodsheds will emerge out of local examples and new local-market forces, rather than by the design of some technocracy. Examples, in fact, already exist:

- In North Dakota, there has been a resurgence of locally owned, value-added processing enterprises in the past decade.
- In Minneapolis, Minnesota, the Upper Midwest Organic Alliance is currently experimenting with a project in local labeling. Before a manufacturer or retailer may use the "Midwest" logo, at least 50 percent of the ingredients in the product must come from the five-state region covered by the project.
- Local microbreweries have enjoyed such success in the marketplace that major breweries have decided to enter the microbrew market. Interestingly enough, major breweries have attributed microbrewers' success exclusively to the quality of the product. The success of microbrews may have as much to do with community as with product

quality. Part of the attraction to microbrews is sitting in local pubs drinking beer with your neighbors, watching beer being brewed!

• Community-supported agriculture and farmers' markets are moving us in the direction of regional foodsheds. Increasingly, people prefer fresh food, locally produced, to highly packaged and processed food shipped thousands of miles.

• A few communities have started to purchase the food consumed in local community institutions from local farmers. Hendrix College, for example, now has a policy of purchasing at least 30 percent of the food served in its cafeteria from local farmers. If local citizens decide that tax dollars earmarked to purchase food for local hospitals, schools, or prisons should be used to purchase locally grown food, this may help to create the local infrastructures needed to stimulate local food purchasing. Furthermore, communities might urge local nutritionists (also often paid with local tax dollars) who plan the menus for local hospitals, schools, and other institutions to create nutritious menus that use locally produced foods.

From the Ground Up

This vision of sustainable agriculture may seem naive and unattainable. Forces favoring a global industrialized food and agriculture system seem too great to allow locally vested food systems to survive. I take issue with that argument.

First, historically, trends seldom prevail over the long term. In fact, cycles rather than trends may be more relevant for providing clues about the future.

Second, because ecological systems are more in harmony with the process of evolution, they are more sustainable than industrial systems. Evolution has driven the course of nature for billions of years. Ultimately, industrial systems depend upon ecological systems for necessary resources.

Third, food is different from any other commodity. We can all get along without computers, cars, and fax machines. We are not vested in those commodities in the same way we are vested in food. People become passionately involved in food issues. That may be one reason why people are increasingly buying their food in direct markets.

Another reason may be that the industrial food system has succeeded in alienating people from the food they eat. People have no connection with the places where food is grown, no knowledge about how it is handled or processed, and their food choices are reduced. This sense of alienation, perhaps more than anything else, motivates people to regain connection with their food and the source of its production.

As people become more connected to the source of their food, their views about other aspects of life are influenced. This simple fact bodes well for the ecological revolution.

Alice Waters, founder of San Francisco's Chez Panisse restaurant, said the following in a letter to President Clinton and Vice President Gore:

> If we choose to feed ourselves responsibly, if we feed ourselves with fresh, living, local food, we have to interact with purveyors who are trying to live on the earth in a harmonious and responsible way. After several years of buying food from such people . . . one has all kinds of understanding: about agricultural economy and risk, and the heroic effort required to husband the land and its life-sustaining resources; about who the farmers are and what they grow best; and about the freshness and seasonality of food and what things smell and taste like. And these kinds of understandings contribute to the health and stability of local agriculture and to a real sense of belonging to a local community.[37]

These are the powerful forces that can create local foodsheds, support local economies, and create healthy soil, ecological neighborhoods, and human communities.

The Role of Independent Beef Producers in Rural Development

Suddenly everyone is interested in developing us. The January/February 1997 Kerr Center newsletter announced that it was adding "rural development" to its program.[1] The lead article in the newsletter points us in a rural-development direction, but it cannot possibly lead to any real rural development. It suggests that the beef industry's problems could be solved through vertical integration, much like the swine and poultry industries. Producers would be paid a salary to raise calves to a specific weight and would receive a bonus for good performance. The article asserts that "raising cattle is a hobby and not a business" when herds are only 100 cows or less, although it is my understanding that 50 percent of the beef cows in the United States are in herds of this size.

I would have expected something like this in *Beef* or the *Farm Journal*. I was really surprised to find it in a "sustainable agriculture" newsletter. Apparently, the author of the article, a "livestock specialist," is not aware of several facts. For example, the economic viability and environmental benefits of herds of less than 100 cows that are fully integrated in crop/livestock systems are well-established. Several North Dakota State University studies on integrated crop/livestock systems demonstrated that:

• When sixty beef cows were integrated into a cropping system so that the cows could make use of corn stover and other crop residues, the return for labor was $22 per hour. Feed costs were low because cows consumed crop waste, and crop production costs were lowered by ma-

A version of this piece was originally published in the newsletter of the Center for Sustainable Agricultural Systems, Institute of Agriculture and Natural Resources, University of Nebraska, March–April 1997, 1–6.

nure applied to crops. Any time farmers can turn waste into income and make $22 an hour doing it, they are on the path to economic sustainability.

• When eighty-five cows were added to a cropping system, the return to the cropping system increased by $24,000 annually in conventional farming systems and $27,000 annually in conservation tillage systems.

• When crop residues were fed to cows, 71 percent of the nitrogen consumed by the cows was returned to the field in the form of manure.

Crop/livestock integration is one of the key ways to improve economic and ecological sustainability, and herd size can be well below 100. Furthermore, it is precisely such integrated crop/livestock systems that enable producers to develop ecologically elegant systems, surely one of the hallmarks of sustainability.

Contrast this with the model Lathrop proposes: the broiler industry. In a recent article in *Time* magazine, farmers who had contracted with Tyson to produce chicken had become "serfs on their own land."[2] Because Tyson was the only market, farmers were in no position to bargain or auction for better prices. They had not received an increase for their labor in eleven years, despite the fact that their costs had increased by 50 percent. In the processing plants, workers received minimum wages in extremely harsh working conditions that now make "fowl processing one of the nation's most hazardous jobs." Furthermore, the manure overload from the massive concentration of chickens creates an intolerable waste disposal problem with numerous detrimental environmental impacts. Is this the "sustainable" future that Lathrop sees for beef producers and the rural communities in which beef is produced?

Our 3,100-acre grain and livestock farm has 114 beef brood cows. The beef cattle are fully integrated into the cropping system. We feed our cattle no cash grain, only forages and crop residues. We generate, on average, $300,000 gross revenue annually, and we haven't borrowed any operating funds in twenty years. I assure you this is not a hobby farm. Over the past ten years we have always received top dollar for our back-grounded calves—not because we are part of a vertically integrated, industry-managed quality-control system, but because our calves are healthy, grass-fed, and ready to perform well when they hit the feedlot.

Lathrop does suggest that producers need to cooperate. I agree. But they need to cooperate with one another (not with corporations), develop direct markets where possible, and pool their capital to capture market segments that companies such as Iowa Beef Processors cannot compete with, such as high-quality grass- and forage-fed beef. However, farmers will need to build locally owned processing plants to create the products that will be attractive to specific market niches. Wealth generated by beef enterprises that stays in local communities instead of being drained off to distant investors is real rural development.

Foreword to *Farming with the Wild: Enhancing Biodiversity on Farms and Ranches*

As a farmer, I have had a relationship with wild things that has been fraught with ambiguity. I grew up believing that wildness was the enemy of agriculture. I didn't like blackbirds eating our sunflowers, coyotes attacking our calves, or weeds robbing our crops of nutrients and moisture. So I had an almost instinctive inclination to tear all the wildness out of our farm. I was ready to use any tool or scientific management tactic available to eradicate wild things from the farm.

A part of me even felt morally justified in harboring that attitude because it is deeply entrenched in our culture. The early Puritans who settled on New England's shores considered it part of their manifest destiny to "tame the wilderness" and "build the Kingdom of God" in this "new land." Cotton Mather (1663–1728) considered the wilderness to be the "devil's playground."[1] It was, therefore, part of his God-given responsibility to urge his fellow Puritans to replace the wilderness with nice, neat rows of corn. For good or ill, that Puritan ethic shaped much of the culture in North America once Native Americans were driven from the land. I am a product of that culture.

Like the generations of farmers and ranchers before me, I have lived, in part, by this wilderness-eradication ethic and have caused devastating harm to natural ecosystems. Meanwhile, conservationists have adopted a countervailing ethic in order to protect the wilderness. In response to centuries of abuse, conservationists promoted designating certain regions as wilderness areas to protect them from human activity. Only with great difficulty have wilderness advocates managed to keep a small proportion of our country

This is an edited version of the foreword to Daniel Imhoff, *Farming with the Wild: Enhancing Biodiversity on Farms and Ranches* (San Francisco: Sierra Club Books, 2003).

(approximately 5 percent) free from industrial intrusions (though not free of livestock). But by eliminating humans from certain parts of the landscape to preserve it, we have also inadvertently consented to humans using the rest of the landscape without any regard for its wildness.

We now know that this dual approach to land use is dysfunctional on both counts. Wildness cannot be "maintained" in isolated pieces of the landscape, and farms cannot be productively managed without wildness. Just as wild organisms need the connectivity of natural ecosystems to thrive, so agriculture needs the wildness of soil organisms to maintain soil quality and pollinators to grow crops—both necessary elements for productive farming. So in the interests of both productive farming and robust wilderness, we need to revisit our dualistic mentality.

Because producing as much as possible in one part of the landscape while preserving everything in its natural state in another part of the landscape is not working, and the real goals of conservation—preserving the integrity, stability, and beauty of the biotic community—have been betrayed, we now must face our fundamental role as *Homo sapiens* within the biotic community. The essential fallacy in our dualistic thinking is that in both cases, wilderness and agriculture, we assumed humans were separate from nature. Isolating wilderness areas from human activity assumes that wilderness thrives best without human intervention. Indeed, large areas uninhabited by people, such as the Brooks Range of Alaska, provide powerful testament. That assumption, however, while probably true in the modern, industrial context, serves only to deepen the schism between humans and wild nature. Isolating wildness from agricultural landscapes presumes that humans, acting separately from nature, can control production systems purely with human ingenuity and technology. Neither assumption encourages the sort of healthy reintegration into the biotic community that humans must achieve—for our own sake and the sake of all life on Earth. Behind that dualistic fallacy lies another, namely that nature is a given, that it has evolved into a state of equilibrium (that it will remain essentially the same) and that we can either manipulate it at will (agriculture) or preserve it in a natural stasis (wilderness). No empirical data justify such assumptions. And this both encourages the alienation of humans from nature and represents a serious underestimation of nature.

Fifty years ago, Aldo Leopold attempted to overcome this flawed, dualistic thinking by introducing a new paradigm: ecological consciousness.

The role of *Homo sapiens,* he suggested, had to be changed from "conqueror of the land-community to plain member and citizen of it."[2] This way of thinking, he suggested, transforms our relationship within Nature. It "reflects the existence of an ecological conscience, and this in turn reflects a conviction of individual responsibility for the health of the land. Health is the capacity of the land for self-renewal. Conservation is our effort to understand and preserve this capacity."[3] When our understanding stems from this perspective, the boundaries between domesticated agriculture and wilderness begin to soften.

Our society's failure to appreciate the need for an ecological consciousness is evident not only on industrial farms, but on organic farms as well. We have, unfortunately, come to think of organic farms as isolated enclaves that have little or no connection with the ecology of the landscape in which those farms exist. Organic farms, treated as isolated enclaves, cannot maintain the rich biodiversity necessary for a healthy farm, any more than an isolated wilderness can preserve the biodiversity of a healthy ecosystem. If we hope to create an agriculture that ensures the land's capacity for self-renewal, or a wilderness that perpetuates the native biodiversity of a region, then humans who possess an ecological consciousness need to be part of the landscape.

Our dualistic thinking has led us to believe that the "environment" exists of its own accord. It is just "out there." In truth, however, the environment is constantly being constructed by the organisms (including humans) that live in it. As Harvard evolutionary biologist Richard Lewontin reminds us, all organisms "are in a constant process of altering their environment. Every species, not only *Homo sapiens,* is in the process of destroying its own environment by using resources that are in short supply and transforming them into a form that cannot be used again by the individuals of the species."[4] In other words, if it were not for the activity of organisms in nature modifying their environment—and, in doing so, destroying part of it—there would be no environment.

As one species destroys part of the environment, opportunities for other species are created. Cows eat grass, but the by-product of that activity is manure, which provides food for dung beetles and other organisms, who in turn destroy the manure, and in so doing create nutrients for the soil to produce more grass. Lewontin explains that "every act of consumption is also an act of production." The appropriate role of humans, then, is to engage in a dance with other species in the biotic community in a manner that enables the community to renew itself—both its wild and domestic parts.

Applying this view to twenty-first century agriculture will require a radical shift in our relationship with nature. We must reclaim our solidarity with the ecosystems in which we farm through "place-based reinhabitation." As David Abram has written: "It is only at the scale of our direct, sensory interactions with the land around us that we can appropriately notice and respond to the immediate needs of the living world."[5] Our mission as farmers and ranchers must evolve from providing adequate, affordable, nutritious food and practicing good conservation to taking responsibility for the "health of the land." Our concept of science must change from reliance on technological innovations to solve human problems to engaging in locally based conversations with nature. Our notions of organic farms must change from enclaves of purity to habitats within ecosystems. The certification of individual farms must give way to standards and monitoring systems for certifying entire watersheds. At that point, agriculture's relationship to wildness will move from production enclaves to wild farm alliances, restoring interconnected, healthy ecosystems.

On our organic farm in North Dakota, we have begun to appreciate the role of wildness. We now use livestock breeds that have retained some of their "wildness." Our beef cows possess the instinct to protect their calves from coyotes until the youngsters are old enough to fend for themselves. We have discovered that maintaining habitats for pollinators and beneficial insects increases the productivity of our cropping system. By using crop rotations to mimic the succession inherent in wild systems, we have eliminated the need for costly herbicides to control weeds. We hope that someday perennial polycultures will replace annual crops, eliminating the annual disturbance of agricultural lands. We are convinced that many additional benefits lie hidden in the vast resources of the prairie ecology in which we farm. After decades of research and education devoted to controlling nature, we have a lot of catching up to do. We need to comprehend how the prairie ecology functions so that we can access nature's free ecosystem services while improving the land's self-renewal capacity. With that understanding, our farm will become more profitable and sustainable.

Fossil fuel depletion, inability of our farming regions to sustain further agriculture-related degradation, and expanding human population and impacts on biodiversity may force many of the above changes to take place. But this will require that we abandon our dualistic thinking, adopt an ecological consciousness, and erase the hard boundaries between tame and wild in our minds.

On Being an "Objective" Farmer

Can I put this together?[1]
—Barry Lopez

I was born in a farmhouse south of Medina, North Dakota, a small rural town that is now struggling to survive. My parents began farming on that land in 1930, so they spent their first years as a young farm couple in the midst of the Dust Bowl. Those were hard times that taught harsh lessons. At times my father wasn't sure he would be able to feed his young family. He learned to be extremely frugal—perhaps too frugal, he later thought. And he vowed that what had happened to his land in the ravages of the Dust Bowl would "never ever happen again." Eventually he became, by any standard, a successful farmer. The operation expanded from five cows, a team of horses and 120 acres of rented land in 1930 to a 2,400-acre farm with 200 head of cattle by 1970, all of which was owned and debt-free.

My father achieved all of this without relying on any science-based research. He learned by observation and through direct experience. His learning was guided by his passions: to be "the best farmer in Stutsman County," and to provide his land with the best care possible.

My father became a serious conservationist, but on his own terms. He introduced farming practices that prevented his land from suffering any further loss of soil due to wind erosion. But in his efforts to raise fifty bushels of wheat per acre, he plowed up a lot of native prairie that most conservationists, including myself, were convinced should have been left in grass.

This is an edited version of an article that first appeared in Zachary Michael Jack, ed., *Black Earth and Ivory Tower: New American Essays from Farm and Classroom* (Columbia, S.C.: University of South Carolina Press, 2005), 224–30.

I grew up in that environment. While I often found myself disagreeing with my father on specific details, I always marveled at his ability to anticipate and prepare for events that seemed wholly unpredictable to me. It seemed he had developed some kind of clairvoyant ability to foresee problems and opportunities before they occurred.

In high school and college I learned about the scientific method and how scientists had to remain "value-free." They had to maintain a certain detachment from what they wanted to know in order to prevent their own biases from distorting the data. This new way of knowing presented me with a puzzle. If detachment and rigorous adherence to the scientific method constituted the only true way of knowing, how did my father consistently anticipate problems and opportunities and take appropriate actions without the benefit of that approach? With only a sixth-grade education, he knew what he knew by immersing himself fully in that which he sought to know, and he filtered his knowledge through the screen of his passion.

In graduate school I encountered a variety of methodologies for knowing. I also began to marvel at the ability of those who combined science-based knowledge with experience-based intelligence. For example, Aldo Leopold wrote openly about his passion for a reconnection with nature and insisted that an ethic was essential to insuring the health of the land. After graduate school I pursued a career in higher education but always maintained my farming connections. I talked regularly with my father and always spent summer vacations on the farm. In one form or another, those conversations inevitably ended up exploring the way he knew what he knew and how it differed from the way the academy claimed it "knew" what it knew. He had great respect for the academy, but he also harbored deep suspicions of it. Whenever the "science" seemed to contradict what he had learned through field experience, he suspected that the scientists "hadn't picked enough rocks"—his favorite expression for people who lacked field experience to corroborate their academic conclusions.

I continued to search for more mentors. Among philosophers, I found the phenomenologists particularly helpful. I ran across Edmund Husserl's contention that pure objective reality (usually a given to modern science) was not the concrete basis underlying all experience; rather, objective reality was in fact a *theoretical construction* that constituted a kind of unwarranted idealization of an intersubjective experience. It occurred to me that there might be a third way to understand how we knew what we knew.

Neither the subjective experience I thought my father represented nor the objective experience modern science represented told the full story of how we actually know what we know. Husserl, and later the work of Michael Polanyi, taught me that the "real world" was not a pure object or a fixed and finished reality from which we could strip all subjective qualities, but rather a complex matrix of perceptions and experiences lived from many different perspectives. What we call "objectivity" is the mutual understanding that emerges from our continual exploration and our ongoing search for consensus with others who are trying to understand the same reality.

The role of "others" in this knowledge dance, I learned later, is not strictly limited to other *humans,* but includes all the "others" of the biotic community. My father, the scientists in their lab coats, and the ants dragging a grain of wheat through the stubble are all partners in the dance of knowledge.

After fifteen years in the academy, I returned to manage the farm, where I encountered my father's unusual wisdom almost daily. How did he "know" we should trade in that combine this year, just before the engine blew up? How did he "know" that the brown-spotted cow was likely to give birth to her calf within twenty-four hours and that she "might have trouble"? How did he "know" that next week would provide better all-around conditions to start planting wheat than this week? It was almost painful to watch other young, enthusiastic farmers in the neighborhood, fresh from agricultural colleges, depending almost exclusively on computers to make essential management choices—and then to watch them, one by one, go out of business because of bad decisions. My father simply shook his head.

Shortly after I returned to the farm, I joined the North Central Sustainable Agriculture Research and Education (SARE) program as a member of the Administrative Council, where I found a rare opportunity to explore these disparate ways of knowing. By design, the SARE program brought together farmers and academic researchers to identify, design, and carry out research projects, a unique circumstance that blended field experience and the "objectivity" of the academy.

The first meetings were tense. Farmers, not unlike my father, weren't sure they trusted the academics. How could academics "know" what things were like on a real farm? Academics were equally distrustful. Would farmers, with their subjective biases, distort or interfere with the objectivity of their work?

Eventually farmers and academics began to appreciate their varied perspectives and found real value in comparing the different knowledges they each contributed to a better understanding of the whole. Appreciation ultimately gave way to recognition that these differing perspectives were, in fact, *essential* to improving the work of *both* farmers and academics.

Participating in the SARE program opened other doors for me to develop close working relationships with research and extension personnel in my own community. I began to work closely with several researchers in two of our extension field stations. The apparent chasm began to narrow between the way my father "knew" what he knew and the way academics "knew" what they knew. Researchers developed a real appreciation for the perspective that farmers brought to the table. Farmer "advisory boards" began to provide real input into the selection, design, and evaluation of research work conducted at the station and on farms. Farmers began to appreciate the data generated by computers, laboratory data, and field trials. Together farmers and researchers struggled to determine the best way to apply their combined knowledge on real operating farms and in the marketplace.

Now I've returned to the academy. In July 2000 I accepted the position of director of the Leopold Center for Sustainable Agriculture at Iowa State University. I'm still managing the farm, mostly by cell phone, as I work closely with three young men who take care of the farm's daily operations. But most of my time is spent with the Leopold Center's programs at the university. I find myself immersed in a new set of tensions that still revolve around some of the same old issues.

Land-grant universities, I think, are caught in a peculiar set of circumstances, partly due to the social changes that have transpired over the last several decades. The apparent intention of the Morrill Act of 1862, which founded the land-grant university system, was to establish a "permanent" agriculture by providing better education to the "industrial classes." Farmers would take better care of both land and people, thereby creating a stable agricultural system and stable communities.

That goal was partly undermined, however, by a social contract with agriculture that was established early in the twentieth century. That contract invited farmers, with the help of research at the land-grant universities, to produce all of our food and fiber with a dramatically reduced labor force. This would "free" people to work in industry and professional associations in order to improve our shared quality of life. While this may have been a worthy social goal at the time, it is hard to imagine that society still benefits from pushing more farmers off the land. I would argue that if we want to care for farmland in an ecologically sound manner, we need *more* farmers on the land.

Nevertheless, government officials, agribusiness firms, and farmer commodity groups still largely operate out of the old paradigm of maximizing production with as little labor as possible in order to compete in a global economy. Land-grant universities are following suit by pursuing one-dimensional research that helps farmers and agribusiness industries meet that singular goal. But many scholars in the land-grant university system question the validity of this conventional wisdom on both scientific and practical grounds. One reason for the perceived need to shift paradigms is that the unforeseen side effects of the conventional approach can no longer be ignored.

By some estimates, 36 percent of the world's cropland is losing topsoil at a rate that undermines its productive capacity. Excess nutrient runoff from agricultural fields is a major contributor to the evolution of fifty-three dead zones in the Earth's water systems. [Editor's note: the count reached 400 by 2009.] Major aquifers are being depleted due to irrigation-dependent production systems. In the meantime, science has begun to realize that the single-tactic, single-gene approach to solving agriculture's problems has failed. Using a pesticide to control a target pest is often successful in the short term, but it fails in the long term. There is a growing recognition that all problems are evolutionary in character and require a systems approach, rather than a one-dimensional approach. The complexity of living systems does not allow problems to be readily solved by applying single-gene, single-tactic solutions.

But paradigms are very powerful. Once we see the world through a particular set of lenses, it is often difficult to view it from a new perspective, especially if the current view is vested with business interests that provide financial gain to its proponents. In such circumstances, innovators are often punished, sometimes intentionally and sometimes unintentionally. Research grants often go to those whose research helps substantiate the current view of things, or those who find new fixes so that the old way of doing things can survive a little longer. Those who want to explore alternatives often are ignored or are given signals that what they are doing is less relevant. The science declared to be "sound" is often the science supporting the prevailing paradigm. In such circumstances, it is especially dangerous to base one's position on experience-based knowledge or to be guided by one's passion.

I find myself, then, in much the same quandary as the naturalist. In much the same way that my father experienced his farm, naturalists understand nature through direct experience and deep immersion in that part of nature they are trying to understand. And they are often driven by an unrelenting passion. Barry Lopez explains that the naturalist is in an uneasy position. Immersed in nature, the naturalist experiences the loss and pain of the damage we have done to nature. But science demands that one remain detached. How, then, does one "manage emotional grief and moral indignation in pursuits so closely tied to science, with its historical claim to objectivity"?[2] Lopez observes that "the modern naturalist, acutely, even depressingly, aware of the planet's shrinking and eviscerated habitats, often feels compelled to do more than merely register the damage. The impulse to protest, however, is often stifled by feelings of defensiveness, a fear of being misread. . . . Almost every naturalist has borne the supercilious judgments of various sophisticates who thought the naturalist a romantic, a sentimentalist, a bucolic—or worse; and more latterly, the condescension of some scientists who thought the naturalist not rigorous, not analytical, not detached enough."[3]

My father's ways of knowing were met with similar suspicions. The same condescension is often directed at farmers and scientists who are struggling to discover a new paradigm for agriculture: one that enables farmers to be more productive and profitable while restoring and protecting the ecological health of the land. According to Lopez, "The bugbear in all of this is the role of field experience, the degree to which the naturalist's assessments are empirically grounded in firsthand knowledge. . . . What part, of what the naturalist has sworn his or her life to, comes from firsthand experience, from what the body knows?"[4] The naturalist, like the farmer/academic, lives in two worlds that he or she constantly struggles to reconcile. On one hand, one must honor the knowledge that comes from firsthand experience, knowledge that one is never sure one understands because the more it is pursued, the more mysterious it becomes. On the other hand, one must honor the need to corroborate perceptions with the work of scientists who use analytical tools. As Lopez asks, "Can I put this together?"

Farmers and naturalists share another challenge. Lopez, again, puts his finger on the problem: "Firsthand knowledge is enormously time consuming to acquire; with its dallying and lack of end points, it is also out of phase with the short-term demands of modern life. It teaches humility and fallibility, and so represents an antithesis to progress."[5] And nothing could be more anathema to modern agriculture than appearing to be against progress!

Firsthand knowledge also is out of phase with the demands placed on university researchers to obtain most of the funding for their research from outside the university. Most of these grants support research that yields quick results that lead to profitable technologies. Very little money is available for research that helps us to better understand how systems function or how we can redesign systems to make farming more productive while reducing the costs to the farmer and the environment.

The task, then, for this farmer/academic, is to envision a new agriculture for the future. This must be an agriculture that is profitable for farmers, that restores the natural habitat of which any farm is a part, and that contributes to healthy landscapes and human communities. The new agriculture must be open to others, not disparaging of the current worldview of other farmers and entrepreneurs, and it must emphasize the importance of remaining immersed in the firsthand knowledge of direct experience and the mystery it reveals. The new agriculture must also embrace the passion that makes it all worthwhile.

This is not to assume that it will all be easy. As Lopez reminds us, "Historically, tyrants have sought selectively to eliminate firsthand knowledge when its sources lay outside their control. By silencing those with problematic firsthand experiences, they reduced the number of potential contradictions in their political or social designs, and so they felt safer."[6] Many academics and industrialists may feel threatened by the new agriculture that is emerging, but they are certainly not tyrants; they just feel safer with the old paradigm and will, in their own ways, resist change. What is needed, then, are farmers and scientists who are willing, as a National Academy of Sciences study put it, to accept the "tensions in the research agenda" through "sustained vision, leadership and political will."[7] That will require a level of engagement that goes beyond the old paradigm of "detachment."

Being at Home

Knowing the nature and behavior of fire, water, air, stars, the heavens, and all the other bodies which surround us . . . we can employ these entities for all the purposes for which they are suited, and so make ourselves masters and possessors of nature.[1]
—René Descartes

It is tempting, even for scientists, to get carried away by success stories. Science has popularized the view that humans are at the top rung of Earth's evolutionary "ladder" and that with technology we have stepped outside the framework of evolution. . . . These views underestimate the Earth and the ways of nature.[2]
—Lynn Margulis and Dorion Sagan

Once the Universe becomes a machine, no longer alive, once human beings are defined as the only intelligent life-form, a unique kind of isolation enters human lives, a kind of loneliness.[3]
—Stephen H. Buhner

Homelessness . . . is both a physical and psychic condition. We are not so much at home on *earth as we are* home *as earth.*[4]
—Larry Rasmussen

What does it mean to be at home? For most of us, being at home simply

---

This was originally a lecture prepared for the Journey's Home lecture series, sponsored by the Washington College Center for Environment and Society, the Maryland Center for Agro-Ecology, the Eastern Shore Land Conservancy, and Adkins Arboretum, March 24, 2004.

means being in an apartment or house or condo where we usually sleep and where, once in a while, we eat meals with our family members or watch television. Home is mostly an enclosure that protects us from the rest of the world, sometimes with help from security personnel and technology. The "homeless" are those who are deprived of such amenities and find themselves sleeping under bridges, on sidewalks, in parks or in homeless shelters. But is the ownership of a structure or having contractual rights to reside in one really what it means to have a home?

Some of us claim to be more "at home" in certain ecological niches. I often refer to myself as a "prairie boy" because for some strange reason I feel more like I belong on the prairies of North Dakota than I do in the mountains of Colorado or on the beaches of Florida. Could it be that we become conditioned to a place by virtue of birth or upbringing or evolutionary history, making us more "at home" in one ecological neighborhood than another?

For that matter, are we, members of the human species, "at home" on planet Earth in any case? An old gospel song tells us that "this world is not my home, I'm just a-passin' through," and some religious traditions have taught us that our short tenure on planet Earth is simply a "pilgrimage," a kind of tutorial to prepare us for another life in an altogether different venue, a "heaven" that these traditions tell us is our *true* "home."

Religious traditions, however, are not the only sources suggesting the existence of an elevated world superior to the one in which we dwell. According to David Abram, mathematicians going back to Pythagoras believed in a "higher world, untainted by the uncertainty and flux of mortal, earthly life." The prospect of such an "ideal" world inspired Plato to expand this superior world from "just numbers and mathematical relations" to include "truth, justice, and beauty" in which "the ideal form of each such notion enjoyed the purity of an eternal and transcendent existence outside of all bodily apprehension."[5] Are such conceptions—in which we appear stuck in a somewhat bellicose physical environment while longing for a more ideal life in some "higher" world—pathological distortions or expressions of some deeply held precognition?

From an evolutionary perspective, we may question whether planet Earth is truly "home" for the human species. We are latecomers and may not yet be well-adapted to the place. Furthermore, many species that came before us apparently did not find the planet much of a home either. Mass extinctions (five in the last 500 million years) killed off 10 to 50 percent of existing species each time. One suspects the planet didn't feel very "homey" to those species while they were being wiped out. Evolutionary biologists tell us that 99.99 percent of all of the species that have ever existed on this planet are extinct now.[6,7] Earth didn't become "home" on a permanent basis to those species. There is no particular reason to believe that the human species is exempt from a similar fate. Our planet will likely continue to change over time, with or without our help, and it may change in ways that will make it difficult for us to adapt. Just what does it mean to be "at home" here under such potentially threatening circumstances?

From the perspective of evolutionary biology, the human species may not hold a particularly salutary place on the planet. We may be simply one of many experiments that microbes have devised to ensure their own survival. After all, bacteria were the first living inhabitants of our planet. It seems that for the first 2 billion years of life on the planet, bacteria were the sole occupants. All of the rest of life emerged in the subsequent 1.7 billion years. We have been around for *far less than 1 percent* of that time! So it may be that all of Earth's "higher" plant and animal species are simply "homes" for the microbes—tenants who may well decide to switch homes when it suits them. If further planetary changes make it difficult for us to adapt, the microbes might replace us with some as-yet unimagined new species.

Microbes, practicing fermentation, photosynthesis, nitrogen removal, and oxygen breathing, made existence on the planet by higher life forms (including us) possible in the first place. Their ongoing activity *continues* to make our habitation possible. Our continued existence on this planet absolutely depends on the microcosm, as it always has.[8] That doesn't place us in a particularly enviable position. If we go back further, to the very beginning, some 15 billion years ago, when planet Earth first flared forth at temperatures 6,000 degrees hotter than our sun, the planet certainly wouldn't have seemed much like home to us. Or would it?

Our Perception of Ourselves

Isn't it really a matter of perspective whether we are "at home" here? Being at home on this planet depends on our perception of ourselves and our relationship with the rest of the cosmos. Our contemporary perception suggests a rather strange and limiting relationship. Most of us seem to think that the Earth exists solely for our benefit; it must serve our needs in order for us to feel at home here. This egocentric image of our relationship leads us to vacillate between two epistemological errors: we apprehend the world as a hostile place, a place that we must modify, tame, or manipulate to suit our purposes; or at the other extreme, we perceive it as a "harmonious place," a place that will benignly nurture us if left alone.

Neither perception is consistent with current cosmology, ecology, or actual lived experience on the planet. Being eaten by a lion, bitten by a poisonous snake, or consumed by an infectious disease is not a particularly harmonious relationship. Moreover, incredible synergies and synchronies within nature provide all of the food we eat, the air we breathe, the water we drink—all the essentials for life. And it is all provided absolutely free. This hardly fits the description of an enemy that has to be subdued or a collection of inert raw materials that have no value until we manufacture them into something useful.

A key component missing from our understanding of our planet is that everything in the cosmos, now as from the beginning, is part of the same fabric. We are not *separate* from the plants, animals, insects, or microbes. Nor are we separate from the soil, rocks, water, or air. We are not separate from the quarks that constituted the stable elementary particles that formed the protons and neutrons, which formed into nuclear particles and the first atoms of hydrogen and helium, and finally into molecules and cells and then into lions and tigers and bears—and us! It is all part of the same dynamic, evolving drama. Consequently, as Larry Rasmussen reminds us, the question is not whether we are *at* home *on* Earth; it is rather that we *are* home *as* earth.[9]

Cosmologist Brian Swimme gives poetic expression to this unitary nature of the cosmos:

> That which blossomed forth as cosmic egg fifteen billion years ago now blossoms forth as oneself, as one's family, as one's community of living beings, as our blue planet, as our ocean of galaxy clusters. . . . For we know this body of ours could have been a giant sequoia. We know in a simple and direct way that we share the essence of and so easily could have been a migrating pelican. Our astonishment at existence becomes indestructible, and we are home again in the cosmos as we reach the conviction that we could have been

an asteroid, or molten lava, or a man, or a woman, or taller or shorter, or angrier, or calmer, or more certain, or more hesitant, or more right or wrong.[10]

Anthropologists have suggested that being at home is rooted in our awareness that the human body and the body of the land share a common language.[11] But coming home in our cosmos transcends these important insights. We not only share a common language; we are embedded in the same cosmic fabric. We are interchangeable with asteroids, lava, and pelicans. We not only share a common language; we are a common *community*. As Aldo Leopold reminded us, this awareness requires us to enlarge our understanding of the boundaries of "community" to "include soils, waters, plants, and animals, or collectively: the land."[12] He might have said, collectively: the cosmos.

In the most fundamental sense, being at home on this planet of ours is recognizing that we "are home as earth." We and soil, we and rocks, we and water, we and air, we and bacteria, we and trees, we and stars, we and galaxies, we and insects, we and grass are all part of the same prolific, numinous energy. There is, in fact, no "we" and "them." Only a thin layer of skin separates us from the rest of the cosmos. The same essence that blazed into existence 15 billion years ago still gives birth to our grandchildren today. To recognize this is, as Brian Swimme puts it, "to taste the joy of radical relational mutuality."[13] It is, in other words, to be *at home*.

From this perspective, being at home is more complex, profound, troubling, and perhaps more satisfying than we might think. Home is not simply the castle, house, cave, or cardboard box under a railroad bridge where we reside. Home is not reduced to an ecological niche—prairie, woodlands, mountains, or seaside. Home is not just the common language between our bodies and the land, or the meaning of the landscape we occupy. Home is not just a particular place on the evolutionary ladder. Home is not defined by how well the Earth fulfills our needs or by the prospects it offers for us still being around a few billion years from now.

Being at home has more to do with recognizing that we truly are radically connected to everything else in the cosmos. When we *are* home *as* earth, we are inseparable from a cosmos in which *everything* belongs by virtue of its common cosmic origins and its interdependent, ongoing evolution.

It may be hard to accept that we are but one tiny organism in a vast community of organisms, in which no one gets to sit on top of the evolutionary ladder. We are one tiny member of a vast community of galaxies that continue to expand in ways we find hard even to imagine. As a species, we are part of a cosmos in which particles, including us, are constantly disappearing into an "all-nourishing abyss" from which new particles are constantly being created.[14] Our solidarity with the rest of the cosmos is assured precisely because we are part of this ongoing cosmic dance of life and death. Embracing this reality may be the only way for us to be at home as earth.

We are embedded in a reality in which stars and moons, as well as earthworms and rocks, become one with us as a community. As David Abram puts it, "there is an intimate reciprocity to the senses; as we touch the bark of a tree, we feel the tree *touching us*."[15] If we are at home as earth, we cannot imagine ourselves separate from it, let alone in *control* of it. Perhaps only if we recognize that we are an infinitesimally small member of a cosmic community and of the cosmic dance of death and resurrection, which invites us into that "radical relational mutuality," can we be at home as earth.

Being at home has ecological, spiritual, and social dimensions. Failure to consider what it means to be at home from these three dimensions diminishes our lives, blinds us to the enormous blunders of which we are all too capable, and plunges us into profound loneliness. In the long run, failure to recognize that we are home as earth may contribute to our own undoing.

Being at Home Ecologically

For more than four centuries, we (at least in the Western world) have characterized our relationship with the rest of the planet community primarily from the perspective of *control management*. We see ourselves as "masters and possessors of nature," a role that René Descartes thought entirely appropriate. We see ourselves as *separate* from the rest of the world, acting *upon* it rather than dwelling *in* it, standing *over against it* rather than being embedded in it. This perception of how we physically engage the world we live in has profound implications for us and the rest of the cosmic community. At the very least, it is a prescription for homelessness.

Quantum physics and evolutionary biology remind us that the causality theories of classical physics can no longer be defended. Classical physics was grounded in the notion that nature could be reduced to matter and motion, that it existed in a state of equilibrium, *and that it was therefore controllable.* Quantum physics, however, demonstrated that we are not detached, objective observers. We are always embedded in the thing we observe. Our behavior and consciousness always become *part of* whatever experiment we may be performing, according to Werner Heisenberg.[16] We are always sensuous participants in the world we are trying to understand.

Control management is particularly ill-suited on Earth because Earth is essentially a bacteria-based planet, and bacteria can adapt to our technological interventions with amazing speed. Bacteria can run through approximately fifty generations in just twenty-four hours; control management is unlikely ever to be effective in such dynamic conditions. Even *problems* are dynamic; they are systemic and nonlinear, and they have an evolutionary character. They continue to change while we are trying to solve them. Ecologists have urged us to abandon control management as unworkable and embrace adaptive management instead.[17] Attempts to control pests and diseases with pesticides work only until the pests develop resistance, usually a matter of a few years. Adaptive management seeks to understand *why* pests emerge and employs self-regulating dynamics already present in the biotic community to suppress the pests.

Our tendency to characterize our relationship to the world in terms of control management is rooted in our refusal to recognize the true ecological dimensions of our existence. Once we recognize that we are one member of a very complex, interdependent community, we are likely to give up the illusion of control management. Recognizing the ecological dimensions of our relationship to the land "changes the role of *Homo sapiens* from *conqueror* of the land-community to *plain member and citizen of it,*" as Leopold so famously and elegantly reminded us.[18]

Such a shift in our thinking changes our entire relationship to the biotic community. As conquerors, we can be seduced into believing we know how to manipulate nature to our liking, despite much evidence to the contrary. As plain members and citizens, we understand the need to attend to the other members of the community and the dynamic relationships among them. We are more likely to recognize that we *can't* know all of the complex connections and interdependencies of the various members of the community or how they will evolve. We are less likely to manipulate one part of the community and more likely to enhance the *entire* community's health, especially because our *own* health depends on the community's health.

This ecological awareness also is consistent with the insights of the emerging science of networks. This relatively new science not only is reminding us that we can never fully understand systems in terms of their component parts, but also that "weak links" in a system (which we usually ignore) often hold the key to system health. Applying these insights to ecology, we find that a complex network of species often behaves differently than we might expect from observing individual species, because it is not only the individual species but also the interactions among species that determine how the community evolves.

Mark Buchanan offers an example of such complex relationships. When Atlantic cod populations collapsed due to overfishing, the Canadian government suggested hunting expeditions to kill North Atlantic harp seals, because the seals were known to eat cod. It was assumed that eliminating the seals, a principal cod predator, would allow the cod populations to rebound. What the government failed to realize was that the cod/seal relationship was affected by many other less prominent species in the system. The seals, for example, not only fed on cod but also on 150 other species, many of which also fed on cod! So there simply was no way of knowing in advance whether reducing the seal population would actually produce more cod or less cod. In food webs involving as few as eight species, there can be "more than 10 million distinct chains of cause and effect that would link the seal to the cod."[19] How can we ever exercise effective control management in such complex, dynamic communities?

The lesson for conservation implicit in these dynamic networks is obvious: "If we wish to preserve an ecosystem and its component species then we are best to proceed as if each species is sacred."[20] It is interesting that designating a species as "sacred" is proposed as a tool for achieving ecological health. It suggests that being at home *ecologically* propels us rather quickly into the realm of being at home *spiritually*.

Being at Home Spiritually

In modern western culture, engaging in meaningful discourse on the subject of spirituality is problematic. The same mechanistic worldview that isolated us ecologically from the rest of the cosmos has also divided the visceral from the cerebral, the body from the mind, and tacit knowing from cognitive knowing. We accept that precise, measurable, cognitive analysis, relegated to the purview of science, is reliable. On the other hand, experiential, sensual, and visceral experiences, which have been assigned to the realm of religion or art, are suspect. Even to raise the subject of spirituality tends to discredit the discussion.

However, in order to come to terms with what it means to be at home, the spiritual dimension is critical. As Larry Rasmussen reminds us, homelessness is "both a physical and a psychic condition."[21] In other words, our state of homelessness is at once both ecological and spiritual. Spirituality is, of course, grounded in the human capacity for inspiration and affection, and it can be experienced only through sensual, bodily knowing. Cognitive knowing can analyze inspiration and affection, but these experiences cannot be "known" through pure analysis. To experience the joy of sex, one has to engage in it; one can't know it by analyzing data.

Sensual body knowledge is the primary way in which infants experience their world, as Morris Berman points out. An infant experiences the world almost entirely through its mouth. It literally comes to know the world by tasting it: "Its entire body, and thus its entire world, is sensualized."[22] No wonder, then, that children experience their world as a magical place, see stars as something to "wish upon," and bond with plants and animals in ways that are identical to human bonding. Infants do not experience the separation that comes from the perception that we are special, different, or threatened. Consequently, they tend to be more spiritually and ecologically "at home."

As a child's cerebral functions develop, it begins to analyze its visceral experiences. For the rest of our lives, our knowing consists of a "from-to" process: we attend *from* our bodily encounter with the world *to* our analytical attempts to understand what we have experienced. Alienation or homelessness sets in once we deny the validity of the sensual and insist that only the analytical has value. The denial of the sensual is the beginning of our spiritual malaise.

This spiritual bankruptcy is at least partly responsible for our psychic homelessness. Because only that which can be reduced to matter and motion has intellectual legitimacy, and because "objectivity" is required for our knowledge to be credible, we disavow all sensual connection with the world around us. We alienate ourselves from the inspiration and affection that bond us to the cosmos. We acquire tons of knowledge *about* our cosmos, but we seldom allow ourselves to have a spiritual connection *with* it. Despite the fact that we know more about our world than any generation that has ever existed, we seem less at home in it than ever before.

What does this tell us about being spiritually at home in our world? Spirituality is grounded in the visceral, physical experience of touch, taste, and smell and is critical to a full appreciation of our place in the world. We can only experience the "joy of radical relational mutuality," which is essential to being at home in our world, by opening ourselves to the sensuous encounter of fully dwelling in the world of the spiritual.

Those of us who grew up in a religious culture that tended to draw a hard line between the physical and the spiritual, or between pleasure and religious duty, may find it hard to accept this. For us, spirituality belongs to the realm of the ideal; it suggests we rise above the world of the flesh and dwell in the world of the spirit. Much of Western Christian theology, especially theology inspired by the Puritan faith, advocates such a sanitized spiritual life.

Shannon Jung, a professor of rural ministry, suggests that one might glean another interpretation from the biblical and theological traditions of the Christian Church. The core themes concerning food and eating in the biblical text focus on the twin ideas of "delight and sharing." These twin realities are especially celebrated in the Eucharist, which commemorates the delight of sharing a meal while binding it to the good that comes from *giving* one's life as a means of *saving* it.[23]

Such notions may seem contradictory to the egoistic rational mind fixated on the sole objective of securing its own welfare. However, the notion of giving one's life to save it is entirely consistent with a cosmos in which particles are constantly disappearing into a nourishing abyss from which new particles constantly emerge. It is consistent with a planet on which almost all of the species that ever existed are now extinct but that simultaneously exhibits an incredible capacity to renew itself. Recognizing that we are an integral part of this drama of death and resurrection, of sharing and delight, of giving to receive, is a crucial step to being at home as earth.

Being at Home Socially

Sharing and delight are deeply rooted in bodily functions and therefore ecological. But they are also deeply social. We delight in good food, especially when good food is eaten in the company of good friends and conversation.

The Eucharist is about sharing and delight, but also inclusiveness. Those who betray that vision are not excluded from the table. We are more at home when *everyone* is invited to the table. Exclusiveness not only separates the other from us; it also separates us from the other. Alienation and homelessness are part of exclusiveness, just as being at home requires inclusiveness. Sharing recognizes the need to surrender what is "ours" so that we can live in community. Hoarding separates us from others and fosters loneliness and homelessness. Sharing bonds us to the other and fosters community. Delight and sharing, both physical activities, generate spiritual connections that enable us to be at home, but they also have profound social implications.

Perhaps it is obvious that any real sense of being at home as earth will require some kind of social community. However, Western industrial culture has emphasized the rights and importance of the individual to the exclusion of the welfare of the cosmos or the commons. Consequently, most of us seek a home with boundaries that extend no further than our own welfare, or, at best, the welfare of our immediate families.

We have adopted a convenient economic theory of self-interest that says if each pursues his or her own individual economic wealth, the good of the whole will somehow be served. We adhere to such theories even though there is no factual evidence to support them.[24] Economics has become our theology and the market our new god. We are asked to believe, as old hymns have put it, that the "light inaccessible" is currently "hid from our eyes," but not to worry because "further along we'll understand why."[25,26] The result is a culture of self-indulgence that makes it impossible for us to ever be at home psychically or socially. We are running on a treadmill to find individual satisfaction, in isolation from the very social and ecological bonding that can provide it.

In a desperate search to find meaning and satisfaction through self-indulgent behavior, we demand more, hoard more, accumulate more, and we find ourselves less and less at home. In the *Odyssey,* Odysseus goes to Hades to visit the seer Teiresias to seek his help in finding the way home after a twenty-year search for the Self. Teiresias suggests that a life that is tantamount to "burning" probably should be given up.[27] Cut off from our ecological connections to the cosmos, our spiritual connections to the inspiration and affection that such ecological bonding provides, and the social bonding that comes from sharing and delight, we are homeless, all the while burning out ourselves and our planet in a desperate search to be at home.

Finding Our Way Home Again

So how do we find our way home again? How do we overcome our ecological, spiritual, and social alienation? How do we escape from a failed culture that has seduced us for several centuries? How do we shift from a Cenozoic Era, in which placental mammals replaced the world of reptiles and dinosaurs of the Mesozoic Era, to an "Ecozoic Era" in which human/Earth relationships are mutually enhancing?

There are several theories of cultural change worth considering. Thomas Jefferson suggested an Enlightenment approach in which people who are free to do the right thing and equipped with information will do the right thing. This approach implies we can find our way home again through education and political freedom. The "incentives" approach, favored by Adam Smith, proposed that even when people are free to do the right thing and have information, they are still unlikely to do the right thing unless given incentives. Thus, in addition to political freedom and information, we need an opportunity to pursue something we value as an incentive to find our way home.

But major changes often take place because of events beyond our control. The planet, after all, did not shift from the Mesozoic to the Cenozoic because someone planned for it to happen. Neither freedom nor incentives had anything to do with it. These planetary events were beyond the control of dinosaurs or mammals. Can we imagine future events that might cause us to move into an Ecozoic Era and help us find our way home? Possibilities include climate change, environmental degradation, the end of the fossil-fuel era, a dramatic increase in infectious diseases, or significant decreases in biodiversity due to our human economies. Any one of these, or a combination of them, could radically change our self-indulgent ways and lead us to an ecological, spiritual, and social revolution. A bit of death and resurrection may be involved along the way.

In his engaging book *The Lost Language of Plants,* Stephen H. Buhner tells the story of lying on the bank of a pond deep in rural Indiana with his great-grandfather, who had taken him there for his first taste of wild water. He tells of the impression that moment made upon him—how that simple moment of ecological engagement stayed with him, shaped his relationship to the cosmos, and informed his spiritual life. He describes part of that journey in moving terms:

Later my mother caught me drinking wild water and told me it would kill me and began to instill in me a fear of the wildness of nature. And later still my great-grandfather died and my days began to be filled with TV dinners and the flickering half-intimacy of television. The years passed and the voices of my ancestors began to fade from memory; I became used to the taste of domesticated water.

It was long and long again before I tasted wild water once more, before the seeds that my great-grandfather and the land had laid within me began their slow growth. Even more years before I was no longer afraid wild water would kill me. The journey back to wild water is a long one—for our species, for each of us. In making that journey we must find a way to heal within ourselves a wound laid down long ago, a wound that came from a certain decision our species made, from a certain way of thinking—a wound that can be most easily distinguished when remembering puppies.

It is easy to remember what a puppy looks like, perhaps even to imagine one on the other side of the room you are in now. He is smelling the floor, looking around, filled with the newness of life as puppies often are.

The puppy looks up and sees you ("that's a good boy" you say) and his whole body begins to wag. "It's you," the puppy seems to be saying, "It's you!" And in that moment something passes between you and the puppy. It is as if something leaves your body and enters the puppy; as if something leaves the puppy and enters you. And the most important thing then is to touch the puppy, to pet him, to hold him. And the puppy seems to want nothing more than these things as well—perhaps, in addition, to lick your hands or your face.

This is an experience that nearly all people know, yet we have no word for it in our language. (*Love* is too broad in its possible meanings, too overworked.) Once, people experienced this exchange with everything on earth. The experience was understood, expected, a natural part of human life—this deep interaction with the nonhuman world—this exchange of essence.[29]

Perhaps a child *will* lead us, but it may be more likely that the *inner* child of our great-grandparents, bonding not only with our children but with all of the children of all of Earth's species, will show us the way home. In the book's epilogue, Buhner tells the story of passing along this ecological and spiritual bonding to the next generation:

> In my turn I have walked with my son in the deep forest. I have lain next to him and felt something leave my body and enter his. He needs it less often the older he becomes. Still, sometimes he is unsettled and paces the floor and a peculiar look comes over his face. Agitated, he will ask if he can lie next to me. And in silence I hold him and something in him opens up and a flood flows out of me into him. The color and tone of his skin change and his breathing slows and deepens and eventually he sighs and is filled once more. And I know that in his time he will pass this on as it was in turn passed into me. And perhaps also, one day, he will bend over and cup his hands, and ask his child or grandchild or some child: *"Here, have you ever tasted this water?"*[30]

Although drinking water from the ponds of Indiana may not be a good idea today, we do need to reawaken the spiritual bond that still exists between us and the rest of the cosmos. Being able to drink the wild water from the ponds of Indiana, or Illinois, or Iowa may be much more important than we had realized. Conversely, being deprived of such simple, sensuous pleasures may be preventing us from finding our way home. We must face what we are doing that *prevents* us from drinking the wild water, and, by extension, prevents us from experiencing all of the other simple delights that could send us home again.

The Pleasure of Good Eating

For most of us the pleasure of good eating probably consists of chowing down on a steak, a delicious pork chop, fresh vegetables with taste-bud-exploding flavors, or a savory tree-ripened peach that melts in your mouth. But in truth, the pleasure of good eating consists of much more than tasty treats.

When I was growing up on our farm in North Dakota, almost everything we ate was produced on the farm. We had a large garden where we produced all of the vegetables and condiment ingredients, and most of the fruit, that we ate in season or canned for the winter months. Wild plums and chokecherries provided additional fruit from which we made jam and wine. All of our meat came from the farm (beef, pork, lamb, chicken, turkey, goose, and duck), we milked cows for our own milk and cream, and we made all of our own butter and cheese. Once a year we bought 400 to 500 pounds of flour from which we baked all of our own bread.

There was only one rule at our table: we were expected to never be *schnagich*. *Schnagich* was a Russian German word for which there is probably no exact translation. But even if you didn't understand its exact meaning, the sound of the word was so harsh that you knew it was something you never wanted to be. To be *schnagich* was to be finicky, but it was much more than that. It was about being disrespectful. At our table we were expected to show appreciation for the food that was provided, for the labor of those who produced and prepared it, for the animals and plants that gave their lives for it, and for the land that was the gift that made it all possible.

Of course, there was a lesson in all this: The pleasure of good eating was

---

This is an edited version of a keynote address given at the annual Food Alliance Dinner, Portland, Oregon, February 17, 2006.

about much more than the taste of the food. It was about a deep appreciation for and connection with everything on our plates.

The reason why our family had this appreciation was that we were intimately connected with the food we ate. With the industrialization of our food system, to many people food is like any other commodity. Somewhere along the way we came to expect our food to be fast, convenient, and cheap. "Factory food" is no longer a strange concept, but it has taken us down some peculiar paths. Fruit farmers routinely are told the only thing that matters is color and shelf life. Some food scientists suggest that one day we may manufacture food pills containing all of the nutrients we need so that plants and animals will not be needed for food.

In a future food-factory scenario, Rogoff and Rawlins envisioned a food system not requiring farms or farmers at all.[1] Their proposal would have us discontinue the inefficient method of producing food from crops and animals. Instead, a perennial biomass would be reduced to a syrup and piped to urban centers, where it could be manufactured, using transgenic technologies, into any food item the market desired.

While no one has yet tried to operationalize such futuristic scenarios, we have industrialized our food system in ways that are almost as bizarre. We have turned food-citizen-customers into "consumers" expected to be passive recipients of whatever the industry decides to produce, even when much of the food has virtually no nutrient value, let alone any kind of a story that consumers might want to support. As my friend Bill Heffernan puts it, if the industrial food system today were to choose an appropriate logo for itself, it would be "just eat it."[2]

To make matters worse, we not only want consumers to just eat it; we're also trying to *force* them to eat it. John Ralston Saul says we are now at a point where we as citizen-eaters must arrive at the "hardest of hard scientific evidence" just to "not put something into our collective stomachs" that we choose not to eat.[3] This is hardly a recipe for the pleasure of good eating.

Fortunately, things are changing, and major food industry players are beginning to recognize this. Rick Schnieders, president and CEO of SYSCO Corporation, said that the pleasure of good eating is not about *fast, convenient,* and *cheap,* but about *memory, romance,* and *trust.* He reminds us that if we want to be successful in today's food market, we need to have a product so good that when customers eat it they say, "Wow, where did that come from, I want that again" (memory). We also need to provide customers with a genuine story so they can feel good about eating a food, such as who produced it; the type of environmental stewardship practiced in growing, processing, and transporting it; how animals were treated; and so on (romance). Customers also want to be active participants in the food chain, to access information and have a relationship that reaches back to the farmer who produced the food (trust). Dan Barber, one of the nation's leading chefs, says he spends more time acquainting his servers with the story behind every item on the menu than he does preparing food, because the food story entices customers to return to his restaurants.

This does not mean that to enjoy the pleasure of good eating we have to become intimately connected to everything we eat. It means we need to retrieve those values and make them part of our modern food system.

John Thackara reminds us that the next challenge for capitalism is to manage "relationship value."[4] Capitalism needs to shift from emphasizing stuff to emphasizing people. When we were euphoric about moving beyond the "industrial" era into the "information" era, we forgot one important thing: who we were as human beings. The information age was short-lived because it physically isolated us from each other by connecting us virtually. We need to be physically present with one another to do the intimate things that fulfill our lives. And next to making love, eating is one of the most intimate things we do. We cannot have the pleasure of good eating without "being there," as Thackara puts it. I would add two more requirements for success in today's food market: intimacy and affordability.

Simply having information on a package or Web site about where the food comes from, important as that is, will not substitute for "being there." In the long run, our food and agriculture systems need to be more decentralized. In the interest of energy conservation and food security, we may be driven to decentralize anyway, but decentralization also is essential to the pleasure of good eating.

As to affordability, we simply must begin to address the gross inequity deeply entrenched in our global society, especially as it relates to food. Almost half of the world's citizens live on less than $2 a day, making social unrest inevitable and peace unlikely. Capitalism must shift its wealth-creation strategy from wealth *concentration* to wealth *expansion*. As long as one-sixth of the world's population is malnourished, there is little chance that any of us can enjoy the pleasure of good eating.

If we are to sustain the pleasure of good eating, our food systems must consist of a new kind of value chain that connects the farm to the table. Such a value chain would make those connections by:

- fostering a food system that honors the labor of all involved throughout the global village by compensating everyone fairly for their part in putting food on our tables
- nurturing a land ethic that respects the gift of good land, including soil, water, plants, and animals
- creating opportunities for intimacy, not only among eaters but among all participants in the food chain
- producing, processing, and distributing food with life-giving stories
- providing wonderful, delightful, good-tasting, healthful, nutritious food that is so good the flavors explode in our mouths

I suspect this is the modern version of not being *schnagich* at our food tables worldwide today.

Is Sustainability in Our Energy Future?

On December 18, 2005, I finished the first draft of the year-end economic analysis of our North Dakota farm in anticipation of filing our 2005 tax return. One number stood out with unpleasant clarity: our total farm fuel bill for 2005 was just over $30,000. In 2004, it had been just under $20,000.

Yes, we added 110 acres to the operation, but we also bought a new tractor that was demonstrably much more fuel-efficient than the one it replaced. The significant increase in unit fuel costs was just too great. Fortunately, our year-end financial statement was not hit with similar cost increases for fertilizer and pesticides (both tightly linked to fossil-fuel resources) because we had transitioned our farm to a closed-nutrient-cycling, self-regulating pest-management system almost thirty years ago.

To me, the 50 percent increase in our fuel bill was a loud wake-up call. Our farm is still too dependent on fossil fuel to be sustainable much further into the future. I am, of course, aware that there is still a debate raging about when we will reach global peak oil production (the point at which we will have produced as much oil per day as we will ever produce). We reached that point in the United States in 1970. In the late 1950s, M. King Hubbert, the legendary geologist with the U.S. Geological Survey, predicted that oil production in the United States would peak between 1965 and 1970. Hubbert was ridiculed for his predictions, but he turned out to be remarkably accurate.

While Hubbert's method may not be a foolproof way of predicting peak oil production worldwide, there is one thing about his analysis that seems irrefutable: peak oil production is tightly linked to peak oil discovery.

This piece is edited from the original, which appeared in *The Practical Farmer: Practical Farmers of Iowa Newsletter,* Winter 2006.

Peak oil discovery in the United States occurred around 1930, and Hubbert calculated that peak oil production takes place 40 years, more or less, after reaching peak oil discovery.[1] We reached peak global oil discovery in the late 1960s. Do the math.

While Red Cavaney, president and CEO of the American Petroleum Institute, still argues that new technology will postpone the reckoning day of peak oil production for a long time, I wouldn't bet the farm on it.[2] We need to be working right now to find ways to make our farm less energy-dependent. So, what should we do?

Shiyomi and Koizumi raise an interesting and important question all farmers have to wrestle with as we approach a farming era devoid of cheap and abundant petroleum supplies. "Is it possible," they ask, "to re-place current technologies based on fossil energy with proper interactions operating between crops/livestock and other organisms to enhance agricultural production?"[3] If so, "then modern agriculture, which uses only the simplest biotic responses, can be transformed into an alternative system of agriculture in which the use of complex biotic interactions becomes the key technology."[4]

On a small scale, we already know the answer to their question. In Japan, Takao Furuno transformed his fossil-fuel-dependent, monoculture rice farm into a highly productive mixed rice/fish/duck/fruit farm and now uses almost no fossil fuels at all.[5] The resources for the exceptional productivity of his farm result from species interactions that "influence each other positively in a relationship of symbiotic production." More than 10,000 farmers in Japan have now adopted his system. Joel Salatin in Virginia, whose operation has been featured in numerous publications, has developed a rotational grazing system that supports seven or eight species of animals, all interdependent in ways that have dramatically reduced his reliance on fossil fuels.[6]

We also have examples in Iowa. Jeff Kuntz has developed a system involving corn, grapes, and pheasant that generates more than $10,000 of income per acre and uses very little fossil fuel.[7] Francis Thicke's rotational grazing dairy farm is another example of an Iowa farm that is more knowledge intensive than energy intensive.[8] Boone's Dick Thompson now rotates his prime farm land into pasture three years out of six and reports that he makes more net profit during the years that the land is in pasture then he does with corn and soybeans. In all of these operations biological synergies replace fossil-fuel energy.[9]

So how does all of this knowledge apply to my farm in North Dakota, or to farms in Iowa—especially on the scale on which most of us are operating? I don't know yet. Unfortunately, almost none of our public research dollars is devoted to this kind of research. Consequently, we know almost nothing about the ecological wealth, encapsulating our farms in the form of various natural organisms, that could be linked to biological synergies that could drive our productivity. How could any of us have known, before Matt Liebmann and his Iowa State University colleagues did the research, that the common prairie deer mouse is a voracious consumer of weed seeds and, under the right circumstances, can dramatically reduce the weed populations (for free!) in our fields during the winter months?[10]

I know almost nothing about the natural prairie ecology in which my North Dakota farm is embedded, so I am largely ignorant of the possibilities for developing proper interactions that could operate between crops, livestock, and other organisms to enhance agricultural production. Like most farmers, I make decisions without adequate knowledge. I suspect that I must dramatically reduce the acreage currently devoted to raising annual crops, increase the acreage devoted to rotational grazing, and cultivate a greater diversity of animal species. But what is the right combination of species? What is the most positive relationship among them to optimize symbiotic production in that particular ecology in North Dakota? We will probably have to learn by trial and error, but I am convinced that biological synergies will have to largely replace intensive energy use if our farm is going to be sustainable very far into the future.

A Journey toward Sustainability

Truth is forward-looking, and a society can claim to have found it only when the society's practices and institutions sustain its people indefinitely on the land it inhabits.[1]
—Bryan G. Norton

When I started to transition our North Dakota farm to organic production in 1977, the concept of sustainability was not yet in the public domain, nor had I heard of it. At the time I also was unaware that a special market existed for organic production. I was motivated entirely by the fact, brought to my attention by my former student David Vetter, that well-managed organic farms could dramatically improve soil quality.

The motivation to improve the soil quality on our farm was imbedded in me by my father, who always insisted that "taking care of the land" was the most important task entrusted to any farmer. He came by that conviction from living through the Dust Bowl of the 1930s and seeing farmland everywhere decimated by it. So he took great pains to implant the importance of taking care of the land into his young son's conscience.

It wasn't until the 1980s that "sustainability" became part of the public discourse on agriculture. However, coming up with a definition that everyone could embrace was elusive. I remember attending my first conference on sustainable agriculture at the University of Nebraska in the late 1980s and seeing eight different presenters offer eight varying definitions. Eventually students of sustainability came up with the "three-legged stool" concept of sustainability. To be sustainable, an activity had to be "economically viable," "ecologically sound," and "socially acceptable" or "socially just." While that threefold principle seemed satisfying to many in the sustainability movement, a universal prescription for sustainability on the farm has continued to elude us. What practices will make a farm truly sustainable?

At first a few intellectuals attempted to simplify the definition, boiling it down to specific practices. A U.S. Department of Agriculture official who owned a farm in Indiana, for example, asserted in a news article at the time that his farm was sustainable because he practiced no-till. Meanwhile, many organic farmers started to claim that they were sustainable just because their products were organic.

As I wrestled with the concept of sustainability on my own farm, I initially succumbed to this same prescriptive approach. I believed that there had to be a core set of practices that farmers could adopt on their farms to make them sustainable. If you practiced crop rotation, included green-manure legumes in the rotation, composted your manure, and spread it on your fields, your farm would be sustainable. On my own farm, I recognized that such a prescriptive approach to sustainability was deeply flawed.

The first lesson I learned was that no two farms are alike; consequently, any universal prescription for sustainability was inapt. A farm is not a factory that operates in accordance with stable, uniform management practices. A farm is a biological organism, and, like all biological organisms, it has its own unique aspects, including the uniqueness of the farmer. Therefore, no two farms can be managed exactly alike. While some *principles* of sustainability may apply to all farms, how those principles are actualized may differ significantly from farm to farm. Practices that enhance sustainability on my central North Dakota farm could be dysfunctional in California.

The second important lesson I learned from my farm is that sustainability is a moving target. Farms are constantly evolving biological organisms. Accordingly, strategies for achieving sustainability have to keep changing. Sustainability is ultimately about sustaining something indefinitely into the future. To address sustainability, one has to constantly anticipate emerging changes and get a head start in preparing for them. "Steady state" sustainability, according to Joseph Fiksel, is an oxymoron.[2]

For me this was perhaps the most important lesson I learned from my own farm. When I took over the management of our farm in 1976, the energy crises of the early 1970s were already receding into the background. Importing huge quantities of oil seemed to solve the energy problem. Energy sustainability was not high on anyone's list. Of course, I had always wanted to reduce my diesel fuel consumption and was able to cut farm usage by about 20 percent after transitioning to organic farming. And, of course, I was pleased that we weaned ourselves from off-farm crop and livestock inputs by developing a closed nutrient-cycling system and adopting appropriate husbandry practices. But beyond that, energy sustainability was simply not on my radar screen. Now, as we reach the tipping point of peak oil, it is near the top of my list.

The third lesson I learned on my own farm is that it is futile to think that the farm can be sustainable if the ecosystem in which it exists is not sustainable. Like any farm, my farm depends on a vibrant, resilient ecosystem for vital ecosystem services that are critical to the farm's productivity. Pollinators are just one example. A farm is not an isolated entity; it is a complex set of relationships. Any farm is part of the ecology of the landscape in which the farm exists. This is the most fundamental reason why agriculture and conservation, or agriculture and environmental health, cannot be viewed as separate enterprises.

Even more fundamental is the awareness that the human community and the rest of the biotic community are not separate entities. As Aldo Leopold reminded us, we are not the "conquerors" of the land-community but rather "plain members and citizens" of it.[3] So either it is all sustainable, or none of it is. Reflecting on my own journey toward sustainability, both the experience-based education I received from my father and the academic education I received at the University of Chicago prepared me for my own journey toward sustainability.

Methodology and Intimacy

In addition to imbedding a land ethic into my conscience, my father also taught me to be wary of untrammeled objectivity on the farm. Intimacy was also required. My father appreciated objective data that told him, for example, which variety of wheat contained the best yield and quality characteristics. Yet he also had learned that on a real operating farm the highest yields of a particular crop in a given year did not necessarily result in a profitable farm or the farm's long-term survival.

His animals taught him similar lessons. He initially heeded the advice of extension specialists who recommended big-framed animals because their big calves would reach weaning weight more quickly. But he discovered that in the context of a real operating farm, the big-framed cows did not breed back as efficiently as the rest of his herd, and they consumed proportionately more feed.

Over time, I became intimately acquainted with the whole farm and learned how it functioned, which made it possible for me to manage the farm for sustainable productivity. Alfalfa, for example, did not necessarily produce the highest short-term return, but it improved soil quality and reduced input costs, which contributed to the farm's long-term profitability. I also became convinced that diversity was an essential part of sustainability. My father often said the reason he liked to have cows on the farm was that they did not get "hailed out." If a hail storm wiped out your crops, you still had livestock to see you through tough times. As in the rest of nature, biodiversity and genetic diversity are essential to resilience on a farm.

While I was at the University of Chicago, many of my faculty mentors stressed the importance of selecting the right "methodology" for any phenomenon you were trying to understand. They helped me appreciate the fact that the method chosen to examine any phenomenon determined, to a large extent, the data one collected. If your goal is to determine what actually happened during a particular period of history in a given place, you can focus on major events, such as wars or famines, and you get one picture of the past in a particular time and place. If, instead, you focus on what ordinary people were reading in a given time and place, or the tools they were using in their communities, you might get a different picture. So it is always important to be clear about methodology.

How did my insights about these two principles—intimacy and methodology—help me on my journey toward sustainability? Acknowledging the importance of methodology always leads one to question assumptions. Industrial agriculture, it seemed, operated on the assumption that maximum yield and short-term return were the only relevant goals of farming. Specialization, simplification, and concentration appeared to be the most efficient ways to achieve significant short-term returns.

The industrialization process led to the demise of smaller, more diversified farms in favor of large, specialized operations because the latter had the potential to produce higher gross short-term returns. Crop yields, pounds of milk per cow, or hog weight gain in the shortest amount of time increasingly became the goals of industrial farms.

While not discounting the importance of such indicators in any farming operation, my training in methodology led me to question whether judging a farm's performance in this way was appropriate for reaching the goals I wanted to achieve. Would operating my farm by that method lead to sustained profitability? Would a farm operated by that method be resilient enough to thrive under adverse conditions? It led me to question whether maximum yield and short-term returns were consistent with the goal of long-term sustainability. And I wanted my farm to thrive over the long term.

Furthermore, ecologists had begun to question the impact of industrial agriculture on the environment. As Wendell Berry put it, "I know that 'technological progress' can be defended, but I observe that the defenses are invariably quantitative . . . and I see that these statistics are always kept carefully apart from the related statistics of soil loss, pollution, social disintegration, and so forth. That is to say, there is never an effort to determine the *net* result of this progress."[4]

But it wasn't just the ecological "net" result that was at issue. Even farmers' net *income* was not always well served by the "produce as much as possible" mandate that is central to the industrial agriculture doctrine.

At the time when I was wrestling with these issues, a new farmer club was formed in North Dakota with the help of a few creative extension specialists. They called themselves the Maximum Economic Yield (MEY) Club. While the MEY Club focused on short-term returns, they encouraged farmers to ask somewhat different questions. They looked at how farmers could achieve maximum *net* economic return, not just gross yield per unit of production. While I never joined the club, I followed their research results closely because they were questioning the *method* by which conventional agriculture judged its success.

Research conducted by the MEY Club demonstrated, to the farmers' chagrin, that investment in additional technologies to achieve maximum yield often reduced net economic return. The expenses incurred to produce the additional 5 or 10 percent yield gain often cost more in inputs than the farmer gained in financial returns. The MEY Club data suggested to me that a new methodology might be in order.

So my father's experience-based wisdom, my university training, and the MEY Club's on-farm research led me to explore a different methodology for managing our farm. The strategy for developing a new methodology that ultimately appealed to me was to combine the best wisdom from the past with the best science available. Using that method, could one come up with a new system of farming that would be more sustainable? In 2002, I discovered that a farmer in southern Japan had been wrestling with some of the same issues and had come to a similar conclusion in 1987.[5]

Nature's Farming

Deciding to combine past wisdom with current science led me to explore some of the thoughts of agriculturalists who, early on, had sensed the weaknesses in the movement to industrialize agriculture. Among them were Sir Albert Howard, J. I. Rodale, Lady Eve Balfour, F. H. King, and Rudolf Steiner. These visionaries, along with others at the time, ascertained from their experiences in farming that the industrialization of agriculture was ultimately not sustainable.[6] Sir Albert Howard referred to industrialization as a kind of "banditry" because it threatened to rob future generations of the healthy soil they would need to sustain themselves.[7]

Howard articulated his proposed alternative to industrialization clearly and succinctly at the very beginning of his 1943 classic work, *An Agricultural Testament*. It was precisely this graphic description of a different way to farm that captured my attention: "The main characteristic of nature's farming can therefore be summed up in a few words. Mother earth never attempts to farm without livestock; she always raises mixed crops; great pains are taken to preserve the soil and to prevent erosion; the mixed vegetable and animal wastes are converted into humus; there is no waste; the processes of growth and the processes of decay balance one another; ample provision is made to maintain large reserves of fertility; the greatest care is taken to store the rainfall; both plants and animals are left to protect themselves against disease."[8]

Here, it seemed to me, was a well-articulated method of farming that was grounded in principles of long-term sustainability rather than short-term return. Of course, I knew that short-term return could not be ignored, and it seemed logical to assume that our farm would produce more "stuff" if we followed the industrial method of farming. Yet it seemed equally clear that adopting nature's method of farming was much more likely to assure the farm's long-term success. Nature, after all, has been around for a long time and seems to be relatively resilient.

I'm not implying that a farmer can ignore the need to produce quantity. I need, and appreciate, good yields as much as any farmer, and improving yields is certainly one of the goals of our farm. But there are limits to rates and intensity of growth, and those limits are set by nature. Ultimately, a farm's success depends on the ecological health of the land in which the farm exists. And ecological health is best defined as the land's "capacity for self-renewal."[9]

Nature can deceive us easily in this respect. It may seem to the farmer that nature possesses an unlimited capacity for self-renewal and abundance. But, as Howard observed, while nature may appear lavish, she actually works on small margins. The whole of nature may seem luxurious to us, but "natural surpluses are made up of minute individual items: the amount contributed by each plant or animal is quite tiny: it is the additive total which impresses us."[10] Here, he said, "we may find our principal warning. The pursuit of quantity at all costs is dangerous in farming. Quantity should be aimed at only in strict conformity with natural law, especially must the law of the return of all wastes to the land be faithfully observed. In other words, a firm line needs to be drawn between a legitimate use of natural abundance and exploitation."[11]

Farming, Howard had observed, was ultimately dependent on the gifts of nature, and these gifts were tied to a complex, interdependent web of life composed of everything from soil microorganisms and worms to plants and mammals. And this web of life is sustained by the law of return. The health of the soil, which is the foundation of all life, is sustained by the return of all of the "waste" generated by the web.

Based on this wisdom from the past, we adopted six fundamental principles for managing our farm:

- Diversity is essential and is best accomplished with a mixture of crops and livestock.
- Managing for soil health is essential.
- The law of return must be obeyed. There shall be no waste.
- Managing for moisture conservation is critical, and is tightly linked to soil health.
- Natural selection will be the principal tool for improving the health of the farm.
- The farm will be conducted by the principles of *adaptive* management, rather than *control* management.

Applying the Principles

Of course, adopting principles is the easy part. Learning how to apply them in a particular time and place is the challenging part. What is the right mixture of crops and livestock in our particular ecological neighborhood? How many animals can we reasonably support on our farm during the winter months, given limited groundwater? About 1,000 acres of our farm is in native prairie, so what is an appropriate stocking rate, taking drought periods into account? What crops are best suited to our soil and climate conditions? How do we design a crop rotation that best protects and restores soil quality, conserves moisture, can be marketed profitably, and meets the needs of the diverse life of the farm? How can we design a system that is as self-renewing and self-regulating as possible?

Trying to answer all of these questions on my own probably would have been futile. David Vetter, who had returned to his own farm near Marquette, Nebraska, continued to be a source of inspiration and information for me. Since farming in southern Nebraska was significantly different from farming in south-central North Dakota, David could not give me very many specific suggestions for my own farm.

Fortunately other farmers in the northern plains at the time also were wrestling with these same issues. We found each other at a 1979 conference sponsored by a fledgling natural fertilizer company in Bismarck, North Dakota. A small group of us decided to continue learning from each other, and we formed the North Dakota Natural Farmers Association to plan educational conferences and field days so we could interact on a regular basis. Over time the association grew to include farmers from surrounding states and Canadian provinces. Subsequently, we renamed the organization the Northern Plains Sustainable Agriculture Society. It continues to serve as a vehicle to bring farmers and others together to educate each other. Learning from each other's mistakes and successes has proven to be the best education.

The Kirschenmann Family Farms Journey

There was an irony about my father's farming. While he was obsessed with taking care of the land, he was equally obsessed with being "progressive." He was driven to be the best wheat farmer in Stutsman County, which, of course, meant producing the highest yields of the best-quality wheat in the county. So when fertilizers became readily available in North Dakota right after World War II, he was both intrigued and concerned. The potential for increasing crop yields was attractive to him, but he worried about the effect synthetic fertilizers might have on his land.

I remember, as a young boy, traveling with him one winter as he sought information from extension specialists and other farmers whose judgment he valued. He asked them whether the application of synthetic fertilizers would "hurt his land." Everyone he talked to scoffed at the idea. It could only improve his land because it would improve the nutrient value of his soil, he was told. On the strength of that evaluation, he became the first farmer in our township to begin using fertilizers. Given the immediate response to fertilizer that he witnessed, along with the ability to simplify his farming system, my father declared that he "could never farm without fertilizers again." Of course, as a result our farm gradually drifted toward a more monoculture wheat operation, and that inevitably led to the need to apply pesticides to control weeds.

By the time I met David Vetter two decades later and learned about the connection between well-managed organic practices and improved soil health, my father had noticed the disappearance of earthworms from our farm as well as other characteristics that he associated with deteriorating soil quality. That concerned him deeply and led him to become a skeptical but strong supporter of transitioning the farm to organic management when I left a career in higher education in 1976 and returned to manage the farm. And thus our transition journey began.

The journey was not without its pitfalls. While I understood and embraced the six principles of nature farming that we developed, I did not fully appreciate what was involved in applying those principles on the ground. My early attempts to develop a crop rotation were crude at best and dysfunctional at worst. We suffered significant yield declines as a result. Gradually we learned from our mistakes, and within three years our yields had returned to normal.

Of course, one of the first realities that any farmer designing a farming system has to consider is climate, because it largely determines which species can thrive on a farm. How to fit the farm into the climate's seasons is a prime consideration. Several decades ago, a Texan stationed at one of North Dakota's air force bases wrote a book about North Dakota that he titled *July, August, and Winter*.[12] While we actually have four seasons in

North Dakota, the Texan's book title highlighted our short growing seasons, which limit the crops we can grow, the crop rotations we can design, and the animal breeds that thrive there.

Market availability is, of course, another significant crop-rotation constraint. No matter how ecologically ideal it may be to include a certain crop in a rotation, farmers can't afford to grow a crop if there is no market for it. Since the industrial economy has developed a very specialized food system, with just four crops—corn, wheat, soybeans, and rice—supplying 90 percent of the ingredients in processed foods, it is almost impossible to design an appropriately diverse crop rotation system on any kind of scale. Consequently, developing a crop rotation continues to be one of our biggest challenges.

A few examples of how we have applied the six principles of nature farming over the past thirty years may serve to paint a picture of part of our journey. After experimenting with different crop sequences, we eventually settled on a crop rotation pattern that appeared to meet the demands of our six nature farming principles:

- Alternate cool-season and warm-season crops to control weeds. Regularly alternating cool- and warm-season crops prevents both cool- and warm-season weeds from establishing themselves by continuously producing seeds and taking over the landscape.
- Alternate grassy and broadleaf plants to disrupt disease cycles.
- Alternate between shallow- and deep-rooted plants to use soil nutrients more efficiently.
- Incorporate a leguminous green-manure cover crop or forage crop into the rotation pattern to fix nitrogen and restore organic matter.

In addition to maintaining soil health, this rotation pattern also helps diversify risk. Different crops are vulnerable to different weather and disease events. Given our diverse crop mixture, only a modest portion of our farm's crops are ever vulnerable to any single threat. Because nature is not always benevolent, adaptive management on the farm is more successful than control management. Using adaptive management, we pay attention to how nature functions and then adapt the farm as fully as possible to nature's functioning. Trying to control nature is usually a fool's errand.

After learning this lesson through experience, I was later inspired by ecologist C. S. Holling, who also provided the scientific justification for adaptive management.[13] And for anyone still tempted to be nostalgic about farming with nature—or, for that matter, optimistic about controlling her—I would suggest reading Gary Larson's book, *There's a Hair in My Dirt.*[14]

Yet, despite the complexity and challenges, an appropriate crop rotation is simply one of the best ways to apply nature farming and adaptive management on the farm. The following are typical crop rotation sequences we have used on our farm:

- Year 1. Yellow blossom sweet clover is incorporated into the soil for green manure. Composted livestock manure added in the fall. A year devoted to restoring soil health. The clover also serves as an emergency source of forage to serve as winter feed for livestock during drought periods.
- Year 2. Hard red spring wheat. Cool-season, grassy crop.
- Year 3. Winter rye. Wintertime grassy crop with allelopathic effects to suppress weeds.
- Year 4. Sunflowers. Deep-rooted, broadleaf, warm-season crop. Sweet clover is interseeded during last cultivation.
- Year 5. Return to Year 1.
- Year 1. Alfalfa. We generally leave a field in alfalfa for three to four years, harvesting the forage each year for winter feed for our animals. It will accumulate nitrogen in the soil and protect soil from erosion. The second cutting of alfalfa is incorporated into the soil in the summer of the final year, and composted livestock manure is added.
- Year 2. Flax. Cool-season broadleaf crop.
- Year 3. Durum wheat. Grassy crop.
- Year 4. Buckwheat. Broadleaf warm-season crop. Clover interseeded.
- Year 5. Yellow blossom sweet clover is incorporated for green manure, and composted livestock manure is added.

Oats or barley is sometimes seeded in place of winter rye; millet can replace buckwheat as a warm-season crop. We have generally grown eight or nine different crops in various rotation schemes in a given year. All of the crops we grow are relatively quick to mature and work well in our short growing season.

Over time, various events have forced us to eliminate or add crops to our rotation. For example, we used to raise canola in our rotation as a cool-season broadleaf plant; it was well-adapted to our climate and was quite profitable. But once Roundup Ready canola was introduced into our neighborhood, we had to abandon the crop. Organic standards do not allow transgenic inputs, and it became impossible to prevent cross-pollination of our own seed or to obtain seed with sufficient purity from seed suppliers.

We also had to give up raising sunflowers a few years ago. Blackbirds use wetlands in North Dakota as their nesting habitat and tend to congregate in early September to prepare for the winter migration to the south. By early September sunflowers are one of the few crops left standing in the fields that blackbirds can feed on, and they are definitely the birds' preferred food. As long as most of our neighbors also raised sunflowers, we all shared our sunflowers with the migrating birds. With a little careful management, we could limit our losses to the birds to 5 or 6 percent. However, because federal crop subsidies increasingly favored corn and soybeans, and seed companies developed earlier-maturing varieties of these crops, most farmers rationally switched from sunflowers to corn and beans, leaving our sunflower fields as the only feed source for thousands of blackbirds. During the final two years that we raised sunflowers we lost more than 60 percent of the crop to blackbird predation and could no longer afford to include the crop in our rotation.

We also experimented with multicropping. One of the things I learned from Takao Furuno's farming operation in Japan is that monocultures are horribly inefficient and always require significant energy inputs. Why produce only one food commodity from an acreage that requires intensive energy inputs in the form of fertilizers and pesticides to achieve production goals, when one can produce five or six food commodities off the same acreage and use far less energy due to the synchrony made possible by a multispecies system?

Our experiment was not nearly as sophisticated as Furuno's. We planted wheat and flax together in some fields, and lentils and flax together in others. The production part of the experiment worked quite well. In the flax/wheat combination, wheat is clearly the dominant species, and the flax has no adverse affect on wheat yields. And while flax yields in this combination tend to be modest at best, there is no additional labor or input cost, aside from the seed. In the case of lentils and flax, one can give the comparative advantage either to the lentils or the flax by adjusting the seeding rate for each crop. Again, there is little effect on the yield of the dominant crop and no additional cost from adding the recessive crop except for the seed.

These crop combinations work well as companion plants, and the flax can be separated easily from the wheat or lentils. We simply run the combined harvested crops through a rotary screen cleaner. However, because flax is the smaller seed, most of the foreign materials that are part of any harvested crop end up in the flax bin. Naturally, processors don't like to process the flax with all of the added foreign materials, especially because flax is difficult to clean in any case. Someday we may install a seed cleaner at our farm so we can clean the flax ourselves and continue experimenting with companion planting. During the winter months, things slow down on our farm, and we could take the time to run the flax through our own cleaner and deliver a pristine product to our customers.

"There shall be no waste" is the one principle out of the six that has always most intrigued me. We started integrating our crop and livestock systems early on in an effort to implement that principle. As a result we managed to close our nutrient cycle and eliminate most "waste" on the farm. I put quotation marks around the word "waste" because, from the perspective of the law of return, there is no waste. As Rattan Lal has observed, calling crop residues a "waste" is "a dangerous trend" because "it is not a waste. It is a precious commodity and essential to preserving soil quality."[15]

As our crops are harvested, we run our grain through the rotary screen cleaner to remove broken and shrunken kernels, weed seeds, and other foreign materials from the grain. On farms without livestock, such screenings are often deposited in landfills. We put these screenings into a separate bin, and during the winter months we grind and feed this "waste" to our animals as an additional protein supplement to their forage diet. The basic rule at our farm is that we *never* feed any crops to animals that are suitable for human consumption. All of our grain crops that meet human food quality standards are sold into the organic food market.

In the summer months, our animals graze on our native prairie lands. These lands are not suitable for cultivation or crop production because they are too hilly, too rocky, or have too many wetlands. But they are perfect for grazing. During the winter months, we place our animals into large loafing areas near the farmstead where they have access to barns during inclement weather. Deep straw is put in the barns and spread on the feeding areas to provide bedding and absorb the urine and manure deposited by the animals. Their diet consists of forages: alfalfa, native prairie hay, and straw. On our farm, forage is a by-product of the alfalfa that fixes most of the nitrogen required by our crops.

In the spring, after the animals return to the prairie, we begin composting the rich mixture of straw, manure, and urine that has accumulated over the winter months. This mixture is piled in windrows approximately six feet tall and six to eight feet wide at the base. By fall, the composting process is completed, and we spread the compost on cultivated fields. The "waste" from the animals becomes food for the crops. This ensures that waste from one part of the farm always becomes food for another part of the farm. Crop waste becomes food for the animals. Animal waste becomes food for the crops.

This waste-to-food system goes a long way toward reducing our energy consumption. We have purchased no crop or livestock inputs on our farm since 1980. Once we began viewing our farm as an intimate set of relationships, rather than a series of individual enterprises managed to maximize short-term productive capacity, we observed opportunities to reduce our energy consumption and increase our ecological capital. The soil health of our farm continues to improve. The law of return works!

However, as we approach peak global oil production, we know that new challenges lie ahead. We still use too much diesel fuel on our farm. Our grain and livestock are shipped hundreds and even thousands of miles, part of a system that still relies on cheap energy. We need to prepare quickly for a new energy future based on energy exchange rather than energy input. Again, nature farming principles can guide us here. It is becoming clear to me that we now need to explore new ways to develop interdependent biological synergies among species on our farm so that the waste of one species becomes the energy for another, the way nature does it.

Creating a synergistic energy exchange system on our farm will likely require a much more creative system of crop/livestock integration. While we have integrated our crops and livestock by turning waste into food, we have not explored deeply the biological synergies that might be possible in our prairie ecology. I am intrigued by systems that farmers like Takao Furuno and Joel Salatin have designed, wherein the waste of each species on the farm becomes food (energy) for another in ways that require very little external energy input. These farming systems truly mimic the way nature uses energy. I need to learn more fully how to apply those strategies to the northern plains prairie ecology. And we need our public research institutions to conduct far more research to support the development of these new farming systems. As Wendell Berry has said, "if one lives on the prairie, one must learn to farm by studying the prairie."[16]

Nature farming depends on systems that are as self-regulating and self-renewing as possible. That is the way nature functions. In this regard, husbandry becomes extremely important, and good husbandry is not possible without intimacy. Let me cite one example from our farm.

When I returned to the farm in 1976, our beef cattle were managed in a fairly traditional manner. Like other farmers and ranchers in our area, we bred our cows to give birth in early spring, late February and March. I think this tradition was born out of the desire to get the calving out of the way before spring field work begins in April. From the perspective of labor efficiency, this is eminently sensible. From the calf's point of view, however, there could hardly be a worse time to be born. In the spring, calves are born into cold, wet conditions, perfect for developing many diseases, such as pneumonia. They all crowd into barns to protect their little bodies from the cold, and in so doing they readily contract diseases from each other. Not surprisingly, during calving and for a month or more thereafter we were constantly administering therapies to fight calf diseases of one kind or another, and we routinely lost 5 to 10 percent of the newborn calves.

When I looked at this situation from the calf's point of view and pondered how nature did it, it occurred to me that a much better time and place for the calf to be born would be in June or July, out on the prairie. When cows begin labor, they instinctively leave the herd, give birth, and nurse the calf, all in isolation from the herd. They only bring the calf into the herd after it has nursed for several days and has gotten its share of disease-fighting immunities contained in the cow's colostrum.

Once we made this shift in our birthing routine, we eliminated virtually all calf disease problems from our herd. We have not used a needle on a calf in more than twenty years. Furthermore, we have dramatically reduced birthing difficulties. We attribute this to the fact that the cows are in better condition due to the increased exercise that they get from grazing on the prairie. Of course, there are predators (such as coyotes) on the prairie, and I initially thought we might lose calves to predators. To decrease that likelihood, we began slightly modifying the genetics of our cows by cross-breeding certain breeds into our herd that have excellent mothering instincts.

Our herd has always been composed of mixed breeds, though Black Angus is the dominant breed. But I had learned from breeders that the Tarentaise breed tended to have good mothering instincts, including protecting their calves. They appear to create a safe zone around the newborn calf and tend to keep any animals away from the calf. They also are good nurturers and urge their newborn calves to get up and begin nursing as soon as possible, encouraging them to obtain the first colostrum as quickly as possible. So we maintain a small amount of Tarentaise genetics in our herd to encourage better mothering instincts. Our cows now do an excellent job of protecting their calves from predators. To my knowledge, we have never lost a calf to coyotes.

These management strategies are simply a way of applying the principle of adaptation rather than control to our animal operation. We use natural selection aggressively with our herd. Any cows that do not thrive in our prairie ecology are culled and replaced with better-adapted heifers. This improves herd health as well as the resilience of our animals. Aside from pregnancy-testing our cows once a year, we never need a veterinarian on our farm. Howard's principle of leaving "both plants and animals to protect themselves against disease" may initially seem naive or even cruel, but the concept is sound. Building natural immunities and managing animals so that they develop their own defenses is, in the long run, much more humane than constantly intervening with therapies to restore their failing health. And certainly Howard did not promote neglect. Sick animals need to be cared for, but therapeutic intervention at the expense of ecosystems management creates a system that fosters disease and that is, in the long term, less humane than allowing them to "protect themselves against disease."

So our journey, I believe, has taken us on the right path. While our profit margins are slim, as they are for any farm in today's rural economy, the farm has been sufficiently profitable to be debt free. We have not borrowed any operating funds since 1980. And, more important, the soil quality has improved dramatically. In 1987, despite one of the severest droughts on record in North Dakota, we managed to harvest an average wheat yield of seventeen bushels per acre. Not great, to be sure, but some of our conventional-farming neighbors never even pulled a combine out of the shed, because their crop dried up before it could mature. So we were satisfied with what our land provided. Independent research has shown that healthy soil with increased organic matter absorbs and retains more moisture.[17,18] The experience on our farm during drought conditions seems to corroborate such research.

Of course, on our farm we need to continue to anticipate the coming changes and get a head start on preparing for them. The challenges of peak oil, climate change, declining freshwater resources, and reduced biodiversity will make all farms more vulnerable. While the diversity and self-regulating systems we have put in place may shield us from some of the looming threats, we are still at risk in many respects.

We began taking small steps in the spring of 2008 to prepare for our new future. We have begun converting some of our annual crop acres to perennial grasses, and we are slightly shifting the crop/livestock balance of our farm. We will be increasing the perennial/animal component of our farm and decreasing the annual/crop portion. Perennial grasses and livestock seem to be more resilient than annual crops in the face of more unstable climates, and they require less energy. Perennial plants have deeper roots and are therefore better equipped to withstand drought. They maintain living cover on the land and therefore sequester more carbon and protect the soil from erosion during periods of heavy rains. So the perennial/livestock part of the farm is simply more resilient. It harks back to my father's old rule: "Cows don't get hailed out."

Of course, no farm story is complete without including a conversation about markets. The modern food system has become extremely specialized and concentrated. Mass marketing of undifferentiated commodities leaves little room for individual farmers to make independent decisions that respond to the needs of their farms, their families, or their communities.

However, new trends in the food market are providing emerging opportunities to produce highly differentiated food products and retain part of the value of those unique products at the farm gate. I have written about these new supply-chain market opportunities in other essays in this volume.

In the 1980s, some of the farmers in the Northern Plains Sustainable Agriculture Society had the good fortune to work with entrepreneur Michael Marcolla, who created an early version of value-chain marketing. This process gave us a voice in the prices we were paid and provided information about the products our customers needed. Each partner in the chain valued the relationship we developed because each party benefited from the relationship. Farmers got a fair price for their products and a stable market. Our customers got a fair deal and a reliable source of supply for the products they needed. As the organic industry matured and became more commoditized, some of the companies, unfortunately, drifted away from that business arrangement. However, our farm has established good business relationships with companies such as Eden Foods, Roman Meal Milling, and Rockwell Organic. We continue to do business by some of those values principles to this day, albeit as an individual enterprise rather than through a farmers' marketing network.

I am now part of a coalition that recognizes the need for values-based value chains, in which all participants work as partners to grow and market products of superior value, sharing the risks and rewards. The "value" to the food customer is the quality of the product, the food story that comes with the product, and the trusting relationship created by linking the customer with the rest of the players in the chain. It follows the philosophy of John Thackara, who stresses "relationship value."[19]

One of the other delightful benefits of being a farmer on one's own farm is the opportunity to produce almost all of the food we consume. Most farmers today buy processed food from big-box stores, like everyone else; but we decided to produce almost all of what we eat from our own farm more than a decade ago. At first it seemed impossible to produce the variety of foods that are essential to the pleasure of good eating, owing to our short growing season in North Dakota. To our surprise, we were able to cultivate many varieties of fruits and vegetables acclimated to our climate, giving us incredible flavors we never experienced from our local supermarkets. And, of course, the beef from our own animals continues to be exceptional.

Another challenge that we share with many other farmers today is transitioning the farm to the next generation. My sister and I both have children who love the farm but have no interest in managing it. Fortunately, we have two young families that have been with our farm for almost twenty years. They attend to most of the day-to-day farm management while I spend most of my time with the Leopold Center for Sustainable Agriculture at Iowa State University and the Stone Barns Center for Food and Agriculture near New York City. We have taken steps to enable these two families to own livestock on our farm and some of the land. In today's farm economy, few beginning farmers have sufficient capital to own their own land. We need policies to enable beginning farmers to obtain low-interest loans and access to land through land trusts. We need to increase the low percentage of young farmers in American agriculture today. As of the 2002 U.S. agricultural census, only 5.8 percent of U.S. farmers were younger than age thirty-five.

Many challenges face our food and agriculture system in the twenty-first century. It is important to remember what Sir Albert Howard said in the 1940s: soil health and the law of return are the basis for a healthy, productive agriculture.

PART 2

Cracks in the Bridges

Inspecting the Industrial Food System

On Learning to Farm
Ecologically on the Prairie

The Changing World of Agriculture

No one would argue that major changes are taking place in agriculture. The question is, of the many directions agriculture could take, which will best serve farmers and society? The choices facing us are really just two: industrial agriculture or ecological agriculture. Industrial agriculture is primarily driven by a productionist ideology, in which increasing production is an intrinsically desirable social goal. In the ecological paradigm, adequate production is folded into a larger social goal. Ecological agriculture weighs the benefits of increased production against the ecological and social consequences of such increases.

Ecological agriculture is not new. Herbert C. Hanson came to the North Dakota Agricultural Experiment Station in 1930 and later served for a brief time as its director.[1] Hanson published an article in *Ecology* magazine that was remarkable for its time.[2] Noting the increased interest in "ecological concepts and procedures" in other fields of study, Hanson stressed the importance of ecological approaches for "planning improved relationships of people to the land."[3] Addressing the challenges facing agriculture, he suggested that the "concepts and tools needed are methods of achieving harmonious relationships of organisms between themselves and their environment, the concept of the natural tendency of community development

This piece is based on two presentations, the first given at the Carrington Research and Extension Center, Carrington, North Dakota, October 1993. Another version of this talk was the keynote address at the Sustainable Land Management conference, Preparing Professionals for Leadership, held in Bryan, Texas, February 1994. The talk was published in the conference proceedings, Texas A&M University, College Station, Texas, February 1994, 62–72.

toward stabilization with the environment, and the need for natural areas as checks, or standards, by which the values of effects of tillage, irrigation, drainage, grazing, lumbering, and other uses may be measured."[4]

To make his point about the need for such holistic thinking and research in agriculture, he told a story about an experiment in the Laramie River Valley in northern Colorado. In an effort to reinvigorate grass production in the valley, extension agents decided to experiment with limited burning of sagebrush. The experiment appeared successful. Phenomenal increases in the growth of grasses were observed where the sagebrush had been burned. Soon experiment station circulars urged ranchers to improve their grass stands using the burning method.

Then objections began to appear. First, concern was registered that fires might spread into the forest. Next there were complaints that sagebrush-burned areas farther west were followed by vigorous growth of annual weeds instead of grass. While the sagebrush could at least be used as emergency forage and was useful as a snow catch, the weeds were worthless. Shortly thereafter, farmers began to report a dramatic increase in curly top virus, a disease that caused heavy losses in sugar beets, beans, and other irrigated crops. Reports of increases in loss from this disease came from as far away as California.

Investigations revealed that the beet leafhopper, the vector transmitting the disease, increased its population in annual weed habitat. Soon the connection between burning sagebrush, increased annual weed production, and loss of crops to curly top became obvious. "A practice considered beneficial in one area," wrote Hanson, turned out to "have serious consequences in another area. . . . Burning of sagebrush . . . may result finally in the distant, irrigated farmer losing his crops of sugar beets and beans."[5]

These ecological insights led Hanson to draw two conclusions about agriculture. First, "permanent agriculture must be in adjustment with the environment."[6] Second, "unless a satisfactory farm life can be developed on the basis of the resources of that region, no amount of modification of the physical environment will be worthwhile."[7]

New Ways of Thinking

Hanson was not alone in pressing for ecological initiatives in agriculture. Twenty-five years earlier, Liberty Hyde Bailey, dean of agriculture at Cornell University, wrote that "a good part of agriculture is to learn how to adapt one's work to nature. . . . To live in right relation with his natural conditions is one of the first lessons that a wise farmer or any other wise man learns."[8] At about the same time, agricultural visionaries in other parts of the world were stressing a similar path. Sir Albert Howard of Great Britain, Rudolf Steiner in Austria, and Mokichi Okada in Japan all emphasized the importance of farming in concert with nature. These early overtures, imploring agriculture to adopt more ecological methods, represent part of a larger epistemological shift that has gradually been taking place in all fields of study since the turn of the century.

In the field of quantum physics, it is not possible to separate the knower from the known. The frame of reference from which a researcher addresses a problem affects the outcome of the conclusion. Experiments to determine whether light was a particle or a wave, for example, showed that the results depended on how the researcher set up the experiment to capture the light. Such relationships led Heinz Pagels to conclude that in the quantum world, "the ordinary idea of objectivity fails."[9]

In the environmental field, deep ecology has taught us the importance of attending to all of the connections in the environment and not simply the welfare of one species or the conservation of one resource. In the field of medical science, somatic therapies have taught us that the mind and the body ultimately cannot be separated and that one can have a profound effect upon the other.

In all of these fields of study the shift has been from:

- Parts to wholes
- Detachments to relationships
- Seeing things only from the outside to seeing them from both inside and outside

This shift has led us to begin thinking about ecosystem health, rather than the productivity of isolated parts of the system. That shift will profoundly affect agriculture and agricultural research in the next century. Moving in the direction envisioned by Hanson in 1939, this shift will blur many of the traditional lines between basic and applied research, research and extension, and researcher and farmer.

Science from a New Plateau

I am not suggesting, however, that we discard research and extension work conducted primarily on the premise of reductionist detachment and seeing things only from the outside, the method introduced by René Descartes, Francis Bacon, and others more than three hundred years ago. Instead, I propose we examine Albert Einstein's analogy of how scientific work progresses. Progress in scientific thought, Einstein argued, was not like tearing down an old barn to build a new one. It was rather more like climbing a mountain in which each new plateau provides an increasingly clearer view of the landscape. It is always easy, from the vantage point of a new plateau, to see that one might have taken a better path to climb the mountain. But it is pointless to curse the path one took to get there. On the other hand, one should reassess one's position from the new plateau and make midcourse corrections before continuing the climb. An example of this approach can be found in the course correction made by the International Rice Research Institute (IRRI), one of the keystone research centers of the so-called green revolution (GR). The IRRI made enormous contributions to that agricultural revolution, not least of which was the development of new rice varieties and production technologies that doubled and even tripled rice yields in the developing world.

Yet, viewing its work from a new plateau and assessing its accomplishment from a more comprehensive perspective, IRRI now believes that the successes of its program have been overrated, while the problems have been underrated. According to a report released in 1993, IRRI recognized a number of problems associated with the GR strategy.[10] First, high-yielding seeds need to be "pampered with expensive fertilizers, pesticides and irrigation," making producers in developing countries dependent on unaffordable technologies. In addition, the new seeds displaced "traditional specially adapted rice varieties, resulting in an erosion of the crop gene pool" and increasing rice-production vulnerability to environmental changes. The GR strategy also brought on a "wide range of ecological problems . . . increasing soil infertility, chemical pollution of land and water resources, pesticide poisoning and pest immunity to agro-chemicals." Furthermore, in their rush to improve yields, agronomists "neglected to calculate the value of other crops and activities carried out in the farm areas of traditional systems. Villagers across Asia grow fruit trees on their rice fields, or use submerged paddy fields to raise fresh water fish."[11] The monocropping strategies of the GR largely ignored such companion production.

The GR strategy also produced serious social and economic consequences. The IRRI study showed that when increased farmer health costs were added to production costs, GR farmers fared no better economically than traditional farmers. Finally, it is now recognized that the GR strategies "mainly benefited rich farmers, who took maximum advantage of the size of their holding and their ability to invest in new inputs." As a result, the Food and Agriculture Organization of the United Nations has concluded that it is no longer possible to develop a stable, sustainable agriculture in the developing world "without carrying out land tenure reform."[12]

Had IRRI insisted on seeing their work only from the plateau of productionist ideology (producing as much rice as possible), they would never have seen these other related factors. Looking at their work using ecological connections, they were able to assess their work with fresh insight.

Insights That Will Shape the New Agenda

Five ecological issues appear to be emerging for agriculture in the twenty-first century.

The ecological connections of the ecosystem are much more complex and subtle than previously understood. The way we farm in one region may affect not only the welfare of farmers in other regions, but also the economic, environmental, and social matrix in which we and other species live. Farming practices can affect the ability of future generations to secure adequate food supplies for themselves. Water, soil, and the quality of life in human communities are affected by the structures and practices of the agriculture we choose. If we are concerned about the consequences of agriculture beyond the bottom line of a single growing season, we must begin analyzing the long-term effects of industrial agriculture.

Hanson's notion that a "permanent agriculture must be in adjustment with the environment" has taken on a more comprehensive and compelling meaning than even he had surmised.[13] Everything in the ecosystems in which we live and farm is connected to everything else, and these embedded ecological connections can either work for farmers or against them. Our efforts to conquer nature in farming, forestry, fishing, and mining are proving costly and counterproductive. Over the past century we have ignored many of those costs, which we have paid for with abundant cheap energy. The costs are now catching up with us.

For example, assessments of pesticides usually only focus on direct crop returns and ignore environmental and economic costs. The benefits of pesticide use must be evaluated against all of the costs associated with its use: human health effects, domestic animal poisonings, destruction of natural enemies, pesticide resistance, crop-pollination problems, honeybee losses, crop and crop product losses, groundwater and surface water contamination, wildlife and microorganism losses, and governmental expenditures to reduce the environmental and social costs of pesticide use.[14]

Although the ecological connectedness of ecosystems can cause widespread and unanticipated detrimental effects, these connections can be harnessed to benefit farmers. For example, we can use nature's principle of diversity and integrate livestock into a crop farming system. The waste from the livestock operation fuels the cropping system, and wastes from the cropping system feed the livestock, a double economic return with minimum waste or pollution. Ecological connectedness gives livestock manure a multiplier effect. It adds nutrients to the soil, improves soil structure, adds soil organic matter, and increases soil biological activity. It improves overall soil quality in ways that we don't yet fully understand.

Ecological farming enhances and uses diversity, rather than limiting and destroying it. Beneficial insects to control insect pests help achieve balanced predator/prey relationships that can reduce future pest problems. Insecticides destroy target and beneficial insects and increase future pest problems. A diversity of crops in a rotation to control weeds and maintain fertility, in place of a single-species monoculture, can have similar benefits.

The more diversity we add to the system, the less "brittle" the system is. Vulnerability to disease, weather-related losses, and economic forces can all be mitigated through diversity. Ecological connectedness is the principal reason for this stability. It makes more sense to cooperate with nature's ecological diversity and work with it than to conquer or destroy it.

We are now more aware of the limits to growth. "In many parts of the world, the sources of food (land, soils, waters, soil nutrients) are falling and the sinks of pollutants from agriculture are overflowing."[15] In these places, agricultural throughput already exceeds sustainable limits. Without rapid change, the Earth's booming population will have to feed itself from a degraded resource base.

The severe impact that limitless growth has already had on the planet means that our century-long productionist ideology needs to give way to a more comprehensive outlook. Of course, the productionist ideology was phenomenally successful, measured in terms of quantity of output. But we never paid enough attention to the social and ecological costs of producing that output. The cost in soil loss and groundwater depletion alone should have led us to question the benefits. Even if we could continue to ignore those costs, we can no longer ignore that we are running out of oil and that the levels of pollution are no longer acceptable to society.

The wisest thing to do now is to transition from an oil economy to a solar economy and from a polluting economy to a recycling economy. In some instances, we already know how to do this in agriculture, although in many other respects we need much more research. We should start preparing now to farm without oil and without loading any more pollutants into the groundwater.

We now have a new social mandate for agriculture. Society's mandate for agriculture during the past century was to produce as much food and fiber as cheaply and efficiently as possible. For the next century, the mandate will be preserving the resource base, protecting the environment, and treating animals humanely. Increasingly, this mandate will include preservation of biodiversity and protection of the atmospheric gases that make up the Earth's envelope.

University research and extension programs have a vital role to play in finding new ways to farm and in bringing together farmers, environmental organizations, and politicians to develop ecological farming systems. Public policies are also needed to help end the silly feud that often erupts between farmers and environmentalists. As long as farmers and environmentalists see each other as enemies, we have little hope of meeting the new social mandate for agriculture.

We have to get past simplistic thinking and work together to produce an agriculture that meets our food and fiber needs without destroying the resource base or further degrading the environment. We cannot have economically healthy farms or rural communities if we destroy our natural capital. Farmers and land-grant universities should welcome the new mandate of the twenty-first century and work together to develop farming systems to meet it, as they did to meet the productionist mandate of the twentieth century.

Designing an agriculture that is "in adjustment with the environment" is uniquely regional. Agricultural practices that achieve ecological goals in one region will likely not work in another region. Recognizing ecological and social differences will be crucial to success. Efforts to "harmonize" agriculture on a global scale will probably fail. While the federal government can set national goals, it cannot manage natural resources. Because nature is dynamic and every regional ecosystem is unique, proper management can only be executed by local managers who understand local systems and who can modify management strategies to accommodate local changes in nature. David Ehrenfeld says assessing ecological health is "a judgment that can be made only by someone who has been intensely familiar for a long time with what is being judged. Each living system is unique, and there are too many variables to let us expect that the mere application of scientific formulas will do the job."[16]

This same principle holds true for farming. Farming involves managing a biological system within a local ecosystem. Conservation biologist R. Edward Grumbine noted that the key problem in natural resource management is "how, specifically . . . to marry our developing knowledge of species' needs and of a dynamic nature with a new sense of ourselves as part of the community of life."[17] He suggested we have two problems, one scientific and the other ethical. We are still biologically illiterate concerning "species' needs and how nature evolves." And we are still addicted to the notion that we are somehow separate from nature. The challenge to overcome these deficiencies is exactly the challenge facing agriculture.

A global, extractive economy creates negative impacts on rural communities. The industrial economy driving agriculture for the past century has insisted on cheap labor, cheap raw materials, and few environmental restrictions as a "friendly" climate for doing business. This "free market" economy largely ignored the ecological and social costs of doing business.

The result has been a triple dagger to the heart of rural economies. First, it degraded or depleted the natural capital of rural communities—their ultimate source of wealth. Second, it exported raw materials from rural communities to add value elsewhere and then imported expensive value-added products back into the rural community. The result is that very little wealth stayed in rural communities to produce multiplier effects. Third, the farm share of the agriculture economy gradually decreased, while the market and input shares increased.[18]

This extractive economy has left rural communities in perpetual economic depression, social destabilization, and ecological ruin, which highlights the difficulty of achieving economic health, apart from social, ecological, and human health. If the health of rural communities is to be restored, the farming sector of agriculture (still one of the principal economic enterprises in most rural communities) must wean itself from external inputs and stop exporting cheap raw materials to add value elsewhere.

Dependence on off-farm inputs and the siphoning off of value-adding market activities into the market sector reduced the farm share of agriculture's economic activity from 44 percent to 9 percent between 1910 and 1990. Stewart Smith has predicted that if these trends don't change, the farming sector will disappear by the year 2020.[19]

If this scenario plays out, the land-grant universities could disappear along with the farming sector. Industry is not likely to pick up the tab for a science-based institution because it will be much cheaper for corporations to simply create their own research laboratories to produce the technologies they need. The public is not likely to support a land-grant university whose only clientele is big business.

Expensive off-farm inputs can be replaced by on-farm cultural practices. Intensive rotational grazing instead of bovine growth hormone is a good example of such a strategy in dairy, as Smith points out. The farming sector must also find ways to recapture part of the market sector activity. The recent development of grower-owned processing cooperatives is a hopeful sign of such a market shift in North Dakota. Because these kinds of shifts have the potential to revitalize rural economies, we need more research and extension work devoted to such efforts.

What Do Farmers Need?

I want to turn my attention now, more specifically, to what farmers need to farm ecologically. Here we must be very clear about the question, which is what farmers *need*—not what farmers want.

Farmers have traditionally wanted to take care of their land, to raise their children on farms and have them become farmers, and to be part of a rural community life. Recently, farmers have been seduced by the productionist ideology, wanting only to produce more. Frederick Buttel views farmers as reluctant cooperators in this seduction, but they were seduced, nevertheless.[20] Consequently, many farmers believe their only salvation lies in producing more. Such farmers now want more magic bullets from their land-grant universities, to help them produce more. But if the productionist ideology has played itself out for the reasons noted above, then what farmers want and what farmers need may be two very different things. This is not to discount the importance of production. But how do we sustain productivity?

A new vision of the prairie. What farmers need from an ecological perspective, rather than a purely production perspective, is related to the ecosystem in which the farming is practiced. In the Great Plains, that ecosystem is a prairie. If prairie farming is to succeed over the long term, it has to be adapted to the prairie environment. As Hanson argued, the prairie must serve as the standard against which we evaluate the effects of farming.

Accordingly, in the Great Plains, answering the question "what do farmers need?" from an ecological perspective has to begin with updating our vision of the prairie. Freyfogle points out that while the vision of the prairie cherished by European settlers "switched its clothing several times," it was, throughout, a "battered image."[21] Europeans believed that the prairie needed to be conquered. Bent on conquest, they ignored the connections and interdependencies integral to understanding the prairie. Early European settlers misunderstood prairie fertility because trees, not barren grasslands, were a sign of fertility to them. Prairie settlers simply wanted to know what could be used for grazing and what could not, what could be used for raising crops and what could not. They had no interest in comprehending the prairie or its complexity.

Eventually, European settlers modified their image of the prairie. They discovered that prairie soils were as rich as soils in woodlands. They began to divide the prairie into two camps: friend and enemy. Friendly components supported living on the prairie: plants that could be grazed, wildlife that could be eaten, fields that submitted easily to the plow. Enemies were plants that poisoned domestic animals, wildlife that preyed on them, and rocks, wetlands, or other barriers that stood in the way of crop production.

Given this heritage, we have never understood the complexity of prairie ecology, nor have we cared to. Even after a century of living, farming, and doing research here, we are biologically illiterate about the prairie, especially concerning the use of its rich diversity to support agriculture. We have seen the prairie as a place to be exploited, rather than a place to be understood. Like any other ecosystem, we will, of course, never fully understand the prairie. But we can learn from its wisdom. What we can do, to paraphrase Aldo Leopold, is to begin thinking like a prairie.

If we are going to use the prairie in a manner that preserves its value for future generations, then we must give birth to a new vision of the prairie. Informed by this new vision, "the fresh-plowed field in spring will mean more than beauty and opportunity; it will mean exposure, erosion, and long-term soil loss. The endless expanse of wheat will mean more than harmony and wealth; it will mean monoculture, insect pests, and the inevitable pollution of farm chemicals. The center pivot irrigation system, long a symbol of the blooming drylands, will mix its Eden message with a sense of draining aquifers and slowly poisoned soils."[22]

Farming within the limits of ecological sources and sinks and kindling this new vision of the prairie is essential to maintaining productivity. This new vision of the prairie can help farmers understand and become part of the prairie's productive power while preserving it, instead of doing battle with it and destroying it. This new vision is one of the first things that farmers in the Great Plains need. Meeting this need is a task that could be undertaken by extension, but it is unlikely to be a popular task. It probably won't be funded by commodity groups or the agribusiness industry. If the popular media see the need for such a transformation, then public support for this task might be generated.[23]

A sustainable agriculture perspective. This new vision of the prairie tacitly assumes a transition to a more sustainable agriculture, and not just techniques for farming without chemicals. In our rush to precisely define sustainable agriculture, we have allowed the issue to become polarized into debates over contrasting farming technologies. More is at stake here. The transition to a sustainable agriculture requires the same sweeping change of perception that informs a transition to a more sustainable society as a whole. A sustainable agriculture:

- Cannot deplete nonrenewable resources faster than substitutes can be found, or renewable resources any faster than they can be regenerated
- Cannot produce more pollution than what the planetary sinks can absorb, assimilate, or dissipate
- Must maintain the right people-to-land ratio so that local land users will have sufficient intimate knowledge about the local ecosystem to manage it appropriately

Thus, the new vision of the prairie from a sustainable agriculture perspective is more than a romantic notion of returning the prairie to a buffalo commons and more than alternative technologies and farming practices. Sustainable agriculture is a way of thinking about farming and nature, a radical transformation of our understanding of the proper place and role of the human species in relationship to the rest of the Earth community and how agriculture fits into that community. Increasingly, it will not be enough to concern ourselves only with the resources we need to produce food and fiber. We in agriculture will be required to participate in the emerging effort to enhance and preserve all of the resources on which the total community of species life depends. What farmers need is a new sense of themselves as part of that community.

Agroecological literacy. After farmers acquire a new vision of the ecological neighborhood in which they farm, they will need more information about how to fit agriculture into that neighborhood without destroying it. This task is not as daunting as it may seem because many techniques have already been developed. Some have been practiced in various parts of the world for centuries. Crop rotation, contouring, polycultures, cover crops, composting, and diversification are all well-known strategies that are ecologically and economically effective.

Other approaches need much more research. For example, farmers need information on specific predator/prey relationships and new cultivars that perform well under alternative growing conditions, not just cultivars that are bred to respond to high fertilizer inputs and chemical pest controls.

They need to understand soil quality: how to achieve it, measure it, and maintain it. Farmers need these and hundreds of similar technologies, all uniquely adapted to prairie ecologies.

Juan Izquierdo, regional plant production officer of the United Nations Food and Agriculture Organization, suggests that shifting from productionist to ecological farming will require a new perception of crop science. It will necessitate "an approach to the production of crops based on less uniform plants and is in total contrast to the present trend toward uniformity and standardization."[24] Izquierdo calls this a shift from "vertical" improvement in crop sciences (which have focused on the Mendelian principles of "elimination of defects") to "horizontal" crop improvement. Horizontal improvement focuses on crops that are less uniform, crops containing "genetic mosaics," and the introduction of a greater diversity of crops into the cropping system.

Transgenic strategies, which emphasize monoculture, would give way to a system that enhances biodiversity. This shift makes ecological and economic sense and can help us get off the crop-improvement technology treadmill. Genetic engineering will likely not solve the problems of vertical improvement, Izquierdo warns, because nature develops resistance to uniformity and standardization, even if genetic engineering can develop new forms of vertical integration. The vertical approach, which attempts to control nature, is doomed to failure because it is contrary to nature's evolutionary process. In contrast, a horizontal approach attempts to fit agriculture into nature's evolutionary system and uses nature's own diversity to solve agriculture's problems, increasing its probability of success.

New infrastructures for ecological farming. Meadows and her colleagues assert that "millions of farmers in all parts of the world already follow soil-conserving and ecologically sound agricultural techniques. The challenge is to see that all farmers know and are able to practice these techniques. That is not a technical problem, it is a social one."[25] Thus, besides ecological farming approaches, farmers also need education, community support, and market infrastructures that enable them to adopt alternative production practices. Changing farm production practices to conform to a new vision of the prairie and to meet new ecological goals will not work without transforming the infrastructure supporting agriculture.

Here is where farmers need to begin holding environmentalists and food activists to account. Farmers can't change the infrastructure by themselves. Such changes must become the social agenda of all citizens. Farmers cannot adopt a greater diversity of crops unless there are markets for those crops, and there will never be adequate markets as long as 90 percent of food is manufactured from just four commodities. All eaters and food activists have a role to play in diversifying the food and farming system.

Farmers will not substitute beneficial insects for insecticides unless the beneficials are available. They are not likely to reintegrate farm animals into their farming systems unless tax laws are rewritten to support integrated crop and livestock systems, rather than the concentration of animals in huge feedlots. Nor are farmers likely to introduce a mix of crops that could achieve ecological goals if only a few crops are eligible for federal crop insurance. All citizens can help change the public policies that shape the current infrastructure.

These and other infrastructure changes are needed if significant numbers of farmers are going to adopt more ecologically sound farming practices. Creating new infrastructures will require interdisciplinary cooperation. Nutritionists need to explore and publicize the nutritional value of alternative food crops that fit into the new, more diverse crop rotations. Social scientists need to investigate new community structures that support regional resource management. Political scientists need to explore alternative public policies that provide incentives to farm ecologically. Economists need to explore alternative marketing opportunities that support such farming practices.

New research structures. The isolation and compartmentalization that characterize agricultural research today will not meet the needs of tomorrow's ecological farmers. "Vertical" problem solving lends itself well to reductionist research, carried out by technicians in the isolation of the laboratory. "Horizontal" problem solving, adapted to specific watershed ecologies, will require a different research methodology. Horizontal problem solving will require that more of the research be designed, carried out, and evaluated in the ecologies where the problem occurs. Because there is no known way to simulate all of the variables of a natural ecology in a laboratory setting, the only way to competently design and evaluate ecological farming practices is in the field. This means that on-farm research must complement laboratory and field plot research.

The integral interconnectedness of ecological research and ecological farming will also require new forms of interdisciplinary and multidisciplinary study. Shifts in methodology and location of research will be needed; new research teams will need to be created. A complex ecology can only be understood and studied effectively from a variety of perspectives. That multiplicity of perspectives needs to be represented on the research team. Partnership research will become the watchword of twenty-first-century agricultural research. This will effectively end the working isolation among researchers, extension, and farmers, as well as the functional isolation of academic disciplines.

Working in research teams presents enormous problems. As John Ikerd has pointed out, farmers and scientists don't even share the same research goals: "Farmers need information that will help them reduce the risks of making wrong decisions in managing their farms. Scientists, on the other hand, may be more concerned about the risks of misinterpreting their research results and thus drawing wrong conclusions. . . . Farmers are primarily concerned with decision risks. . . . Researchers . . . with conclusion risks."[26]

Part of the benefit of farmers and researchers working together on teams is becoming aware of and negotiating such differences. Fortunately, farmers and researchers share a common methodology, involving "posing problems (hypothesizing), testing possible solutions for those problems (experimenting), and coming to conclusions as a result of that testing (accepting or rejecting hypotheses)."[27] Kloppenberg and Hassanein contend that the difference between farmer and scientist research is in the practice, not in the principle. This difference is what gives partnership research the potential to enrich the work of both farmers and scientists.

What farmers and scientists both need, therefore, is the evolution of a methodological framework that enables farmers and scientists to work together on teams so that what farmers know can be "used to complement what scientists know, and vice versa." Such a methodology would be based on the "assumption that farmers are sophisticated producers of knowledge" and that farmers can be "partners in the research process from the inception of the project to its completion."[28]

Interdisciplinary partnership research, based on ecological models, could also help reduce some of the secrecy associated with the nondisclosure, trade secrets, and publication delays characteristic of industry-supported research. This secrecy has become increasingly worrisome and is bound to further erode public support for land-grant university research. The purpose of a university is, if nothing else, the free and open development and exchange of information. The need for collegiality in the ecological, partnership research model has the potential to resurrect such freedom of information.

Partnership research could prove to be the most important innovation of the land-grant university in the twenty-first century. It not only has the potential to stimulate new research ideas and test the validity of that research in a real-world setting, it might also reinstate the importance of collegiality in research decisions and evaluations. That could develop much-needed renewed political support and public funding for research as citizens become engaged in, and recognize the value of, land-grant research.

New economic models. Of all the needs that farmers have, none is more pressing than the need for an alternative agricultural economy. Farmers may interpret this need in terms of higher prices for their commodities, more income per acre, or even as becoming more efficient and competitive. However, achieving such goals will not improve the economic position of farmers. Before farm economies can be substantially altered, farmers need changes in at least four economic arenas.

First, we must challenge the central place that neoclassical economic theory occupies in agriculture, together with the presumption that this particular theoretical framework of economics is based on "value-free" science. This philosophy of economics leads us to conclude that present economic trends are inevitable and predictive, and there is only one "objective" way of interpreting economics. In the neoclassical paradigm, the present economic structure is synonymous with reality and the economy is totally self-regulating. These assumptions have been bankrupting farmers and destroying rural communities for decades.

It is beyond the scope of this paper to debunk neoclassical economics or to propose alternatives. Fortunately, the task has already been undertaken by others.[29] As Patrick Madden says, "The challenge before the agricultural research establishment is to . . . create science and technology that will lead to a 'better' society, better according to ethics and values far beyond those embodied in current market prices. With sensitivity to that broader set of ethics and values, as well as to the integrity of natural and living systems, economic analysis can illumine many decisions by predicting the outcome of alternative courses of action."[30]

Second, farmers need full-cost accounting to escape the economic treadmill on which they are constantly chasing new technologies.[31] Costs of pollution, resource depletion, and social upheaval will have to be added to the cost of doing business in agriculture. Farmers who are operating on the assumption that those costs will continue to be "externalized" are headed for a rude awakening. Already some insurance premiums are beginning to reflect pollution liability.

In a truly free-market economy, every technology should pay its own way. If an insecticide produces human illness or causes environmental damage, then the health care and environmental restoration costs associated with the insecticide should be added to the cost of its use. If livestock manure accumulations from the concentration of livestock in huge feedlots causes high nitrate levels in groundwater, then the cost of such pollution should be added to that method of producing meat.

If we were to institute true cost accounting, the invisible hand of the free market might change the way we determine efficiency and give us a very different kind of agriculture. Estimating calories of energy expended to put a calorie of food on the table is a much better way of determining food production efficiencies. By that formula, modern industrial agriculture does not fare very well. For example, it takes an estimated 100 calories of energy to put a single calorie of potato chips on the table. If all of the costs were included in bringing a hamburger produced on rainforest land to a U.S. consumer's table, the burger would cost $200. If we took other efficiencies as seriously in agriculture as we take labor efficiency (for example, energy efficiency and land efficiency), our rural communities might look very different.[32]

David Pimentel and others have done excellent work highlighting these hidden costs.[33,34] Now we need economic models that internalize all the costs of doing business. When we defer external costs to the future, depreciate our natural capital, ask farmers to accept substandard wages for their labor, and subsidize exploitive agriculture, we conduct agriculture on the premise that someone besides the end user should pay the bill. To assume that costs don't exist because we have "externalized" them is to believe in economic magic. We need to charge and pay for the true cost of food and fiber, and give farmers a fair return for their labor.

Third, farmers need an economic structure that retains more value locally. The farming sector and rural communities have been victimized by a global economy that extracts raw materials from and sells expensive value-added goods back to the community. Such economies produce no sustainable, wealth-creating activities and deplete rural communities' local, natural capital. The margins retained are inadequate to sustain a vibrant economy, leaving rural communities in perpetual economic depression. Increasing exports, finding markets for products manufactured from farm commodities, and making farming more efficient by further "industrializing" it will not help farmers or rural communities.

John Ikerd has outlined why this is true. According to Ikerd, changes in farm-level productivity do not have a major impact on consumer food costs. If the efficiency of farm-based production were increased by an additional 10 percent, which would be a significant technological achievement, total food production costs would drop by only about 1 percent. Likewise, a 10 percent reduction in farm-level efficiency would raise food costs by about 1 percent. The farmer's share of total consumer expenditures, including food and all other items, is even less significant: less than 1.5 percent. Thus, a 10 percent drop in farmers' claims to total consumer expenditures would amount to less than 0.02 percent of total consumer expenditures. Farm-level production innovations of this magnitude would likely become lost in aggregate economic statistics.[35]

Increasing farmers' productivity through the development of new technologies, or increasing demand through expanded exports or alternative uses of farm commodities, will not help farmers or consumers. The farmer's share of consumer expenditures is simply too small for such strategies to have much impact on farmers' economic welfare or the welfare of rural communities. Most of the wealth extracted from rural communities leaves in the form of the larger margins enjoyed by input and market sectors.

So what farmers need is research and development that helps them own and retain the wealth inherent in their production by adding value to their commodities before they sell them. They also need research and education that will help them replace expensive value-added purchased inputs with on-farm cultural practices.

Fourth, farmers need research and extension programs that can help them begin to protect themselves from the economic power vested in the oligopoly structure of the food and agriculture industry. This will not be easy.

Rural sociologist Bill Heffernan has focused public attention on the power that multinational food corporations wield in the marketplace. He pointed out, for example, that during the 1980s, while farmers experienced an unprecedented economic crisis, ConAgra experienced unprecedented growth and profit. Net sales increased by 1,730 percent, net income by 1,054 percent, and total assets by 1,280 percent. In each year during the 1980s, ConAgra yielded a return on equity exceeding 20 percent.[36,37]

Such phenomenal growth and profit is made possible by the consolidation of agriculture in the marketplace. This consolidation has vested power in a few food and agriculture corporations who largely control agricultural markets. Most poultry is produced under contract, most of it with one corporation. This kind of contract farming turns farmers into factory workers.

With the development of genetically engineered and patented seed, the grain sector can also be converted to contract farming. If seed is engineered to perform for specific end uses, and the seed and market are both owned by the same corporations, then farmers will be forced to contract for the seed in order to secure a market for their production. Unit prices and production practices will be dictated, as is currently the case in the broiler industry. Such oligopoly control does not portend well for either farmer or consumer. Unless we can envision and implement an alternative food system, farming as we have known it—with food produced by independent entrepreneurs within rural communities, with land cared for by local owners, and with local people empowered to hold local practitioners accountable for local land use—will likely disappear.

The time is ripe for citizens (and perhaps land-grant universities) to set priorities for a new food production and marketing system. Increasing citizen dissatisfaction with our present food system includes lack of confidence in the ability of government to protect them from risks associated with a global food system, resource depletion, environmental contamination, devastation of rural communities, and rural and urban hunger. Ken Taylor of the Minnesota Food Association recently outlined these priorities:

- Using ecologically sound practices to grow safe, nutritious food products
- Creating new local and regional avenues for processing and marketing these products
- Capturing the greatest possible production values at the local/regional level
- Reducing the number of transactions taking place between farm and final market[38]

While such priorities may not transform the global food economy, they could, if supported by research and development, help evolve local models of food economies that retain value on the farm and in rural communities. If such models promoted ownership at the local rural community and farm level, they could stimulate local investment and reinvigorate rural economies.

Conclusion

I am optimistic about the future of agriculture. While many formidable forces are working to keep agriculture on the path of global industrialization, many other forces are moving it in an ecological direction.

Society's mandate to transform agriculture from cheap production to affordable production within a context of humane, environmentally sound, resource-based care will continue to gain momentum. Farmers are becoming increasingly disenchanted with the industrial model. The "technological treadmill," as well as the hazards to which this system exposes them, is becoming increasingly loathsome. Furthermore, society will not continue to allow industry to "externalize" costs that the public and future generations will have to pay.

So the real question is not whether we will farm ecologically in the future. We will. The question is: will we combine the resources of farmers and land-grant universities to proactively meet this new mandate for the next century now, or will we be forced to accept it as a result of ecological disasters and citizen revolt?

Can Organic Agriculture Feed the World? And Is That the Right Question?

Thomas Malthus, an English clergyman and political economist, published a treatise in 1798 that riveted the world's attention on the "problem" of human population growth.[1] Malthus argued that population growth was bound to outstrip food production, because human population would increase geometrically while the food supply could only grow arithmetically. Malthus's powerful thesis has been used to justify many social doctrines ever since, everything from "survival of the fittest" to the "green revolution" (GR).

The question "Can organic agriculture feed the world?" is posed against that backdrop. What the question is asking is this: can organic farming methods produce enough food to feed an ever-expanding human population, or will its methods of production reduce yields and therefore hasten the time of the massive famines envisioned by Malthus? The question usually raises a moral issue as well as a technical one. In his essay in praise of Norman Borlaug, Gregg Easterbrook blames all those who oppose GR agriculture for the starvation of people in Africa.[2] Borlaug is, of course, the agronomist who helped develop the high-yielding grain varieties (and the input-intensive technologies required to produce those yields), ushering in the new era of industrial agriculture. The moral implication of Easterbrook's essay is clear: those who oppose high-input agriculture will have starving millions on their conscience.

Description of the Problem

Posed this way, the food/population issue appears to be a simple matter of producing enough food and inventing the technologies capable of pro-

---

This is an edited version of an essay that first appeared in *For All Generations: Making World Agriculture More Sustainable,* edited by J. Patrick Madden and Scott G. Chaplowe, 154–72 (Glendale, Calif.: OM Publishing, 1997).

ducing it. However, the imbalance of humans relative to the millions of other species with whom we coevolved now disrupts the biotic community and the delicate ecological relationships that have evolved over billions of years. This disruption and deterioration now threaten the food supply of the human species. The reason we need to consider an alternative is that our current model of industrial agriculture is contributing, dramatically, to this ecological disruption. So while the green revolution may have enjoyed success in increasing the yields of a few crop varieties for the short term, it now threatens the ability of future generations to feed themselves.

In other words, the question "Can organic agriculture feed the world?" is a much more complex question than is often implied. This is not simply a question of whether or not the technologies to farm organically can outperform the technologies to farm industrially. The question is, how do we regain and maintain the evolutionary stability of the various ecological neighborhoods in which we humans live? Apart from such stabilization, we will lose the "ecosystem services" that provide not only food, but all of the life-sustaining elements that make human life possible on this planet.[3] So, the "agriculture" question (inside that larger question) is: What kind of agriculture can best mirror and maintain that evolutionary stability?

Niles Eldredge gives us some examples of our utter dependence on these complex biological relationships. Insects, which humans generally hold in low regard (we'd love to expunge many of them from the face of the Earth altogether), are so important, says Eldredge, that "humanity probably could not last for more than a few months" without them.[4] Most of us would probably support a proposal to eradicate termites from the face of the Earth. But Eldredge reminds us that termites, because of their symbiotic relationship with spirochete bacteria, are one of the few creatures on the planet that can digest cellulose. Consequently, we humans are absolutely dependent on termites for a huge portion of the recycling of the world's biotic material. "No recycling, no ongoing life," he says.[5] Put another way, without termites you can forget about the problem of producing enough food. There wouldn't be any humans—or much of any other kind of life as we know it—to feed!

What is often posed as the food/population problem can more accurately be described as a population/ecology problem. In other words, the real problem with the unprecedented increase in human population is that it has led to the disruption and deterioration of the natural functioning of

Earth's biotic community, and that is what threatens our future, not lack of production.

The Ecology/Food/Population Connection

When the technologies we use to increase the production of a few species of crops and livestock accelerate ecosystem disruption and deterioration, we only hasten the time when food shortages become inevitable. In short, we are now on a downward spiral of an ever-increasing population and an ever-decreasing capacity to produce food, our powerful technologies notwithstanding. If we are to survive, we must both reduce the growth of the human species and transform agriculture so that it enhances, rather than further deteriorates, the ecological neighborhoods in which we farm.

Reducing the population of the human species is, of course, a formidable task, given its current rate of growth. Before agriculture was invented, about 10,000 years ago, the total human population on the planet had reached an estimated 10 million people over its entire evolutionary history. After agriculture was invented, the human population jumped from 10 million to about 50 million in just 3,000 years. Thereafter, the human population doubled at an ever-increasing rate. In the pre-Christian era, it took 1,600 years for the human population to double; the population went from 50 million in 3000 B.C. to 100 million in 1400 B.C. The most recent doubling took just thirty-six years, from 1969 to 1996.

Not surprisingly, the disruption of the natural functioning of biotic communities has increased along with population. But population growth, up to now, is not the major cause. The disruptions are caused by the way an increasing number of us relate to the rest of nature and how we feed ourselves from it.

For the past five years, the United States has seen the worst declines in honeybees in its history. Many states have seen bee kills as high as 85 and 90 percent. The immediate cause of the bee kills is, of course, the varroa mite, but the mite's impact might have been minor had the industrial system of agriculture not provided an environment in which it could do its damage. Derrick Jensen describes the real problem:

> The collapse was inevitable anyway. In February, the hills surrounding Modesto, California, roll with white-blossomed almond trees. Although monocropped miles of almond flowers may be beauti-

ful, they're as unnatural as Frankenstein's monster; the staggering number of blooms to be pollinated grossly overmatches the capacity of wild pollinators like bumblebees, moths, wasps, and beetles to set fruit, causing almond ranchers to pay distant beekeepers up to $35 per hive to bring in bees for the four-week bloom.

Almonds aren't the only crop needing pollination. Apples, cherries, pears, raspberries, cranberries, blueberries, cucumbers, watermelons—each of these densely packed crops requires similarly densely packed beehives to set fruit. The strengths that have made modern beekeeping the foundation upon which the agricultural infrastructure rests are precisely the weaknesses that have made beekeeping, and modern agribusiness, vulnerable to something as tiny as the mite.[6]

Thus, industrial agriculture, with its successful productivity in a few crops, has caused the ecological imbalance that now threatens the productivity of those same crops. Jensen's analysis of the honeybee destruction helps us to see that if we are truly interested in feeding the world, then we have to face up to a host of complicated questions often missing from the "feeding the world" debate.

Even the debate between Lester Brown, the World Bank, and the UN Food and Agriculture Organization (FAO) is oversimplifying the issue. Their debate hinges primarily on whether future technologies will be able to continue to increase production. The World Bank and the FAO argue that such technologies are on the horizon. Brown argues that they probably aren't.[7] Posing the question this way implies, again, that the issue can be reduced to our capacity to produce more grain through technology. However, the problem is much more complicated.

The Manifold Dimensions of the Problem

The weather factor. In *The Genesis Strategy*, climatologist Stephen Schneider demonstrated that both crop yields and low variability are due at least as much to weather as to technology.[8] I suppose most any farmer could have told him that: "Don't worry and fret about the crops. After you have done all you can for them, let them stand in the weather on their own."[9] Because weather is such a significant factor in our capacity to produce high yields, Schneider argues that if we want to keep the world fed, we need to implement the strategy of Joseph in the Bible, who urged Egypt's pharaoh to store part of the abundance of the seven good years, to assure themselves food for the seven bad years. Because small changes in atmospheric conditions can cause major changes in weather patterns, we should not use farming practices that help destabilize delicately balanced atmospheric conditions. Global warming may radically disrupt global weather patterns and cause dramatic increases in severe weather changes and violent storms. Those changes can dramatically alter our ability to produce food.

Insurance companies worldwide have taken note of the increased insurance losses due to weather-related natural disasters since 1980. In the entire decade of the 1980s, insurers paid only $17 billion for all weather-related natural disasters. By the end of the first half of the 1990s, insurers had already paid out $57 billion for such damages. No wonder insurance companies often stand shoulder to shoulder with environmentalists lobbying for legislation that has the potential to reduce climate change.[10] Farmers and food-related industries might do well to follow their example. After all, "If the crop of any one year was all, a man would have to cut his throat every time it hailed."[11]

Ecological farming practices, which seek to mirror and maintain the ecological neighborhoods in which they exist, are much less likely to contribute to climate change than industrial agriculture, which alters natural ecological neighborhoods for the sake of short-term yield increases of a few specialized crops. Industrial agriculture accelerates global warming through forest destruction and use of ozone-depleting chemicals, such as methyl bromide, as a soil fumigant. To the extent that organic agriculture remains true to its ecological roots, it may do a better job of feeding the world.

It's not just about grain. Sixty percent of the world's population today depends on fish and seafood for 40 percent of its annual protein.[12] Insects provide "the major source of protein to roughly 60 percent of the world's population."[13] These and other vital food sources are often ignored in the feeding-the-world debate. In fact, there is a tendency to equate grain yields with food production. Easterbrook, for example, credited Norman Borlaug with saving "more lives than any other person who ever lived" because Borlaug increased grain yields of a few crops two- and threefold.[14] But it is well known that the very technologies that accomplished the increased grain yields have seriously damaged seafood ecologies. So an important question has to be asked: did we really increase food production when we increased wheat and rice yields at the expense of seafood?

According to the International Rice Research Institute (IRRI), increased rice yields may not have improved the quality of life in the developing world that much.[15] The institute concluded that pesticides induced resistance to pests, created new pests by destroying natural predators, and increased health problems from farming with pesticides. Farm families have lost "more money from getting sick than the chemicals save by killing bugs in the field."[16]

Furthermore, the IRRI scientists expressed doubts that the GR methods had actually produced more food. While using the GR technologies, rice yields doubled and even tripled, but those same technologies killed fish previously raised in the rice paddies and fruit trees previously producing fruit on the periphery of the rice paddies. Despite increased rice yields, more food was probably not produced. As a result, the UN FAO has established farm schools to teach ecological methods to the same farmers that had previously learned GR practices from IRRI.

Vandana Shiva points out similar problems with the GR in India.[17] While the GR "miracle seeds" were more responsive to chemical fertilizer and irrigation inputs, their overall performance was inferior to the indigenous seeds selected and bred by India's farmers for centuries. She argues that considering all factors, the GR has diminished rather than enhanced India's food security.

In the industrial paradigm of agriculture, the way to feed the world is by reinventing nature to increase grain production. One has to question this paradigm because much of the increased grain production goes into alcohol and animal feed, and is not used to directly feed humans at all.

The role of animals. Much of our capacity to feed the world is wasted because we feed grain protein to animals instead of feeding it directly to humans. However, that is not a good reason to eliminate animals from the food system altogether, as Rifkin has argued.[18] Animals play a key role in keeping the world fed and help maintain the ecological health of the neighborhoods in which we live. Ruminant animals are the only creatures capable of transforming grass into protein that can be digested by humans. Consequently, if it weren't for animals, more than a billion acres in the United States alone could not be used for human food, because that acreage is unsuitable for annual cereal grain production, with which industrial agriculture would feed the world.

Furthermore, without animals many other foodstuffs not suitable for human consumption, such as crop residues and weather-damaged grain, could not be turned into protein for humans. Nevertheless, industrial agriculture unnecessarily feeds animals huge quantities of grain. The principal reason for feeding large quantities of grain is that industrial agriculture has concentrated animals in large feedlots and in hog and poultry barns, and concentration makes it inefficient to feed animals either forages or crop residues. Transportation costs dictate that protein fed to animals must be in concentrated form, primarily corn and soybeans.

Concentrating animals also means that animal manure becomes a huge, environmentally damaging waste-disposal problem rather than a rich source of fertilizer and organic matter to improve soil quality. Large concentrations of animals also deplete water resources in the ecological neighborhoods where they are confined and make grazing difficult, if not impossible. Disease problems and pathogen resistance are increased, which lead to increased use of antibiotics to control the increased disease. Thus, antibiotic-resistant pathogens are more likely to end up in the food system.

Organic farms that remain true to their ecological roots integrate animals into the farming system to help close nutrient cycles on the farm. The wastes from the cropping system are used as food for animals, and the wastes of animals are used to feed the crops. Integration and dispersion of animals throughout ecosystems is a much better way of maintaining ecological health and feeding the world over the long term.

The ecological disruption/food supply connection. Since the era of industrial agriculture began, we have lost approximately half of our topsoil, and the quality of the remaining soil has seriously deteriorated. High-yielding crops require large quantities of water. Irrigation is depleting our groundwater sources faster than nature can replenish them. Inadequate water supplies may be more of a problem than inadequate food supplies for an expanding human population. Water quality has been seriously damaged through fertilizer and pesticide runoff. Biodiversity has been reduced as a result of industrial agriculture practices. These effects of industrial agriculture are well known and documented. Their potential to seriously jeopardize our capacity to produce food in the future is obvious.

Many other adverse consequences are not as well known. In a recent *Science* magazine article on nitrogen use in Minnesota, nitrogen loading was found to be causing environmental disruptions. The study showed that "after 12 years of N addition, species richness declined by more than 50 percent."[19] Such deterioration of the biotic community, plus the atmospheric changes caused by concentrations of nitrous oxide (which is a long-lived greenhouse gas and a destroyer of the ozone layer), can seriously disrupt our ability to produce food.

Arsenic poisoning in India has been traced to irrigation.[20] Prior to the GR, arsenic, naturally present in the soil, posed no problem to humans or other animals. But irrigation concentrated the arsenic so that it caused major health problems. Although industrial agriculture increased grain production in India, it did so in some locations at the expense of human health.

Dramatic increases in world trade augment the likelihood that new pests, "invader species," will hitchhike to new ecosystems in which they did not evolve.[21] Without the natural enemies with which they coevolved, these exotic insects, nematodes, mites, and weeds can quickly become disastrous pests. In addition, industrial agriculture now depends on only about fifteen varieties of plant species worldwide for 90 percent of the calories used to feed the world.[22] The specialization of industrial agriculture (resulting in very brittle ecosystems) and increased potential for invader species disrupting brittle ecologies is a prescription for food-supply disaster. The nineteenth-century Irish potato blight and the corn leaf blight of the 1960s in the United States remind us how vulnerable genetically uniform cropping systems can be. Increased risk of invader species moving into genetically uniform ecologies may make the bee kills resulting from the hitchhiking of the varroa mite into the United States seem like a minor incident by comparison.

Contrary to Easterbrook's vision for saving Africa from starvation, the National Research Council has concluded that Africa may need to return to its more than 2,000 indigenous species of grains, fruits, vegetables, and roots to reduce the continent's vulnerability to food shortages.[23] That advice may become more critical if local ecosystems, dominated by monoculture agriculture, are disrupted by invasive species. Destabilization by invasive species could be further exacerbated by the introduction of novel, transgenic organisms, which some scientists have referred to as "aliens with a capital

'A.'"[24] The ecological risks of introducing genetically engineered organisms are similar to the problems created by introducing non-native organisms into new environments.[25,26] A diverse, ecologically integrated agriculture practiced by organic farmers may do a better job of feeding the world.

Production vs. power. In a report to the Bruntland Commission, the issue of food and population was put into proper perspective. The report said, "The problem is not one of global food production being outstripped by population. The problem has three aspects: where the food is being produced, by whom, and who can command it."[27] Reducing the problem of hunger to adequate production simply misconstrues the problem, either inadvertently (due to a lack of understanding) or purposefully (to protect vested interests). The fact that 800 million people are starving on the planet when we have the capacity to feed everyone makes it clear that hunger is not a production problem. The global food market responds to money, but most of the 800 million who are starving have no economic power. One does not have to go to Africa to see this problem at work; in the United States, 12 million children go to bed hungry every night.

Daniel Quinn suggests that agriculture has always been totalitarian.[28] If so, then agriculture has always been more about power than about feeding people. While it is difficult to substantiate Quinn's claim historically, modern agriculture is clearly about power. Power is perhaps also the reason we talk about this subject in terms of "feeding the world" rather than "keeping the world fed." "Feeding the world" suggests someone is responsible for feeding someone else, which increases dependency. Under such terms, there can be no food security. "Keeping the world fed," however, implies that people are empowered to feed themselves, which is essential to long-term food security. Organic farms integrated into local ecologies and rooted in communities have more potential to keep the world fed than large, corporate farms owned by distant investors.

Energy to feed the world. The industrial food system is, of course, made possible only by the availability of cheap, abundant energy, which is used at all levels: production, processing, and distribution. From the perspective of calories of energy consumed to put a calorie of food on the table, it is one of the least efficient systems known to humankind. As sources of cheap, nonrenewable, stored energy continue to be depleted, it will become increasingly necessary to rely on much more current, efficient energy sources. In a study comparing the energy efficiency of actual operating organic, no-till, and conventional farms in North Dakota, organic farms were 70 percent more energy-efficient when all energy use was calculated.[29] Ultimately, an ecological agriculture that incorporated perennial polycultures, in a manner similar to that being explored by the Land Institute in Salina, Kansas, would have an even better chance of keeping the world fed without destroying the resources upon which agriculture depends.

Can Organic Agriculture Feed the World?

So what is the answer to the question, "Can organic agriculture feed the world?" First, we should not delude ourselves into believing that the human species can continue to reproduce itself at anything like its present rate without dire consequences. The human species is part of an intricate biotic community; thus, we have to maintain some kind of equilibrium within that community if we are to survive with any kind of quality of life. Feeding itself from that community is only one of a very complex set of problems which an overburdening human population poses. Maintaining the ecological relationships between diffusely coevolved species is essential to survival.

Therefore, if our population increases, we have to use fewer of our ecosystem resources and services to restore and retain the health of our ecological neighborhoods. The only kind of agriculture that can hope to keep the world fed is an ecologically oriented agriculture that mirrors and maintains the natural ecology in which it is located.

From Farm to Fork: Reorganizing the Food System

However, organic agriculture, inserted into the current industrial food system infrastructure, will fare no better at feeding the world than industrial agriculture. Apart from a radical restructuring of the food system, we will have little success in keeping the world fed. Meeting maximum production goals of a few crops and livestock in a few regions of the world, to be marketed into the global economy, cannot keep the world fed. In keeping with the sentiment of the Bruntland report, the best way to achieve food security is evolution of a people/food/land equilibrium based on local culture.

Helena Norberg-Hodge provides an intriguing example of a food system rooted in local culture.[30] Despite scarce resources and extreme climates, the Ladakh people who live in the desert highlands of the western Himalayas are well-nourished, usually healthy, and free of social and environmental stresses. The Ladakh experience corroborates one of the principles for ending hunger outlined by Francis Moore Lappé: "While slowing population growth in itself cannot end hunger, the very changes necessary to end hunger—the democratization of economic life, especially the empowerment of women—are key to reducing birth rates so that the human population can come into balance with the rest of the natural world."[31]

We still don't know the capacity of people in a local ecological neighborhood to feed themselves, once they are empowered to properly use local resources and sound ecological farming systems. Different ecological neighborhoods have different capacities, depending on such factors as local climate and land- and sea-based food resources. Exporting surpluses from one foodshed to another could, of course, always continue to be part of the new food system. But the first priority in the new food system is food self-sufficiency in every ecological neighborhood.

Furthermore, local food systems, tied to local ecological neighborhoods, would tend to create people/food/land equilibriums through local culture as it has among the Ladakh. This vision of the restructuring of the global food system may seem bizarre in our world of global markets and global competitiveness. Regional foodshed concepts, until recently, were largely endorsed only by grassroots groups and a few prophets in the wilderness. More recently the idea is being endorsed by the U.S. Congress in programs like the Community Food Security Act and by a few faculty in land-grant universities.

Jack Kloppenburg and his colleagues at the University of Wisconsin claim that regional foodsheds are not only desirable but feasible. Bill Heffernan at the University of Missouri has suggested for some time that farms need to understand the global food market and then unhook from it. Cornelia Flora at Iowa State University suggests that food systems should integrate into the new economy, rather than follow the model of "Fordism," or mass production of uniform commodities at low prices.

The new economy relies on the production of differentiated products produced on a much smaller scale but designed to be innovative and flexible to meet the fast-changing demands of a discriminating consumer.[32] The post-Fordist economy shortens supply lines and responds to local markets. It doesn't attempt to compete in the global mass market. This localized, site-specific concept of the economy can be adapted to empower local people to feed themselves.

Furthermore, the idea of local foodsheds is catching on in many communities, especially among poor neighborhoods. Hundreds of communities are creating new food and farming markets. Organic farmers are collaborating with community organizations to exchange food for labor, community gardens are linked with local school systems to provide food for poor families and teach kids organic gardening, and businesses work with nonprofits to make food available in communities without grocery stores.

These fledgling enterprises, along with the growing farmers' markets and community-supported agriculture, are indications that the global industrial food system is not working for a growing number of people. New food systems, grounded in local culture, sound local ecological management, and local control, are likely to make up an increasing portion of the food system of tomorrow. Making such fundamental shifts in the food system is, however, bound to run into opposition. Because agriculture today is about power, corporate interests will oppose these new initiatives and continue to claim that only their way can prevent world starvation.

A Final Observation

Awareness that sound ecological farming and local empowerment are essential to feeding ourselves leads to a conclusion that industrial farming is fundamentally about something other than "feeding the world." Perhaps Wendell Berry said it best:

> But the *real* products of any year's work are the farmer's mind and the cropland itself.
>
> If he raises a good crop at the cost of belittling himself and diminishing the ground, he has gained nothing. He will have to begin over again the next spring, worse off than before.
>
> Let him receive the season's increment into his mind. Let him work it into the soil.
>
> The finest growth that farmland can produce is a careful farmer.
>
> Make the human race a better head. Make the world a better piece of ground.[33]

Biotechnology on the Ground

What Kind of Future Can Farmers Expect, and What Kind Should They Create?

A pragmatic assessment of any technology is complicated by the cultural love affair with technology that we have nurtured in our society since the dawn of the Industrial Revolution. By now, farmers must comprehend that not all new technologies will be beneficial. Indeed, Willard Cochrane demonstrated how new technologies can be detrimental to farmers with his concept of the "technology treadmill." Even when a technology appears to be beneficial to farmers, like tractors replacing horses for greater labor efficiency, it will put a good number of farmers out of business.[1]

Whether eliminating farmers from farming has been, or continues to be, a social benefit is a subject for a debate that we have never had in any democratic forum. But to argue that every new technology is a sign of progress and bound to benefit farmers is a proposition of mythology, not sound business or social policy.

While every new technology usually benefits someone, not every new technology benefits everyone. Farmers need to ask whom genetic engineering will benefit. The likely beneficiaries are the corporations developing the technologies and their investors. They wouldn't invest billions of dollars otherwise. The biotechnology industry claims that farmers will also benefit. The alleged benefits can generally be subsumed under three categories. The technology will:

- Enable farmers to feed a world of expanding human population. This claim mostly promises farmers an opportunity to achieve a social

This is an edited version of a talk presented at the National Agricultural Biotechnology Council meeting, Lincoln, Nebraska, June 7, 1999, and later published in *National Agricultural Biotechnology Report #11* (Ithaca, N.Y.: National Biotechnology Council, 1999).

goal, but it is generally assumed that it would also provide them with economic benefits.

- Simplify farmers' pest-management problems in an environmentally benign way. This claim promises to benefit farmers directly and to enable them to achieve a social goal.
- Increase farmer profitability and make them more competitive in the marketplace. This claim promises direct benefits to farmers.

Are these claims true? I argue, from a farmer's perspective, that farmers will unlikely experience these benefits, given the way the technology is currently applied.

Genetic Engineering Will Feed the World

There is a fundamental flaw with the claim that genetically engineered foods will feed the world. Hunger is not caused by food availability, but by food entitlement. In other words, hunger is not caused by an insufficient quantity of food, but by insufficient access to food. Feeding the world is therefore largely a social and economic problem, not a production problem.[2,3]

Ironically, continuing to assert that hunger is a production problem without considering entitlement issues only exacerbates the problem and ends up hurting farmers economically. For example, soybean production in Brazil has increased dramatically in recent years. But the soybeans are produced primarily for export, where they are used for animal feed, which denies local Brazilians entitlement to the food-production capacity of their own country. Consequently, while soybean production has exploded, the number of malnourished in Brazil has increased from one-third of the population to almost two-thirds. Brazil's increased food requirements will not be supplied by U.S. exports because malnourished Brazilians cannot afford them.

The expansion of soybean production has pushed soybean prices down to $4 per bushel and has decreased the availability of land for local food production in Brazil. This is not a formula that feeds the world or brings benefits to the majority of farmers. Converting all the soybeans grown in Brazil to genetically engineered varieties won't change that.

Furthermore, focusing on more food as the single solution to feeding expanding human populations distracts us from a host of other problems that further overcrowding by still more humans on the planet will surely create:

- Increased disease
- Destruction of ecosystem services
- Increased fragility of the entire ecosystem

To my knowledge, no one ever asked farmers if they wanted to take on the responsibility of feeding the world or asked them how they wanted to do it, if they did.

Genetic Engineering Will Solve Pest-Management Problems in an Environmentally Benign Manner

The fundamental flaw with the claim that genetic engineering will help farmers manage pests without harming the environment is that this strategy adheres to the same paradigm that led to futility in pest management with toxic chemicals. Joe Lewis of the Agricultural Research Service's Insect Biology and Population Management Research Laboratory argues that our predominant paradigm for pest management has been one of "therapeutic intervention." He and his colleagues argue that "this approach attempts to eliminate an undesirable element by applying a "direct external counterforce against it."[4] That paradigm is now being widely questioned in agriculture, medicine, social systems, and business management enterprises.

Peter Senge's work on systems dynamics reinforces this view. He has explained that externally imposed solutions that ignore the functions of the system generally lead to creating the problem we are trying to solve.[5] The reason is simple: "Pushing harder and harder on familiar solutions, while fundamental problems persist or worsen, is a reliable indicator of nonsystemic thinking—what we often call the 'what we need here is a bigger hammer'" approach.[6] Farmers can certainly relate to that with respect to pest management. In fact, it is precisely this principle that led Robert van den Bosch to coin the phrase "pesticide treadmill" more than twenty years ago.[7] An external solution applied to a pest problem generally disrupts the natural balance that keeps pests in check and develops resistance in the target pest, thereby increasing the need for more of the solution. While that certainly benefits the company selling the solution, it hardly benefits farmers or the environment.

Not only is the therapeutic interventionist paradigm ineffective in providing sustainable relief from pests; it also makes the farmer more dependent on the supplier of the intervention and shifts economic empowerment from farmers to the provider of the therapy. Such a scenario does not benefit farmers. To assess the long-term benefit of any pest-management strategy for farmers, it must be measured against the "fundamental principle" that Lewis articulates so succinctly:

> Application of external corrective actions into a system can be effective only for short-term relief. Long-term, sustainable solutions must be achieved through restructuring the system. . . . The foundation for pest management in agricultural systems should be an understanding and shoring up of the full composite of inherent plant defenses, plant mixtures, soil, natural enemies, and other components of the system. . . . The use of pesticides and other "treat-the-symptoms" approaches are unsustainable and should be the last rather than the first line of defense. A pest-management strategy should always start with the question "Why is the pest a pest?" and should seek to address the underlying weaknesses in ecosystems and/or agronomic practice(s) that have allowed organisms to reach pest status.[8]

According to Lewis, this principle holds for molecular biology as well as toxic chemicals. Because genetic engineering conforms to the same interventionist strategies used in chemical pest control, farmers should not expect long-term pest management benefits from this technology. We now have corn that has been genetically modified to produce an insecticide called Bt; but we also know that resistance to Bt will develop and render Bt corn and similar pest-management strategies ineffective, complicating future pest-management efforts and destroying an effective and environmentally benign pest-management tool that farmers have used for decades. If a recent study reported in *Science* magazine is correct in demonstrating that the genes encoding resistance to Bt in European corn borer are dominant (rather than recessive, as previously thought), then the high dose/refuge strategy recommended to postpone resistance will fail.[9] The high dose/refuge strategy is the practice of inserting high doses of Bt into the transgenic plants to obtain maximum kill and simultaneously requiring that farmers plant at least 20 percent of their crop to conventional, nontransgenic varieties on which no pesticides at all are used, to serve as a breeding ground for insects unaffected by Bt.

Genetic Engineering Will Increase Farmer Profitability and Make Them More Competitive

The claim that genetic engineering will make farmers more money is even more questionable than the previous claims. Farmers are unlikely to see much profit from genetic engineering, because of the cost of planting refugia to postpone resistance, the yield drag of some genetically engineered varieties, and the technology fees that farmers are required to pay. One might argue that transgenic crops might still pencil out despite these downsides, if one takes a long-term view. Conventional farming magazines often make such claims.[10] Perhaps they are correct, but I'm skeptical.

There is a more fundamental principle that farmers need to consider when assessing the profitability of any technology. Stewart Smith, an agricultural economist at the University of Maine, articulated that principle clearly almost ten years ago. For most of this century, farmers have been taught to believe that profitability is strictly a matter of price and yield.[11] Indeed, Paul Thompson at Purdue University has suggested that farmers have been so indoctrinated into the higher-yield school of profitability that they now operate out of a single ethical principle: "produce as much as possible, regardless of the cost."[12] But Smith suggests that while farmers' fortunes are, to some extent, linked to price and yield, those factors ultimately do not determine farmer profitability.

Profitability is determined more by the share of the agricultural economic activity that farmers command than by the quantity of commodities they produce or the price received for them. The farm sector's share of agricultural economic activity has steadily eroded for most of the twentieth century, shrinking from 41 percent to 9 percent from 1910 to 1990. Coincidentally, during that same period the input sector's share of agricultural economic activity increased from 15 percent to 24 percent, and the marketing sector increased from 44 percent to 67 percent.[13]

Technology plays a key role in determining who gets what share, of course. Smith points out that "technology is the primary cause of farming activity loss." The kind of technology that has been promoted by both private and public sectors is technology that shifts economic activity away from farming to the input sector. These technologies exert an external, corrective action on a problem rather than developing self-regulating systems. The reason that the private sector develops such technologies is understandable: it increases the profitability of the corporations producing the technologies.

The reason that the public sector promotes this paradigm, according to Smith, is because it is strongly influenced by private funding.

Genetic engineering advances this scenario another quantum leap. Not only does the technology conform to the same paradigm of exerting an external corrective action on the problem, but it is instrumental in speeding up the merger mania in the input and market sectors. These developments portend a future wherein farmers become contract workers for these large input/market conglomerates. The farmer's only role will be to grow out the firm's seed for the firm's market, much like tenant farmers.

If anyone thinks that farmers will become economically empowered in this system, they haven't looked at the broiler industry lately. The only hope farmers may have of retaining any voice in their own economic welfare will be through some kind of universal collective bargaining. Farmers already pay something like union dues in the form of check-off dollars, although the funds are misdirected. Farmer check-off programs seem to be based on the flawed notion that farmers can produce their way out of this problem. Airline pilots never use their union dues to get more people to fly. They use them to get a fairer share of transportation profits.

A more immediate way to empower farmers economically, however, is to implement Smith's suggestion regarding the use of public funds. Public funds should be directed toward farming systems that "displace purchased inputs." These technologies should create self-regulating pest-management systems and on-farm nutrient-cycling systems. These shifts would replace economies of scale with economies of scope and would put farmers in much more control of their own costs.

The way farmers do business has to change. Instead of mass-producing undifferentiated raw materials for the global economy, they must produce identity-preserved products that are marketed as directly as possible. Such enterprises need to be owned and operated by farmers, with direct retail links that conform to consumers' changing demands.

What Kind of Future Should Farmers Create?

The farm sector is developing into two very different kinds of farms. Approximately 163,000 farmers now mass-produce 61 percent of the undifferentiated commodities that are sold as raw materials into the global market. These farms are likely to continue increasing in size and decreasing in number as they become vertically integrated into the food system through contractual relationships. It does not seem far-fetched to say that farmers' numbers will decrease to fewer than 50,000 in the next decade.

The production paradigm of industrialized farms is not likely to change. Genetic engineering will increasingly be the "direct external counterforce" used to solve farming problems. In the short term, these technologies will be successful in solving some production problems. Eventually, we will see the technologies become ineffective and increasingly ecologically worrisome. But even if they question the long-term effectiveness of transgenic technologies, industrial farmers will be required to use them because of contractual relationships. Industrial farmers should not expect to generate increased profits, with or without genetic engineering, unless they can develop some kind of effective collective bargaining to claim a larger share of food-system profits.

Industrialized farms, in my opinion, will ultimately fail due to three fundamental reasons:

- These farms are highly centralized, routinized, and specialized, which leaves little room for flexibility, diversity, or innovation. History gives us no examples of successful farming systems designed on those principles. Increasingly, industrial production systems will attempt to force the market to change (witness efforts to get Europeans to accept genetically engineered food and hormone-fed beef) rather than adapting to changing markets. That is not likely to succeed. Consumer acceptance must be part of the equation.
- The routinization of farms will dictate that the preferred technologies will be used as a direct external counter-force to solve problems, rather than using methods that facilitate adaptive management. There is no reason to believe that molecular biology will be any more successful as an external counterforce than chemistry has been in solving pest management problems.
- Genetic engineering will increase the specialization and routinization of these farms, further reducing their biodiversity and the ecosystems in which the farms exist. Reduced genetic and species diversity makes farming systems increasingly vulnerable to new pests and diseases.

Although farmers, like the Sinners in Casselton, North Dakota, have begun filling the market niches created by the consumer backlash against genetic engineering,[14] precious little research and technology have been funded to support this alternative direction. Market infrastructures have not been developed, and public policies, for the most part, favor the old paradigm. Public policies that put alternatives to industrial production on a level playing field would help farmers gain a foothold in this new economic future.

Questioning Biotechnology's Claims and Imagining Alternatives

[Humans] are only fellow-voyagers with other creatures in the odyssey of evolution. This . . . should have given us, by this time, a sense of kinship with fellow-creatures; a wish to live and let live; a sense of wonder over the magnitude and duration of the biotic enterprise.[1]
—Aldo Leopold

The controversy surrounding transgenic technologies appears to be based on different assessments of the technology's merits. Proponents argue that transgenic technologies will help us feed the world, cure diseases, and solve many other problems facing the human species. Opponents argue that the projected benefits are exaggerated and that the technology poses many risks that have not been adequately assessed.

But these quarrels lead to circular arguments. We won't know, *for sure,* whether transgenic technologies can feed the world until we try it, and if it doesn't, it's too late. Developing other options for self-sufficient food systems will have been ignored. We won't know, *for sure,* if transgenic organisms will create ecological havoc until we release them, and if they do, it's too late. We won't be able to put the genie back into the bottle. In the meantime, we debate the technology's potential risks or benefits, relying on our personal or collective judgments and biases about the technology's efficacy and capabilities. It may be more fruitful to examine the assumptions underlying the technology's promises and problems. If the assumptions are faulty, the conclusions may be unreliable as well. In fact, I do find many

This is an edited version of a paper first published in Frederick H. Buttle and Robert M. Goodman, eds., *Of Frankenfoods and Golden Rice: Risks, Rewards, and Realities of Genetically Modified Foods* (Madison, Wis.: Wisconsin Academy of Sciences, 2001).

assumptions weak, which leads to the second topic of this paper: an examination of alternatives to biotechnology.

Prevailing Ideology

The first questions to consider are: What is the ideology that informs modern science? Is that ideology sound? Richard Lewontin, the prominent geneticist at Harvard University, argues that our modern optimism regarding the ability to solve many of our social, medical, and agricultural problems with transgenic technologies is based on what he calls "biological determinism." This ideology, he says,

> makes the atom or individual the causal source of all the properties of larger collections. It prescribes a way of studying the world, which is to cut it up into the individual bits. It breaks the world down into independent autonomous domains, the internal and the external. Causes are either internal or external, and there is no mutual dependency between them.
>
> For biology, this worldview has resulted in a particular picture of organisms and their total life activity. Living beings are seen as being determined by internal factors, the genes.[2]

But this ideology completely ignores the actual relationship that exists between organisms and their environments. He suggests that four rules govern "the real relationship between organisms and their environment":

- Environments do not exist in the absence of organisms but are constructed by them out of bits and pieces of the external world.
- The environment of organisms is constantly being remade during the life of those living beings.
- Fluctuations in the world matter only as organisms transform them.
- The very physical nature of the environment as it is relevant to organisms is determined by the organisms themselves.[3]

Thus, organisms are not the isolated entities assumed when we fantasize about feeding the world by manipulating a few genes in a few plants or animals, or healing debilitating diseases by adjusting a few defective genes. Each individual within a species is a "unique consequence of both genes and the developmental environment in a constant interaction."[4] Human well-being depends on interactions among genes, organisms, and environ-ment: "It is a fundamental principle of developmental genetics that every organism is the outcome of a unique interaction between genes and envi-ronmental sequences, modulated by random chances of cell growth and division, and that all these together finally produce an organism. Moreover, an organism changes throughout its life."[5]

The notion that gene technology can by itself solve problems that are, at least in part, derived from social and environmental interactions illustrates a faith in technological fixes that is not corroborated by experience. For example, it has always been something of a mystery to me how we will be able to "feed the world" of expanding future populations by producing more food with biotechnology, when we presently fail to feed more than 800 million malnourished people in an era of overproduction.[6–8]

Molecular World as Ecosystem

A second underlying question we might ask is this: is it possible to do "just one thing" at the molecular level? We know it is not possible to do "just one thing" in the ecosystems in which we live. Even when we have made good-faith efforts to improve the resilience of our ecological homes, we have often miscalculated the extent to which, and the manner in which, species within ecosystems are interdependent.

Ecologist Yvonne Baskin provides a chilling example of this kind of miscalculation. In an effort to boost the numbers of salmon that swim up-stream from Montana's Flathead Lake to spawn in Glacier National Park's McDonald Creek, state fisheries officials stocked the upstream portions of the watershed with exotic opossum shrimp to provide food for the salmon, which would in turn provide more food for eagles, bears, gulls, mallards, golden eyes, coyotes, minks, otters, and other species that feed on salmon and their eggs.[9]

But, "the plan overlooked an important bit of natural history of both shrimp and fish."[10] The salmon, it seems, feed on zooplankton near the surface during the day, while the shrimp spend the day near the bottom, pretty much out of reach of the fish. "At night, the shrimp migrate upwards to feed on zooplankton themselves—the same zooplankton, unfortunately, that serve as the chief food for [the salmon]." Consequently, "rather than supplying a new food resource for the [salmon], humans . . . unwittingly introduced a competitor." As a result, "zooplankton quickly declined, especially populations of daphnia, or water fleas, which are a favored food of both the [salmon] and the shrimp. Within just a few years, the [salmon] population in the lake had collapsed, too. One hundred kilometers upstream in McDonald Creek, the disappearance of the spawning [salmon] eliminated a food resource that had once fortified eagles for their winter migration and fattened bears for hibernation. It also brought to an end a wildlife spectacle that had boosted off-season tourism revenues for the park and neighboring communities."[11]

In less than nine years, the population of 100,000 salmon was reduced to fifty. If our judgment is this bad, are we really ready to begin modifying the genome?

The same ecosystem dynamics that are at work on the organism level are most likely at work at the molecular level as well. In fact, diversity and interconnectedness of the world of single-celled microbes is astonishing. Robert Service has used gene-typing techniques to compare gene sequences of different organisms. He said, a "pinch of soil can contain 1 billion microbes or more," and the world of microbes is a "thimble-sized rainforest." Moreover, he said it is "virtually impossible" to describe the "ecological structure" of this biodiversity.[12]

Such observations, made possible by DNA evidence, confirm Richard Lewontin's suggestion that the ecosystem metaphor is more appropriate for biotechnology than the software "operating systems" metaphor that the biotech industry prefers. Evelyn Fox argues that given the dynamic, ecosystemic nature of the genetic world, the major lesson we are likely to learn from our further research in genetics is "humility."[13] As Lewontin says, "You can always intervene and change something in it, but there's no way of knowing what all the downstream effects will be or how it might affect the environment. We have such a miserably poor understanding of how the organism develops from its DNA that I would be surprised if we *don't* get one rude shock after another."[14]

I am not suggesting transgenic research be abandoned. All species, after all, do modify their environments. Environments are constructed by living organisms out of the bits and pieces of the external world available to them; the environment wouldn't even exist if it were not for organisms modifying it. But if we continue to ignore the ecological dimensions of our modifications, as we seem to regularly do with genetic engineering, we are likely to experience many unpleasant surprises.

Because ecosystems dynamics are at work even at the molecular level, we need to proceed more cautiously than most molecular biologists have thus far, and we should not ignore fundamental ecological principles in the process of our modifications. We can no longer blithely continue to assume that our proposed modifications are "safe" simply because we have convinced ourselves that:

- Genetic engineering is no different from ordinary sexual reproduction
- Nature will always keep all populations in balance
- Transgenic organisms will always be ecologically competent
- Because the host has been domesticated, it is so genetically debilitated that the transgenic organism will not pose an ecological problem

None of these assumptions serves us well.

The Basis for Assessing Risk

What is an appropriate basis for determining whether to release a transgenic organism into the environment? In an essay published in *BioScience,* Mario Giampietro suggested that such a decision must be analyzed on at least three different levels: individual, social, and biospherical.[15]

At the individual level, we would ask whether a transgenic organism would be beneficial to individuals: to the company that develops it, the individual who will use it, or the organism that has been altered. At this level, it is relatively easy to quantify risks and benefits. It is also the level at which most industries want to make decisions.

At the social level, things are more complicated because we need to examine how the transgenic organism will impact the overall well-being and stability of society. What type of health risks does it pose to human populations, and what economic benefits or damages will be created in the community in which it is released?

At the biospheric level, we encounter a wide range of issues that are extremely difficult to assess through conventional risk/benefit analysis. Because every organism is part of a very complex, well-orchestrated ecosystem that has evolved over several millennia, it is virtually impossible to assess, in advance, how changes in an organism may change the ecology in which that organism exists. How do these changes affect energy flows? How do they affect oscillations in predator-prey relationships over many life cycles?

Do they increase the possibility of one species taking over, as non-native species have done when introduced into new ecologies?[16]

Giampietro suggests that decisions regarding transgenic organisms are made mostly at the individual level, with occasional passing reference to the social level. We rarely make them on the biospheric level. If we are interested in sustainability, then we need to give primary attention to the biospheric level.

Giampietro's analysis also highlights the need to be clear about which problems we are trying to solve with transgenic organisms. For example, if we are concerned only about making more food immediately available to help feed a growing population, we might decide to support the development of genetically engineered organisms that promise to improve yield (the individual level). But we may decide to approach the hunger problem differently if we are concerned about the social inequities and the political structures that prevent people from gaining access to food despite adequate production (the social level). If we are concerned about humanity's ecological footprint on the planet, which destroys the ecosystem services that make food production possible (the biospheric level), then we might completely redefine the problem of hunger. Giampietro's insights help us realize that current biotechnology applications in agriculture are primarily designed to address the problems created by monoculture farming's specialized production systems.

Propping up monocultures and the industrial food system using transgenic technologies is challenging because monocultures are fundamentally at odds with nature. Nature is diverse and complex. Monocultures are inherently unstable and fraught with pest problems. All organisms in nature have learned to adapt to biodiversity. Nature will always find ways to overcome the specialization and simplification of monocultures.

Ethical Issues

What is the ethical basis for making decisions with respect to transgenic organisms? This is a particularly difficult question to answer because in our culture, going all the way back to the seventeenth century, we insist on separating facts from values, which have been relegated to the realm of personal opinion and private faith. Ethics and values have been disconnected from science and facts. That perspective has left us with few disciplined tools for making ethical decisions as a society. New technologies, however, are propelling us into a world in which we no longer have the luxury of relegating ethics to the arena of private and personal choice.

For example, our new-generation technologies in robotics, genetic engineering, and nanotechnology are self-replicating. With them, we run the risk of doing "substantial damage in the physical world."[17] Bill Joy, co-founder and chief scientist of Sun Microsystems, compared the dangers of twenty-first-century technologies with those of the twentieth century:

> Certainly the technologies underlying the weapons of mass destruction . . . nuclear, biological, and chemical . . . were powerful, and the weapons an enormous threat. But building nuclear weapons required, at least for a time, access to both rare—indeed, effectively unavailable—raw material and highly protected information: biological and chemical weapons programs also tended to require large-scale activities.
>
> The twenty-first century technologies—genetics, nanotechnology, and robotics—are so powerful that they can spawn whole new classes of accidents and abuses. Most dangerously, for the first time, these accidents and abuses are widely within the reach of individuals or small groups. They will not require large facilities or rare raw materials. Knowledge alone will enable the use of them. Thus, we have the possibility not just of weapons of mass destruction but of knowledge-enabled mass destruction . . . this destructiveness hugely amplified by the power of self-replication.
>
> I think it is no exaggeration to say we are on the cusp of the further perfection of extreme evil.[18]

This is not the ranting of an end-of-the-world fanatic who foresees Armageddon at every turn, but the observations of someone who has been at the forefront of developing the very twenty-first-century technologies that now compel more careful ethical scrutiny.

For farmers who have worked hard to develop and supply markets with crops that do not contain genetically modified organisms (GMO), there is an immediate ethical problem. As transgenic crops spread throughout the landscape, farmers are challenged to produce GMO-free crops. Mary-Howell Martens discovered GMO contamination at an average level of 0.25 percent in virtually all the non-GMO corn crop (that was tested) produced in the Midwest in 2000.[19]

David Vetter, a veteran organic grower and processor near Marquette, Nebraska, had managed to keep his open-pollinated organic corn free of GMO contamination for the twelve years since he began developing an organic variety. But when he finished his fall 2000 harvest, he tested and found GMO contamination in his corn. Careful management and selective breeding had enabled Vetter to develop an open-pollinated variety of comparable quality to that of standard hybrid varieties, making it a valuable product. Open-pollinated varieties save on input costs, and Vetter's customers prefer them. In addition to the extra costs involved in managing his corn to prevent pollen drift, Vetter now also has to absorb the additional cost of testing all of his corn. Further, now that the corn has traces of GMO contamination, Dave will label his corn to reflect the contamination, something he feels he must ethically do, but also something he is certain will cost him some of his customers.[20]

Seed companies that sell GMO-free seed now want higher GMO residue tolerances of GMO contamination so they can still market their seed as GMO-free. Vetter said he believes this is an indication that the more such seed is planted, the higher the contamination levels will climb. That prospect, plus the expectation that many additional GMO crop varieties will be introduced into the environment, suggests that farmers in the United States will soon be unable to produce any GMO-free—and therefore any "organic"—crops at all.

Specialty markets are critical to the survival of small farmers. Vetter's corn market is a very high-value specialty market that took him twenty years to develop. If he must sell his certified organic corn on the conventional market because his customers reject it, the price differential will be equal to his annual farm income, approximately $17,000 on forty acres. Who pays for David Vetter's loss?

Imagining Alternatives to Biotechnology

Proponents of agricultural biotechnology argue that although some risks may be involved in using this technology, we have no alternative but to forge ahead. Given that the world will add another 3 billion people by 2050, it is the only way to avoid calamity, they argue. Most of that population growth will take place in the developing world in urban centers. By 2030, 57 percent of developing-country populations are expected to live in cities.

The argument that biotechnology is needed to feed exploding populations is advanced by Leisinger, who has argued that "people living in cities are not able to feed themselves through subsistence food production in the same way that people living in rural areas do."[21]

This will have a cascading effect, the argument goes. Exploding populations in urban areas of poor nations will require ever-higher yields. Urban people eat more high-value foods, animal proteins, and vegetables. Higher meat consumption will require more diversion of cereals from food to feed because of the loss of protein involved in the conversion of plant food to meat. Leisinger doesn't tell us why this shift from rural to urban must *necessarily* take place. We do know that the industrialization of agriculture in the industrial world has had the related social cost of pushing farmers off their land by increasing farm size. But the necessity of doing this to achieve production goals is not self-evident. In fact, midsize farms can be more efficient than megafarms.[22,23]

Leisinger argues that higher productivity (which, in his view, can be achieved only with biotechnology) will have positive ecological effects: "If average annual per hectare productivity increases just 1 percent, the world will have to bring more than 300 million hectares of new land into agriculture by 2050 to meet expected demand. But a productivity increase of 1.5 percent could double output without using any additional cropland."[24]

Without biotechnology, the argument goes, we will have to bring fragile lands and wilderness areas into agricultural production, with all of the attendant ecological devastation. However, Leisenger ignores how much land will be taken out of production due to urban sprawl if his scenario comes to pass, or the potential for increased production through successful urban farming ventures. In Cuba, urban gardens produce 50,000 tons of food annually inside the city of Havana, without any genetic engineering.

Nor does Leisinger mention the potential for increasing food availability by decreasing waste. In the United States, an estimated 25 to 40 percent of food is lost due to waste and spoilage between field and table. Nor does he mention the potential of increasing yields by improving soil quality, the most effective way to increase yields, according to the National Academy of Sciences.[25] Nor does Leisinger tell us how people crammed into urban centers, living on annual incomes of less than $400, are going to be able to buy food produced with biotechnology. He suggests that as the economies of developing nations grow, people will eat higher on the food chain. But he fails to mention the fact that as economies grow, the "absolute gap between rich and poor . . . increase[s]."[26]

To his credit, Leisinger calls attention to the challenges associated with maintaining current levels of productivity, such as depleting water resources and soil quality, unforeseen climate changes, and poor governance, issues that biotechnology proponents usually overlook. He fails to mention, however, that many of these problems were caused by the industrial farming methods that he wants to perpetuate. He also fails to acknowledge that food security is negatively affected by two consequences of modern industrial agriculture: pest infestations that result, in part, from the lack of biodiversity and genetic variability, and the failure to initiate land reforms that could put land into the hands of farmers who would produce food for local populations.

Nevertheless, Leisinger believes that agricultural biotechnology is the linchpin to solving the food-security problem associated with global population explosion. His contention, however, is not based on field data, but on conjecture and analogy. He cites a World Bank panel's *prediction* that rice yields in Asia could increase by 10 or 20 percent with biotechnology. He compares the *future* potential of biotechnology with the past yield increases achieved with green revolution (GR) technologies.

Problems resulting from the green revolution, such as waterlogging and salinization of soils, depletion of water resources, and environmental contamination are issues that Leisinger said he feels must now be addressed with biotechnology. He fails to report, however, that while rice yields increased with green revolution technologies, other food sources were destroyed by the pesticide inputs required to make the GR technologies perform. Neither does he mention that in many developing countries, farmers are abandoning GR technologies in favor of integrated pest management and other less invasive agroecological practices, and in many cases they can achieve higher yields with less costly inputs.

Leisinger does acknowledge that we should judge genetic engineering "in the context of a wider technological pluralism." Biotechnology, he argues, should be used only if it proves "superior to other technologies with regard to cost-effectiveness."[27] Fair enough. But cost-effectiveness has to include ecological and social costs. This is where the analyses of agricultural biotechnology proponents such as Leisinger fail. They ignore alternatives for achieving the goals of providing adequate food and fiber within a robust economy, a healthy ecology, and vibrant communities.

Assessing Risk

To assess the social and ecological costs of agricultural biotechnology, we have to begin with the question of risk. Most proponents (and Leisinger is no exception) want to dismiss the problem of risk by claiming that "sound science" has already settled the matter. Leisinger argues, for example, that "there is a scientific consensus" establishing that there is "no conceptual distinction" between biotechnology and classical crop breeding methods, and that the same laws govern both methods.[28] Presumably, that provides prima facie evidence that there is no significant risk.

That assumption led him to conclude that anyone who introduces "speculative risks" into the debate is doing so deliberately in an "attempt to stir up controversy."[29] The debate over risk is reduced to two polarized sides: uninformed "laypersons" who operate out of "angst" and "feelings," and the Nobel laureates in biochemistry and molecular biology who have the "irrefutable facts presented by scientists."[30]

I almost don't know where to begin here. First, the discoveries of quantum mechanics have laid to rest the flawed notion that science can establish anything as an "irrefutable fact." Quantum physicists demonstrated that the world is a world of *probability,* not *predictability.*[31] Risks can never be assessed with any kind of certainty.

Furthermore, science doesn't operate on the basis of "irrefutable facts," but on the basis of consensus of the scientific community. That consensus is arrived at after peer review of data over long periods of time, and it is always subject to review. Whenever scientists discover new data or look at old data from a new perspective, old conclusions can give way to radical new ones, establishing a new consensus and a new "objective" truth. The scientific community's occasional failures to honor this reality and consequently the necessary tentativeness of its conclusions generate public distrust of science. Jim Davidson, research dean at the University of Florida, stated the matter succinctly with respect to agricultural science:

> The distrust on the part of nonagricultural groups is well justified. With the publication of Rachel Carson's book entitled *Silent Spring,* we, in agriculture, loudly and in unison stated that pesticides did

not contaminate the environment—*we now admit that they do.* When confronted with the presence of nitrates in groundwater, we responded that it was not possible for nitrates from commercial fertilizer to reach groundwater in excess of 10 parts per million under normal productive agricultural systems—*we now admit they do.* When questioned about the presence of pesticides in food and food quality, we assured the public that if a pesticide was applied in compliance with the label, agricultural products would be free of pesticides—*we now admit they're not.*[32]

To this list one can add scientists' assurances that there was no link between mad cow disease and Creutzfeldt-Jakob disease, between organophosphates and pesticide poisoning, and between the release of chlorofluorocarbons and the hole in the ozone. One can also add the assurances of scientists that nuclear energy was safe and would be "too cheap to meter" and that thalidomide was a safe drug. Proponents of biotechnology always seem to leave these examples out when they compare opponents of biotechnology to the technophobes who were opposed to railroads and the Model T.[33,34]

The problem here is not with the intelligence of scientists. If that were the case, the solution would be simple: just get smarter scientists. The problem is that scientists sometimes make universal claims based on insular data. We simply cannot make accurate predictions about how a technology will perform in the world of interconnected and interdependent relationships of living systems based on isolated data collected in laboratories. In a world of social and ecological relationships, there will always be surprises, surprises vastly magnified by introducing technologies into ecosystems with which they did not evolve. Discovering the "truth" about how these technologies behave in our complex, interdependent world usually takes a lot of time and careful monitoring. It took forty years to discover that chloroflurocarbons were blowing a hole in the ozone.

How should we think about technological risks? Stephen Schneider suggests, "the bigger the technological solution, the greater the chance of extensive, unforeseen side effects and, thus, the greater the number of lives ultimately at risk."[35] Aldo Leopold proclaimed, "the greater the rapidity of human-induced changes, the more likely they are to destabilize the complex systems of nature."[36]

When Professor Leisinger assures us that agricultural biotechnology does not pose any significant risk, that it is "not very different" from what we have done in the past, and that the only reason there is so much opposition is that "highly sophisticated activists are easily able to mislead a scientifically uneducated public,"[37] we can perhaps be forgiven if we simply disagree. I doubt that Bill Joy, who has been at the forefront of developing powerful new technologies and is urging caution, is an example of Leisinger's "sophisticated activist" intent on misleading an "uneducated public."

I believe we will be better served if we follow the advice of ecologists who have carefully observed the workings of nature rather than the advice of Leisinger, who seems to have observed only the tantalizing promises of a largely untested technology. Ecologists warn that "the level of uncertainty in our understanding of ecological processes suggests that it would be prudent to avoid courses of action that involve possibly dramatic and irreversible consequences and, instead, to wait for better information."[38] Ultimately, the main problem with biotechnology is that it conforms to the same paradigm that has failed us in chemical technology.

The Alternatives

As it turns out, alternatives often exist to the "quick-fix" applications of biotechnology. Managing corn rootworm serves as an example. Corn rootworm has become one of the most difficult pests for corn farmers to manage. The University of Illinois's Michael Gray, one of the leading entomologists in the country studying this pest, reports that Western corn rootworm has not only become resistant to most of the insecticides used against it, but it also has evolved resistance to cultural practices such as crop rotation. So here it would seem we have a perfect candidate for a variety of corn that has been genetically modified to produce the insecticide Bt, to control a problem for which there are no alternatives.[39]

But Gray is not so sure. First, there is the issue of cost-effectiveness. He estimated that farmers will invest more than $400 million annually in technology fees alone to prevent an economic loss estimated at $650 million annually. At best, farmers will earn less than one dollar for each dollar invested, and that assumes that losses due to pest infestation in the refuge acres will be minimal.

The long-term cost to the environment, and eventually to the farmer, could be significant. Bt corn used to combat rootworms could harm beneficial insects, and transgenic Bt may not break down in the soil, harming vital soil organisms and affecting yields. Resistance may develop quickly in rootworms because they feed on the endotoxins of the transgenic plants twice during a growing season, first as larvae on the roots and then as adults on the pollen and foliage. Gray said he believes that apart from careful pest monitoring and selection of fields in which the transgenic varieties are planted, resistance is assured.[40]

But an alternative exists to using Bt corn for rootworm control. Researchers with the Agricultural Research Service at the University of Missouri have developed corn lines with native-plant resistance to corn rootworms, a resistance based on multiple proteins. Transgenic varieties, on the other hand, depend on only one protein. Rootworms will likely develop resistance to the transgenic varieties more quickly than to multiple-protein varieties. The Agricultural Research Service's Bruce Hibbard said that they "aren't necessarily trying to eradicate corn rootworms completely" but rather to simply hold "rootworm damage below the economic threshold."[41] Hibbard's comment suggests an effort to understand why the rootworm is a pest and find ways to alter the system so that it will no longer be a pest, rather than using an external counterforce to eradicate it.

This raises an important question. If we invested research funding for ecological approaches to solving production problems that was comparable to what we spend on the engineering approach, what solutions would we find? Conversely, if we convince ourselves that no alternatives to engineering external controls exist, we guarantee that ecological approaches won't be explored.

Leisinger suggests the possibility of increasing rice yields by 10 or 20 percent with biotechnology. However, in a research project conducted in China, farmers have already experienced an 18 percent yield increase without using fungicides or transgenic technologies.[42] Instead, two varieties of traditional rice that are locally adapted were companion-planted. Another example is the Aigamo method of producing rice, which increases rice yields 20 to 50 percent in the first year.

The Aigamo method involves putting about 200 ducklings into each hectare of rice paddy. The ducks eat insects and snails that attack rice plants, and they eat weed seeds and seedlings. They also oxygenate the water, which encourages rice plant roots to grow. The mechanical stimulation of their paddling makes for sturdier rice plants. Using this method, a farmer's two-hectare farm annually produces "seven tonnes of rice, 300 ducks, 4,000 ducklings and enough vegetables to supply 100 people."[43] The Aigamo method, now being adopted in many developing countries, may help Japan, which currently imports 80 percent of its food, become self-sufficient.

In another example, Brian Halweil has reported that farmers in East Africa have managed to successfully control the Striga weed by planting leguminous trees prior to planting corn.[44] He argues this may be a more useful technology than herbicide-resistant corn, because the corn and the herbicide are too expensive for African farmers. Another approach to increasing food security that does not use transgenic technology comes from the Land Institute in Salina, Kansas. Scientists there are developing perennial polycultures from wild grasses that can reduce soil erosion, use water more efficiently, and reduce planting and tillage costs.[45] John Jeavons, world-renowned for his biointensive methods, has experienced phenomenal yield increases in vegetable production.[46] Jeavons's system involves, among other features, a double-digging technique to loosen the soil two feet deep, which permits higher-density plantings because the roots can go deeper into the soil.

All of these examples have the potential to produce other positive effects. Agriculture that is based on complexities cannot be readily managed in large-scale monocultures. Highly intensive methods may support more people on the land with smaller-scale, highly productive farms. A system that supports more people on the land may slow down, or even reverse, the migration to megacities. Could the Leisinger scenario of continued urbanization be forestalled or reversed?

Richard Manning has concluded that we will never be successful in our efforts to feed the world if we do not take the complexity and diversity of local cultures and local ecologies into consideration.[47] He concluded that genetic engineering may be a limited tool in food production for an expanding human population, but it will not be the solution:

> The genetic engineering business is going to get all the headlines, but these simple matters [attending to the needs of local cultures and local ecologies] are potentially far more earth-shaking. What must happen, and to a degree is happening, in agriculture is also

an information revolution. If there was a key mistake of the green revolution, it was in simplifying a system that is by its very nature complex.

Farming is not just growing food. It is not simply a tool we use to feed however many beings our social structure generates. The way we grow food determines our structure, makes our megacities, makes us who we are. Agriculture is culture. . . . This is about growing good food, but more important, it is about making good lives. We will fail if we attend to the former without considering the latter.[48]

Our current fascination with new-generation technologies may be distracting us from recognizing important human failures. One failure is our tendency to believe we can solve our problems without nature. In Iowa, a cow named Bessie gave birth to a gaur, an oxlike Asian bovine mammal. It was the world's first cloned endangered species, and the experiment was undertaken to help save the species from extinction.

Ellen Goodman suggested that this may be a necessary thing to do.[49] From a whole-systems perspective, however, it raises a number of questions. Why are we willing to expend this extraordinary effort to save one species while we remain oblivious to the destruction of the habitat of hundreds of others? What does it mean to save a species from extinction when its habitat has been destroyed? Do we think that the baby guar can live on an Iowa farm, raised by an Iowa cow, and still be a gaur? We may never know, because the guar born on January 8, 2001, died eighteen hours later.

Biotechnology is never simply a matter of "just adding another gene to what we have already been doing," as Monsanto science fellow and agronomist John Kaufmann put it recently at a biotech conference.[50] According to Stuart Newman, professor of cell biology and anatomy at New York Medical College, there is an "incorrect, but prevalent notion, that genes are modular entities with a one-to-one correspondence between function and a gene."[51]

Another example of the complex relationships that have evolved in nature involves "a chemical laxative in the cherry-sized fruit of a Costa Rican shrub. The drug appears to act on the bowels of the birds, to the plants' and not the birds' advantage."[52] Though we have known that fruits contain laxatives, this is the first evidence that animals are drugged into transporting and dropping seeds more quickly. Plants have evolved a complex mechanism that enables them to control the rate of passage of a seed through birds to give the plants the best opportunity to propagate themselves. We simply have to take such contexts into account as we contemplate changing the world with powerful, self-replicating technologies.

Everyone agrees that biotechnology has the ability to make dramatic changes in nature. If that were not true, then the argument that it has the potential to dramatically increase productivity would be hollow. But if powerful technologies have the potential to radically change complex relationships, thereby potentially upsetting delicate interactions that have evolved over millennia, shouldn't it inspire caution? Bill Joy reminds us of another failure, the common human attitude toward new technologies. As he puts it, we almost never pause to try and "understand the consequences of our innovations while we are in the rapture of discovery and innovation."[53]

Conclusion

What is our prevailing scientific ideology, and how does it affect the assessment of these new technologies? Do we recognize ecosystems dynamics at the molecular level? Can we learn to incorporate the potential consequences of ecosystems functions in our assessment of transgenic organisms? Will we be clear about the level at which we are attempting to solve a problem and properly assess the risk at the individual, societal, and biospheric levels? What are the ethical implications of new technologies, and how do we begin making sound ethical choices in an ethically challenged society? These are all questions we need to ponder.

Why American Agriculture
Is Not Sustainable

A land ethic, then, reflects the existence of an ecological conscience, and this in turn reflects a conviction of individual responsibility for the health of the land. Health is the capacity of the land for self-renewal. Conservation is our effort to understand and preserve this capacity.[1]
—Aldo Leopold

A pervasive criticism of sustainable agriculture is that without a commonly accepted definition of sustainable agriculture, there is no basis for an intelligent discussion of the issue. Some argue that because there is no universally agreed-upon standard set of sustainable farming practices, the entire concept is suspect. The problem here is not lack of definition, but flawed reasoning. The term "sustainable" is a transcendent term that does not lend itself to definition according to a uniformly accepted set of rules or activities. Sustainability is similar to terms like truth, justice, or beauty. Something is just, true, or beautiful depending on the context, but that has never deterred us from using the terms. We just agree that what is true, just, or beautiful in any given situation may differ widely. The same is true of sustainability.

Thus, the sustainability of American agriculture cannot be judged based on the merits of specific farming practices. Moldboard plowing is normally considered an unsustainable practice, but such tillage may be part of a sustainable system in certain contexts. To evaluate American agriculture, it is more useful to identify indicators of sustainability that suggest if we are moving toward or away from agricultural resilience.

This is a revised version of a paper that was first published in *Renewable Resources Journal,* Autumn 2002, 6–11.

In his seminal work *The Ecology of Commerce,* Paul Hawken suggested three guidelines, embodying nature's principles, that serve as indicators of sustainability.[2] His principles can be applied to agriculture.

Hawken's first principle is "waste equals food." Sustainability requires that production systems be designed so that waste from one part of the system returns as food for another part of the system. When waste does not return as food, eventually it will exceed Earth's capacity for absorption, making the practice unsustainable. In agriculture, this principle has long been known as the law of return: "the return of wastes to the soil creates humus, which encourages healthy crops whose remains, properly composted, return to enrich the soil's humus content."[3] Hawken's second sustainability principle suggests that we transition from a carbon-based economy to an economy based on hydrogen and sunshine, moving from borrowed to current energy. Such a shift is necessary because of the depletion of stored carbon energy sources, and because further increases in atmospheric CO_2 levels threaten to undermine the planet's essential life-support systems. The third principle requires that we pay heed to ecological restoration. Restorative behavior is integral to long-term sustainability. Maintaining the capacity for renewal is essential to sustainability.[4]

These three basic principles have led us to move beyond the definition offered by the World Commission on Environment and Development. The commission framed sustainability to mean meeting the "needs of the present without compromising the ability of future generations to meet their own needs."[5] While that definition described a core element of sustainability, it lacked any reference to ecological restoration and implied a distinctly human point of view.

True sustainability must include the element of ecological restoration and be inclusive of the entire biotic community. Any definition of sustainability that limits itself to the welfare of the human community is deeply flawed. The human community cannot sustain itself apart from the health of the rest of the biotic community. All of nature's organisms must meet their own needs now and in the future if the human community is to survive. Accordingly, these three indicators of sustainability—the law of return, current energy, and ecological restoration—helps us assess the sustainability of American agriculture.

The Law of Return

Modern American agriculture largely ignores the law of return. With the introduction of fossil fuels in the 1950s, we shifted entirely from a nutrient cycling to an input/output system of production. We now rely exclusively on exogenous inputs to supply basic nutrients; farms are specialized, standardized, and simplified like factories. Diverse cropping systems and crop/livestock integration, required for efficient nutrient cycling, are no longer necessary. These production systems meet the needs of an industrialized food system, but they depend on fossil-fuel inputs for fertility, pest control, processing, packaging, and shipping.

Nutrient cycling was common until the mid-nineteenth century. Most human and animal wastes were recycled as food for the plant kingdom. As society became urbanized in the mid-nineteenth to the mid-twentieth centuries, human waste recycling became difficult, so we began depositing it in landfills and sewers. As agriculture became industrialized in the late twentieth century and crop and livestock production systems became isolated from each other, recycling animal wastes became difficult and costly, creating unintended consequences such as soil loss, nutrient pollution, and imperiled water systems.

The National Academy of Sciences correctly stressed that "soil degradation is a complex phenomenon driven by strong interactions among socioeconomic and biophysical factors." However, they also recognized soil management as a key factor in improving soil quality.[6] Specializing in a few crops with minimal diversity in the cropping system leads to biological, physical, and often chemical soil degradation. According to the National Academy study, "soil degradation may have significant effects on the ability of the United States to sustain a productive agricultural system."[7]

In Switzerland, biological and physical properties of soils in both organic and conventional systems were evaluated over a twenty-one-year period. Organically managed soils, whose nutrients were replenished with green and livestock manures, had higher soil quality, including "greater biological activity" and "10 to 60 percent higher" soil aggregate stability.[8] Unacceptable levels of nutrient pollution also result from failure to apply the law of return. In specialized animal-production systems, animal wastes concentrate near feedlots and animal factories and are overapplied to nearby fields.

Meanwhile, manufactured nutrients are applied in excess to crops on fields from which animals have been removed; these nutrients find their way into surface and groundwater, causing eutrophication. The dead zone in the Gulf of Mexico is created by nutrient runoff, primarily from crop and animal systems in the midwestern Corn Belt.[9] Soil and water quality are, of course, tightly linked, because conserving or enhancing soil quality is fundamental to improving water quality: "Reducing losses of nutrients, pesticides, salts, or other pollutants will be impossible or difficult if soil degradation is not controlled. Indeed, use of nutrients, pesticides, and irrigation water to compensate for declining soil quality may be an important cause of water pollution."[10]

Current Energy

Suggesting that agriculture must rely on current, rather than borrowed, energy to be sustainable may have seemed like an extreme concept prior to the era of peak oil. For more than a century, fossil-fuel energy has been convenient, abundant, and cheap, while sources of current energy—such as wind, solar, and biomass—were cumbersome, inefficient, and costly. As we enter the twenty-first century, we must move beyond our fossil fuel–based agriculture and to do so, we will need to rely increasingly on interactions between organisms and the environment. Shiyuomi and Koizumi argue that sustainable agriculture must be based on species interaction and interdependence, that is, synergy and synchrony.[11]

Modern agriculture, which uses only the simplest biotic responses, must be transformed such that complex biotic interactions become the key technology. While direct evidence to substantiate that synergy and synchrony can replace fossil-fuel inputs may be scarce,[12] research in this area could be the most fruitful avenue to future productivity. Studies by David Tilman and his colleagues suggest that possibility.[13–15] Farmers such as Takao Furuno in Japan and Joel Salatin in the United States have explored such systems and find them highly productive and profitable.[16,17] As farmers in many parts of the world discover the benefits of these systems and learn how to manage them, they begin to adopt them.[18]

This paradigm shift, however, faces several challenges. Throughout most of the fossil fuel–based agricultural era, farmers have viewed biological diversity as a constraint to be overcome. Fossil fuel–based systems sought to eliminate all species from the landscape except for the one species being cultivated for production. Consequently, "little attention has been paid to the complex networks of biological interactions." It is now difficult for us to understand "the complex effects operating between organisms themselves or the organisms and the environment."[19] There has been very little effort to understand, let alone determine how best to use, biological diversity to increase productivity. Furthermore, farmers have limited experience managing interspecies systems and won't easily adopt these new practices.

Ecological Restoration

The concept of ecological restoration may be new to proponents of sustainable agriculture because our focus has been on ecological soundness, conservation, and stabilization. Given the state of environmental deterioration and the increasing impact of human populations on the environment, ecological restoration must now become an integral part of any strategy for making agriculture durable. A recent National Academy of Sciences study indicates that human demand on the planet now exceeds Earth's regenerative capacity by at least 20 percent.[20] Agricultural production is a key component of that disparity. If we are to avoid drifting toward an increasing state of decline, ecological restoration is an especially urgent task in an era of fossil-fuel depletion. The soil degradation caused by industrial systems is masked by heavy use of fossil fuel–based fertilizers. As these inputs become prohibitively costly, we will have to rely more on soil quality to maintain productivity, which will require redesigning farming systems to maintain the capacity of the soil to renew itself.

We will need to pay much closer attention to the web of life and how it functions in nature. For example, photosynthate from healthy forest trees that grow in full sunlight will travel down and across mycorrhizal fungi (which serve as bridges) to bolster the nutrition of weaker shaded trees.[21] Biologists at the University of York reported that modern, intensive agriculture disrupts this very web.[22] We must pay more attention to synergistic and symbiotic relationships so that we can employ them in a more sustainable food-production system.

The Socioeconomic Factor

Sustainable agriculture has long subscribed to a threefold formula of sustainability: economically viable, ecologically sound, and socially responsive.

Hawken's principles of sustainability are largely focused on the ecological part of the equation. The economic and social components are equally important.

Of course, agriculture must be economically viable in order to be sustainable. But a deeply rooted assumption in current economic philosophy contends that economic viability is largely limited to economic efficiency. Nobel Prize–winning economist Amartya Sen calls this the "engineering-based" approach to economics because it concerns itself only with the "logistic and engineering problems within economics" instead of the economic wealth and well-being of society. While the engineering-based approach predicts that societal well-being will automatically be served, that assumption, according to Sen, rests more on theory than on empirical verification.[23]

Classical economists, like Adam Smith, insisted that economic freedom and power affected economic viability as much as efficiency. Economic power in our food and agriculture system is now so heavily concentrated that neither free-market competition nor efficiency is evident. Such concentration does not serve the best interests of either producers or consumers. Farmers are increasingly forced to provide bulk commodities below cost of production, and the potential benefits of market efficiencies are no longer passed on to consumers. This scenario hardly lends itself to a future that is economically viable or sustainable.

Our current economic philosophy also has made it difficult for us to address the third component of the sustainability formula, social responsiveness. Our laissez-faire economic ideology regards any interference in the free market to achieve social goals as "social engineering" and therefore suspect. But it is impossible to achieve either the economic or environmental goals of agriculture without the "proper functioning of those social institutions which are essential to satisfactory farm life."[24] To ensure a durable and economically healthy society, the state and civil society must be equal partners with free markets. As Aldo Leopold reminded us, the "economic parts of the biotic clock" will not function well without the "uneconomic parts."[25]

Thus, the economic, ecological, and community components of agricultural sustainability are interdependent. If we focus only on economic viability while ignoring farm ecology, soil quality will degrade, requiring more fertilizer, which affects the economic viability of the farm. Likewise, if we ignore community welfare, the public services that support the farm economy, such as public roads and quality local education and local re-search, will deteriorate and affect farm viability.

Similarly, if we only attend to the ecology and the community and ignore the farm's economic viability, then the deteriorating economy of the farm makes it impossible for the farmer to actively support the community or properly care for the ecology. These three components are inextricably linked, and one cannot imagine a sustainable agriculture without acknowledging the interdependent whole.

A New Land Ethic

This leaves us with a final question. Can we achieve agricultural sustainability without an underlying ethic to direct our agricultural activities? More than fifty years ago, Leopold argued that we could not. He observed that we usually rely solely on economic motives to stimulate sustainable behavior. However, most members of the biotic community (many of them essential to a healthy ecology) have no immediate economic value. Thus, any system designed to achieve sustainability that is "based solely on economic self-interest is hopelessly lopsided. It tends to ignore, and thus eventually to eliminate, many elements in the land community that lack commercial value, but are (as far as we know) essential to its healthy functioning."[26]

Our tendency, then, is to "relegate to government many functions eventually too large, too complex, or too widely dispersed to be performed by government."[27]

Leopold's insight truly was profound. We know more fully now than we did fifty years ago that the entire biotic world is indeed a "community." We know that local ecologies are highly site-specific and do not respond well to ecological management from centralized bureaucracies or corporations. According to Hawken, restorative behavior is best achieved through standards and incentives that "release creativity and productivity," rather than through regulation, and "by smaller enterprises" rather than by "larger, unwieldy corporations."[28]

Modern biology suggests that Leopold's conclusions regarding the biotic community were on target. Harvard geneticist Richard Lewontin outlines four facets of organism and environmental interactions that are consistent with Leopold's ethic.[29]

First, each organism determines which aspects of the environment are relevant to it and accordingly selects a habitat suitable to it. Each organism in the environment finds a "special and temporal juxtaposition of bits and pieces of the world that produces a surrounding for the organism that is relevant to it." Second, each organism actively "constructs" a world around itself, thereby creating the environment. Third, each organism is in a "constant process of altering the environment." And fourth, organisms adjust some of the properties in their environment to adapt to fluctuations that could threaten the organism's survival. Plants, for example, store energy in underground tubers so the next generation can begin from internally stored energy. Without the activity of organisms within the environment, many of which have no immediate economic value, there would be no environment. And there would be no agriculture!

These dynamic interactions in the biotic community suggest how we might relate to our world in the interest of sustainability. We cannot "save the environment," "stop extinctions," nor maintain some kind of presumed "balance" in nature. The dynamic, complex, interdependent activities taking place in the biotic community simply make such objectives unrealistic. "What we can do," writes Lewontin, "is to try to affect the rate of extinction and direction of environmental change in such a way as to make a decent life for human beings possible. What we cannot do is to keep things as they are."[30]

These observations are consistent with Leopold's land ethic. Leopold noted that the concept of the "balance of nature" does not adequately describe how nature works. The "biotic pyramid," he suggested, was a much "truer image" because it recognized that "each species, including ourselves, is a link in many chains."[31] This biological bond led Hawken to suggest that "biological knowledge and understanding will soar in demand because it will provide the means to integrate human needs with the carrying capacity of natural systems."[32]

Historically, we have adopted numerous ethical positions with respect to nature. At one point we assumed that nature was the enemy, something evil that had to be tamed. There are still those among us who regard nature as an adversary that we must "fight" if we are going to have a healthy economy. Then, through most of the industrial era, we regarded nature as a collection of objects that functioned in accordance with mechanical laws. It became our role as humans to engineer those objects into a functioning whole for the sole benefit of the human species. Until recently, we also regarded nature as a stable system that had achieved a state of equilibrium through a long process of evolution. Our responsibility as a human species, it was then assumed, was to prevent the destabilization of nature and to preserve its harmony. Modern evolutionary biology suggests that these ethical perspectives are now dysfunctional. Lewontin and Leopold both suggest that what we can do is nurture the ecological health of the environment, ecological health being understood as "the capacity of the land for self-renewal."[33]

How Can We Make Agriculture More Sustainable?

If the above observations are valid, making agriculture more sustainable cannot be reduced to some kind of universal prescription for changing farming practices, such as switching from chemical to biological inputs. Nor can we condense sustainability to a simple formula for increasing the yields of a few commodities to "feed the world." In broad terms, what we can do is to redesign our food and agriculture system so that its functions are more consistent with our best understanding of how the biotic community works. We can seek to provide adequate amounts of food by nurturing the potential for increased productivity inherent in redesigned multispecies systems. It seems imperative to pursue four objectives to that end.

First, we should refocus our public-research agenda to investigate the synergies and synchronies of the diverse species in each agricultural watershed. We need to evaluate how they can be employed to increase our agricultural productivity, while simultaneously enhancing the capacity of local ecologies to renew themselves. We need to use ecological screens to determine what technologies to employ and how best to employ them to achieve these larger objectives.

Second, we should expand our research agendas. We need new food-marketing relationships that enable farmers to produce more value and retain a larger share of that value in the economy of the farm and the local community. There can be no sustainable future for an agriculture that only expects farmers to produce undifferentiated raw materials as cheaply as possible, with the value of that production accruing to distant shareholders. The federal Sustainable Agriculture Research and Education program might well be expanded to include such total-food-systems research.

Third, we need new federal and local policies that support new production and marketing systems, so that farmers can transition out of the unsustainable systems of the past. If the health of our economy, ecology, and community are to be achieved in concert, then our public policies must be redesigned to achieve that larger, integrated goal. We cannot continue to support bulk commodity production of just a few crops, using flawed farming practices, that are sold at untenable prices. In the face of declining fossil-fuel resources, ecological restoration must be a centerpiece of the new policies. As Leopold and Hawken both argue, such policies should be geared to promoting smaller enterprises and creativity, rather than consolidation and regulation. Sound ecological management can be carried out only by people living in local ecologies long enough and intimately enough to learn how to manage them well.

Finally, we need to launch a nationwide educational program to foster a national ecological conscience. As Leopold said, "Obligations have no meaning without conscience, and the problem we face is the extension of the social conscience from people to land." Our ethical imperative must be broadened from one limited to human-to-human relationships to one that encompasses the entire biotic community.[34]

What Constitutes Sound Science?

Both religion and science have always been in a state of continual develop-
ment. . . . Science is even more changeable than theology. No [person]
of science could subscribe without qualification to Galileo's beliefs, or to
Newton's beliefs, or to all his own scientific beliefs of ten years ago.[1]
—Alfred North Whitehead

The vast growth of science in the last 300 years proves . . . that new aspects
of reality are constantly being added to those known before.[2]
—Michael Polanyi

Marion Nestle has argued that the public no longer receives the best scientific information regarding diet and health. Nestle is a renowned nutritionist with years of experience working on nutrition and dietary guidelines for the Food and Drug Administration (FDA) and the U.S. Department of Agriculture (USDA). She outlines in her provocative book, *Food Politics,* how the food industry regularly stifles the scientific community when its findings conflict with the financial interests of the industry.[3]

Nestle, in fact, comes to a disturbing conclusion. Science, she suggests, is now often used to defend a position already adopted rather than to discover new or truer descriptions of reality. It is science designed to persuade, rather than science meant to explore and enlighten. One can see this phenomenon at work in the genetic engineering debate. Both sides in the debate regularly attempt to use science to sustain positions they have already adopted, rather than encouraging scientists to freely investigate and pursue a fuller understanding of the biological world.

This talk was presented at the annual Sigma Xi lecture, Iowa State University, December 5, 2002.

Barry Commoner points out that substantial scientific evidence exists to question genetic engineering's core idea, the "central dogma," which is the "one-to-one correspondence of gene to protein" and the corresponding belief in biological determinism. But despite the fact that the one-to-one theory has now been largely invalidated, the dogma still stands. The reason for this intransigence, Commoner suggests, is not just the "traditional scientific economy of prestige and generous funding that follows it" but that money has distorted the entire "scientific process," which was once a "purely academic pursuit" and has now "been commercialized to an astonishing degree by researchers themselves."[4] So, has money simply corrupted science?

Evelyn Fox Keller, from MIT, notices an even greater incongruity: "The basic fact is that, at the very moment in which gene-talk has come to so powerfully dominate our biological discourse, the prowess of new analytic techniques in molecular biology and the sheer weight of the findings they have enabled have brought the concept of the gene to the verge of collapse."[5]

How could the biological sciences be dominated by a dogma that is largely discredited? Keller argues that the problem is rooted in "gene talk." Scientists, she says, "are language-speaking actors," and "the words they use play a crucial role in motivating them to act, in directing their attention, in framing their questions, and in guiding their experimental efforts." She suggests that "what is missing, and would be absolutely required for understanding the role of language in biological research, is a far deeper investigation of the material, economic, and social context in which that language functions."[6] The problem is not just with money, but also the culture of science.

The debate over how best to "feed the world" in the face of an exploding human population entails similar problems. Under the spell of the central dogma, some scientists maintain that only by increasing the yield of a few commodity crops through technological innovation will the hungry be fed. Supported by powerful economic interests, our culture of science continues to maintain that our most complex societal problems can be solved only with technological innovations.

However, recent research in biology, physics, and sociology reveals a more complex world than previously imagined. Emerging complexity does not lend itself well to linear technological manipulation, indicating the need for more humility in our interactions with the environment. As Keller concludes, "It is a rare and wonderful moment when success teaches us humility, and this, I argue, is precisely the moment at which we find ourselves at the end of the twentieth century."[7]

But humility is seldom evident among scientists who use science primarily to produce technological innovations. For example, in defending his position that the world's hungry can only be fed with transgenic technologies, Norman Borlaug insists that science has already given us all the information we need to establish the soundness of his position, and that opposition to it is based on "fear born of ignorance."[8] Such arrogance inevitably leads to the position that the science one uses to validate one's own position is sound, while the science used by one's opponent is junk.

How did we get here? How did we come to believe that science is a discipline that produces irrefutable facts and that its role is to defend those "facts"? What happened to science as process and science that encourages questioning established dogma? What happened to science that continually discovers new ways of interpreting the world around us? We need science that probes rather than proves.

What Is Science For?

How we got here can be determined, in part, by tracing the history of U.S. public science policy after World War II. The war cemented the importance of technological innovation in the public consciousness. Superior technology, we believed, enabled us to win the war. So when the Cold War emerged, we readily turned to science and technological innovation as the keys to outcompeting our new enemies, thereby proving the superiority of our economic and political system. The technological innovations required to conquer space became key symbols in the new war. Outperforming our enemies economically and developing technological innovations to win this peculiar new "war" became central to our defense strategy.

The quality of science in the United States was evaluated almost exclusively in terms of its ability to deliver technological innovation. Scientists were rewarded for developing new technologies, not for discovering how the world worked or how the synergies and synchronies of nature functioned.[9] This trend was also supported by political and business leaders and the public, all of whom wanted to explain science in simplistic terms that could be easily quantified and justified—and funded.

President Franklin D. Roosevelt requested a report on science policy, which Dr. Vannevar Bush, director of the Office of Scientific Research and Development, published on July 25, 1945. The report, titled "Science, the Endless Frontier," began with this statement: "New frontiers of the mind are before us, and if they are pioneered with the same vision, boldness, and drive with which we have waged this war, we can create a fuller and more fruitful employment and a fuller and more fruitful life."[10]

While the report pays lip service to the importance of basic research, referring to it as "scientific capital," such research is never regarded as valuable in its own right. Rather, it is seen as "essential to the achievement" of the goals in the report. And those goals are the technological advances that will "create more jobs," "make new and better and cheaper products," and create "more abundant crops," among other things.

The report also proposes that "the government should foster the opening of new frontiers." And it suggests that the "modern way of doing it" is to extend government support to "industrial research" and "provide suitable incentives to industry to conduct research." That could be accomplished by making research tax-deductible and by strengthening the patent system. While the report strongly supports freedom of inquiry so that "scientists are free to pursue the truth wherever it may lead," even this caveat is couched in terms of industrial competition.

This new vision for the role of science set the stage for the next fifty years of research. It launched a research funding structure that created partnerships among industry, government, and universities for the primary purpose of increasing economic competitiveness. In the 1980s, three new laws further propelled science into the business of doing research to promote private financial benefits. In 1986, Congress passed the Federal Technology Transfer Act, which amended both the 1980 Bayh-Dole Act and the Stevenson-Wydler Technology Innovation Act. These legal changes were designed to increase U.S. productivity and give the United States an advantage over foreign competition.[11] Benefits of publicly funded research were shifted from the general public to private industry, on the assumption that the public would benefit *indirectly* as a result of increased jobs, higher wages, and improved quality of life.

As a result, science has become even more narrowly focused. Efforts to understand and explore the complexity of nature have been superseded by efforts to develop technologies that could extract economic benefits from nature. Research agendas began to favor powerful industries and organizations that can demonstrate technological success, such as putting a man on the moon. As a result, centralized, linear organizations with greater power to determine the direction of future research have emerged. Winning has become more important than understanding. Applied research leading to utilitarian results was given preference over basic research leading to enhanced intellectual capacity, a transformation now generally referred to as the industrialization of science.

Overall, research is most valued if it contributes to technological advancement. Increasingly specialized, single-discipline-based inquiry that results in new and powerful technologies is favored over multidisciplinary approaches to increase wisdom. Qualitative measures to determine collective well-being are less important than quantitative measures to evaluate singular, technological tactics. The value of research is now judged almost exclusively on utilitarian results. If a research project produces a pesticide that kills a target pest, it is successful and rewarded, even if it doesn't reduce the overall amount of crop loss due to pests. Our interest is in the technological capability of killing pests, not in understanding the more complex biological systems within which pests emerge.

Utilitarian science has resulted in at least three unintended consequences that plague science today. First, utilitarian science tends to misapprehend the true nature of problems because it assumes that (1) the structure and composition of ecosystems can be simplified to achieve the efficient production of goods and services, (2) problems lend themselves to technological solutions, and (3) control management is effective.

But most problems are systemic, nonlinear, and evolutionary in character. Social and biophysical problems are dynamic and complex, and they seldom lend themselves to technological solutions or control management.[12] Most observant farmers know this well. Consequently, the public is often disillusioned by the long-term results of scientific research, despite being initially enamored by short-term successes. This tends to undermine public confidence in science.

A second unintended consequence of the utilitarian approach to science is separation from nature. Nature is something to be used, not something to which we belong. This has alienated the public from nature and science.

Science belongs to the experts. Science is something the experts use to extract benefits from nature for our benefit. It is not something that *we* use to better understand nature or our place in it.

Third, by focusing on short-term, utilitarian results, science tends to ignore potential, long-term ecological consequences. Science focuses on the immediate potential benefits of developing a technology like DDT, but it pays little attention to exploring the potential long-term effects of the release of DDT into an environment composed of millions of very complex, interdependent, living, emergent organisms. The failure to recognize these ecosystem complexities and emergent properties has led to numerous incidents in which technological innovations caused harm to human health and the environment, despite initial assurances by scientists that the technologies were safe. This tends to erode the public's trust in science.

Jennifer Wilkins, at Cornell University, examined how land-grant university educators "view complex and interrelated issues related to GE [transgenic] food crops."[13] Wilkins's study revealed "a growing constituency that questions the extent to which LGUs are upholding their original mission to improve the lives of rural people and to bring benefits to a broad constituency of common citizens."[14]

The idea that research should enhance economic competitiveness has become so entrenched in the culture of science that it is difficult to even find a venue for discussing alternative values for science. But as we enter the twenty-first century, I argue that we should emphasize research that:

- Enhances global *cooperation* rather than research that increases *competitiveness*
- Is multidisciplinary and increases our understanding of evolving complexities and interdependence of our social and biological lives, rather than disciplinary research focused on producing more new technologies
- Focuses on more secure and efficient distributive, decentralized, flexible systems rather than the highly coupled, centralized, linear systems that evolved out of our economic competitiveness research
- Pays closer attention to the "ecological overshoot" of our human economies, rather than bolstering the economy with technologies that negatively affect the planet

Such reassessments were called for in a highly publicized presidential address by Jane Lubchenco at the annual meeting of the American Association for the Advancement of Science on February 15, 1997. In that talk she called for an entirely "new social contract for science."[15] She argued that given the magnitude of the impact that humans now have on the planet's ecosystems, and our increased realization of the "intimate connections" between ourselves and the ecologies in which we live, science can no longer ignore that it now has a new, if unspoken, mandate. Lubchenco suggested that the new contract needs to "more adequately address the problems of the coming century than does our current scientific enterprise."[16] She argued that the new contract must be predicated on three assumptions. The new contract would assume that scientists should:

- Address the most urgent needs of society in proportion to their importance
- Communicate their knowledge and understanding widely in order to inform decisions of individuals and institutions
- Exercise good judgment, wisdom, and humility

There is that word "humility" again.

Lubchenco also said that "the contract should recognize the extent of human domination of the planet. It should express a commitment to harness the full power of the scientific enterprise in discovering new knowledge, in communicating existing and new understanding to the public and to policy makers, and in helping society move toward a more sustainable biosphere."[17]

Lubchenco's call for a new social contract is a challenge to radically transform the scientific community as we enter the twenty-first century. The scientific community is called to emphasize the "pursuit of knowledge about how the world works" over manipulating pieces of nature for purely human benefit, especially when such manipulations place additional burdens on the planet. The scientific community is asked to emphasize serving the public with wisdom and humility as opposed to serving narrow economic interests. The scientific community should reorder its priorities to "investigate more complex, interdisciplinary problems that span multiple spatial and temporal scales."[18]

In the years since Lubchenco issued her challenge to the scientific community, not much has changed. Why not? Does this new vision *not* constitute good science?

What Is Good Science?

The industrialization of science hardly began with Vannevar Bush or World War II. The foundation for a science that evaluates its success in terms of the technological innovations it produces has deep roots in Western culture, reaching back at least to the sixteenth and seventeenth centuries. The central dogma behind industrial science is rooted in the mathematics-based science of René Descartes, who articulated his philosophy of science in *Meditations,* published in 1641. Descartes believed that one could, and must, separate the thinking mind (or subject) from the material world (or object). By doing so, he believed one could establish objective certainty, wholly determinable and free of any subjective judgment. It was on this basis that Descartes could speak of material reality in strictly mechanical terms. His belief formed the basis of the "disinterested" sciences that produced the knowledge and the technologies, as well as the culture that made industrial science possible.

Descartes' description of the world as a mechanistic "object" represented an emerging culture at the time. Francis Bacon, a contemporary who espoused this same mechanistic philosophy, promoted the idea that nature could be controlled and manipulated for the exclusive benefit of humans. It was Bacon who first proposed the idea that it was our responsibility to "bend nature to our will." No longer was nature a teacher to whose ways we must conform; nature was a passive object that we must manipulate for our own benefit. Casting nature as an objective reality separate from us, and promoting the belief that nature could be controlled and dominated for our benefit, laid the foundation for the modern industrialization of science.

At the time even conservationists adopted Bacon's point of view. William Derham, a student of Bacon's, declared that we can "penetrate into the bowels of the earth, descend to the bottom of the deep, travel to the farthest regions of this world, to acquire wealth, to increase our knowledge, or even only to please our eye and fancy."[19] Derham even described how we should conduct research to achieve those ends: "Let us cast our eyes here and there, let us ransack all the globe, let us with the greatest accuracy inspect every part thereof, search out the inmost secrets of any of the creatures, let us examine them with all our gauges, measure them with our nicest rules, pry into them with all our microscopes."[20]

Descartes' worldview has, of course, been largely discredited, although the culture of modern science seldom acknowledges it. Descartes' assertion that it is possible to separate the thinking mind from the material world has been invalidated in philosophy by both existentialists and phenomenologists, and in science by physicists, following the discovery of quantum theory and the theory of relativity. In philosophy and physics that transformation is essentially complete, and in the field of biology it is just under way. Although the basic concepts that underlie industrial science have largely been abandoned, the segment of science engaged in technological innovation appears to still be largely unaffected by that transformation.

We now know that mass is a form of energy, and particles are not like tiny billiard balls but are more like bundles of energy that are constantly changing. We now know that organisms are not wholly determined by their genes, but by complex interactions within and among organisms, and between organisms and their environment.[21] Yet we still continue to develop technological innovations as if the world consisted of static, linear, isolated, determinable functions.

Perhaps the reason that it is so difficult for us to translate our scientific knowledge into practice is that our new knowledge about how the world works seems contrary to our ordinary experience. Our situation is not unlike that facing Copernicus in the sixteenth century. Copernicus had the difficult task of convincing his contemporaries that the Earth revolved around the sun, contrary to their everyday experience, which seemed to suggest that the sun moved around the Earth. We have the difficult task of convincing our contemporaries that we are plain members of the biotic community, when everyday experience seems to suggest that we are in charge.

In the interest of good science, we must continue to explore how the world works and adapt our technological innovations to those discoveries. Basic science is not simply the "science capital" that drives innovation, but the essential framework that determines the appropriateness of the innovations we pursue. Adapting our technological innovations to the best information that basic science can provide is particularly important when innovations have the potential to cause irreversible harm.

An Alternative Epistemology

All of this could be dismissed as so much philosophical rhetoric were it not for the fact that the way we *perceive* the world has profound effects on the way we *relate* to the world, and therefore on how we act upon the world.

David Abram put it succinctly: "Ecologically considered, it is not primarily our verbal statements that are 'true' or 'false,' but rather the kind of relations that we sustain with the rest of nature. . . . A civilization that relentlessly destroys the living land it inhabits is not well acquainted with *truth,* regardless of how many supposed facts it has amassed regarding the calculable properties of its world."[22]

What is scientifically true or false is not the facts we utter, but how we live in the world. Adopting a way of knowing that assumes we can act upon the world in which we live without consequences, separates us from nature, and makes us arrogant can have dire outcomes, not only for ourselves but for all the organisms in the biotic community for all generations. Living truthfully, in an ecological sense, is one of the most important decisions we all make. But how do we *know* what it means to live truthfully in an ecological sense?

Insights from the work of Michael Polanyi, a twentieth-century Hungarian physicist/philosopher, are useful for rethinking the epistemological paradigm for science for the twenty-first century.[23–26] Polanyi, who has written extensively on the epistemology of science, provides four key components of sound science:

Indwelling. Contrary to the objectivist science of Descartes, Polanyi argues that it is never possible to separate the knower from the known. We always indwell what we know. Such indwelling is not to be confused with subjectivism, however. Subjectivism and objectivism are both victims of the same fallacy. Objectivism assumes the knower can separate himself from what he experiences *externally* and therefore can establish certitude, while subjectivism assumes that the knower can separate himself from what he experiences *internally* and therefore can establish certitude. Both ignore the fact that no knowledge exists apart from the participation of the knowing person (the subjective side) in the knowing target (the objective side).

The only way we can know anything is by dwelling in the clues that point to a meaning we are struggling to understand. This is true of all knowing, whether one is struggling to understand the meaning of a black hole or the most commonly accepted mathematical formula, such as 2 + 2 = 4. Even the most explicit scientific data become knowledge only as the knower dwells in the data to understand its meaning. Apart from the participation of the knower, the data only exist as markings on a piece of paper.

All knowledge contains three poles. All knowledge is an activity that contains three poles: the knower, our subsidiary awareness (a multitude of our experiences, beliefs, memories, and sensory operations), and our focal awareness (the focus of our attention—that which we are striving to understand). All knowledge thus exists in a from-to relationship.

Given the threefold nature of the knowing process, knowledge can never be precise information. Knowledge is always a skillful act performed by the knower in which the knower is perpetually relying on what she tacitly holds to be true in order to attend to what she is struggling to understand. This means we always live in the tension between what we are and what we are seeking to understand.

Discovery. We are in a constant state of discovery. All sentient beings are inclined to struggle continually for more coherent and comprehensive integrations of meaning and satisfying interpretations of reality. The knowing process, therefore, is not a mechanical accumulation of exact, precise findings, but a heuristic enterprise that includes many false starts and many surprises.

For Polanyi, this means there is no such thing as dispassionate, value-free inquiry. Our inclination to constantly find new integrations of meaning is driven by passion, and that passion is always shaped to some extent by our tacit awareness. Einstein was convinced that the theory of relativity was correct long before he could produce scientific evidence to substantiate his conviction. His passion to discover new integrations of meaning rather than accumulating objective facts led to his discovery.

Commitment and risk. The knowing process, according to Polanyi, always begins as an act of faith. Since truth can never be established independently of the knower, the knower always has to begin with certain assumptions —that words have meaning, that the scientific method is reliable, and the truth we seek to discover exists.

Thus, all knowledge involves risk, which Polanyi describes as an unavoidable tension between our conviction that we know something and our awareness that we may be mistaken. Given this tension, we cannot escape personal vulnerability in the knowing process. Driven by passion to constantly discover higher integrations of meaning, we state our findings, despite the hazards involved. There is no way that an outside observer can compare another person's knowledge of the truth with the truth itself; he can only compare it with his own knowledge of it.

Our dependence on the perceptions of others to validate our own conclusions mandates the need for a scientific community—or what Polanyi liked to call "the society of explorers." Because we all act out of our own tacit awareness, which is by definition personal, we cannot escape our own personal histories and biases any more than we can crawl out of our own skins. There is no way that we can verify the "truth" of our perceptions without subjecting them to the perceptions of others who are focused on the same knowledge we are trying to understand. This makes a "community" of scientists indispensable to good science and humility essential to the scientific enterprise.

Implications for Good Science

Polanyi's analysis has important practical implications for the way we do science. According to Polanyi, claiming to be objective in science can be a dangerous illusion because it impedes scientific progress and emphasizes observational accuracy at the expense of understanding subject matter.[27] Once scientists have convinced themselves that a phenomenon is an irrefutable fact, they will no longer explore its veracity; thus, they will deprive the scientific community and society of any potential benefits derived from further exploration. The effort to establish irrefutable facts focuses science on quantitative analysis at the expense of higher levels of understanding that could be more beneficial to society in the long run.

Therefore, understanding *why* a pest is a pest could lead to more effective pest management than simply inventing a pesticide that can kill a measurably larger number of target pests. Attending to the complex set of factors that make farms profitable or not might help farmers more than inventing yet another technology to increase the yield of a single crop. While the latter is infinitely more quantifiable, it is less likely to help farmers understand the "truth" of the condition of their farms.

Polanyi's concept of "indwelling" invites the knower to become personally involved in what he is struggling to understand, because indwelling is essential to achieving real meaning. In fact, the detached knowing inherent in Cartesian epistemology, together with its attention to particulars at the expense of integration, prevents us from achieving real understanding and alienates us from the thing we are trying to understand. We understand things not by looking at them but by dwelling in them. The "belief that, since particulars are more tangible, their knowledge offers a true conception of things, is fundamentally mistaken," writes Polanyi.[28] Science that recognizes the importance of indwelling and integration in all knowledge might be better equipped to tackle some of the complex issues facing us in this ecological era.

Adopting Polanyi's approach could affect how science is carried out. Instead of focusing on the invention of a particular technology to be transferred to farmers, scientists might dwell in the world of farmers to gain a fuller understanding of the implications of the technology for farmers, farms, and the social and biotic communities in which farms exist.

Polanyi's way of knowing requires that scientists be free, within the bounds of professional standards. What makes freedom necessary in good science is the unspecifiability inherent in all discoveries. Any master plan for science would stifle discovery. The very act of developing a specific set of objectives and directing how science is to achieve them prevents science from following a free and consensual process. Good science is not likely to result from a prescription. Since it is the nature of science to pursue what no one yet knows, any effort to direct science ends up destroying science.

Adopting Polanyi's epistemological posture reduces the likelihood of using science to defend a position one had already adopted. Instead of using science to persuade farmers to adopt what we have invented, we might use science to revisit current systems of farming and explore alternatives.

- Because a community of scientists is essential to good science— owing to the vulnerability of our personal knowledge—any proprietary information in the knowing process is by definition bad science. All of our findings, arrived at through the process of knowing, which is grounded in our own tacit awareness, must be submitted to others who are likewise struggling to understand similar phenomena.

Thus, any science claiming validity that has not been scrutinized by a community of independent scientists exploring similar data cannot be considered good science.

- Because we always live in the tension between our convictions that we know something and our realization that we could be wrong, humility is essential to good science.

- The nature of sentient beings is to continually struggle for more coherent and comprehensive integrations of meaning. Any science that limits its investigations to linear, reductionist observations at the expense of struggling to understand the more complex, interdependent realities of which these observations are a part cannot be called good science. Despite all the technological innovations that surround us, our world is still a living, vibrant, biotic, and constantly changing community. Good science tries to make that world more transparent to our experience.

Of Science and Conversation

The environment in which we live exists only by virtue of millions of organisms modifying their environment out of the bits and pieces available to them. In the course of this activity, they create challenges and opportunities for those other species that share their space in an ecosystem.[29] The most appropriate science in such a world should not lead us to detach ourselves from this community in the interest of some kind of supposed precise information. Appropriate science would not oversimplify the complexity of the biotic community, nor presume we can know all we need to know to proceed with our technological innovations with impunity. The most appropriate science would be one that invites us into conversation with that community in all its complexity.

Stephen Talbott suggests guidelines we might use for such a science of conversation.[30] First, every technique we use, industrial process we initiate, and technology we introduce should be "a question put to nature." With each of our innovations, we are trying to remedy some ignorance, and for precisely that reason we should act with caution and humility. Thus, we should never introduce a technology as an answer to a problem, but as a question put to nature to ascertain its appropriateness.

Second, in a conversation we are always to some extent "compensating for past inadequacies." So part of any conversation involves an attempt to heal what we have harmed in prior conversations. It is always better to admit this at the outset. Ignoring the harm we have done in the past will likely lead to similar or even worse errors in the present. Part of the task of good science, then, is to learn how to continually enhance the health of the biotic community as we converse with it. And, as Aldo Leopold reminded us, health, in this context, is the capacity of the biotic community to renew itself.[31] Our task is not to "save" the environment, nor to preserve things as they are (neither of which is possible), but to enhance environmental capacity for renewal.

Third, in a conversation there is never any single right or wrong response. This is where creativity comes in. The alternatives that exist depend in large part on the alternatives we encourage. Good science is inventive. Declaring that there is only one way to feed the world is bad science.

Fourth, conversation always takes place in the particular. We cannot have a conversation with an abstraction. We can only have conversations with particular individuals. We cannot reasonably save a species, we can only engage in the work of restoring a particular habitat of a particular species. We cannot reasonably feed the world, we can only engage in activities that improve the food security of particular villages or communities.

Conversation is a useful metaphor for describing good science and good soil management, although the science of the industrial world has been a monologue rather than a dialogue. *We* decide what technological innovations to introduce, based on what we believe will enrich *us* without regard for the impact our innovations will have on the larger biotic community. In introducing innovations, we assume we know all we need to know to proceed without caution. We behave as if the biotic community belongs to *us,* rather than entertaining the possibility that together with all other organisms, we belong to the biotic community. Nothing that we now know about the workings of the biotic community justifies continuing down that path.

Good science in the future should spend more resources mapping nature's interconnections and not treat organisms like arbitrary collections of interchangeable parts. It should ensure the future productivity of agriculture by learning to understand the complex relationships among organisms and between organisms and the environment, and it should abandon the effort to invent new technologies to address singular production problems or singular pest problems.

In this regard, good science also is local. As David Abram reminds us, "We can know the needs of any particular region only by participating in its specificity—by becoming familiar with its cycles and styles, awake and attentive to its other inhabitants."[32] That suggests that good science is more likely to be conducted in the context of local cultures and local ecologies, rather than in some abstract, universal global community.

And Then What?
Attending to the Context of Our Innovations

In the domain of emergence, the assumption is made that both actual systems as well as models operate by selection from immense space and variability of the world of the possible, and in carrying out this selection, new and unanticipated properties emerge. . . . Emergence leads to novelties. . . . Nature yields at every level novel structures and behaviors selected from the huge domain of the possible by pruning, which extracts the actual from the possible. The pruning rules are the least understood aspect of this approach to emergence, and understanding them will be a major feature of the science of the future.[1]
—Harold J. Morowitz

David Hurd, former CEO of the Principal Financial Group, told an audience that, as the head of his company, he had learned to insist on an important procedure. Whenever anyone in his company suggested any kind of innovation, he would ask, seven times, "And then what?" This simple exercise, he contended, saved his company from many unintended negative consequences that might otherwise have caused the company significant losses.[2]

From a pragmatic perspective, Hurd's caution is an appeal to common sense. We should try to foresee as many of the unanticipated consequences of our actions as possible before we engage in them. However, Hurd's pragmatic management strategy also is consistent with recent scientific insights about the complex, dynamic, and unpredictable nature of the world in which we live.

Presented at Iowa State University as part of the Department of Chemical Engineering's 2002–2003 Seminar Series, January 16, 2003.

The New Science of Caution

Hurd's strategy also corresponds with recent observations by physicists who suggest that if we took *both* Laws of Thermodynamics seriously, we might rethink the way we introduce technologies into the universe.[3] The first Law of Thermodynamics stipulates that the amount of energy in the universe is constant: it can neither be created nor destroyed. The second law stipulates that entropy increases irreversibly in all processes. Jack Hokikian contends that these two laws affect all physical, social, environmental, economic, and intellectual processes. He asserts that humanity would be better served if we devoted more of our energy to the development of knowledge and attitudes that help us understand and address the problems of the emerging world in which we live: "The poor and hungry of the world do not need complex and high-entropic devices, such as computers, which give them information about food. They need low-entropic food. The homeless and the destitute of the world do not need sophisticated Web sites that show them beautiful pictures of expensive homes. They need shelter."[4]

Based on insights reaching back at least to Descartes, Newton, and Galileo, we have come to view the world as a static, mechanical, and predictable system. Nature, we assumed, existed in a state of equilibrium and functioned much like a clock. It was believed that we could predict nature, and our interventions in it, with certainty. Human intervention in nature for the sole benefit of the human species was morally mandated. Pursuing technological innovation to replace or improve upon natural occurrences came to be regarded as the proper role of the human species.

Today we understand that nature is anything but clocklike. With each stage of the evolutionary process, things become more complex and more dynamic, and emerge with increasing speed. Life first appeared on our planet as single-celled creatures about 4 billion years ago. It took almost 2 billion years before nuclei began to appear in cells. It only took a few hundred million years for multicellular organisms to emerge. Then things really start to speed up. An explosion of diversity occurred a few hundred million years later. Within a couple of hundred million years of the present day, large plants and complex animals were already on the scene. Hominids evolved from the great apes roughly 5 or 6 million years ago.

Then a species emerged about 35,000 years ago that was not only artistic, as attested to by cave paintings, but also had developed capacities to dramatically change its environment and to rationalize its behavior. Harold Morowitz traces the emergence of everything through twenty-eight steps, from the big bang to the spiritual, with the spiritual phase enabling us to understand all the previous stages of emergence.[5]

In the context of a dynamic, emerging world, David Hurd's pragmatic management protocol makes good business sense and also suggests a vital way of living in the world. Asking "and then what?" at least seven times recognizes that we can never introduce innovations into the world without setting in motion a series of related consequences rarely apparent at the time or place of introduction. The future welfare of the human species may therefore hinge on such cautionary action. Asking "and then what?" seems especially prudent as we contemplate introducing a new generation of technologies that are self-replicating and easily accessible. Thoughtful scientists are, in fact, now calling for exactly such restraint.[6]

Of Arts and Sciences

Literary artists have, of course, urged such caution for millennia. Ancient as well as modern writings are replete with warnings about the indiscriminate introduction of new technologies unaccompanied by the exercise of appropriate wisdom. Greek mythology recounts the story of Daedalus, "the cunning one," who fashioned wings out of feathers and wax so that he and his son, Icarus, could escape from the labyrinth that he himself had constructed for King Minos, and within which the king later imprisoned him. Before launching their flight with the newly invented wings, Daedalus warned his son to fly "the middle way"—not too high, lest the heat of the sun melt the wax in his wings, but not too low, lest the tides of the sea catch him. Daedalus flew the middle way and escaped to safety, but Icarus became intoxicated with his new power, flew too near the sun, and plunged to his death. New technology can be useful—it can even save us from previous technologies—but without appropriate caution, it can destroy us.

The ancient Hebrews were even more explicit in their warnings. The Garden of Eden story in the book of Genesis portrays a bit of Hebrew mythology about how people should live in creation: *on creation's terms*. If they succumb to temptation and arrogantly assume they know better (the Tree of Knowledge) than the ecology of nature (the Tree of Life) how the garden should be managed, then they will experience one curse after another and eventually be expelled from creation's fecundity.

Many similar literary examples are familiar to us. The tale of the sorcerer and the servant who misuses his master's magic has been told in many forms. Johann Wolfgang von Goethe captured the story in a powerful poem entitled "The Magician's Assistant" in the late eighteenth century. In the late twentieth century, Nancy Willard created a poem for children titled "The Sorcerer's Apprentice."[7] This tale depicts a wise magician who has the power to make dramatic changes in his environment. The servant or apprentice releases these powers indiscriminately, causing great destruction. The lesson, as Willard suggests, is that masters learn by their failures and discover that unnatural changes must be undertaken with care. Fatal consequences can ensue from any lapse in common sense.[8] In her nineteenth-century novel, *Frankenstein,* Mary Shelley spins a similar cautionary tale.

We don't have to believe in scary scenarios about runaway new technologies to comprehend the need to use caution when introducing novelties into the universe. On-the-ground examples of ecological backlash from technologies we have already released into the environment provide ample rationale for adopting Hurd's precautionary approach to introducing novelties into the universe.

Ecological Failures

Barry Commoner has outlined examples of ecological failures that have resulted from technological innovations we have introduced.[9] Irrigation projects, for example, have resulted in dramatic disease outbreaks, geophysical changes, and a *reduction* of agricultural potential. Because irrigation systems increase the amount of standing water near villages and work areas, they also increase the prevalence of life-threatening, waterborne diseases such as malaria. Waterlogging and salinity problems associated with irrigation have rendered soil unusable for food production. Similarly, synthetic pesticides introduced to control agricultural pests *increased* pest problems as resistance increased and natural predators were eliminated.

Ecological failures associated with the introduction of novel technologies were already well understood in the late 1950s and early 1960s. Yet we remain reluctant to employ adequate ecological screens to determine whether a new technology can be released into the environment without causing ecological harm.

Today we can, of course, readily add many more ecological failures to Commoner's list. Fossil-fuel burning has exacerbated global warming, and chlorofluorocarbons have depleted the stratospheric ozone layer, exposing life on Earth to harmful ultraviolet radiation. Synthetic chemicals likely interfere with the reproductive process of many animals as well as the developmental processes of humans, especially children. Use of PCBs and DDT from decades ago continues to threaten the health of numerous organisms. Nuclear power has exposed human societies to many incalculable risks and incurred numerous unanticipated costs. A source of energy thought to be "too cheap to meter" turned out to be too expensive to use.[10] Nuclear energy, in fact, serves as a chilling example of our failure to ask "and then what?" before introducing a technology into the environment. No one even addressed the problem of decommissioning nuclear power plants before they were constructed. "The International Atomic Energy Agency did not hold its first meeting on decommissioning until 1973, almost twenty years after the first reactor was built."[11]

Commoner reminds us that all of the innovations introduced into international communities in the 1950s and 1960s were thought to be "technological advances" that would spur international development and certainly were not expected to cause harm. But as it turned out they were "powerful intrusions on large-scale geophysical and ecological systems" that often ended up causing more harm than good.[12]

Accidents vs. Design Failures

Commoner asserts that these ecological failures were *not* the result of random accidents but were inherent in the way modern science and technologies are conducted. We fail to anticipate the unintended consequences of our technological innovations because our sciences have been "dominated by an intensely reductionist approach" and that such an approach is "a poor guide to the understanding of those realms of nature which are stressed by modern technology."[13]

Reductionism, Commoner argues, leads us to believe that "the most fruitful way to understand life is to discover a specific molecular event" rather than to understand the "biology of natural systems." It leads us to explore new ways to use nitrogen but to think little about the "fundamental biology of soil nitrogen."[14] Reductionism leads to questions about a new detergent's washing properties, but not its impact on aquatic organisms. Reductionism, in other words, fails to ask, "And then what?"

The failure of reductionism has, of course, been acknowledged in many fields. Richard Levins and Cynthia Lopez point out that while reductionist science has given us many technologies to attack diseases, it has fallen far short in promoting human health. The fundamental reason is as follows: "It is at the level of complex interactions that our science has been least successful. Fragmentation of knowledge prevents us from seeing the whole, and reductionist methodologies encourage explanations within the confines of single disciplines, assigning relative weights to 'factors' rather than elucidating their interactions."[15]

Reductionism is, of course, not an evil science. We need to reduce complex phenomena into fragments to understand how the world works. We get into trouble when we use those bits of information to design solutions to problems without considering the context of the dynamic, emerging world of which those bits are merely ingredients. Reducing atoms to nuclei, which led to the discovery of nuclear fission and nuclear fusion, was not the problem; using the knowledge to convert mass into energy was problematic because we were able to alleviate energy shortages without considering the disorder (the entropy) that the introduction of the technology into the environment would cause. Our failure to attend to the *context* of our innovations, *not* the potential for innovation produced by reductionist science, is what causes unanticipated ecological failures.

It is as if we believed that we could "step out of" our ecological neighborhoods —that we could ignore Mother Nature.[16] We largely ignore the context into which we introduce our innovations. We assume that the way a particular technology works to solve a particular problem—like killing a target pest (the part)—has little to do with the emergent world in which the pest lives (the whole). What is particularly unsettling is that we continue to behave this way as we contemplate introducing a new generation of powerful, self-replicating technologies. We focus almost exclusively on the solution that a particular technology might bring to a problem and, at best, assume that strict regulatory measures will prevent the technology from producing unintended consequences. The Second Law of Thermodynamics challenges that assumption.

An Alternative Approach

Ironically, another approach to problem-solving exists that we seldom consider, an approach that promises more sustainable, long-term results. Joe

Lewis outlines this approach with respect to pest management.[17] In industrial agriculture, we address pest problems by introducing technologies to get rid of the pest rather than trying to understand the system failure that allows the pest to emerge. And it hasn't worked! Instead of asking, "How do I get rid of the pest?" he suggests we should ask, "Why is the pest a pest?" According to Lewis, "application of external corrective actions into a system can be effective only for short-term relief. Long-term, sustainable solutions must be achieved through restructuring the system. . . . The foundations for pest management in agricultural systems should be an understanding and shoring up of the full composite of inherent plant defenses, plant mixtures, soil, natural enemies, and other components of the system. . . . The use of pesticides and other 'treat-the-symptoms' approaches are unsustainable and should be the last rather than the first line of defense."[18]

Lewis contends that this principle of pest management holds true for molecular biology as well as toxic chemicals. Approaches that subscribe to the principles outlined by Lewis, such as the green chemistry movement, take a fundamentally different approach.[19] Traditionally, we have limited exposure, by regulating the use, handling, and disposal of chemicals, an approach that has largely failed to protect the environment. Green chemistry attempts to minimize hazard by designing or selecting chemicals that are benign. It is a way of taking the "And then what?" question seriously.

Green chemistry made several other interesting discoveries from studying natural systems. Nature uses very few chemicals to accomplish a host of tasks. In contrast, we use a host of chemicals to accomplish a few tasks. Similarly, while we were busy with mechanical engineering, we failed to notice that plants had already mastered organic chemistry.

The biomimicry movement is another example of solving problems by redesigning the system rather than introducing an external counterforce. Popularized by physicist Janine Benyus, the governing principle is that nature, by virtue of its long evolutionary journey, has already solved most of the problems we are grappling with. Consequently, biomimicry suggests that we explore nature as a reservoir of solutions to be discovered, rather than a series of defects to be corrected.[20]

Since life's emergence on this planet some 4 billion years ago, nature has solved a lot of problems by extracting the "actual from the possible." As

Morowitz reminds us, "nature yields at every level novel structures and behaviors selected from the huge domain of the possible by pruning."[21] Since nature has done this pruning, solutions to many of the problems we want to solve are already available.

Forests serve as a permaculture design of edible landscapes using many-storied cropping systems. What potential might that have for designing agriculture systems that depend less on exogenous inputs and disrupt natural systems less? Marshes serve as models for constructing wetlands that function as waste-treatment facilities while providing refuges for wildlife. Providing habitat for wildlife can provide free ecosystem services to agriculture; more pollinators come to mind. As the Land Institute has demonstrated, the prairie serves as a model for perennial cropping systems that are more resilient, ecologically restorative, and economically profitable than annual monocropping systems that hardly mimic nature at all.

These are all ways of redesigning systems to potentially *eliminate* problems rather than introducing external counterforces into systems in an effort to *solve* problems. Redesigning systems to mimic nature represents one way, and perhaps the best way, of asking "And then what?" before introducing a novel technology. With respect to agriculture, Wendell Berry counseled such an approach more than a decade ago:

> An agriculture using nature, including human nature, as its measure would approach the world in the manner of a conversationalist. It would not impose its vision and its demands upon a world that it conceives of as a stockpile of raw material, inert and indifferent to any use that may be made of it. It would not proceed directly or soon to some supposedly ideal state of things. It *would* proceed directly and soon to serious thought about our condition and our predicament. On all farms, farmers would undertake to know responsibly where they are and to "consult the genius of the place." They would ask what nature would be doing there if no one were farming there. They would ask what nature would permit them to do there, and what they could do there with the least harm to the place and to their natural and human neighbors. And they would ask what nature would *help* them do there. And after each asking, knowing that nature will respond, they would attend carefully to her response.[22]

The Precautionary Principle

Asking "And then what?" before introducing a novel technology is another way of saying "better safe than sorry," which is the heart of the "precautionary principle." This principle suggests a framework for decision-making when we wish to introduce a new technology and its potential impact on the environment is uncertain. Under the precautionary principle, we should act to protect the environment *before* scientific proof of harm can be established. Green chemistry and biomimicry are proactive ways of applying the precautionary principle. In other words, we can reduce the uncertainty surrounding the introduction of a technology by removing the intrinsic hazard if we stick to technologies that have already been selected by nature. This approach reduces or eliminates the need for regulation and the associated costs of regulation.[23] That is perhaps the most productive way of asking "And then what?"

But does that mean we can never use a technology that hasn't been "pruned" by nature? The short answer is that for the foreseeable future *we will.* Until we conduct more research focused on approaches similar to green chemistry and biomimicry, we have to continue introducing technologies that did not evolve with nature. What benchmarks might we then use to select appropriate technologies that will not produce unacceptable, unintended consequences?

A few years ago I wrote an essay wrestling with this question as it related to the introduction of technologies in agriculture. I proposed four principles that could be applied to all technologies:[24]

- If the *magnitude* of potential harm is limited, we might say yes to the technology. If the effect of the introduction of a material or practice could last for generations, if it doesn't disappear in one generation, we should say no.
- If the *geography* of the potential harm from the technology is limited, we might say yes to the technology. The larger the area affected by the introduction of a material or practice, the more safeguards we must use. For example, if the technology to be introduced is airborne, waterborne, bioaccumulative, or in other ways ubiquitous to the environment, we should say no.
- If the *biology* of the potential harm is limited, we might say yes to the

technology. Because all species in a biotic community have coevolved, we consider the welfare of all affected species. If the introduction of a material or practice potentially threatens the integrity or capacity for renewal of the biotic community, we must say no.

- If the potential *social cost* of the technology is limited, we might say yes. Often we say yes to a new material or practice because the short-term economic gain is attractive, or because of potential economic gains for one sector of society. But rarely are these gains weighed against the long-term economic costs. If the introduction of a technology compromises future economic well-being or is achieved in one sector of society at the expense of another sector, we should say no.

Unfortunately such precautions are seldom considered; indeed, some sectors of our society are hostile toward them. We should be asking "And then what?" at least seven times before we proceed much further. And we should probably all hope that the next stage of emergence on our planet is the emergence of wisdom within the human species!

Food as Relationship

What would happen, for example, if we were to start thinking about food as less of a thing and more of a relationship?[1]
—Michael Pollan

In his classic study of soil fertility, *An Agricultural Testament,* first published in 1940, Sir Albert Howard presented his case for connecting problems with food and health to a failure in soil management. The key to proper soil management, he argued, was "the law of return," which is returning all wastes to the land (preferably properly composted). It was the return of wastes to the land that insured proper levels of humus in the soil. The effect of humus on the crop, and ultimately on human health, he asserted, is "nothing short of profound."[2] Humus is the "well-decomposed part of soil organic matter which holds on to some essential nutrients, storing them for slow release to plants."[3] Our failure to attend to this critical component of soil stewardship, Howard argued, is the source of disease in the soil, plants, animals, and eventually ourselves.

In 1947 Howard published his second classic volume, *The Soil and Health,* in which he warned that the industrialization of agriculture was taking us in the wrong direction. Industrial agriculture, which focuses on "quantity at all costs" by adding artificial fertilizers to the soil (the "NPK mentality"), paid almost no attention to the health of the soil. The lack of attention to managing soil for health, he argued, led to "mining the land," which he considered a "form of banditry."[4] This led Howard to assert "a simple principle" that "underlies the vast accumulation of disease" that affects our world. That principle

A version of this article first appeared in the *Journal of Hunger and Environmental Nutrition* 2–3 (2008): 106–21.

"operates in the soil, the crop, the animal, and ourselves" and "the power of all these four to resist disease appears to be bound up with the circulation of properly synthesized protein in Nature. The proteins are the agencies which confer immunity on plant, animal, and man."[5]

Howard reminds us that nature evolved no means of shielding us from disease, and therefore all of our efforts to develop therapies to ward off diseases are unlikely to keep us healthy. What *did* evolve in nature was the means to produce health-promoting foods from healthy soils that invigorate our immune systems, which can keep us healthy.

Based on these ecological observations, Howard asserted that if we would manage our soils to "build up proteins of the right type," there would be "little disease in soil or crop or livestock, and the foundations of *the preventive medicine of tomorrow* will be laid."[6] Today, of course, we know that a complex set of nutrients and proteins are involved in healthy soil, but the overall principle that Howard proposed is still an interesting health-promoting option to explore. Simply stated, Howard proposed that proper soil fertility that builds appropriate levels of humus in the soil "is the basis of the public health system of the future."[7]

Spending on health care keeps increasing as spending on food decreases, suggesting Howard was right. The proportion of personal income spent on health care for a typical U.S. citizen (when Medicare taxes are included) has increased to 18 percent, while the percent spent on food decreased to 10 percent.[8] Of course, health problems are exacerbated by undernourishment, which often accompanies poverty.

Astonishingly, in the sixty years since Howard made his case for the connections between soil health and human health, very little has been done to test his thesis. A few studies have been conducted to determine whether "organic" foods are more nutritious or health-promoting than "conventional" foods, but we have not explored whether soils with appropriate humus levels have an impact on human health.

Because farms today can obtain organic certification simply by substituting natural inputs for synthetic ones, soil humus levels could be ignored just as easily on an organic farm as on a conventional farm. Given Howard's perspective, I doubt that he would have presumed any beneficial health effects in products from an "organic" farm that ignored humus enrichment. Injecting natural inputs while ignoring the law of return would still yield "artificial" returns. Hence, it is unsurprising when such studies show mixed results.

The truly provocative idea in Howard's work is the notion that the quality of food and health is determined by relationships. Food is not an isolated thing, a commodity composed of a list of ingredients, but part of the ecology in which it is produced.

Food in the Industrial Economy

The soil/food/health connection is not the only relationship we ignore in our modern food system. Our modern industrial culture tends to view food, like the rest of reality, as a collection of fragments (things) rather than a web of relationships. Modern philosophers trace this tendency to the seventeenth-century scientific revolution. René Descartes wanted science to become a "universal mathematics" which, of course, tended to reduce reality to measurable *things* and ignored dynamic *relationships*. It should not be surprising that we have reduced our understanding of healthy food to an ingredient list.

Today we are discovering the dysfunctional aspects of our tendency to reduce food to a thing rather than appreciating it as a relationship. The constant stream of (sometimes conflicting) recommendations suggesting that we will all be healthy if we eat a sufficient amount of a particular ingredient (remember oat bran?) is but one example of this disconnect with nature. Our failure to explore intertwined relationships between soil health and human health is another example of a skewed food culture.

Our tendency to neglect relationships with respect to food has led us to ignore many of the unsustainable social, ecological, and economic components of our modern food system. Our food system exists within the industrial economy, which operates as if it were a bubble floating in space with unlimited natural resources entering the bubble to fuel the economic activities and unlimited sinks in nature to absorb wastes.

Herman E. Daly has long argued that this is the basic flaw in the industrial economy. He has warned that our human economies are, in fact, *subsystems* of larger ecosystems and must function within ecosystem constraints.[9] The natural resources that have fueled our food and agriculture systems are now in a state of depletion, and nature's sinks are saturated. The bubble will soon deflate. There are at least four natural resources that have fueled our industrial food system that are now in steep decline.

Most of the *energy* that is used to produce and process our food comes from fossil fuels.[10] The nitrogen used for fertilizer is derived from natural gas. Phosphorus and potash are mined, processed, and transported to farms using petroleum-based energy. Pesticides are manufactured from petroleum resources. Farm equipment is manufactured and operated with petroleum energy.

Furthermore, cheap energy in the form of fossil fuels offers a comparative advantage to large, concentrated monocultures that are energy-intensive. Cheap energy is then used to ship commodities to similarly large concentrated processing facilities, where modern food processing is equally dependent on fossil energy. Having centralized the production and processing of most of our food, it also must then be shipped thousands of miles using petroleum energy to reach the end customer.

Our modern food system may be labor-efficient, but it is one of the least energy-efficient food systems known. Anthropologist Ernest Schusky reminds us that from an energy-efficiency perspective, hunting and gathering weren't such bad ways to feed ourselves.[11] We simply gathered food, prepared it, and ate it.

Approximately 10,000 years ago, with the advent of the Neolithic revolution, we began domesticating plants and animals. While such agricultural practices were much less energy-efficient than hunting and gathering, they allowed our ancestors to live in settled societies instead of hunting a region's resources to depletion and then moving on.

The more significant shift in our food system occurred much later. Around 1930 we embarked on a new era of agriculture that Schusky calls the "neocaloric era" because it is based almost entirely on "old calories," namely fossil fuels. The defining characteristic of our modern food system is that it replaced human and animal energy with fossil-fuel energy. From an energy-efficiency standpoint, it is the least effective food system ever designed. The industrialized food system consumes more energy than it produces. Schusky cites one egregious example: it takes "about 2200 calories of fossil energy in order to produce a one-calorie can of diet soda," which he suggests is "downright embarrassing to human intelligence."[12]

Fossil fuels are indeed old calories, and they are now being rapidly depleted. Most independent scholars agree that we either have already reached peak oil production or will do so shortly. The era of cheap energy is over, and the end of cheap energy will force us to begin redesigning our food economy as a subsystem of the ecosystem.

In the ecology of nature, species multiply in relationship to the energy available to sustain them. If temporary energy availability causes a population of species to overproduce, eventually natural processes restore its balance with other species in the biotic community. Our species is unlikely to be exempt from this law of ecology.

Of course, alternatives to fossil fuel energy are available, such as wind, solar, and biofuels. But our industrial economy was created on a platform of stored, concentrated energy that produced a very favorable energy-profit ratio—the amount of energy created compared to the amount of energy expended to make it available. Alternative energy, on the other hand, is based entirely on current, dispersed energy that has a much lower energy-profit ratio. The primary sources of stored, concentrated energy are coal, oil, and natural gas; other sources of stored, concentrated energy are not likely to be available on the planet. Consequently, systems that depend on cheap energy are not likely to fare well in the future. The depletion of fossil-fuel resources will require that we revert to alternative fuels to produce, process, and deliver our food, and that we transition to a new energy system. The truly challenging energy transition that we face is moving from an energy-*input* system to an energy-*exchange* system.[13,14]

A second natural resource that has fueled our industrial food system over the past century is a relatively *stable climate.* We often mistakenly attribute industrial agriculture's "production miracle" of the past century entirely to the development of new production technologies. In fact, our robust production was due at least as much to unusually favorable climate conditions as to technology. Because such stable climates are atypical, this temporary condition is limited (and fleeting).

A National Academy of Sciences Panel on Climatic Variation reported in 1975 that "our present [stable] climate is in fact highly abnormal."[15] The report called attention to the fact that "the global patterns of food production and population that have evolved are implicitly dependent on the climate of the present century."

Climate change is likely to be particularly harsh on our industrial farming systems. While it is impossible to predict exactly how climate change will affect agricultural production in the near term,[16] most climatologists agree that we can anticipate greater climate fluctuations, including "extremes of precipitation, both droughts and floods."[17] Such instability can be especially devastating for the highly specialized, genetically uniform, monoculture systems characteristic of industrial agriculture.

A third natural resource that will challenge the limits of our modern industrial food system is water. Lester Brown points out that while we each require four liters of water to meet our daily liquid needs, given today's industrial agriculture it takes 2,000 liters per day to produce each of our daily food requirements. Agriculture consumes more than 70 percent of our global freshwater resources for irrigation. We use twice the amount of water to supply agricultural irrigation today as we did in the 1960s. We have been drawing down our freshwater resources at an unsustainable rate.

Such water depletion is especially troubling in China, where 80 percent of grain production is dependent on irrigation, and in India, where 60 percent requires irrigation. In some parts of China aquifers are dropping at the rate of ten feet per year, and in India at twenty feet per year. Some farmers in China already are pumping irrigation water from 1,000 feet deep, and in India from 3,000 feet.[18] Water tables in the Ogallala Aquifer, which supplies water for one of every five irrigated acres in the United States, are being overdrawn at the rate of 12 billion cubic meters per year (3.17 trillion gallons). To date, water withdrawals are estimated at 325 billion cubic meters, or the equivalent of eighteen times the annual water flow in the Colorado River.[19] According to some reports, this fossil water bank is now half depleted.[20]

Reduced snow packs in mountainous regions due to climate change will decrease spring runoff, a primary source of irrigation water in many parts of the world, further impairing our food production capacity. This is just one of many examples demonstrating the close interdependence of our natural resources.

A fourth limited natural resource being depleted is soil. Soil, of course, possesses very dynamic properties and has been both accumulating and eroding for millennia.[21] Soil erosion due to human activity has for centuries been a major contributing factor to humankind's failure to maintain civilized societies.[22] However, soil erosion on U.S. cropland overall actually *decreased* by 43 percent between 1982 and 2003, according to the Natural Resources Conservation Service. Erosion rates dropped from an average soil loss of 4.0 tons per acre in 1982 to 2.6 tons per acre in 2003. (Certainly some of this improvement in soil conservation is due to the Conservation Reserve Program, which has taken millions of acres of highly erodible land out of production and seeded it to perennials.) Yet 103 million acres (28 percent of all U.S. cropland) are still eroding above soil-loss tolerance levels.[23]

While soil loss due to erosion contributes significantly to our diminished soil quality, a more troubling aspect of soil loss as we enter a world devoid of cheap energy is the draw-down of much of the remaining soil's "stored fertility," Howard's term for humus-rich soil.[24] Unfortunately, cheap fossil-fuel energy enabled us to increase food production using artificial inputs without attending to soil quality.[25] Having subscribed to the NPK mentality, we ignored the law of return and now are left with soils that are essentially depleted of soil health. And as recent research has reconfirmed, soil health is not likely to be restored without the return of organic inputs in the form of cover crops, manure, and other organic materials.[26]

Toward a Postindustrial Food System

So how shall we now proceed? Can we envision and create a sustainable food system that indefinitely maintains the health of the soil, produces an adequate amount of health-promoting, affordable food, and provides us with the pleasure of good eating, in the face of depleted natural resources? I think we can, but it will require a rather radical transformation of our present food system. And given the potentially devastating impact of long-term climate change, we have a limited amount of time to implement the necessary transformations.

First, we need to transform the way we manage soil on the farm. Although we have not verified Howard's assertion that our own health is tightly linked to humus-rich soil, he was correct that soil properties are all functionally interrelated. Soil is a living, complex web of relationships that, when properly managed, provide enormous benefits.

Because farmers have been indoctrinated to believe that maximizing yields by inserting a few artificial nutrients (the NPK mentality) is an all-purpose solution, and no-till is the silver-bullet solution to cure all soil depletion, they are not prepared to manage soil as a web of relationships. Managing soil as a thing to be manipulated utterly fails to appreciate both the complexity and the possibility inherent in the soil profile.

Soil is "not a thing" but "a web of relationships" always unique to its time and place.[27] Soil, as Hans Jenny described it, is "part of a much larger system that is composed of the upper part of the lithosphere, the lower part of the atmosphere, and a considerable part of the biosphere." The living organisms in the soil then become part of soil formation in relationship to all the other factors, including climate, topography, parent material, time, and nitrogen content. In other words, life in the soil adapts to its place much as other life forms do, such as microbes, vegetation, animal life, and humans.[28] Soil is a dynamic, emergent property.

Managing soil properly is as much art as science and depends on the intimate relationship that the farmer has with the soil. Soil managed as a complex web of relationships, including the use of green manure and livestock manure, can solve many of the production problems that our industrial farming systems attack with costly inputs that seldom address the root of the problem and require excessive energy use.[29]

Approaching pest management from an ecological perspective always involves a web of relationships and has connections with soil health. For example, "problems with soil erosion have resulted in major thrusts in use of winter cover crops and conservation tillage. Preliminary studies indicate that cover crops also serve as bridges/refugia to stabilize natural enemy/pest balances and relay these balances into the crop season."[30]

Other benefits flow from improved soil health. John Reganold and his colleagues have demonstrated that soil managed in accordance with the law of return develops richer topsoil, more than twice the organic matter, more biological activity, and far greater moisture absorption and holding capacity.[31] In short, natural systems management can revitalize soil health, reduce weed and other pest pressures, get farmers off the pesticide treadmill, help conserve precious water resources, and begin the transition from an energy-intensive, industrial farming operation to a self-regulating, self-renewing one.

Such soil management serves as an example of how we can begin to move to an energy system that operates on the basis of energy *exchange* instead of energy *input*. But greater innovation is needed. Nature is a highly efficient energy manager. All of its energy comes from sunlight. Through the process of photosynthesis, carbon is combined with other elements to create molecules that store energy, which is then released through the metabolism of living organisms who exchange energy through a web of relationships.

Bison on the prairie obtained their energy from the grass, which absorbed energy from the soil. The bison deposited their excrement back onto the grass, which provided energy for insects and other organisms, which, in turn, converted it to energy that enriched the soil to produce more grass.

These sorts of energy-exchange systems provide guidance for postindustrial farming systems, but currently very little research is devoted to exploring such energy exchanges on a farm level.

Fortunately a few farmers have already developed such energy-exchange systems and appear to be quite successful in managing their operations with very little fossil-fuel input.[32] Converting more farms to this new energy model will require a major transformation. Our highly specialized, energy-intensive monocultures will need to be converted to complex, highly diversified operations that function on energy-exchange principles. The practicality and multiple benefits of such integrated crops/livestock have been established through research,[33] but further study is needed to explore how to adapt this new model of farming to various climates and ecosystems.

These new farms of the future likely will be smaller than the huge monoculture operations that now dominate the landscape. The new operations will be knowledge-intensive and will require an intimate knowledge of the ecological neighborhoods in which the farm is located. They will need to feature management solutions based in husbandry rather than therapeutic intervention. This does not imply that higher transaction costs are inevitable. Some farmers already have shown that they can manage their farms by these new principles, maintain a modest size, and aggregate their production through marketing networks featuring their own brand, thereby bringing their product into the marketplace as efficiently as do large farms. For example, Organic Valley Family of Farms has more than 1,200 growers and produced in excess of $432 million in annual sales in 2007.[34]

This new "ecosystem management" will require more farmers and a new farmer culture. The notion of "freeing" people from the "drudgery" of farming so that they can move to more interesting jobs in the industrial economy to improve their quality of life no longer fits our new world. The notion that farming is drudgery is still deeply ingrained in our culture. Responding to Wendell Berry's criticism of his glowing analysis of "Our Biotech Future," Freeman Dyson envisions a future in which we will be "liberated from the burdens of subsistence farming" and "science will soon give us a new set of tools, which may bring wealth and freedom." He does not say from where the cheap energy to create and operate those technologies will come.[35]

Ecosystem-sensitive farming will attract a new generation of farmers who are highly skilled in ecology, husbandry, and evolutionary biology, and who seek opportunities to work closely with nature. We can create a new food culture that increases the "wealth of communities," described by Bill McKibben.[36]

This new farming future means that we will need to invest in a new kind of training at all levels of our education system. We should begin now to involve all elementary school children in school gardens, agriculture in the classroom programs, and other learning experiences that engage them in the experience of growing food and the excitement of learning about the web of relationships and energy exchanges that can provide their food for them. Such education truly would "leave no child inside." We also need to introduce more college courses in agroecology and provide internship opportunities for experience-based learning in ecosystems management on real farms.

Whether 40 to 50 million people will be engaged in producing food in our new postindustrial world, as Richard Heinberg suggests,[37] remains to be seen. While the exact number of new farmers needed may be debated, the challenges we face clearly require that innovative, creative, and imaginative students will become farmers.

All of this, of course, raises the specter of cost. Will food be more expensive? If we use the current calculations of cost in our industrial food system, it may well be. But such calculations are deeply flawed. We often are told that we have a "cheap food policy" that is the cornerstone of our quality of life and therefore non-negotiable. But I would argue that we really do not have "cheap food" in our current industrial food economy. There are several flaws in the "cheap food" myth.

While we do spend less of our earned income on food than most other countries, that is not a clear indicator of food costs. Because our earned income also is higher than most other nations, the percentage of disposable income really doesn't tell us much about the true cost of food compared to other nations. A few years ago Chuck Benbrook, the former director of the Board on Agriculture of the National Academy of Sciences, did a quick calculation of the cost of food in various countries using a cost-per-calorie metric. By that calculation, twenty-two countries have cheaper food than we do.[38]

But even that estimate fails to provide us with a true assessment of the cost of our food. A more appropriate indicator would be the cost of food per *nutrient value.* And this is important because many people who live in resource-poor communities only have access to food from convenience stores and liquor stores, since they are among the few business establishments that locate in their communities. These stores mostly handle highly processed food that has very little nutrient value and therefore turns out to be very expensive food.

Furthermore, the price we pay for food at the supermarket counter does not include many of the external costs that are part of our industrial food system. A study by Erin Tegtmeier and Michael Duffy at Iowa State University determined, for example, that if the environmental impacts of crop and livestock production from our current industrial agriculture system were included, the additional cost per cropland hectare would be between $29.44 and $95.68 annually. Those are costs that affect environmental and human health and must be absorbed by the public.[39] A similar study was conducted in Great Britain that showed even higher external costs associated with our industrial farming systems.[40]

An additional "cheap food policy" issue needs to be exposed. We in fact do *not* have a cheap *food* policy. What we have is a cheap *labor* and cheap *raw materials* policy. Our industrial food system acquires its labor and raw materials as cheaply as possible so that more economic value can be added further up the food chain. Farmers on average earn virtually no net income from their farming enterprises. As Ken Meter has pointed out, all of the cash receipts that farmers earn from farming are absorbed by their high production expenses.[41]

Because our new farming future will need to significantly increase investments in human capital to transform from an industrial food system to an ecological food system, this cheap labor/cheap raw materials policy requires scrutiny. As long as this policy dominates our culture, we will have to choose between investing in our farmers and thereby driving up food prices, leaving more resource-poor people without food, or squeezing farmers even more so that resource-poor people can afford to eat. Another way to solve this problem is to pay laborers a living wage so they can afford to buy nutrient-dense foods, and to provide farmers with the necessary resources to create the new food system that can ensure food security for all.

Finally, diversifying our farms and reducing energy inputs means we also have to diversify the market. We need to develop food markets that enable growers to sell products emerging from self-renewing, energy exchange, plant/animal relationships that mimic nature. We can just as easily create a food market that encourages citizens to enjoy food varieties by diversifying what we produce locally as we can by importing kiwi fruit from New Zealand in January.

Our food system will need to become more localized, with more community involvement. Fortunately, emerging trends in the market suggest such innovations are possible. Researchers have suggested practical models for relocalizing the food system that could provide numerous benefits to local communities.[42]

In addition to farmers' markets, community-supported agriculture, and Internet sales, demand is growing for highly differentiated food products among health care institutions, school systems, restaurant chains, and other food-service vendors. These markets demand food with better taste, health and nutritional attributes, positive food stories (e.g., good environmental stewardship, appropriate animal care, knowing where the food comes from), and a trusting relationship that preferably extends back to the farmer who produces the food.

If we can respond to new market demands, develop public policies that put agroecological initiatives on a level playing field with our current industrial food system, and devote at least 30 percent of our public research dollars to researching new production and marketing models, we may create a new food system that meets the challenges of our postindustrial era. It can be a food production system that is more resilient, secure, and energy-efficient, and that provides us with healthier food and more pleasurable eating than what the industrial food system currently offers us.

Along with Richard Heinberg, I too "believe that the deindustrialization of agriculture could be carried out in a way that is not catastrophic."[43]

Is the USDA Accounting for the Costs to Farmers from Contamination Caused by Genetically Engineered Plants?

I would like to thank the chair, Representative Kucinich, the ranking member, Representative Issa, and the members of the subcommittee for this opportunity to speak on this matter which so greatly affects the livelihoods of the U.S. organic producer.

My name is Frederick L. Kirschenmann. I am a professor of religion and philosophy currently serving as a Distinguished Fellow at the Leopold Center at Iowa State University, after having been the center's director since July of 2000. However, I appear before you today as an organic producer and manager of our family's 3,500-acre mixed-crop and livestock farm located in south-central North Dakota. Of those 3,500 acres, approximately 1,000 are still in native prairie, which our family uses to graze livestock in the summer months. The remaining 2,500 acres are cultivated.

Approximately one-third of the cultivated land is in leguminous cover crops—alfalfa and clover. Alfalfa serves as a forage crop for our animals, and the clover is a green manure crop that provides essential nutrients for other crop production. The remaining 1,700 to 1,800 acres are planted into small grains that are part of a complex crop rotation plan that I will discuss at great length later in my testimony. We compost all of our livestock manure and apply it to our fields to improve the health of our soil.

This farming method has proven very successful for our farm family, especially since we made the transition to organic farming in 1976. We

This is a slightly revised version of Frederick Kirschenmann's statement before the U.S. House of Representatives Committee on Oversight and Government Reform, Domestic Policy Subcommittee, March 13, 2008. Appreciation is expressed to Bill Wenzel, national director of the Farmer to Farmer Campaign on GE, for his research assistance in developing this statement.

have been certified organic since 1980, and due to our stable production achieved by virtue of our rotation scheme, we have not borrowed operating capital since the certification was received.

I do not come here today pretending to represent organic producers. However, I do have extensive experience in agriculture that complements my work at the Leopold Center and in the management of my farm, which provides unique insights into how shortcomings at the USDA in the regulation of genetically engineered crops have significantly affected organic producers economically.

I assisted in the formation of Farm Verified Organic, Inc., a private organic certification agency, and the Northern Plains Sustainable Agriculture Society. I was appointed to and have served on USDA's National Organic Standards Board, the USDA's North Central Region Sustainable Agricultural Research and Education Administrative Council, and the board of directors of the Henry A. Wallace Institute for Alternative Agriculture. I also serve as president of the Stone Barns Center for Food and Agriculture at Pocantico Hills, New York. The Stone Barns Center, initially funded by David Rockefeller and his family, is a demonstration and education center in sustainable agriculture. I am a member of the National Commission on Industrial Farm Animal Production operated by the Johns Hopkins School of Public Health, funded by Pew Charitable Trusts, and I am the convening chair of a multistate task force, Agriculture of the Middle, that focuses on research and markets for midsize American farms. This group is also responsible for establishing the Association of Family Farms to create standards and markets for the farms that are the focus of Agriculture of the Middle.

In order to understand the monumental challenges posed by genetically engineered crops to the management and profitability of an organic farming system, you need to have a basic understanding of the system itself.

Successful organic farming depends in large part on putting together a mix of crops in a complex crop rotation plan. Because organic producers do not use agricultural chemicals, the mix and sequence of crops in a rotation must help control weeds, suppress pests and diseases, help recycle nutrients, and be profitable in agricultural commodity markets. Naturally, the crop choices available to accomplish this multifaceted set of goals are determined by climate, soil type, available markets, and practical considerations such as availability of necessary machinery and equipment. We have discovered that coming up with the right mix of crops to achieve these multifaceted objectives is the most significant challenge in developing a successful organic farming operation.

Once a farmer finds that delicate balance in the crop rotation scheme, any changes to the system are very difficult to make without incurring financial costs, because each crop performs several functions that enable the entire operation to be economically successful. It is very important to understand this phenomenon in organic farming, because it is never a simple matter of substituting one crop for another.

On our North Dakota farm, given its soil and climate constraints, we have found four crop rotation patterns that can achieve the multifaceted objectives that I discussed earlier. On our farm, we alternate cool-season crops and warm-season crops to help control weeds. If you plant cool-season crops several years in a row, cool-season weeds establish themselves, producing seeds and making it very difficult to control those weeds after just a few short years. We alternate broad-leaf and grassy plants. Planting the same crop in successive years makes it very difficult to control pests and diseases. We also alternate leguminous and nonleguminous plants so that we can produce a variety of food crops and to "fix" sufficient nitrogen in the soil to sustain crop production. Finally, we alternate shallow-rooted and deep-rooted plants to more efficiently use the nutrients throughout the soil profile. The loss of any crop in this complex crop rotation system presents significant management problems and the loss of an income-producing crop. Given the climate and soil types in North Dakota, and available markets, very few options exist to replace crops lost to our crop rotation.

Canola was a critical crop for us in our complex rotation scheme. Canola is one of the few crops that grow in our climate and soil types and is both a cool-season and a broad-leaf plant. It is also very attractive because high-quality organic canola oil is in big demand in the organic market. We marketed our canola through a farmer-owned cooperative that had long-term contracts with several companies on the West Coast. Prior to the forced removal of canola from our crop rotations, 20 percent of our crop income came from canola.

We were not alone in our use of canola as a major income producer. Many crop producers, both conventional and organic, in the northern plains in the United States and in the southern provinces of Canada, relied on canola to provide a significant source of income. Prior to the commercialization of genetically engineered (GE) canola, Monsanto's Roundup Ready (RR) variety, organic producers were receiving a 100 percent price premium when compared to conventional varieties and agricultural economists were touting the potential for significant market expansion. As stated in *Nature Biotechnology* (June 2002), the introduction of transgenic herbicide-tolerant canola in western Canada destroyed the growing market for organic canola. While the commentary in this article was focused on the economic impacts of GE canola in Canada, this scenario was identical to that experienced by U.S. organic canola growers.

In the environmental assessment (EA) conducted in accordance with the petition to deregulate RR canola, the USDA noted that Brassica is an open and self-pollinating crop in the "mustard" family that includes more than 375 genera and 3,200 species. The EA acknowledged that the plants are capable of self-fertilization and intraspecific cross-fertilization; that partial sexual compatibility exists among members of the Brassica family and other closely related species outside the genus; that gene movement is possible to other members of the plant family; and, that honeybees were its primary pollinators. Despite the existence of all these potential avenues of contamination, the USDA concluded that the commercialization of RR canola did not present a plant pest risk, nor did the potential exist for impacts to the human environment through its use in agriculture. Specifically, the USDA determined that:

- Neither the introduced genes and their products nor the regulatory sequences controlling their expression present a plant risk.
- RR canola is neither a weed nor has any significant potential to become a weed and does not transmit weedy characteristics to sexually compatible plants.
- RR canola will not cause damage to agricultural commodities.
- RR canola will not have a negative impact on agricultural and cultivation practices.
- RR canola will not be harmful to threatened or endangered species, including bees.

One area of personal aggravation is that the USDA totally failed to consider the impacts of RR canola contamination on organic producers in the EA process. In assessing the potential impacts of RR canola on agricultural or cultivation practices, the agency acknowledged that volunteer seeds and plants could pose a problem but concluded that RR canola would not negatively affect those practices. This determination that volunteers did not represent a significant adverse impact was based on the premise that the problem could be eradicated through the use of 2,4D or sulfonylurea-type herbicides. Clearly, the impact of volunteers on organic producers was not even considered in reaching that conclusion.

The conclusions reached in the EA defied logic, reason, and reality to those of us with experience in growing canola. The fact that canola is open-pollinating, with its pollen dispersed and transmitted by bees, animals, wind, or other mechanical means over great distances, was clearly indicative of a significant probability that contamination could occur. Canola is a very sturdy and prolific plant. That is one of the reasons it is so attractive to farmers in harsh northern climates. From the outset we knew that the potential for trouble was great.

Farmers were not the only ones concerned about the potential for contamination. The scientific and the canola industry had concluded that cross-pollination, volunteer issues, and gene movement made contamination a virtual certainty and focused on farm management strategies to minimize contamination.

Within two years after RR canola was commercialized, cross-pollination had resulted in the development of a canola hybrid resistant to Roundup, Liberty, and Pursuit. In the *Nature Biotechnology* article previously referred to in my testimony, the authors acknowledged that although the canola industry had predicted that this would occur eventually, this triple-resistant hybrid was created by variety cross-pollination in just two years. The fact that the scientific community felt that contamination was a virtual certainty was also apparent in a *Toronto Globe & Mail* article titled "A New Breed of Superweed." In that article, Phil Thomas, a researcher at Alberta Agriculture's Field Crop Development Centre with thirty years of experience, stated that GE canola can *easily* outcross between varieties, with bees and other insects carrying the sticky pollen from one plant to another. Wind also transports the pollen and all the genetic modification that it contains from one field to another. Seeds from the new outcrossed varieties can be carried by wind, animals, birds, humans, and truck and tractor tires to other fields where their pollen can migrate to yet another type of canola. "This was to be anticipated," Thomas concluded. Apparently, the cross-pollination and subsequent hybridization was anticipated by everyone but the regulators at the USDA.

When RR canola was introduced into our community, I talked with neighbors who planned to use it. While the USDA minimized the potential for contamination, we knew a huge potential existed for that to occur. Similar to the approach being considered by canola crop scientists, our focus was on creating a buffer of sufficient size to minimize the potential for contamination.

We worked cooperatively with our neighbors to try to ensure that our organic canola fields were at least two miles from neighboring fields where RR varieties were being grown. Because canola is an insect-pollinated crop, such distances were critical, according to bee apiarians who regularly place bees on our farm. We felt that this approach could work on our farm as long as we could fit our canola fields into rotation patterns that kept the entire system in balance and were are least two miles from neighboring RR canola fields.

After two short years, RR canola began to be adopted more heavily in our area, and it became impossible to find fields on our farm that could meet the two-mile buffer requirement and also fit into our rotation patterns, despite the fact that our farm fields extend over a twenty-mile range. Additionally, contamination had become an immense problem for canola growers in our area. Organic producers who did not maintain the two-mile buffer were increasingly becoming contaminated, resulting in the loss of lucrative markets and premiums for organic canola. In that short time, contamination had become so pervasive that there were no seed dealers in the area that were willing to guarantee that their seed was GE-free. Our only option was to remove canola from our farming system. What USDA had determined was a virtual impossibility became a reality in two growing seasons. For anybody that farms for a living, this result was totally predictable.

Removal of canola not only meant the loss of a crop generating one-fifth of total farm income; it also presented a whole new set of challenges in finding a new crop that would fit into our complex rotation system. An alternative broad-leaf, cool-season crop that was marketable simply did not exist. Consequently, we were left with no other option than to eliminate the broad-leaf, cool-season crop component of our crop rotation and spread the canola acres among our other crops, reducing the effectiveness of our entire rotation scheme. While it is hard to estimate the long-term economic loss that resulted from the compromise of our rotation system, the short-term economic loss sustained as a direct result of the removal of canola was $50,000 in annual income.

Organic canola producers throughout the northern plains of the United States and the provinces of Canada were similarly affected. Although I do not have statistics for U.S. producers, an estimated $1 million was lost to Canadian organic canola producers. As has been the experience with virtually every GE crop approved for commercial use, contamination cost us valuable markets. In the spring of 2000, GE canola was found in a breeder's lot of canola seeds imported by Advanta (Winnipeg, Manitoba). Advanta quickly determined that the GE contamination had been caused by gene flow from GE foundation seeds planted in neighboring fields. Despite the fact that Canadian seed growers had followed isolation rules, the genes still moved into conventional foundation seed. This not only created havoc in valuable European markets but resulted in an inability to find non-GE canola seed. While this contamination occurred in Canada, the same scenario occurred in the United States.

Canola producers were not the only ones who lost valuable markets as a result of GE canola contamination. In 1999, the EU detected unapproved GE proteins in a shipment of honey. As a result, honey shipments to the EU dropped $4.8 million between 1998 and 2000—or by 55 percent.

While the loss to our farm from the loss of organic canola was sobering, it pales in comparison to the way the introduction of GE wheat or GE alfalfa would affect our operation. Wheat is the lead income-producing crop on our farm. Typically, about one-third of our 1,700 acres planted to small grains is in wheat. Most of our hard red spring wheat is sold to buyers in Europe. All of our buyers have already warned us that if GE wheat is introduced in the United States, they will source their organic wheat from other countries because they have no confidence in our ability to prevent contamination. These buyers have made it clear that their customers are adamant about organic products being GE-free. In many cases the fact that products are GE-free is the sole reason that these customers buy organic, according to those buyers.

Contrary to representations by the USDA, process-based certifications that products are "organic" and that no GE crops were used in the production of those products are insufficient in this day and age. Organic buyers and processors increasingly utilize strict testing regimens to ensure that the crops they are purchasing are GE-free. We sell the vast majority of our durum wheat to Eden Foods of Michigan. Eden Foods makes a commitment to its customers and guarantees that no genetically modified organisms (GMOs) are contained in their products. In addition to requiring organic certification, Eden Foods rigorously tests all incoming grains to make sure that they are free of any GE content, utilizing tests to detect contamination to the lowest level possible with existing technology. They routinely reject any incoming truckloads of grain that test positive for GMOs. Product testing is rapidly becoming an industry standard in both foreign and domestic markets.

Consequently, the introduction of GE wheat presents an enormous potential loss of income for our farm. This year (the 2007 crop) we are selling our organic wheat crop for $24 to $29 per bushel, largely due to global shortages in supply. We normally harvest 19,000 bushels of wheat per year. Losing this year's wheat crop would mean a $494,000 loss to our farm. There is simply no substitute for wheat in our crop rotation. The loss of our organic wheat market would effectively put us out of business.

The introduction of GE alfalfa would have comparable consequences. Alfalfa is one of the few legumes that we can produce on our farm, given soil and climate conditions, that can both serve as a nitrogen-fixing plant and a source of forage for our livestock during the winter months. While we also produce some Yellow Blossom sweet clover to fix nitrogen, it cannot be used as the sole source of forage because feeding clover on a constant basis can cause a poisonous disease in the rumen that can kill cattle. Accordingly, clover can only be used for about 10 percent of our forage needs. The loss of alfalfa due to GE contamination would result in the loss of our primary source of nitrogen for our crops as well as our principal source of winter feed for our livestock. Once again, there is no substitute for alfalfa, and its loss would put us out of business.

Organic producers simply cannot afford the business-as-usual approach to regulating and approving GE crops. The USDA currently serves no valuable purpose other than to rubber-stamp the biotech crops in the pipeline for commercialization. There is no confidence in the assessment process among farmers, buyers, or the marketplace. The lack of an effective regulatory system hurts everyone in the food chain, from field to fork.

I am hopeful that the result of these hearings will provide an awakening at the USDA to the fact that no one benefits from the status quo. A strong regulatory program for GE crops can benefit all concerned. I am appreciative of the subcommittee's interest in this topic and their commitment to support the economic livelihoods of the farmers who are dependent on an effective regulatory system for GMOs.

Placing the Pew Commission Report in Context

When I accepted the invitation to serve on the Pew Commission on Industrial Farm Animal Production, I knew it would be a controversial undertaking. While the meat and animal industries have made huge investments in infrastructure to create the mainstream industrial farm-animal production system—and while they quite rationally want to protect that investment—a growing population of consumers, environmentalists, rural residents, and, yes, farmers, are opposing the evolution of this system because of unintended consequences that are degrading things they care about.

I decided to join the commission because I take a longer-term view and am increasingly concerned about the fact that we are not helping farmers to prepare for future challenges that will make our entire industrial farming system, including our industrial animal system, increasingly untenable. Such challenges include increasing energy costs, depleting water resources, and more unstable climates. I represented that perspective on the commission and was invited, by commission members, to write a concluding segment to the Pew Commission final report, which I titled "Toward a Sustainable Animal Agriculture."

Let me say, first of all, that I was honored to serve on this commission. I have never worked with a group of people who were as dedicated to their task or worked as hard as this incredible collection of people—both commission members and staff.

The commission was made up of fifteen individuals who represented many different points of view, including veterinary medicine, public health, agriculture, animal welfare, food industry, and rural society. The commission also included a former U.S. Secretary of Agriculture and was chaired

This piece was originally published in *Practical Farmer,* 2008. Available from the author.

by a former state governor. Despite this diversity, we agreed at the outset that the only recommendations that would go into our report would be those on which we had reached *consensus*. There would be no "minority reports."

This meant we often debated issues long and hard and listened to each other intently. We commissioned five groups of scientists to research and write a report in each of the study areas that we identified, and we used their reports in our deliberations. We pored through thousands of pages of documents, visited numerous sites around the country, and listened long and hard to many hours of testimony by a wide spectrum of industry representatives, farmers, government officials, and citizens who came to public hearings we conducted throughout the country.

The commission was formed in March 2006 and issued its report in April 2008. The core question we addressed was, "How do we feed the world without destroying the environment, risking the public health, inhumanely treating farm animals, and threatening the future of our rural communities?" We tried to answer that question with a series of recommendations designed to reduce the negative effects of industrial farm animal agriculture. In sum, our recommendations are as follows:

- Restrict the use of antimicrobials in food production animals to medically important treatments in order to reduce the development of resistance to medically important antibiotics and other antimicrobials
- Implement a disease-monitoring program for food animals that allows a forty-eight-hour trace-back of those animals by means of a fully integrated national database
- Treat industrial farm animal production systems more like other industrial operations, and implement a new system for dealing with farm waste to protect the public from adverse environmental and human health hazards
- Phase out the most inhumane animal production practices within a decade to reduce the risk to public health and to improve animal well-being. (Gestation crates and battery cages are specifically mentioned.)
- Amend and enforce federal and state laws to provide a level playing field for farmers when entering contracts with integrators
- Increase funding to expand and reform animal agriculture research

The commission's 124-page assessment noted that while industrial farm animal production systems have increased the speed of production and lowered costs to consumers, "the intensive confinement production system creates a number of problems. These include contributing to the increase in the pool of antibiotic-resistant bacteria because of the overuse of antibiotics; air-quality problems; the contamination of rivers, streams, and coastal waters with concentrated animal waste; animal welfare problems, mainly as a result of the extremely close quarters in which the animals are housed; and significant shifts in the social structure and economy of many farming regions throughout the country."

Some have criticized the report for ignoring "science-based" conclusions on which the animal industry claims to have constructed its operations. In my humble opinion, that is an illegitimate argument. The term "science-based" is regularly used in the media today to convey the notion that science is a discipline that comes up with incontrovertible conclusions. Nothing could be further from the truth. Science is a process, not a fixed set of conclusions. Scientific conclusions are always based on the best information available at any given moment, the scope of work undertaken, and the majority consensus of scientists involved. And those conclusions are constantly subject to challenge based on new discoveries, new perspectives, and emergent properties. Our report is simply part of that process. The entire report, plus an executive summary, is available at http://www.ncifap.org/.

Redefining Sustainability

From "Greening" to Enhancing Capacity
for Self-Renewal

"Going green" seems to be the new sustainability slogan designed to save the planet. The question is: if we all go green, will that get us to sustainability?

A typical dictionary definition of "sustain" is "to maintain," "to keep going," "to keep in existence." As a broad overview, that is a useful definition, because it calls into question exactly what it is that we want to maintain.

In today's discourse, we generally view sustainability from a quantitative perspective. How can we maintain or improve crop yields? How can we maintain the growth of the economy? How can we improve the energy-efficiency of our vehicles so we can continue transporting goods from one part of the world to another in the face of rising energy costs? How can we increase the cod population to maintain our seafood industry? Both environmental and commercial sectors have been captured by this approach to sustainability.

More recently we have added the "greening" component to this quantitative perspective. Recognizing that we are reaching certain thresholds that could fundamentally change the functioning of the planet, we are beginning to focus on improving efficiencies, reducing our greenhouse gas emissions, switching from fossil energy to renewable alternatives, and recycling more of our wastes. On the surface these seem like laudable activities, but will they lead us to sustainability?

Inspired by the insights of ecologists like C. S. Holling, a new professional society has emerged during the last fifteen years called the Resilience Alliance. Following Holling's description of natural systems and how they function, the Resilience Alliance has concluded that this quantita-

A version of this article was originally published in the *Networker,* July/August 2008, available at http://www.sehn.org.

tive approach to sustainability is "based on false assumptions. In a world characterized by dynamic change in ecological and social systems, it is at least as important to manage systems to enhance their resilience as it is to manage the supply of specific products."[1] Using the quantitative approach, the Alliance claims, "We have assumed that we could manage individual components of an ecological system independently, find an optimal balance between supply and demand for each component, and that other attributes of the system would stay largely constant through time."[2]

Given how both social and ecological systems function, that is a fundamentally flawed assumption. All social and biophysical systems are constantly changing. The basic message from the resilience thinkers is that doing more of the same—new technologies, greater efficiency, more control and command, more intensification, more single-tactic strategies, without addressing the resilience of systems—will not lead to sustainability. A central problem is that the kind of efficiency that leads to optimization tends to eliminate redundancies, the key ingredient of resilience. Additionally, the achievement of such efficiencies tends to cause rebound effects. More fuel-efficient cars inevitably lead to more driving.

The kind of greening that pushes the pedal to the metal a little harder—more efficient technologies, better command and control, input substitution—ends up creating the problem we intended to solve. We delude ourselves into believing that working smarter will solve the problem. More often it reinforces the problem, because we have not approached it from a dynamic social/ecological systems perspective.

The central issue is that we can never control whole systems; nor can we totally control any part of a system in isolation. Consequently, while greening may bring about desirable short-term results, it will never lead to sustainability. Our world is a complex adaptive system that is interconnected, interdependent, and constantly changing. All systems are unpredictable and proceed in a nonlinear fashion. We can never hold a system in an optimal sustainable state. We can only design systems to enhance their capacity for self-renewal.

Sustainability from a resilience perspective operates at two levels. All systems (biophysical and social) operate within a certain structure and function. A shock or disturbance may cause a system to cross a threshold into a new structure and function. For example, recent flooding in Indiana caused a disturbance for Jim Lankford, a farmer who raises corn and soybeans in Indiana. The current "stable" form of agriculture in the Corn Belt is monoculture corn and soybeans, leaving large swaths of soil vulnerable to soil erosion. Unusually heavy rain falling in a short period of time caused the river that flows by Mr. Lankford's farm to erode "a new route for itself during June's flooding," leaving ditches with "twelve-foot banks at the edge of some of Lankford's corn fields" and large swaths of crop and soil washed out of his fields.[3] If such flooding continues in coming years (likely as a result of climate change) these fields will "cross a threshold" and be pushed to a different kind of structure and functioning.

From the perspective of resilience, therefore, sustainability is critical in two ways. Systems should be designed that are unlikely to cross thresholds from one state of equilibrium to a different configuration, or if they do (which, over time, all systems will), they are sufficiently robust so that they reorganize themselves into a new structure and function that continues to provide the services required. This second resilience role makes maintaining diversity and redundancy especially important. Only sufficient diversity and redundancy will enable systems to retain their capacity for self-renewal.

Maintaining redundancy and diversity incurs costs of foregone efficiency, so we seldom consider this approach to sustainability. In addition, assessing the costs and benefits of dynamic systems is difficult. We can never accumulate sufficient predictive knowledge. How does one assess the costs and benefits of preparing for a 500-year flood as opposed to the cost of ignoring it in the interest of greater efficiency? In our industrial culture, if you can't prove that costs outweigh benefits, you don't dare interfere with the market.

Aldo Leopold recognized that most members of the biotic community are not economically valuable, but many play an unseen role in maintaining ecosystem integrity and stability.[4] He also recognized that we could not "preserve" the biotic community in any given state of equilibrium. Conservation as an activity to preserve things in their "natural" state is an exercise in futility. What we can do is understand and preserve the biotic community's capacity for self-renewal, and that, according to Leopold, requires the nurturing of a certain kind of conscience: "A land ethic, then, reflects the existence of an ecological conscience, and this in turn reflects a conviction of individual responsibility for the health of the land. Health is the capacity of the land for self-renewal. Conservation is our effort to understand and preserve this capacity."[5] Nurturing this concept of conservation is essential to any quest for sustainability.

PART 3

Envisioning an Alternative Food and Farming System

What's an Education For?

A friend of mine told me a story a few years ago about an incident that had taken place between his father and himself when he was a young lad. As Bernie tells the story, he and his friend were playing catch in their backyard. Bernie said that he had what could generously be described as a "bedsheet with fingers on it" for a baseball glove, a glove that had been handed down by two older brothers. His friend had just gotten a brand-new mitt. Bernie was complaining about the glove and how hard it was to catch the ball with it when he suddenly realized that his father was standing behind him.

"What seems to be the problem?" his father asked. "This," said Bernie, pointing to the glove.

"I still don't see the problem," said his father, "I see a glove."

"Well, there is nothing to it," complained Bernie.

"Well, I have never played baseball," said his father, "but tell me what you think a baseball glove is for."

"It's to help you catch a ball," said Bernie.

"Then I still don't see the problem," said his father. "In what way *doesn't* yours help you catch the ball?"

Bernie told me that the answer to that question was obvious to him, so he quickly replied, "It doesn't protect my hand."

"Ah," said his father, "it seems to me that that is where you are wrong. It seems to me you ought to be able to catch the ball barehanded. The way I look at it, you don't use a glove to protect your hand, but to give you a bigger hand to help you catch balls that are more difficult to reach. It seems to me that you only need a glove to give you a bigger hand to catch baseballs you might otherwise miss."

This is an edited transcript of a commencement speech given in the 1960s at the Milton High School Awards Day Program, Milton, Massachusetts.

I think that Bernie's encounter with his father can serve to help us refocus the debate that has been taking place since the mid-1960s concerning the value of education. Economists and journalists tell us that education isn't worth the price we are paying because we cannot establish a clear correlation between a college education and successful employment.

I'm still not quite sure why it took an economic analysis to tell us that. Most of us who urge young people (and for that matter older people) to get as much education as possible know there is no simple correlation between a college education and success. We could never have promoted such a fantasy in a world where so many men and women have succeeded without the benefit of a formal college or university education, and where so many others *did* go to college but succeeded in fields other than the ones they majored in while they were in college.

Buckminster Fuller, one of the most creative futurologists and inventors of our time, never finished college because he was twice kicked out of Harvard—once for irresponsible conduct because he went to New York and spent all of his tuition and expense money on a party that he threw for the Ziegfeld Follies cast, and once for exhibiting "no noticeable interest in education," as far as the Harvard faculty could determine.

John James Audubon, the greatest artist-naturalist in this country and the man for whom the famed Audubon Society was named, never went to college or an academy of arts. He was, in fact, considered a failure at the age of thirty-five and was thrown in jail for not paying his debts. Alexander Hamilton also never earned a college degree. He began working full-time at age ten in an import-export office. Later he wanted to go to college, and he studied under a private tutor to prepare for the college entrance exam, only to have his college education interrupted by the Revolutionary War. He never returned.

So there is no clear correlation between education and success. However, the conclusion that education is therefore not worth the investment is a false conclusion. That is like arguing that a baseball glove is worthless if it doesn't protect your hand. What's a glove for? To protect your hand? No. It's to give you a bigger hand so you can reach baseballs you might otherwise miss.

What's an education for? To protect you from reality? To get you a better job? To make life easier? No. *It's to enlarge your vision and increase*

*your wisdom so that you can catch more of life than you would be able to reach
without it.*

While many economists conclude falsely that education isn't worth it
because it doesn't lead to better jobs, another economist in our midst takes
a very different view. In *Small Is Beautiful: Economics as If People Mattered,*
E. F. Schumacher argues that education, far from not being worth it, is, in
fact, our greatest and most critical resource because it holds one of the main
keys in our struggle for global survival with quality.[1]

Schumacher argues that one of the primary reasons that our world is
in trouble today is that we are operating on the wrong premises. He contends we make decisions based on six "big ideas" that we inherited from the
nineteenth century, ideas that do not recognize the need to cooperate with
the environment and all peoples of the world. As a result, we make decisions that are inappropriate to our real situation, and we threaten to destroy
ourselves with our own decisions.

Education, argues Schumacher, is our greatest resource because it challenges wrong ideas and fosters a different set of assumptions that can lead
to *new* decisions that will help us save the planet for ourselves and our
grandchildren.

Viewing education from this perspective changes how we determine
its value. It is not enough to get an education that results in a better job,
enriches us culturally for pure private enjoyment, or enrolls us in the social
registers of the powerful and the wealthy. An education that does no more
than this for us is indeed not worth it. The only kind of education that is
worth the price is one that will enlarge our vision and increase our wisdom
for the purpose of saving the planet for ourselves and our children.

If this is what education is for, then I think education should be committed to the development of at least six key competencies. I would urge every high school graduate to challenge the college or university of his choice
to respond to his or her need to achieve these six competencies.

*The competence to challenge and critically analyze the basic assumptions (the
"big ideas") that shape our lives and the lives of those around us.* This is a matter of utmost urgency. We don't have much time left to rethink our basic
relationship with the environment and the people in it. The decisions we
make in the next ten or twenty years may determine whether we survive the

next hundred years. Some scientists are already convinced we have passed the point where any strategy for global survival is possible.

The competence to make increasingly complex decisions on a daily basis. We are already being asked to make difficult decisions at the polls. Should we vote for or against the bottle bill? The spray can? The right to die? The right to an abortion on demand? Even more complicated decisions will follow. How shall we use, limit, and conserve our energy resources? What kind of alternative energy shall we develop? How will scarce resources of every kind, including water, be allocated?

The competence to understand and appreciate the interconnections of everything. Our world, like our bodies, is an intricate system. When we tinker with one part of it, it can affect other parts that seem, to our usual linear way of thinking, totally unrelated. In his recent book Stephen Schneider stated the issue regarding the climate: *"Every place on earth is connected to some extent by the climatic system of every other place"*[2] (italics his). This principle is true not only of the climate but of every system and every aspect of our life on this planet.

The competence to cope with rapid change. The fantastic rate of change in our society is a fact. Some of us seem to prefer to ignore change and bumble into the future. Others try to predict future changes and prepare for them. Neither course of action seems very effective for dealing with change. A more appropriate posture is to learn to cope with change and to attempt to influence it in directions that will benefit our planet for the good of all.

The competence to simultaneously perform effectively in the profession of one's choice and to critically evaluate that profession in terms of the larger global issues of the day. It is no longer sufficient to simply be competent in what we do. It is also necessary to be able to make sound judgments about the way in which our chosen profession influences the environment and the people in it. Does the profession of your choice promote the global welfare, or does it serve narrowly conceived self-interests? How can you work within your profession to make it sensitive to the former and avoid the latter?

The competence to continually promote personal enrichment. Studs Terkel indicates that more than 90 percent of people in all professions are unhappy with their jobs.[3] The reason has more to do with *themselves* than with their jobs. We need more competence in the art of developing a rich, personal center in our lives that will enable us to intensify our own sense of self-worth. Certainly Jack Arbolino is right when he reminds us that at least a part of our education "is to ensure that later on in life when you knock on the door of yourself somebody answers."[4] I would add, so that somebody answers that you *like*!

What's an education for? It is to enlarge your vision and increase your wisdom so that you can catch more of life than you would be able to reach without it. I invite you to get as much of that kind of education as you can, and to join me and thousands of others who are struggling to apply their vision and wisdom to making global survival, with quality, possible. So, "ease on down the road," and I wish you a good life.

Resolving Conflicts in American Land-Use Values

How Organic Farming Can Help

Why do Americans, and especially American farmers, use (or abuse) the land the way we do? I assume land is used in accordance with a set of values, expectations, and perceptions developed over time. That may seem so obvious that it appears trivial, but it is an important point.

All too often we approach land-conservation issues through the concept of "good guys" versus "bad guys." The "good guys" plant trees, install grass waterways, strip crop, and use no-till farming. They do everything possible to keep their soil from being exposed to erosion. The "bad guys," conversely, bulldoze trees, rip up wetlands, cultivate whole quarter-sections as a single field, fall plow, and appear insensitive to eroding soils.

Accordingly, the task of land conservation is reduced to converting, cajoling, or coercing the "bad guys" into complying with the conservation practices of the "good guys." This is a simplistic and incorrect analysis of the problem and perhaps one of the reasons why our solutions are often ineffective. In America we have developed a philosophy of land use that contains conflicting values. I think that understanding the tension caused by those conflicting values will help explain why some try to preserve the land while others abuse it.

Prosperity vs. Virtue

People of European descent who came to this country were caught up in a "dream of destiny." They believed that they came to these shores because they were especially called and chosen by God to build a new "kingdom of God on earth." In *The Lively Experiment,* Sidney Mead demonstrated

---

This is an edited version of a paper published in the *American Journal of Alternative Agriculture* 3 (1988): 43–47.

how this sense of destiny among Americans is rooted in the early Puritan theocracy.[1]

But this mandate had two prongs. On the one hand, early settlers considered it their destiny to clear the land, tame the wilderness, and make the land productive. Breaking up the prairie and planting nice, neat rows of corn was a moral obligation and one of the reasons God had placed them here. The extent to which they "progressed" in this way was, in fact, considered a "sign" that they were fulfilling their destiny. The Native Americans who had refused to "improve" the land were considered "lazy" and therefore not deserving of the land they inhabited.[2] This set of values, expectations, and perceptions about land use is deeply embedded in our history, and we have all inherited it. We feel morally obligated to make the land as productive as possible, to "prosper" on it, to make it yield its maximum potential.

On the other hand, early settlers also regarded it as their destiny to preserve and protect the land. This land was, after all, a gift from God, entrusted to them as a place of freedom: to worship God, develop moral character, and fabricate a body politic that resembled the kingdom of God. Thus, preserving, protecting, and safeguarding the land was seen as a moral obligation and as another of the reasons why God had placed them here. The extent to which they preserved the land as a heritage and as a place to pursue the virtuous life was a "sign" that they were fulfilling their destiny. This second set of values, expectations, and perceptions of land use are equally embedded in our history, making us feel morally obligated to preserve and protect the land for future generations.

These two facets of our destiny spawned philosophies of land use about which honest, responsible people could disagree. In fact, these historical circumstances have created conflicting feelings about land use within most of us. Consequently, whenever economic needs and the desire to prosper appear crucial, we make fragile land available for logging or crop production and relax restrictions that preserve and protect the land. Whenever the need to preserve our heritage for the future appears crucial, we restrict the mining of our natural resources and intensify measures to protect and preserve the land.

But the interesting thing is that whenever conflicts over land use arise, each side tends to regard the other side as immoral. Land developers who level trees and create perfect green lawns regard environmentalists who interfere with their creation as meddling obstructionists. Environmentalists who try to save trees and preserve the environment in its natural state regard land developers as greedy destructionists. But, in reality, it's not a case of good guys versus bad guys. It's a matter of conflicting convictions about how the land should be used.

I experience these conflicting values in myself. On the one hand, I'm motivated to do the best job of farming that I can. It's a moral obligation. I feel that I *must* put in place those practices that will enable my land to produce to its maximum potential. Anything less would be irresponsible. So, if my land produces best when I fall plow or drain sloughs or break up a piece of prairie, then that is what I feel obligated to do.

On the other hand, I'm motivated to do the best job of taking care of the land possible. I feel I *must* protect the land so that future generations can use it to develop a quality life. If protecting the land means leaving stubble and using good conservation practices, then that is what I feel obligated to do.

Material gain is also a motivating factor in the way we use land. We probably all have a streak of this motive in our characters; thus, we all sometimes use land to satisfy material ambitions, but this is probably not the primary cause of land abuse. The need to prosper, demonstrate progress, make improvements, or have the best wheat field in the county are more typical motives of most land users.

Private-Property Rights vs. Stewardship

A second set of conflicting values, also embedded in our history, determines the way we use land: the obligations to protect private-property rights and to practice stewardship. The rights of private property, including land, were close to the hearts of the framers of our Constitution. The Sixth Amendment made it clear that land belongs to individuals and that the rights attending such ownership were not to be easily interfered with by the state. From the beginning, Americans felt a moral obligation to protect the right of the individual to use his land as he sees fit. However, because the early settlers felt chosen to build a kingdom of God on Earth, they also had a strong sense that the land did not belong to them at all, that it was only entrusted to their care. They were not so much owners of the land as stewards. These conflicting values are also part of our philosophy of land use—part of *my* philosophy of land use.

On the one hand, I view my land as *my* property, the place where I decide what is best without outside interference. It is important for me to protect that right, not only for myself but for my neighbors and for future generations. On the other hand, I view my land as a trust, something that never really belongs to me, that was here before I came and will still be here long after I'm gone. The land was placed in my care for a brief time.

Because both values are part of me, I can passionately endorse this well-known proverb: "Treat the land as if you borrowed it from your children, rather than as if you inherited it from your ancestors." I can endorse with equal passion the outburst of a farmer confronted by a wildlife officer when the farmer wanted to drain a slough on his land: "Get the hell off my land! I don't need some bureaucrat telling me how to farm."

Inevitably, of course, some of us are more influenced by the values of developing a virtuous life and practicing stewardship, while others are more influenced by the values of prosperity and protecting the rights of private property. Consequently, in any area of the nation, conflicts over how land should be used are almost certain to arise.

These conflicts grow out of opposing values that are part of our national philosophy of land use and are deeply carved into the moral fabric of the nation. Our conflicts do not represent a division between "good guys" and "bad guys." Once we recognize this, we can begin to reconcile our differences and move toward a comprehensive land conservation program.

Some practical approaches exist to reconcile land-use conflicts that arise from these two sets of values. First, we need to replace short-term thinking with long-term thinking. Second, we need to discover and disclose the inherent connections between economy and ecology.

Short-Term and Long-Term Thinking

A trait deeply ingrained in American culture is our tendency to seek quick and easy short-term solutions. This trait can probably be attributed to the availability of space and resources throughout most of our history. Settlers in a new land seldom had to negotiate their way out of a difficult problem or concern themselves with the long-term effects of their actions. The option of leaving an unpleasant situation to start over in a new location on the frontier was usually available. Americans learned that they could mine any situation for its wealth in the short term without worrying about the consequences in the long term.

That short-term thinking also has become an integral part of our philosophy of land use. Prior to the introduction of synthetic fertilizers, farmers on the plains tended to "use up" land by breaking up sod, farming it until the soil nutrients were depleted, and then moving on to a new piece of sod. There was little incentive to devise a soil-building system that restored and preserved the soil, let alone protected it from erosion.

After the appearance of synthetic fertilizers, purchasing inputs became the new quick short-term solution. It never occurred to most of us to consider the long-term effects of making agriculture dependent on these external inputs nor to assess the long-term effects of applying these synthetic materials to the soil.

But in the 1980s, we have run out of new space. We are forced to look hard at the long-term effects of the way we use the nation's land. Rather than being negative, however, this fact has the potential of leading us to reconcile the conflict in our land-use values. Wendell Berry hinted at the possibility of reconciliation when he wrote: "A people cannot live long or well at each other's expense, or at the expense of their cultural birthright."[3] One of the lessons of history is that whenever a civilization mines its soil to enjoy short-term prosperity, that civilization suffers long-term famine and poverty.

This inherent long-term connection between prosperity and conservation was recognized by a group of German scientists commissioned by the Bonn government in 1979 to research future directions for agriculture in Germany. They recommended that the government deemphasize short-term profitability in favor of long-term adaptability. They concluded by saying that "ecology is long-term economy."[4]

Viewed in the long term, preserving the land's natural ecology for future generations is the most prosperous way to use the land. A healthy bottom line for a few years doesn't necessarily add up to a prosperous farm. Prosperity can only be maintained when the soil and its environment are properly cared for, not when prosperity is derived at the expense of the soil. When we look at land use in the long term, the potential conflict between prosperity and virtue disappears.

Viewing land use in the long term can also begin to resolve the conflict between private property and stewardship. Once we begin thinking in the long term, we begin considering our children's children. Consequently, the "rights" we want to ensure for ourselves within our private-property protections begin to join with the welfare of our offspring and the stewardship required that will provide them the same rights.

However, part of the solution to the private property/stewardship dilemma lies in simply recognizing that *both* values are in each of us. If both those values were clearly introduced into discussions between farmers and wildlife officials over "swampbuster" regulations, for example, it could help both sides recognize that the conflict is between two land values and not two groups of people. That could help to remove some barriers and enable everyone to work together toward some kind of compromise solution.

Organic Farming

Organic farmers generally are committed to preserving the environment, and they are also keenly interested in prospering. And while they want to be good stewards of the land, they also value their property rights. Organic farming is one way to embrace the best part of both sets of values in our heritage.

The key differences between organic and conventional agriculture are clear. Organic agriculture seeks to cooperate with nature's system of production, while conventional agriculture seeks to create its own system of production alongside (and even against) nature's system. Organic farmers, instead of purchasing synthetic inputs, attempt to:

- Supply plants with basic nutrients by creating self-regenerating systems so that each part of the farm's operation feeds into and enriches other parts, thus enriching the soil and creating a nutrient-rich growing environment for plants
- Control weeds by using crop-rotation systems to deprive weeds of the conditions they need in order to thrive
- Control insects by relying on natural predators to keep insect populations in check

In short, instead of spending money to fight against nature, upsetting her well-balanced system, we try to cooperate with nature and let her work for us. These ecological and economic connections in organic farming are illustrated in this true story. In Grass Range, Montana, a young rancher by the name of Tom Elliot owns and manages a large cattle ranch. Several years ago, Tom noticed that leafy spurge was starting to take over his rangeland, so Tom called chemical advisors to help him develop a program to eradicate the spurge. They agreed on a program, and helicopters came and sprayed the spurge. The price tag was $25,000.

Almost immediately after the application, the spurge began to curl up and die. But the next spring the spurge was back. So Tom brought back the chemical advisors. Together they developed a follow-up program. Once again the helicopters came. Once again the spurge began to curl up and die. Once again the price tag was $25,000.

The next spring Tom noticed that the spurge had diminished somewhat, but it was still coming back at unacceptable levels. He also noticed that his pine trees were dying and that he had an abnormal number of diseased cattle, many of them carrying diseases they had never had before. So Tom decided that chemical sprays were not the answer.

One day a neighbor told Tom that while cattle wouldn't touch spurge, sheep loved it. Tom called another neighbor who had a large herd of sheep and inadequate grazing land. The neighbor had been leasing rangeland some distance away and was eager to find pasture closer to home. Tom and his neighbor drew up a lease agreement that allowed the neighbor to graze his sheep with Tom's cattle. The spurge provided excellent pasture for the sheep, and they kept it in check. Because the sheep preferred the spurge, they didn't deplete the rest of the pasture for the cattle. And Tom received a handsome income from the lease.

I'm not suggesting that all of agriculture's problems can be solved so neatly. But the story serves to illustrate that if we look for alternatives to quick, short-term fixes and try to discover and disclose the connections between economy and ecology, sometimes there are solutions right under our noses that make sense for our pocketbooks and the environment. Overall, such solutions also help resolve some of the conflicting values we have inherited about the land in America. With these approaches, we may find effective land-conservation practices that Americans could support over the long term.

What About the Next Twenty Years?

Or "It's Turtles All the Way Down"

Stephen Hawking, in *A Brief History of Time,* tells a delightful story about a well-known scientist who once gave a public lecture on astronomy. In the lecture, the scientist described the universe, with the Earth orbiting around the sun, and the sun, in turn, orbiting within a vast collection of stars called a galaxy. When he concluded his lecture, a little old lady in the back of the room got up and said, "What you have told us is rubbish. The world is really a flat plate supported on the back of a giant turtle."

The scientist, with a somewhat arrogant smirk, responded to the woman's outburst by asking, "But what is the tortoise standing on?"

The woman replied, "You're very clever, young man, very clever, but it's turtles all the way down."[1]

I suspect that one of the reasons this story amuses is that it portrays a double truth. On the one hand, we recognize the scientist's truth. We know from accepted rules of evidence—observation, experience, and replicated experiments—that the Earth is indeed round and revolves around the sun. But, on the other hand, the woman also represents a different kind of truth. She stirs in us the awareness that reality is never as precisely and omnisciently knowable as the scientist implies.

We have, of course, always known the woman's truth, but since the dawn of the modern era we have ignored it. We have instead adopted René Descartes' naively optimistic assertion that humans are capable of knowing everything with certitude and that they can solve all the problems that could ever confront the human mind. More recently, science has adopted a much more constrained posture. With the emergence of quantum physics

---

Talk given at the twentieth anniversary celebration for the Center for Rural Affairs, Walthill, Nebraska, 1993.

255

in the twentieth century, we now realize that many of the basic assumptions that led to Descartes' optimism are not verifiable at the subatomic level. Consequently, our view of the world has forever changed.

In his quantum physics primer, *The Cosmic Code,* Heinz Pagels graphically describes our post-Newtonian world with a new metaphor. He contends that the proper metaphor for the universe is no longer the Newtonian clock—fully knowable, completely predictable, precisely quantifiable, and rigidly deterministic. Rather, it is the pinball machine, full of probabilities and uncertainties.[2] The stock in trade of the quantum world are the concepts "lack of objectivity," "indeterminacy," and "observer-created reality."[3] These properties of the atomic world, especially the awareness that the observer influences the outcome of measurements, Pagels calls "quantum weirdness."[4] Even science now recognizes that "it's turtles all the way down."

As we celebrate the twentieth anniversary of the Center for Rural Affairs and look to its future, it is important to keep this "quantum weirdness" in mind. Recognizing that we live in a pinball-machine-like world—a world full of indeterminacy, lacking objectivity, and allowing observers to co-create reality—can help us to put the center's work into proper perspective.

It was largely conventional wisdom's failure to recognize this pinball-machine-like nature of our world that led traditional intellectuals to mistrust the center's work. From the beginning, much of the center's work was questioned because it didn't fit the assumptions and frames of reference of classical intellectual thought. And because the classical way of viewing the world was assumed to be "objective," it was considered the only legitimate view.

Consequently, when the center started promoting energy self-sufficiency for small farms, critics presumed the center had adopted a neo-Luddite position bent on turning the technology clock backward. When the center challenged conventional wisdom's views on center-pivot irrigation systems, critics accused them of being opposed to progress and of failing to see the obvious benefits of such great inventions for farmers in the drought-plagued plains. When the center proposed that viable rural communities were an indispensable part of a healthy farm economy, critics inferred that nostalgia prevented the center from realizing that rural communities had outlived their usefulness. When the center focused on the farmer as the critical ingredient to any effective and efficient agriculture, critics supposed romantic nonsense had blinded them from seeing that technology had already replaced human resources in modern agriculture, to the benefit of both farmer and consumer.

According to the center, farmers can improve their economic position and improve their land-stewardship practices by substituting information-intensive management for chemical-intensive off-farm inputs. This could benefit rural communities by retaining more wealth in the local economy rather than allowing it to flow through to distant markets. Critics have dismissed the idea as impractical and unworkable. When the center assumed that farmers and environmentalists shared the same goals and organized them into a working coalition to develop common policies that would benefit both, critics thought it was an impossible marriage.

But in all of these seemingly wrongheaded positions, the center has been right. The reason that the center was able to see what conventional wisdom could not was probably not because folks at the center were smarter. It was, more likely, because they simply saw the world from a different frame of reference. They didn't see the world as just being *there*, objective, determined, following its own course. To the center, the world was not on some transcendent, deterministic course that made the failure of rural communities inevitable, the gigantic size of farms predictable, the globalization of the economy necessary, or the conflicts between environmentalists and farmers unavoidable.

That is perhaps the most significant gift the center has given to rural communities in the past twenty years. The center's capacity to see the world differently from the way conventional wisdom sees it has given new hope and purpose to rural life.

I suspect it is this same capacity to see the world differently that will shape the center's agenda for the next twenty years. Granted, the center has now achieved a certain degree of respectability among its detractors, so it may no longer be as unique and distinctive. After all, Chuck Hassebrook is now being quoted in *Farm Journal,* and I understand that Marty Strange is having lunch with Al Gore these days. Land-grant universities are starting to recognize the center as an institution that speaks with some authority on rural issues. While the university may not be quite ready to baptize the center, it has become a "rural sociology department in exile," as Bill Heffernan put it.

Nevertheless, given its genius for seeing the world in terms of its *probabilities* rather than its *predictabilities,* I think the center will face at least three major challenges in the next twenty years. These three challenges are on a continuum with work the center is already doing.

The first challenge arises from the increasing global pressures to adopt new technological quick fixes to solve the old Malthusian dilemma. In his recent book, *Preparing for the Twenty-first Century,* Paul Kennedy predicted that increasing world population and simultaneous leveling off of agricultural productivity will make biotechnology in food production inevitable. He acknowledged that this will create enormous economic, social, and environmental problems. He has already written the epitaph for farmers—and by implication, for rural communities. Farmers, he wrote, are "threatened with redundancy," and farming as we know it is "on its way out."[5]

While Kennedy made a compelling case, he arrived at his conclusions based on traditional ways of seeing the world. He fails, for example, to count all of the costs of the past technological "revolutions" in agriculture when he credits the green revolution with holding the Malthusian monster at bay during the past century. Had he gone on to count the green revolution's costs in soil loss, environmental degradation, depleted nonrenewable resources, deteriorated rural communities, and disruptions of centuries-old agricultural conservation and production wisdom in developing countries, he might have quickly come to the same conclusion as the center: the course we are on is simply not sustainable.

In fact, when one looks at the agricultural revolutions of the past century from the perspective of sustainability, one is quickly drawn to a question raised by Lois Hudson. In her novel, *The Bones of Plenty,* she asks whether it isn't time to "ponder the tendency, apparently so deep in most of us, to try to fix a problem by doing more of what got us into the difficulty in the first place."[6] Technological quick fixes are seldom a substitute for long-term, humane, ecological discoveries and practices. The biotechnology fix is no exception.

A challenge confronts those of us who believe there is a better way to meet our future food needs, a way that doesn't put the environment at greater risk, destroy rural communities, further concentrate wealth and power in the hands of multinational conglomerates, or diminish the value of human resources. The challenge is to map out clearly and convincingly how a more sustainable agriculture can meet the food requirements of an expanding global population *better* than technological fixes can.

In other words, we need to craft a convincing, realistic scenario of how we propose to keep the world fed using the technologies of sustainable agriculture. An even more perplexing proposition is how to reframe the question of population explosion and food production. We need to give the world a more convivial answer than the one in which we mount a simultaneous assault on farmers, rural communities, democratic economic structures, and the genetic code of Earth's organisms just to feed the human species. Our challenge is to propose an alternative for keeping the world fed that, in the words of Thomas Berry, enables the "human community to become present to the larger Earth community in a mutually enhancing manner."[7] I don't think we've done that.

The second challenge that confronts us is what Wendell Berry calls the "decolonizing of rural America."[8] Berry argues that we will not save the land, agriculture, or rural communities unless we radically restructure the global economy. Rural communities, he said, are colonies: "Virtually the whole landscape of our country—from the exhausted cotton fields of the plantation South to the eroding wheatlands of the Palouse, from the strip mines of Appalachia to the clear-cuts of the Pacific slope—is in the power of an absentee economy, once national and now increasingly international."[9]

The center's mission is to build "sustainable rural communities at home and abroad consistent with social and economic justice, stewardship of the natural environment, broad distribution of wealth and opportunity for all people to earn just incomes and own and control productive resources."[10] To accomplish this mission, the current structure of our global economy has to be reordered. This, of course, is a daunting task. Paul Kennedy suggests that as the biotech revolution makes farming redundant and the robotics revolution makes labor redundant, the multinational companies stand to gain even more wealth and power.[11] While he recognizes that this additional concentration of power and wealth in the hands of a few will cause enormous social and political upheavals, he proposes no alternative scenario.

So how is a tiny group of folks like the Center for Rural Affairs to challenge this economic steamroller? I'd like to suggest that the task may not be so formidable. William Greider reminds us of the "frailties of power" within the citadels of the industrial/government complex. Greider recalls how it has always been ordinary citizens, acting in local communities, that have brought about real social change.[12] He echoes the admonition attributed to Margaret Mead to never doubt that a small group of thoughtful committed citizens can change the world.

I think we have an opportunity to challenge the forces that have colonized rural communities. Farmers, environmentalists, and food customers all share a common distaste for our industrialized food and agriculture system. Farmers recognize that the system increasingly squeezes the farming sector out of agriculture's economic pie. Environmentalists realize that the way food is produced, processed, and transported depletes natural resources, destroys biodiversity, and treats animals inhumanely. Food customers are becoming aware they can create a better world by voting for an alternative food system with their food dollars.

If farmers, environmentalists, and food customers joined hands to create an alternative, sustainable food system, it would change agriculture and revolutionize rural economies. A food system based on *buying* principles instead of *selling* principles would not trade food solely on the basis of price and supply, but would also be based on the principles of protecting the environment, restoring the resource base, ensuring justice for rural communities, and guaranteeing safe, nutritious, wholesome food to all food customers. Expanding our coalition to include the voice of the food customer might be one way of decolonizing rural America. I don't think we've done that.

The third challenge confronting the center is the role of mythology in our work. If whole-system, ecological, mutual-Earth-community-enhancing activity is ever to become a reality, then we have to begin operating out of a new mythology.

In *The Universe Story,* Thomas Berry and Brian Swimme suggest that we lack a comprehensive story of the universe in the modern era.[13] We *do* have a story, of course, but it is far from comprehensive. Our current story allows the human species to dominate and exploit every other member of the planetary community to serve its own narrow interests. That mythology has its roots in the industrial era and the Cartesian paradigm. It is a mythology that assumes that the sole reason for understanding nature is to *subdue* it for purely human ends. That mythology is bankrupt, and it will be the undoing of us and the rest of Earth's community.

Berry and Swimme suggest that the guiding principle for the new story with which we must evolve in the next era is that the universe is "a communion of subjects, not a collection of objects."[14] The basis for this conclusion is not just moral imperative but scientific observation. The interdependent bond of communion that exists among all of Earth's biota is the only logical explanation for the Earth's evolution.

For the last three hundred years, we have assumed that the whole Earth was a collection of objects put here solely for our use. If we want to survive into the next century, we need to act out of a mythology that recognizes that we are part of an intricate web of life that evolved together—a communion of subjects—and that maintaining the integrity of that web is our only hope. We need to give voice to the possibility of living out of that new mythology. I don't think we've done that.

If we choose to see the world in terms of probabilities rather than predictabilities, a real prospect exists for a different future for rural America. To conventional wisdom, steeped in abstract models based on global economic forces and the voracious needs and desires of the human community, farmers and rural communities have already been written off. But to those of us who live in these rural communities and have experienced their power and their promise, we see a different future. Indeed, if there is any place on this planet where folks have the potential to begin living in the Earth community as a communion of subjects, it is in rural communities.

For those who think they have already written the epitaph for rural communities, based on their scientific trends and analyses, we need to simply stand up and say, "Rubbish—it's turtles all the way down!"

Rediscovering American Agriculture

Agriculture since 1492

The quincentennial of Columbus's voyage to the New World produced many provocative reevaluations of American history. This seems a good time to take a fresh look at what has happened to agriculture in this part of the world since 1492. Doing so, I think, will reveal that interpretations of our agricultural history have been flawed. Most of us grew up with the notion that nothing was happening agriculturally until the Europeans arrived, stories of Indians teaching Puritans how to plant corn notwithstanding. The popular view involves Indians eating bison or going hungry. Agriculture is often assumed to have begun when Europeans cleared the forests and introduced the plow.

In fact, agriculture was practiced extensively for thousands of years before Columbus arrived. Once the English settled, they emulated native agriculture. As William Cronon points out, both the English and the Indians in New England practiced an agriculture that was "inextricably bound to the wheel of the seasons, both produced maize as their most important crop, both weeded and hilled their corn, [and] both relied on a wide range of different food sources."[1]

Thus, Europeans did not introduce agriculture per se, nor even a radically different kind of agriculture, but rather a different attitude toward agriculture. According to Cronon, Europeans came with a mosaic in their heads that led them to clear forests and maintain domesticated grazing animals, contrary to the native way of thinking.[2] This difference in attitude is a good starting point for rethinking American agriculture.

Native agriculture "fit in" to the landscape, while European agriculture

A previous version of this piece was published in *Word & Work* 13 (1993): 294–303.

primarily altered the landscape. Perhaps one of the most brilliant explanations of the attitude of European immigrants comes from Frederick Turner, who vividly describes the environment prior to 1492 and the predominant attitudes immigrants had toward land that shaped agriculture here after Columbus. Turner remarked that when the Europeans encountered a landscape teeming with wildlife and thick with foliage, "had they been other than they were, they might have written a new mythology here. As it was they took inventory."[3]

To our forebears, this land was a catalog of resources waiting to be mined:

- Bison waiting to be harvested
- Trees waiting to be logged
- Grasslands waiting to be plowed and planted into neat rows of corn
- Rich, black soil and its nutrients waiting to be used
- Aquifers waiting to be tapped and piped into center-pivot irrigation systems to produce huge quantities of grain on marginal land

This was an agriculture of resource exploitation. Because they approached the land from this perspective, they engaged in the kind of agriculture that became the model for the industrial world.

Initially, as nutrients became depleted in one region, fields were abandoned to plow more virgin soil farther west. Taking inventory, early farmers found there was always more where that came from. When new land became scarce, the strategy shifted from primary resource exploitation to secondary resource exploitation—from mining nutrients directly from the soil to mining them from pockets of mineral deposits and transporting them to our fields. Thus the chemical era in agriculture began. Taken together, the principles of taking inventory, mining resources, and extracting cheap raw materials to produce wealth and power constitute the predominant paradigm shaping U.S. agricultural policy and practice.

This attitude was reinforced by a moral imperative: manifest destiny. Our ancestors believed they had been called to this land to "develop" its rich resources, just as surely as Columbus had been divinely inspired to "discover" it. The Puritans saw it as a moral obligation. They were put here to "build a new kingdom of God on earth," and that included "taming the wilderness" and cutting down trees to plant corn. In their view, clear-cutting forests was not "deforestation"; it was "the progress of cultivation."[4] Native Americans, not prone to taking inventory and inclined more toward an agriculture of restraint, were seen as failing to "develop" the land and exercise their God-given responsibility to make use of it. Consequently, the Europeans felt justified in taking over that responsibility—and with it, of course, the land.

The agriculture of restraint that natives practiced before the arrival of Columbus was likely developed in response to fifteen thousand years of experience. Until quite recently, we had dismissed their agriculture as "primitive" because it seemed so contrary to the "clean cultivation" mosaic familiar to the European mind, and because it didn't appear to fully exploit the rich resources available here. Today we are discovering that many principles of native agriculture are precisely the principles of sustainable agriculture.

In the northern plains, for example, the Ankara, Mandan, and Hidatsa tribes had evolved principles of agriculture that are being closely studied by the Carrington Research and Extension Center at North Dakota State University because of similarities to sustainable agriculture research. Diversity, recycling, restrictive cultivation, moisture conservation, and selectivity based on bioregionalism were among the key strategies for successful agriculture devised by those tribes. All of these principles are now very familiar to advocates of sustainable agriculture. It was an agriculture that was successful then, and we are rediscovering that it can be successful now.

John Gardner, superintendent of the research center, once wryly reminded an audience that "native agriculture was an agriculture that normally kept the villages well-fed, often with surpluses available for trade. It was designed to produce reliably under harsh growing conditions (such as drought and frost). And it was an agriculture in which the men spent most of their time hunting and fishing, the women did all the work, and there were no taxes—and we thought we could improve on it!"[5]

The Success of Industrial Agriculture

No one can dispute that the inventory-taking approach to agriculture, which replaced native agriculture, was enormously successful. The success is not surprising. Mining resources that have been stored up over millions of years, while disregarding the need to preserve or restore those resources, creates enormous short-term economic returns. We have all benefited from this agriculture of exploitation during the past five hundred years.

This agriculture of exploitation gave birth to thousands of farms and rural communities throughout the continent and made them economically successful. Population densities, in fact, exactly matched the number of farmers and ranchers required to manage these resource exploitation enterprises. Rangelands in the West tended to be sparsely populated because mining nutrients from grasslands with roaming cattle required only a few ranchers. Parts of the country suited for truck farming became more densely populated because it required more labor to extract nutrients through vegetable production. On the whole, the resource-exploitation approach to agriculture populated the continent with family farms and thriving rural communities.[6]

As the mechanical revolution began to sweep the countryside, farmers started replacing labor with technology. Modern equipment made it possible for fewer farmers to exploit larger acreages. The addition of off-farm inputs made it possible to control nutrient depletion and pest infestation on ever-larger acreages, enabling farmers to specialize in one or two commodities. The result was increased production that eventually required an aggressive export trade scheme to remove surpluses from bulging government storage facilities.

Overproduction by fewer, larger, more specialized farms resulted in declining rural populations and concomitant decline in the demand for local markets and locally produced inputs. Small rural communities began to lose their "pull" (the ability to attract local business). Less money stayed in local communities to support local activities; money tended to "flow through" rural communities to distant suppliers and processors.

Industrialists, of course, argue that the disappearance of farms and rural communities will not affect the continued success of exploitation agriculture. Many economists see the continuing displacement of farms and rural communities as an inevitable and desirable part of progress and a clear sign of the success of agriculture. The invisible hand of free-market competition weeds out economic inefficiencies. Farmers who didn't make it during the past five decades were dismissed as "poor managers." Disappearing rural communities were explained by advances in communication and transportation technologies. Centralizing the entire food production industry into the hands of two or three multinational conglomerates is viewed as economically desirable and inevitable.

However, the miraculous success of industrial agriculture is measured using simplistic indicators of economic success and efficiency. Record yields per acre and record numbers of people fed by a single farmer have become popular benchmarks for defining success. Ever more fantastic successes for exploitation agriculture in the future through the marvels of high technology are predicted. The result is that most Americans probably still believe that our industrial agriculture is the most successful agriculture in the history of the world. Meanwhile, few have noticed that the agricultural wisdom existing prior to 1492 has been relegated to the dustbin of history.

Trouble

However, a growing number of people concede that American industrial agriculture is in trouble—environmentally, economically, and socially. We now know that many of the efficiencies claimed for conventional agriculture were based on faulty accounting. Determining efficiencies by how many nonfarmers a farmer feeds is politics, not economics. A more realistic economic ruler is how many calories of energy it takes to put a calorie of food on the table. By that measure, industrial agriculture does not fare well, considering, for example, that it takes nine calories of energy to put one calorie of canned corn on the table.[7]

We can no longer ignore the environmental costs of industrial agriculture, costs such as cleaning polluted lakes and streams, removing soil sediment from ditches, and increased health problems, all of which we have tended to ignore or push into the future. These costs need to be traced to their source.

Once we do proper accounting, the efficiencies claimed for resource-exploitation agriculture begin to disappear. The economic problems of resource-exploitation agriculture promise to become more acute in the future. The abundant nonrenewable resources fueling this agriculture are rapidly disappearing. As they become scarce, they will become cost-prohibitive. Finally, they will become fully depleted.

I am always amused when I am asked how long I will be able to mine the phosphorus embedded in the soil of my fields without bringing in additional phosphorus from off the farm. I generally respond by noting that land exists that has been farmed by alternative methods for more than 2,000 years without off-farm inputs. According to projections I've seen, no one predicts that known phosphorus deposits will last anywhere near that long, given the rate at which they are currently being mined.

Borrowing Alvin Toffler's notion of future economic development based on mind rather than muscle, farming systems may come to depend more on knowledge, innovation, and flexibility than on the number of acres on the farm.[8] The farmer who can respond to a microbakery's sudden demand for a particular quality of wheat to produce a bread for a new market may have a distinct market advantage over the farmer locked into producing huge quantities of uniform wheat for the mass market.

On the social front, resource-exploitation agriculture has serious problems. While many may debate whether disappearing farms and rural communities pose a threat to food security, growing evidence suggests this phenomenon could be more troubling than the industrial mind is willing to admit. The next wave of farmers leaving the land will increase centralization of farm management, and field management will be replaced by front-office management. Such a shift in management introduces the problems of Soviet agriculture, which did not suffer from lack of production potential but from inefficient and ineffective management. Such deficiencies have both economic and ecologic consequences.

As Wendell Berry has reminded us: "If agriculture is to remain productive, it must preserve the land, and the fertility and ecological health of the land: the land, that is, must be used well. A further requirement, therefore, is that if the land is to be used well, the people who use it must know it well, must be highly motivated to use it well, must know how to use it well, must have time to use it well, and must be able to afford to use it well."[9]

Nothing in resource-exploitation agriculture—which has succeeded in effecting one of the greatest out-migrations of farmers off the land that the world has ever seen—meets Berry's requirements. Keeping farmers on the land who know the land and have the authority and responsibility for making management decisions in the field is not a nostalgic notion about saving the "family farm" or a social-justice imperative to improve the quality of life for farmers. Farmers are needed on the land to ensure food security for ourselves, our children, and our grandchildren.

Choices

As I see it, agriculture in America is at a crossroads. This land has experienced both an agriculture of restraint and an agriculture of resource exploitation. At this juncture we have three choices:

The first option is to stay on our present course of resource-exploitation agriculture. That would mean we would continue to centralize agriculture and concentrate it in even fewer hands. Many policy makers do not see that as a problem. Indeed, an official from the U.S. Office of Management and Budget recently remarked, "If two or three farmers can bring in all of the food and fiber we need—who cares?" This choice, of course, hinges on the false expectation that we can continue to find, make, and afford the inputs necessary to fuel this kind of agriculture. I don't think this is a very realistic future. I think that the five-hundred-year experiment in resource-exploitation agriculture is rapidly coming to a close.

The second option is to go with the next technological fix. A lot of folks believe biotechnology will save us from the problems facing resource-exploitation agriculture. I'm pessimistic about the prospects for transgenic technologies to rescue us. Briefly, these problems include harmful side effects, ignorance of whole-system issues, and further concentration of power in agribusiness. Quick fixes never work. Early applications of transgenic technologies, from rBGH to herbicide resistance, appear to have little benefit for anyone except the companies introducing them.

Our third option is to return to some model of agricultural restraint. This option would require that we develop a more complete, whole-systems understanding of how nature works and how various parts complement one another. We then would need to fit agriculture into the crannies of that system. This would require readopting principles and attitudes of the native agriculture practiced before 1492, and then applying all of the ingenuity we have acquired since then to enhance that system.

Conclusion

As we contemplate the future of agriculture, we might remember that our reign as humans on this planet has been relatively brief. In the larger scheme of things, our survival does not come with a guarantee. We might increase our odds for success in agriculture if we opt for an agriculture of restraint based on biospherical understanding and a respect that accommodates itself to nature. I don't see a future for an agriculture of inventory-taking that ignores the evolutionary laws of the biosphere and is based on the fantasy that there will always be more where that came from.

A shift in agriculture requires, as Turner suggested, that we "write a new mythology here." Our ancestors may have been incapable of that task because of who they were. But after five hundred years, one hopes that we have learned a few things. Perhaps now we are ready to see what our ancestors could not: the agriculture of restraint that was in place here had evolved over thousands of years of learning to live with this land, appreciate its gifts, recognize its limits, and accommodate its curses.

Lewis Mumford suggested in 1926 that immigrants to North America behaved the way they did out of "cultural necessity." Mumford argued that an empty inner space—the cultural vacuum within—determined their behavior with respect to the environment and each other, rather than the vast geography of the continent, as argued by Turner. As we contemplate the agriculture for the next five hundred years, we might give some attention to that inner space, as Mumford did:

> Now we begin to see a little more clearly the state of mind out of which the great migrations to the New World became possible. The physical causes have been dwelt on often enough; it is important to recognize that a cultural necessity was at work at the same time. The old culture of the Middle Ages had broken down; the old heritage lingered on only in the "backward" and "unprogressive" countries like Italy and Spain, which drifted outside the main currents of the European mind. Men's interests became externalized; externalized and abstract. They fixed their attention on some narrow aspect of experience, and they pushed that to the limit. Intelligent people were forced to choose between the fossilized shell of an old and complete culture, and the new culture, which in origin was thin, partial, abstract, and deliberately indifferent to man's proper interests. Choosing the second, our Europeans already had one foot in America. Let them suffer persecution, let the times get hard, let them fall out with their governments, let them dream of worldly success—and they will come swarming over the ocean. The groups that had most completely shaken off the old symbolisms were those that were most ready for the American adventure: they turned

themselves easily to the mastery of the external environment. To them matter alone mattered.[10]

Rediscovering agriculture in America requires discovering a new mythology that will enable us to abandon the inventory-taking approach to agriculture. And that, Mumford said, "is nothing less than the effort to reconceive a new world."[11] Perhaps it is better to reconceive the old world that was already here when we came, a world we couldn't see because we were who we were.

Spirituality and Cooperatives

Using the word "spirituality" is a problem in our largely secular culture. This problem is rooted in our cultural inclination to compartmentalize things: separating mind from matter, facts from values, and science from religion and art.

Such compartmentalization leads most of us to be suspicious about introducing spirituality into business. We assume that spirituality is a "religious thing" and therefore has no real place in business. At best, spirituality is irrelevant because it cannot be reduced to hard facts and bottom lines. When spirituality has mingled with business, it was often as a scam or charity appeal—or worse, as an appeal to moral duty. Appeals to the business community to "save the family farm" or "preserve rural communities" as a moral duty probably are futile. We always insist that the market should decide. For many, spirituality in business is either irrelevant or unpleasant.

What Is Spirituality?

Let's begin by clarifying the concept of spirituality and how it contrasts with religion. In her wonderful book *Walking a Sacred Path,* Lauren Artress writes:

> Religion is for those who are scared to death of hell.
> Spirituality is for those who have been there.
> Spirituality is the inward activity of growth and
> maturation that happens to each of us.

This text is a modified version of a speech delivered at the North Dakota Association of Rural Electrical Cooperatives and North Dakota Association of Telephone Cooperatives Four Million Dollar Tour, July 13, 1995.

To be spiritually mature is to grow in an ever-deepening sense of compassion, lessening our fear of change, and of the differences between us.[1]

Once we start thinking of spirituality as the capacity to overcome past fears, lessen fear of change, or recognize the unique differences among us as assets rather than liabilities, we are dealing with the fundamentals of successful business ventures, especially cooperatives. Thomas Moore's definition of spirituality points to the central role it plays in our individual and collective lives: "Spirituality is an aspect of any attempt to approach or attend to the invisible factors in life and to transcend the personal, concrete, finite particulars of this world. . . . This spiritual point of view is necessary . . . providing the breadth of vision, the inspiration, and the sense of meaning."[2]

Certainly anyone involved in business recognizes such spiritual practices. Every farmer, for example, knows that farming is much more than the individual, finite particulars of starting a diesel engine, ordering seed, putting seed in the ground, and harvesting grain. To be successful, the farmer needs a vision of the farm, faith that the seeds will grow and harvests will take place. Without the inspiration that comes from producing food, working with nature, or seeing a satisfied customer eating a wonderful loaf of bread, there would be little successful farming. Yet these parts of farming cannot be put into a calculus. They are spiritual practices. The very act of cooperating, of acquiring the breadth of vision necessary to imagine a future wherein community cooperation is more productive than individual competition, is a spiritual practice of the highest order—an "inward activity of growth and maturation." No cooperative can be successful without spiritual discipline.

The Absence of Spirituality in Business and Society

Recognition of spiritual practices in business may be one of the greatest contributions that cooperatives can make to society. The absence of spirituality in our business and social lives has left us lonely, isolated, and cynical. Business role models tend to be the tycoons who have risen above their colleagues. Seldom do we find stories of successful communities who worked together to solve a problem, or of successful coalitions who acquired healthy bottom lines by cooperating rather than competing. Rampant individualism prevails, although it has left us isolated, stressed out, and overburdened, and despite hundreds of case studies demonstrating that cooperation works.

The radical individualism that pervades much of the business world is pathological. Humans cannot exist in isolation and remain healthy. According to John Cobb, "The health of the community in which we participate is crucial to our own well-being. We are persons-in-community rather than isolated individuals unaffected by our relations to others."[3]

Increasingly the business world recognizes the value of cooperation. A National Public Radio story this summer featured Scandinavian business leaders who had formed cooperative relationships to convert the waste of one company into the raw materials of another, benefiting both. Prior to cooperation, each company had to spend thousands of dollars and address hundreds of environmental headaches to get rid of their wastes. By cooperating, they profited from waste disposal. They "borrowed this model from nature," one of the company presidents said. These leaders stressed that their efforts were not altruistic or a response to environmental mandates, but were instead a way to make more money.

In North Dakota farmers understand they can safeguard their economic futures more readily by cooperating than they can by competing against one another. Through cooperatives, they can retain ownership of their raw materials in a value-added enterprise. This enables them to recapture part of the market-sector economy and retain wealth in the farm sector and in their own local communities. Such cooperation is a spiritual discipline.

Cooperative development can dispel some of the cynicism that pervades rural communities. Curt Stofferahn and his colleagues at the University of North Dakota discovered that people predominantly use a cynical "corpse" metaphor when thinking about rural communities.[4] Stofferahn and his colleagues discovered that people remain in rural communities because they believe that economic decline and the death of their community are inevitable, and their role is to help "pull the plug" on the town's remaining life-support system and prepare the corpse for burial. Alternatively, some people believe vitality will be restored by some new industry that will move into town and resuscitate the corpse.

This is defeated spirituality that leads to hopelessness. It is this spiritual death that often causes communities to be cynical about local cooperatives, even when they are successful.

The Destructiveness of Extractive Global Economies

While a defeated spirituality destroys the faith of local communities, extractive global economies bleed them of their indigenous economic resources. I am not arguing that the "global competitiveness" of the free market (in which it is assumed that rural communities are too small to compete successfully) destroys rural communities. Rather, it is the extractive nature of global economies that is destructive.

Global economies become extractive in at least two ways. First, they extract raw materials from one place to generate wealth in another place. The business climate that evolves out of this extractive economy is based on three principles: cheap labor, cheap raw materials, and the fewest environmental restrictions. These conditions are the most conducive to making a profit in the global economy. The more one can keep the costs of labor and raw materials down while externalizing environmental costs, the easier it is to compete in the global market—especially if one doesn't have to *live* in the community from which one extracts such wealth.

But these principles ruin a local community's natural capital, degrade the environment, and reduce a community's wealth by offering only low-paying jobs. The global economy, in turn, sells expensive value-added products to the same community, further draining its wealth. By extracting cheap raw materials (and the community's income via imported value-added products) and insisting on cheap labor, local communities are transformed into colonial economies.

Global companies specialize by producing a lot of one thing, which they then sell to communities who become dependent on distant sources of specialized production. Distant companies seek only profitable investment of capital. There is no business interest in sustaining communities. In the era of "free" trade, the global economy is determined to remove any restrictions that impede this process of exploitation. Cobb asks an important question: "From what is this free market or free trade free?" The restrictions that the global economy seeks to remove, he writes, "will make possible still higher degrees of specialization and will further discourage efforts of local communities or nations to supply most of their own needs. Capital will move freely throughout the world to those places where it can be most profitably invested. Labor, which cannot move as freely, will be at an increasing disadvantage."[5]

Cobb reminds us that this is not the kind of free market that Adam Smith had in mind when he formulated the principles of modern economic thought in the eighteenth century. In Smith's time, local markets operated "within established communities and served them." Cobb suggests that trade is only "free" when a community is "free" *not to trade.* Free trade is free only when a community can trade on the basis of its abundance and self-sufficiency, rather than its scarcity and dependency.

The global economy depletes local communities of their monetary, human, and natural resources, ultimately destroying them. One way local communities can resist such exploitation is to form cooperatives that seek to serve the local community's needs and preserve the community's local resources. This will not be easy, and some argue it may be impossible. But who would have predicted twenty-five years ago that the major breweries would introduce a line of microbrews because local microbreweries were cutting too deeply into their market share? Who would have predicted that local microbakeries would be wildly successful or that a small group of ranchers in North Dakota could form a bison cooperative and process the meat themselves, thereby retaining wealth in their local communities?

These and hundreds of other ventures may prove that Alvin Toffler's "powershift" is already taking place. Toffler predicted that the huge "muscle" industries are dinosaurs in danger of imminent extinction and the new emerging "mind" (spiritual?) industries will replace them.[6] In my view, Toffler does not give sufficient credit to the spirit of community in his vision of these new industries. He still uses the model of the entrepreneurial *individual.* But everywhere today, new human industry is emerging in the context of *community*: community-supported agriculture, community food security, and even microbreweries are successful largely because they are in local communities. Major beer companies who distribute microbrewery labels nationally will probably cut into their own market shares, because major breweries cannot duplicate a local community's loyalty to "their" local brewery.

Cooperatives, Spirituality, and Boosterism

If we are going to develop local economies within local communities by cooperating and working together, it has to be real and not just a faddish attempt to do something different. Incorporating spirituality and cooperation into business plans must be accompanied with sound economic theory, competent feasibility studies, and wise business decisions. Boosterism will not help local communities, and simple belief alone will not create successful operations. Shallow efforts will only further endanger the community's economic health. Spirituality, however, can be a powerful force for change if it is released to work within our local communities. As something real and integral within us, spirituality has too long been denied or suppressed.

Spirituality is no substitute for the hard work of restructuring our economic lives and building new local economic infrastructures. But it can be done; indeed it is being done by local communities everywhere. I'm proud that my state of North Dakota is taking a lead. In "Pride of Dakota" expositions, one can see hundreds of locally produced products, many of them by locally owned cooperatives. A new economy is taking shape that is "free" to trade with the global economy but that is also increasingly free *not* to trade with it because it is becoming self-sufficient. Cooperatives have an innate advantage that will help us, but we have a long way to go.

Parable of Hope from Nature

On this long journey we need support for the difficulties ahead. In this regard I borrow a parable from nature from the wonderful little book *Insight and Action,* in which the authors offer lessons from Milton Olsen's observations about geese. The foreword to their book is titled "Facts about Geese." I think these "facts" can help us ground our hope for the future:

- As each bird flaps its wings, it creates uplift for the birds following. By flying in a V formation, the whole flock adds 71 percent more flying range than if each bird flew alone. *Lesson:* People who share a common direction and sense of community can get where they're going quicker and easier because they travel on the thrust of one another.
- Whenever a goose falls out of formation, it suddenly feels the drag and resistance of trying to fly alone and quickly gets back into formation to take advantage of the lifting power of the bird immediately in front. *Lesson:* If we have as much sense as a goose, we will stay in formation with those who are headed where we want to go and be willing to accept their help, as well as give our help to others.
- When the lead goose gets tired, it rotates back into the formation, and another goose flies at the point position. *Lesson:* It pays to take

turns doing the hard tasks and sharing leadership. As with geese, people are interdependent on each others' unique arrangements of gifts, talents, and resources.

- The geese in formation honk from behind to encourage those in front to keep up their speed. *Lesson:* We need to make sure our honking from behind is encouraging. In groups where there is encouragement to work against great odds, production is much greater.
- When a goose gets sick or wounded or is shot down, two geese drop out of formation and follow it down to help and protect it. They stay with it until it is able to fly again or dies. Then they launch out on their own with another formation or catch up with the flock. *Lesson:* If we have as much sense as geese, we too will stand by each other in difficult times as well as when we are strong.[7]

For those who do not find the goose parable trustworthy, perhaps the Hebrew prophets' basis for hope may be more assuring. The Hebrews believed there was a moral order to the universe that eventually would establish justice for the disempowered. Societies always had the opportunity to reorder their communities in conformity with this universal order. If they failed to do so, after a given period of injustice, Yahweh would bring about "the day of the Lord" and restructure society. This usually involved a painful and devastating collapse. But out of the collapse, Yahweh would bring a new order that would better serve the community.

Because the global industrial system fails to meet the needs of the majority of people in their communities and increasingly wrests control from citizens, it may be headed for collapse. William Greider provides instructive comments in this regard:

> My conviction . . . is that an active faith in democratic possibilities dwells at the very center of the American experience. . . . Among other things, I have seen up close the frailties of power. At the pinnacles of political command, behind the veil of platitudes, I have usually glimpsed a scene of confusion and often chaos . . . folly and misapprehensions of people in charge. . . . History confirms that this is nearly always the reality of power.
>
> This fallibility . . . exists in authority figures of every kind, from corporate executives to church prelates. There is a "reassuring anarchy" . . . in the most exalted realms of power and this encourages

my conviction that rigid arrangements of power are much more vulnerable to intrusion and change than the experts and authorities wish people to believe. The people who are running things are especially prone to error when they are isolated from the shared ideas and instincts of the larger community.[8]

Finally, the global economy is enormously energy-intensive. We need smaller, more dispersed enterprises that are more innovative and capable of responding to new local markets. Local cooperative business relationships, funded with local capital, and designed to meet local needs, appear to have a comparative advantage. Ultimately, cooperation builds community. Life in community nourishes our well-being, not life in isolation. Common health and commonwealth always go together, as Wendell Berry has reminded us. Cooperatives and spirituality also belong together.

In Search of Objectivity, or How to Create a Credible Certification Program

Certification programs in search of credibility have attached themselves to the concept of "third-party" status like a magnet to clean metal. Food customers want assurances that organic certification is reliable. Many leaders in the certification network have responded by assuring the public that if a certification program has "third-party" status, it can be trusted and is credible. Nothing could be further from the truth.

"Third-party" language has probably crept into the industry because it is commonly believed that "distance" assures "objectivity." That belief had scientific validity from the time of Descartes to the emergence of quantum theory. Descartes' scientific doctrine was based on the assumption that one could separate the researcher from the research, thereby eliminating subjective bias and establishing "objective truth."

But with the advent of quantum physics in the early twentieth century, those assumptions were discarded. As Werner Heisenberg put it, quantum theory made it impossible to "disregard the fact that natural science is formed by men" and that therefore "natural science does not simply describe and explain nature, it is a part of the interplay between nature and ourselves; it describes nature *as exposed to our method of questioning.*"[1] As Heisenberg explains, "objective truth" is impossible, and we have to content ourselves with "degrees of truth."

"Distance," consequently, is not an adequate criterion for credibility. To establish the credibility of their findings, scientists must rely on peer review. Michael Polanyi described this scientific community as a society of explorers who are committed to discovering degrees of truth under the scrutiny

---

This paper was given as a keynote address at a national organic inspectors' training event in 1990.

of peer review, which relies on critical and independent evaluation within a community. Truth through "distance" is replaced by truth through communal scrutiny. Each individual in the community is invited to evaluate the data from his or her unique perspective, exposing that perspective to the scrutiny of the community.

The organic industry should take its lead from this transformation in science as it struggles to establish the ground for reliability in certification. No matter how much "distance" between various parties a certification program may claim, it can never achieve objectivity because certification is performed by people. This means the same thing for certification programs as for scientific research. Certification reports are *not* pure descriptions of inspected farms or processing plants; they are instead reports of the interplay between farms and farmers, farmers and inspectors, and inspectors and farms. Instead of "objective" decisions by "third-party" committees, we have outcomes from individuals who interpret inspection reports using their own perspectives.

This means we need to face up to several observations. First, in every certification program, someone always "signs the check." This by itself obviates third-party distance. Anyone working in a certification program would be tempted to indulge the party that signs the check; it makes little difference whether the program is owned by growers, the state, or a commercial company. The only way to ensure that such temptation does not unduly affect the quality of the certification work is by placing all certification activity under the scrutiny of peer review, with a public report of the findings.

Second, artificial distance created through third-party mechanisms can be counterproductive. Creating "distance" ensures a degree of unfamiliarity and fractionalization that can translate into ignorance, blindness, and unreliable data. Advocates of third-party distance have suggested that growers who participate in a certification program should not be allowed to do farm inspections in that program, especially not in their own communities. Distance is thus created between the inspector and the inspection work.

But who is more knowledgeable about the requirements of a certification program than a grower who participates in it? And who is more knowledgeable about the farming practices of a particular community than a farmer who lives in the region? And who is more likely to know what kind of pesticide violations to look for during a farm inspection than another grower in the same community? And who is more likely to be privy to community information regarding the farming practices of organic growers in a given region than another grower in that community? In reality, no one is more qualified to do a professional job of inspection than those ruled out by third-party qualifications.

Another self-defeating regulation is the proposal that no inspector should be allowed to inspect the same farm more than two years in succession, to prevent the inspector from getting too "close" to the farmer to be objective. But this removes the inspector precisely when one might assume he or she has gotten to know the farm well enough to begin doing a competent job of inspection!

The public should be skeptical of any certification program that has not been scrutinized by peer review, no matter how effectively that program has managed to establish third-party status. Even state-operated certification programs, which should be the most objective, have been questioned in this regard. For example, skeptics have questioned whether Texas "hormone-free" beef is really genuine. Apart from an effective peer-review process, there is no way to answer such skepticism.

Of course, some growers may want to be lenient in their inspections of fellow growers, just as some manufacturers may be empathetic toward fellow manufacturers when they inspect their processing plants. However, a built-in incentive exists to constrain cheaters. It is in the growers' interest to allow only genuine organic growers into the program, because that helps limit supply. Similarly, manufacturers want to ensure that all companies operate by the same standards to ensure a fair and level playing field for competition. Both growers and manufacturers have incentives to safeguard the reputation of the program in which they participate, because they rely on the program's credibility to sell their own product. Thus, creating "distance" in relationships between those doing the certification work and those being certified can often serve to lower the quality of certification. Such efforts are unnecessary because strong incentives exist to do credible certification work, despite "closeness" in such relationships.

The most effective way to ensure that certification work is properly conducted is through peer review. Every certification program should be required to undergo independent evaluation by peers for the purpose of ascertaining whether the program meets prescribed standards and procedures at all levels. The Organic Foods Production Association of North

America recently adopted a foundation document for accrediting certification programs that would create such a peer-review program. The accreditation process proposed in that document is modeled after the educational accreditation system used in the United States.

To ensure compliance, a peer-review system would perform periodic, in-depth, on-site evaluations as well as interim spot checks between formal evaluation visits. A small percentage of files, farms, and processing plants in a given certification program can be spot checked using survey instruments, telephone interviews, and on-site visits. Nothing short of such a thorough peer review can ever give assurance that a certification program is reliable. In this type of system, accreditation would be required of certification programs in the same way that schools in the educational system need accreditation, to avoid the stigma associated with nonaccredited status.

This does not dismiss the need for third-party language in certification programs, any more than quantum theory displaced the need for objective research. In both cases, it is a matter of deciding where distance is appropriate. The proper role for third-party separation in certification programs lies in separating *functions,* not in creating artificial "distance." Effective peer review requires a clear delineation between rule making, inspection, decision making, and oversight. Each function needs to be performed by different groups of people selected for their expertise and unique points of view. The proper role for third-party separation is not to create a mythical distance between inspector and inspection but to clarify distinctions among the various functions of certification. Certification loses its professional edge when an inspector not only inspects the farm but also makes the decision concerning the farm's eligibility for certification status. Peer review is only possible when different people occupy the chairs associated with each of the distinct functions of the certification process.

In this sense, "in-house" certification programs are those programs where the *same people* perform all of the functions of certification, because that obviates peer review. No one should ever review their own work. No matter how "objective" we may be, we all need the corrective insights that come from alternative points of view.

Even though the most critical part of the peer-review process is the oversight function, it is still missing from many certification programs. If we want to secure the credibility of the organic certification process, we need to embed this oversight function in all certification work, regardless of the structure of the program, as soon as possible. Ultimately, the credibility of any program depends on its being scrutinized by an independent group of knowledgeable peers who have authority to investigate all aspects of the program and issue a public report on their findings.

Such peer-review evaluation is, incidentally, also the key to making reciprocity between programs work. Once all programs are accredited through peer-review evaluation, reciprocity becomes a simple matter of making appropriate financial, procedural, technical, and administrative arrangements.

On Becoming Lovers of the Soil

I have seen so many delicate shapes, forms, and colors in soil profiles that, to me, soils are beautiful.[1]
—Hans Jenny

As farms and farmers continue to disappear from the landscape in many parts of the world, citizens have increasingly begun to ask themselves whether they should become more concerned about farm issues. This is a good question. Why *should* we be concerned about what happens to farms or farmers? After all, food is more abundant and available in global supermarkets today than ever before. For the most part, our food is safe. Industrialized nations spend less of their earned income on food than ever before. And all this despite the fact that farm numbers have been declining steadily for almost a century. So why should we be concerned about farms and farmers? Isn't everything just fine?

Still, at some level, most of us *are* concerned. But why?

The Heart of the Matter

I think we should be concerned because the issues at stake go to the very core of who we are as human beings on a planet that nurtures our life. If I really want to understand why I should be concerned about farm issues, I have to look beyond questions of food safety and environmental protection. I have to begin exploring my real connection to the soil and how that connection, or lack of connection, affects who I become as a person and the kind of society I create with others.

This is an edited version of an essay that first appeared in *For All Generations: Making World Agriculture More Sustainable,* edited by J. Patrick Madden and Scott G. Chaplowe, 101–14 (Glendale, Calif.: World Sustainable Agriculture Association, 1997).

Our modern industrialized society has gone through a divorce. We have become divorced from the soil. And I submit that until we heal that divorce and become lovers of the soil again, many of our social problems will go unsolved, including our food safety and environmental protection problems.

This essay is an invitation of sorts: it is an invitation to all of us to become lovers of the soil again as a way of healing our soils and our souls. Ivan Illich and some of his friends recently called attention to such an invitation. Their invitation was specifically addressed to colleagues in the field of philosophy. But I would suggest that it is an invitation that applies to us all:

> The ecological discourse about planet earth, global hunger, threats to life, urges us to look down at the soil, humbly, as philosophers. We stand on soil, not on earth. From soil we come, and to soil we bequeath our excrements and remains. . . . Our generation has lost its grounding in both soil and virtue.
>
> We were torn from the bonds to soil—the connections which limited action, making practical virtue possible—when modernization insulated us from plain dirt, from toil, flesh, soil and grave. The economy into which we have been absorbed . . . transforms people into interchangeable morsels of population, ruled by the laws of scarcity.
>
> Commons and homes are barely imaginable to persons hooked on public utilities and garaged in furnished cubicles. Bread is a mere foodstuff, if not calories or roughage. To speak of friendship, religion, and joint suffering as a style of conviviality—after the soil has been poisoned and cemented over—appears like academic dreaming to people randomly scattered in vehicles, offices, prisons and hotels.[2]

Illich and his friends then go on to say that they also lament "the neglect for soil in the discourse carried on among board-room ecologists."[3]

I realize that an invitation to become lovers of the soil is an alien request. We cannot take this request to a national government, the United Nations, or environmental organizations as part of the sustainable agriculture debate. Food activists cannot take this issue to their members. University researchers will not be interested in exploring the topic, and organic farmers are unlikely to be receptive. It is certainly not a project that will attract funding from a private foundation.

However, I submit that becoming lovers of the soil is absolutely fundamental to the work that all of us are doing. Soil is the connection to ourselves. From soil we come, and to soil we return. If we are disconnected from it, we are aliens adrift in a synthetic environment. It is the soil that helps us to understand the limitations of life, its cycles of death and rebirth, and the interdependence of all species. To be at home with the soil is truly the only way to be at home with ourselves and therefore the only way we can be at peace with the environment and all of the species that are part of it. It is literally the common ground on which we all stand.

If soil is the source of life, why have we become so divorced from it? Our arrogance may prevent us from acknowledging our tie to dirt. We are such an elegant, smart, inventive species that it is simply beneath us (no pun intended) to entertain the notion that we are somehow inextricably tied to dirt. But the fact remains that we are tied to it. My friend John Pitney, who has made a career of writing songs about the land, has put it eloquently: "The fact that we are not *now* dirt is only temporary."

This arrogance, which we probably all share and which divorces us from soil, was captured by Earl Butz, dean emeritus at Purdue University and former Secretary of the U.S. Department of Agriculture.

God put the worm in the apple; man took it out.
God put the cockroach in the cracker barrel; man took it out.
God put the potato bug on the potato; man took it off.
God put the cocklebur in the soybean field; man took it out.
God put the Johnson grass in the cornfield; man took it out.
God put the termite in the timber; man took it out.
God put the malaria-laden mosquito in the backyard; man took it out.
God put the mildew on the rose; man took it off.
God put the brucellosis in the cow; man took it out.
God put the parasite in the pork; man took it out.[4]

We may smile at some of Mr. Butz's naiveté. We know that for many of the pests that Mr. Butz claims we have "taken out" with our cleverness, we have actually replaced them with hardier pests, and in the process we have made our groundwater undrinkable and our planet less livable. But who among us doesn't harbor visions of remaking the Earth to suit our pleasure and convenience?

There is, of course, nothing wrong with wanting to make our lives more pleasurable and convenient. We *all* prefer wormless apples and termite-free homes. But too often we forget to ask the ecological questions. How does this way of obtaining wormless apples and termite-free houses affect the rest of the Earth?

There are limits, and many of us would like to insulate ourselves from those limits. Becoming lovers of the soil puts us back in touch with those limits. The fact is, we don't like being tied to the soil's limits. Most of us *like* the idea that modernization insulates us from plain dirt, toil, flesh, soil, and grave. But for that divorce, we have paid a great price—and we will continue to pay a great price.

On Becoming Lovers of the Soil

How do we become lovers of the soil again? Becoming any kind of lover is, of course, a very personal matter. But there are some clues that can help us in our quest to become lovers of the soil. I offer three.

The first clue comes from Clarissa Pinkola Estes's remarkable book *How to Love a Woman*. In her view, loving is about proper eroticism, but it has little to do with sex.[5] Rather, proper eroticism is tied to the ability to really *see* one's lover, both the "inner" and the "outer" levels. Eroticism is tied to really seeing the lover's hair, body movements, and tiniest nuances. To love emotionally means not only listening to words but to all of the silent communications that lie behind and beyond words.

Eroticism, in other words, involves a level of "seeing" that goes behind ordinary sight, to penetrate the soul of being. Loving soil involves much the same kind of sight. To love soil requires that we see more than dirt. It requires that we become intimately involved with soil—that we see its life and beauty, smell its rich aroma, hear its voice.

Not too long ago, soil scientists had reduced soil to "a medium that holds a plant in place" while we artificially feed the plant and control its pests. During that era of soil science, soil was considered "fertile" so long as it contained adequate amounts of macronutrients: nitrogen, phosphorous, and potash. Later, soil scientists began to recognize the importance of micronutrients such as sulfur and zinc. Still later they remarked on the importance of soil structure and its relation to compaction and erosion. Still later, the importance of earthworms was recognized, followed by the importance of the rate of organic matter turnover. Now soil scientists are beginning to talk about "soil quality" and "soil health." This is a progression of "seeing" soil—of seeing it as more than dirt. Scientists are ready to become lovers of the soil, to know it intimately, to care about it. This "inner" seeing helps us understand soil as more than a medium.

A second clue to how to become lovers of the soil comes from Wendell Berry. In "The Pleasures of Eating," Berry suggests that we can overcome our insulation from soil—our industrial eating, as he calls it—by (among other things) growing and preparing our own food.[6] Growing something to eat, even if it's only a tomato plant in a pot, begins to acquaint us with the "energy cycle that revolves from soil to seed to flower to fruit to food to offal to decay, and around again." We will, in other words, begin to "see" the soil as that part of the cycle of life that feeds us and to which we return.

A third clue on becoming lovers of the soil comes from Paul W. Brand, who grew up in the mountains of South India, where rice was grown in terraced paddies on mountain slopes. Each paddy was carefully crafted with a grass spillway that retained water and allowed it to trickle to the next paddy. These spillways were controlled by a senior village elder, who ensured the water was equally shared by all of the villagers. As a child, playing with his friends in the mud, Brand encountered the elder's wisdom:

> We . . . called him "Tata," meaning "grandpa." He was the keeper of the dams. He walked slowly, stooped over a bit as though he were always looking at the ground. Old age is very much respected in India, and we boys shuffled our feet and waited in silence for what we knew was going to be a rebuke.
>
> He came over to us and asked us what we were doing. "Catching frogs," we answered.
>
> He stared down at the churned-up mud. "What is this?" he asked.
>
> The biggest boy among us took the responsibility of answering for us all. "It's mud, Tata."
>
> "Whose mud is it?" the old man asked
>
> "It's your mud, Tata. This is your field."
>
> Then the old man turned and looked at the nearest of the little channels across the dam. "What do you see there, in that channel?" he asked.
>
> "That is water, running over into the lower field," the biggest boy answered.

For the first time Tata looked angry. "Come with me and I will show you water."

We followed him a few steps along the dam, and he pointed to the next channel, where clear water was running. "That is what water looks like," he said. Then he led us back to our nearest channel, and said, "Is that water?"

We hung our heads. "No, Tata, that is mud, muddy water," the oldest boy answered. "And the mud from your field is being carried away to the field below, and it will never come back, because mud always runs downhill, never up again. We are sorry, Tata, and we will never do this again."

But Tata . . . went on to tell us that just one handful of mud would grow enough rice for one meal for one person, and it would do it twice a year for years and years into the future. "That mud flowing over the dam has given my family food every year from long before I was born, and before my grandfather was born. Now it will never feed us again. When you see mud in the channels of water, you know that life is flowing away from the mountains."

The old man walked slowly back across the path, pausing a moment to adjust with his foot the grass clod in our muddy channel so that no more water flowed through it. We were silent and uncomfortable. I had gotten a dose of traditional Indian folk education that would remain with me as long as I lived. Soil was life, and every generation was responsible for preserving it for future generations.[7]

Each of these clues has to do with "seeing." We see by attending, by being in touch, and by cultural memory. A friend and I have talked about developing "rituals of consent" that growers might use before they prepare the soil for seeding, to awaken the consciousness of "seeing." If I ask the soil's consent, I am more likely to attend to its needs, be in touch with its cycles, and invoke a cultural memory of caring for the soil in that place. It might be one way of beginning the long journey back to loving the soil again.

Challenges Facing Philosophy as We Enter the Twenty-first Century

Reshaping the Way the Human Species Feeds Itself

If you destroy the economies of household and community, then you destroy the bonds of mutual usefulness and practical dependence without which the other bonds will not hold.[1]
—Wendell Berry

I'd like to begin with a disclaimer. While my academic training is theology, my energies in the past twenty-five years have been devoted to farming. And while I have tried to emulate Thomas Jefferson's vision of the ideal American farmer who is also a philosopher, I confess I have not risen to his standard of farming by day and reading the classics in Greek at night. So my observations about food and farming are more informed by the earthworm and plow than by Plato or Husserl. I can only hope that what I have to offer in some small way contributes to the legacy of Willard Eddy and to the important work that philosophy needs to undertake today.

Anyone working to reshape the food system as we enter the twenty-first century might be seen as working on a solution for which there is no problem. For decades now, most of our major food-related institutions, such as the USDA, FDA, the American Grocers Association, agricultural commodity groups, and even land-grant universities have assured us that our food system is the envy of the world. Our agriculture not only produces the safest, most nutritious food in the world, it does so more efficiently than any other. Americans now spend less than 10 percent of their earned

This is a transcript of the talk Frederick Kirschenmann gave for the annual Willard O. Eddy Lecture, Colorado State University, Ft. Collins, Colorado, September 28, 2000. During his fifty-six years at Colorado State, Eddy founded the honors program and the philosophy department, and he is credited with promoting interdisciplinary study and international understanding.

income on food, less than any other country in the world. Supermarket shelves bulge with more food than we could hope to eat. Concern about potential food shortages in a world of rapidly expanding human population may be justified, but for the immediate future, farmers are oversupplying most key commodity markets to the point of depressing farm prices below their cost of production. So where is the problem?

The growing number of problems related to our food and agriculture industry can perhaps be clustered into three groups: loss of goodwill, ecological degradation, and too many humans relative to the number of farmers.

Loss of Good Will

First, agriculture has a public perception problem. Throughout most of this continent's history, agriculture was perceived as a public good. For Native Americans, who occupied this continent for almost fifteen thousand years before Europeans arrived, agriculture was perceived as a way to keep everyone in the village fed while disturbing nature as little as possible. For many tribes, the goal was to follow a code of conduct that satisfied both ancestors and descendants for at least seven generations. Agriculture was a critical part of that public trust.

In the early 1600s, the Puritans arrived with a very different vision for agriculture. They considered it their divine mandate to "tame the wilderness and establish the Kingdom of God." Clearing the trees and plowing the prairie to plant neat rows of corn was integral to their perceived destiny to create a new social order in this "new" land. That frame of mind still influences us today. It has remained, as Sidney Mead observed, "a constant part of the ideological structure of the nation."[2] While that peculiar mindset is part of the problem, the Puritans (and many since then) have perceived agriculture's role in taming the wilderness to make room for God's kingdom as a public good.

For most of the eighteenth and nineteenth centuries, agriculture was key to creating a democratic republic. A country of landholding farmers, beholden to no one, would ensure that everyone could speak their minds and vote their conscience. Thomas Jefferson was a principal promoter of this vision, and it was certainly in his mind when he signed the Louisiana Purchase. In the twentieth century, the industrial vision of agriculture focused on producing food and fiber with a dramatically reduced labor force, to "free" as many citizens as possible to engage in other professional pursuits to improve our quality of life. In these visions, agriculture was perceived as a public good. It was never merely a means of producing foodstuff.

Today, agriculture is perceived as more of a public *problem* than a public *good*. If agriculture comes to mind, it is usually in connection with a problem. Agriculture is perceived as the origin of our polluted groundwater, eroded soils, destroyed rain forests, intolerable odors, and dead zones. It is seen as a leviathan force preventing consumers from exercising choice in the marketplace, denying farmers access to markets, and threatening public health because of its implication in mad cow disease, *E. coli*, cancer, and endocrine disruption. Agriculture is no longer perceived as a public good.

Ecological Degradation

But agriculture is troubled by more than a public perception problem; it is directly associated with ecological problems that threaten future food security. Yvonne Baskin cites these issues:

- *Waterlogging and salinization.* Unwise irrigation practices have contributed to waterlogging and salinization.
- *Desertification.* Seventy percent of the world's drylands are threatened by desertification, and no one has found a way to reverse the process once it begins.
- *Depletion of water resources.* One-third of the world's food is produced on irrigated lands and we are losing our capacity to harvest water, much of it due to the vegetation changes created by farming and forestry practices.
- *Soil erosion.* The world's farmers lose 24 billion tons of topsoil each year.
- *Pollution.* With soil erosion, not only do we lose precious soil, but eutrophication occurs as fertilizer—the annual use of which increased from 14 to 143 million tons between 1950 and 1989—runs into lakes and streams, causing algae blooms and the eventual death of all oxygen-dependent life.[3]

Too Many Humans, Too Few Farmers

Our food and agriculture system is also implicated in the dramatic rate of increase in the human population and decrease in the number of farmers. The number of humans has increased relative to other species along with our "ecological footprint."[4] Humans face difficult and complex problems that surpass simply producing enough food to feed the extra mouths.

How do we produce the food needed to feed the additional mouths without doing additional harm to an already-damaged planet? How do we redesign the food system so that the hungry have entitlement to the food produced? Even with more than 800 million malnourished on the planet, insufficient production is not the problem. How do we restore the health and diversity of our ecological communities to mitigate the additional disease that will surely come with several additional billion humans in a world that is already too full? In addition, we are now at a point where, given the consistent decline in farm numbers, the increasing age of remaining farmers, and the decline of young people growing up on farms, we are in serious danger of losing our most important human agriculture resource—the farmer.

We are, as Calvin Beale has pointed out, in a "free fall" situation. Farm numbers in the United States declined from 6.5 million in 1935 to just over 2 million in 1997.[5] More troubling is the fact that of the 2 million remaining farms, 1.3 million are part-time, residential, or retirement farms. While 61 percent of farm sales are captured by just 163,000 large industrial farms, 63 percent of these industrial farms are tied to some kind of value chain through contract with a large corporation, so they aren't farms in the traditional sense.[6]

If all we expect from agriculture is production of food and fiber as efficiently as possible on a global scale, then the United States should consider exiting farming altogether. The United States can't compete with low-cost producers in other parts of the world, according to the argument made by Steven Blank, professor of agricultural and resource economics at the University of California, Davis.[7] He argues that we should focus national resources on higher-value activities and leave the production of raw materials to others.

However, farms are not isolated economic enterprises with the sole function of producing raw materials that can be manufactured into food products. Farms are not merely food factories; they are parts of local ecosystems. They cannot be managed like isolated enterprises. Niles Eldredge reminds us that there is no such thing as a global ecosystem. There are only local ecosystems, and the health of our planet depends on the health of the combined local ecosystems.[8] Preserving the family farm is not an exercise in nostalgia; it is critical to maintaining a resilient agriculture in a full world.

Agriculture is not an isolated enterprise in trouble. We must learn to fit all of our human enterprises into local ecosystems without harming them. The task before us is to reshape the way we relate to the ecosystems in which we live so as to permit renewal and restoration of the ecosystems and the institutions we have created in them, including agriculture. A fundamental paradigm shift in our thinking is required, which is why philosophy has a crucial role to play.

Philosophy and Agriculture

Unfortunately, in our culture philosophy is largely perceived as an esoteric discipline without any relevance to the more "productive" sciences like biology, physics, economics, or agriculture. In most of our land-grant universities, philosophy, if it has survived as a discipline, has virtually no interaction with agriculture. But philosophy plays at least two important functions in human civilization.

The principal role of philosophy is to determine the meanings of things. This endeavor is central to human intelligence because it challenges assumptions and asks the questions that lie behind our prevailing paradigms. It is a role that societies often find threatening, as Socrates discovered. But it is a role that is indispensable to human intelligence—and, therefore, essential to the development of a sound agriculture.

A second important function that philosophy performs in society is to examine the assumptions that inform our actions. Understanding how our assumptions evolved can help us to more intelligently chart our future course. And, again, this task is indispensable to any effort to chart the future course of agriculture.

The Prevailing Assumptions of Today's Agriculture

So what are the prevailing assumptions that shape our modern food and agriculture system? It seems to me there are at least three.

Nature must be controlled. The notion that we can control nature was born out of naive conclusions, articulated in the seventeenth century, that assumed that nature functioned in a mechanical and predictable manner, like a clock. Those assumptions have long since been proven false. The rigid causal theories of classical physics, upon which our optimism for controlling nature is based, have been set aside. Unfortunately, in agriculture we still seem to be addicted to the belief that we can "bend nature to our will," as Francis Bacon admonished us to do.

Furthermore, we have now entered the biological era, with a long history of coming to understand how the planet's life systems evolved. We now know the Earth is fundamentally a bacterial planet. Bacteria provide the essential components for every significant biological cycle on the planet. Bacteria can adapt to almost any threat, probably because they have been around longer than any other living organism and have had more time to develop adaptive mechanisms.

Thus, efforts to control nature to make room for agriculture can only succeed for short periods of time, and control management is expensive because we must constantly invent new control technologies to replace those made ineffective by nature's adaptive capacity. We are applying our new knowledge in molecular biology in a further attempt to control nature, in the face of a new physics that suggests it can't be done. We would be on sounder scientific ground if we used this new knowledge to better understand how nature works and how to fit agriculture into it, rather than trying to modify nature to make room for a mechanistic agriculture. We need to move beyond the single-gene, single-cause, single-effect, control approach in agriculture. We need to move to a more whole-systems, dynamic, probability, adaptive approach. Agriculture might be better served through a combination of agroecology and genomics than by a combination of technological fixes and intensified control mechanisms. In any case, this is a rich arena for some disciplined philosophical exploration.

Our control paradigm seems to misapprehend how problems are constituted. Our seventeenth-century mechanistic philosophy of the world led us to believe that problems were discrete entities that could be singled out and solved in isolation. Most problems are systemic, nonlinear, and evolutionary in character. This is true for problems in ecosystems as well as for those in social institutions. Because problems are complex and dynamic, they seldom lend themselves to quick technological fixes or to control measures. Accordingly, Holling and his colleagues argue that we need to abandon our illusion of control management and replace it with adaptive management.[9]

But the psychology of control is deeply ingrained in our culture, and I suspect that shifting from a control management model to an adaptive management model will be one of the most difficult shifts for us to make as we struggle to craft new ways to feed the human species. Helping society to make that paradigm shift is an appropriate challenge for philosophy.

Economics determines everything. The second assumption that pervades the way we feed the human species is the notion that economics determines all human activity. This assumption is grounded in Adam Smith's contention that with everyone free to pursue their own rational self-interest, we will achieve the greatest social good. In this paradigm, any cost not directly associated with an individual economic activity should be externalized. Although this may have been valid in Adam Smith's relatively "empty" world, in our current "full" world these assumptions are questionable.

Neoclassical economics, as Herman Daly has pointed out, assumes that economic activity takes place inside a bubble with unlimited natural resources coming in, infinite capacity for growth within, and unlimited sinks for wastes coming out.[10] But farms aren't isolated economic bubbles floating in space. Farms are ultimately not factories; they are biological organisms. As such, they are integral parts of the ecosystems in which they exist. As biological organisms, they function in a context of biological constraints that we cannot ignore for very long.

Living in a full world means we no longer have unlimited natural resources to satisfy all our desires or unlimited sinks for the wastes generated by our activities. We no longer live in a world in which the impact of the human species is easily absorbed by the ecosystems in which we live. The size of the "ecological footprint" that we leave today is now so large that we can no longer ignore the impact that our agricultural activities have on our local ecosystems. We simply can no longer afford an economic model that only measures yield per acre in a given field in a given year. We need economic models that measure the productivity of whole farms for at least a decade, as compared to the costs of such productivity to the farmer, the community, and the ecosystem. Every technology has a cost, and our economic paradigm has largely ignored the ecological and social costs of the technologies we use. We need to challenge the assumptions behind that economic paradigm. Philosophy can help meet that challenge.

Ecological standards are alien to agriculture. Driven by economic determinism, modern agriculture is loath to consider any kind of ecological standard to guide its activities. Suggestions that farms operate by goals other than short-term economic performance or that agriculture should internalize the environmental costs of production are unwelcome.

However, crafting acceptable ecological standards is vital to creating a robust and resilient agriculture. We need an ecological standard for agriculture that is at least as compelling as our economic standard has been for the past century. Aldo Leopold's "land ethic" standard still provides us with a good point of departure: "A thing is right when it tends to preserve the integrity, stability and beauty of the biotic community; it is wrong when it tends otherwise."[11] Leopold can perhaps be forgiven if he did not incorporate in his ethical statement a more complex notion of the dynamic changes inherent in evolving ecological, economic, and social communities.

Some ecological agriculture examples are beginning to emerge, such as the rice research efforts in China recently reported in *Science* magazine.[12] Two types of rice, adapted to local growing conditions, were seeded together, replacing the practice of rice monoculture planted with genetically uniform seeds bred for universal application. The result was an 18 percent increase in overall productivity and a dramatic reduction in inputs that are potentially harmful to the environment. This project is interesting because it meets both environmental and production goals without burdening farmers with the costs of additional inputs.

What is the ecological equivalent of this research for more robust and resilient production on the prairies of Iowa, the woodlands of California, or the desert Southwest? One suspects there may be thousands of similar farming practices waiting to be explored in every ecological neighborhood, if we only had a better understanding of how local ecologies function and how agriculture could be adapted to them.

Our tendency to separate ecological and economic benefits is part of our general seventeenth-century tendency to separate humans from nature, mind from matter, and science from values. And that is a philosophical predisposition—one that philosophy can challenge. We need sound, disciplined philosophical discourse that challenges the prevailing notion that ecological standards are alien to a robust and resilient agriculture or that ecologically sound farming must always be at the expense of economically viable farms. On what basis do we continue to insist that ecological standards are alien to an economically viable agriculture? Philosophy is in a good position to challenge these prevailing assumptions.

What Shaped Our Prevailing Assumptions?

In addition to questioning our assumptions, philosophers can help us re-shape the way the human species feeds itself by clarifying how we came to adopt our prevailing paradigms so we can more intelligently take corrective measures. At least three intriguing theories may shed light on how we came to relate to nature the way we do and why we have adopted our current agricultural practices. Each of these theories is explored here.

The culprit is agriculture itself. Niles Eldredge argues that we may have begun to behave differently vis-à-vis nature when we invented agriculture some ten thousand years ago. When we took charge of producing our own food as opposed to simply hunting for it or gathering it, we gained a sense of independence from nature that led us to believe we were no longer tied to the ecological neighborhoods in which we lived.

Anyone who has ever felt the rush of power that comes from getting Mother Nature to do what we want can relate to this theory. There is no good reason to dismiss the notion that agriculture had this unanticipated consequence. However, a strong sense of alienation from nature pervades our culture today. We are ideologically committed to the idea that economically viable agriculture is only possible by controlling nature with our technologies. What else could account for this philosophical commitment?

It's genetic. Another theory is provided in Reg Morrison's *The Spirit in the Gene.*[13] Morrison argues that we are probably genetically designed, through a long evolutionary process, to behave the way we do toward nature.

However, Morrison does not subscribe to the tired proposition that "particular genes code for particular behaviors." (It was my genes that made me do it, your honor.) Instead, his argument is more complex. Through our long evolutionary journey, humans were not well-equipped for either flight or fight. We were no match for either the speed of the leopard or for its fur, claws, and fighting teeth. As our reasoning capability developed, it created a handicap. Pausing to think in the face of an attacking leopard almost ensured being eaten. We evolved an elegant defense mechanism to override our rationality, to help ensure survival in a world in which we were not well-designed to compete.

This defense mechanism, Morrison argues, is the mystical side of our psychology, where we manufacture beliefs. Our beliefs may be totally irrational, but they facilitate genetically advantageous behavior, including fast instinctual reactions rather than thoughtful ones. However, with this mystical survival package, we also developed cultural belief systems that enabled us to delude ourselves. Here is how Morrison summarizes it:

> The ultimate origin of all human behavior resides in our genes, just as it does for all earthly organisms. It is vital, for sound evolutionary reasons, that we not see it this way, however. So in order to maintain nonrational, genetically determined behavior in all matters of evolutionary consequence, our genes are forced to strut their stuff behind a mask of emotion and culture. In this sense, it could be said that our mystically based cultures evolved specifically to counter the massive expansion of the human cortex and offer our genes the perfect antidote to critical analysis and reasoned thought in gene-threatening circumstances.[14]

Morrison suggests that this mystical side of our brains accounts for our numerous irrational actions and our ability to override our rational awareness that the actions are, in fact, irrational. This genetic predisposition accounts for the trappings of civilization that enable us to continue to act in irrational ways despite our rational awareness to the contrary. Morrison offers a poignant example. The inevitability of our present population explosion and the grim consequences that it portends "have been painfully apparent to all educated people for many centuries." Then, "finally, two clergymen, Lutken and Malthus, became aware of the global scale of the threat and tried in vain to warn their contemporaries of it. Nationalistic paranoia, intellectual jealousy, and dogmatic religious beliefs—all good, genetically determined reactions—ensured that few understood, and none heeded, the warnings of those practical prophets."[15]

In the meantime, Morrison argues, nothing has changed:

> Some still argue that humanity, with the aid of education, technology, and a new spirit of cooperation . . . will somehow pull the survival rabbit out of the hat once more. Others argue that our growing intelligence, armed with better information, will eventually save us from the coming holocaust. Sadly, their faith is unfounded. Evolution is without intent and does not progress, and we are indeed normal animals in every sense. Besides, both propo-

sitions fail to take into account a key fact of biological evolution: all species must fail eventually, especially the very successful ones, or the whole system would grind to a halt.[16]

Morrison's proposition is at least as compelling as Eldredge's. Genetic mechanisms may help explain human behavior toward nature and why we have adopted nature-alienating paradigms that drive modern agriculture. Still, some questions remain unanswered. If genetic mechanisms are the only factors determining human behavior, why don't all humans behave the same way? Oral cultures, for example, seem to relate to nature quite differently from cultures with written language.

It's language. That brings us to a third theory that explores why we relate to nature and practice agriculture the way we do. In *The Spell of the Sensuous*, David Abram argues that our modern alienation from nature can be traced to the invention of written language.[17]

Following Merleau-Ponty, Abram reminds us that language is *not* a set of arbitrary symbols that we assign to experience. It is rather a bodying-forth, a living gesture, by which we articulate meaning rooted in sensory experience. Language, then, cannot be isolated from the sensory experience in the world that gave rise to it. Language, as Merleau-Ponty described it, is "a particular way of 'singing' the world."[18]

But our modern view of language, born in part out of the scientific revolution, has reconceptualized language as a set of arbitrary symbols linked together by agreed-upon rules. In this view, once language is committed to paper it contains its own abstract meaning, detached from the real world. Language becomes a way of "*representing* actual things and events in the perceived world, but it has no internal, nonarbitrary connections to that world, and hence is readily separable from it."[19] This has the effect of locating meaning in symbols on a piece of paper rather than in the reciprocal relationship of sensory experience in the world. This shift in attention, *of itself,* alienates us from nature.

Additionally, Abram argues that this view of language, containing abstract and objective truth, emerged as we became preoccupied with "human specialness," the idea that we were "definitely set apart from, and above, the rest of the animate world." Abram linked the need to demonstrate our specialness with our need to justify our increasing exploitation and manipulation of the nonhuman world.

Alphabetic writing undermines connectedness to nature in two distinct ways, according to Abram: "First, reading and writing as a highly concentrated form of participation displaces the older participation between the human senses and the earthly terrain (effectively freeing human intention from the direct dictates of the land). Second, writing down the ancestral stories disengages them from particular places."[20] Written language, interpreted as an arbitrary construct containing objective truth, alienates us from nature and the ecological neighborhoods in which we live while simultaneously justifying our manipulation of the world around us. This development, Abram argues, had a profound effect on the way we relate to the world and therefore how we behave in it.

Next, "once the stories are written down . . . the inked traces left by the pen as it traverses the page [replace] the earthly traces left by the animals, and by one's ancestors, in their interactions with the local land. . . . The human senses, intercepted by the written word, are no longer gripped and fascinated by the expressive shapes and sounds of particular places. The spirits fall silent. Gradually, the felt primacy of place is forgotten, superseded by a new, abstract notion of 'space' as a homogeneous and placeless void."[21]

Suddenly one can see the undeniable parallels in modern agriculture. Agriculture also was once rooted to place. Good farmers paid close attention to the particular nuances of the ecology of the place where they farmed. Now, the felt primacy of place is forgotten. A farmer on a tractor is a farmer on a tractor whether in Illinois, Colorado, or California. Farmers work in a homogeneous and placeless void, seeding genetically uniform seeds, in uniform monocultures, with uniformly prescribed practices.

As we think, so we farm.

Agriculture and Philosophy

Philosophy and agriculture are inextricably related, whether our prevailing culture wants to admit it or not. Our current food and agriculture system is driven by philosophical assumptions. In today's culture it is generally assumed that food is disconnected from nature, biological cycles, and the essential caretaking that makes sustainable food production possible. Our current philosophical assumptions teach us that we do not need to think beyond the bread in the supermarket or the technologies required to produce the wheat that makes the bread. We are taught not to think beyond the lovely woodwork that adorns the wall of our houses or the technologies required to harvest the trees that produce the wood.

Farmers know the technological language required to produce our food and fiber: what size tractor to use, how much fertilizer to apply, which pesticide to use for which pest, how to adjust equipment hooked up to satellites, and how to do it all with incredible precision. But many of us know *nothing* of the language of nature: how life in the soil functions, what free ecosystem services are available to work for agriculture in a particular watershed, or how plants participate in their own defense against pests.

Farming that knows only the language of technology alienates us from the rich resources of nature just as surely as the alphabet markings on paper alienate us from the rich and complex language of sensory experience. This alienation has fundamentally changed who we are as beings in the world. As David Abram put it, "In order to obtain the astonishing and unifying image of the whole earth whirling in the darkness of space, humans, it would seem, have had to relinquish something just as valuable—the humility and grace that comes from being fully a part of that whirling world."[22]

This is part of the reason that agriculture is no longer seen as a public good. If agriculture is purely an industrial act whose only purpose is to manipulate the technologies required to produce some wheat with which we have no connection, ground into flour in some distant factory with which we have no connection, made into frozen bread dough in some warehouse-like bakery with which we have no connection, and placed into a microwaveable plastic container with which we have no connection—all the while harming wildlife and contaminating our water—how could we expect the public to support agriculture?

However, I believe the problems facing agriculture are an opportunity. Because agriculture is now widely perceived to be part of our global ecological crisis, broad public support will emerge to develop a new vision for agriculture that addresses the crisis. Although few philosophers are engaged in this conversation in any direct or vital way, agriculture is on some of the most important social agendas in the world.

Two years ago, Jane Lubchenco, then president of one of the most prestigious scientific professional associations in the world, the American Association for the Advancement of Science, challenged the entire scientific community to rethink its social contract based on the fact that we now, for the first time, live on a human-dominated planet. When Lubchenco issued that challenge, asking the scientific community to "devote their energies and talents to the most pressing problems of the day," easily half of the problems she outlined are directly related to agriculture. Not least among the problems she identified is the fact that "more atmospheric nitrogen is fixed by humanity than by all natural terrestrial sources combined."[23]

We have to address a mounting set of problems, created at least in part by agriculture, if we are going to survive very far into the next century with any quality of life. This is an unprecedented opportunity for philosophers to be part of the solution. Robert Goodman, at the University of Wisconsin, described this challenge: "Unmistakable signs exist that humans must replace the exploitative model manifest in our pesticide-dependent, industrial system of agricultural production. . . . The emerging principles of ecology, integrated with genetics, and wisely used, offer society enormous promise to move toward an agriculture consonant, rather than in conflict, with environmental quality and sustainability."[24]

If these new approaches are to be "wisely used," philosophy has a key role to play. To be effective, philosophy must be engaged in interdisciplinary dialogue submerged in the sensory world. Paula Hirschboeck describes quite eloquently the kind of philosophical interplay we need:

> During many years of my schooling, I felt alienation from the discipline of philosophy. While I was profoundly drawn to the questions it considers, I experienced philosophy as a highly specialized way of thinking about these questions that only a few great minds engaged in. More recently, I've explored the transdisciplinary and interdisciplinary nature of philosophy.
>
> This exploration leads me to ask many questions about teaching, learning, and scholarship in general. What are some of the implications of the fact that originally philosophy was the *precursor* to other disciplines? "Philo-sophia," the love of wisdom, began, as Aristotle said, with the wonder of the mysteries of existence and expanded into life lived in passionate moral and intellectual integrity.
>
> Now, after the centuries that saw philosophy narrowed into a highly specialized field, interdisciplinary transgression could welcome Sophia back into our scholarship in new ways. I am intrigued by the description of Sophia in the book of Proverbs. Sophia is the

wisdom that "cries out in the streets and marketplaces" and is "at play in the world."[25]

Hirschboeck's description of philosophy at play in the world is the kind of interplay we need between philosophy and agriculture. As long as philosophy is itself alienated from the sensory world, imprisoned in language constructs that purport to be the meaning of things without being engaged in the sensory world of things, it cannot help us reshape the way we feed the human species.

This is not to say we should abandon disciplinary efforts. We have learned a lot about the world and ourselves with this incredibly productive method of learning, but we do not acquire all the knowledge we need by that method. As John Cobb and Herman Daly explain, we need to study problems within disciplines and to engage in the disciplined study of problems in the context of the world.[26] To illustrate this problem, Robert Hutchins once quipped that the University of Chicago appeared to be a collection of separate departments connected only by the central heating system.

If philosophy is going to help shape the way humans feed themselves so that we enrich rather than degrade the life-support systems of the planet, we have to find meaningful, disciplined ways to engage with philosophical inquiry. Philosophers must engage us in a manner that, as Abram puts it, "places us in contact with the trembling neck muscles of a deer holding its antlers high as it swims toward the mainland, or with the ant dragging a scavenged rice grain through the grasses,"[27] or (one might add) with the earthworm burrowing its way through the soil.

If philosophy is to resume being the "love of wisdom," it must be involved at the beginning of things, testing assumptions. Philosophy must also help us face who we are as a species and how our feeding habits affect the world in which we live.

As a patch-disturber species, humans as hunter-gatherers tended to forage for food in a given area until the area was hunted and gathered out; then we moved on and allowed the abandoned area to recover.[28] With the advent of agriculture, we remained patch disturbers, but the technology of agriculture allowed us to settle in larger numbers and stay for longer periods of time. These agricultural societies, in many instances, extended the process of ecological decline and the spatial scale. They eventually eroded the soil, their technologies began to fail, and populations declined, bringing about the collapse of the society. Yet some agricultural societies have recognized that they were part of ecological neighborhoods, and they used agricultural practices that preserved the health of their local ecosystems, allowing them to thrive for thousands of years.

What is different in the twenty-first century is that humans occupy every ecological patch on the planet and have disturbed every patch to capacity. There are no new places to move to and no abandoned patches left to recover, and much of the disturbance has now reached the point of no recovery. The planet is human dominated, a full world. We have only two choices. We can begin to recognize our plight and take immediate steps to live within our ecological means, or we can allow our species to follow the inexorable evolutionary pathway assigned to every species that reaches a plague-prone status: collapse. Philosophical discourse that breaks out of its narrow disciplinary boundaries can help us make the right choice.

A Pig's Tale

Marketing Stories for New Value Chains

Any customer can have a car painted any color that he wants so long as it is black.[1]
—Henry Ford

We live in stories. We breathe stories. Most of our best conversations are about stories. The broadcast era is over. Marketing is conversation.[2]
—*The Cluetrain Manifesto*

In conventional business circles, niche markets are suspect because they are vulnerable; they are too small, powerless, and helpless to matter. Niche markets are considered high-risk ventures that will not survive. We admire major mass markets that control billion-dollar inventories. Economies of scale reflect economic power, and economic power suggests market resilience and reliability. Why, then, would anyone propose—much less attend —a conference on niche marketing?

Perhaps we tend to devalue niche markets because of the way we define "niche." Although we think niche means small, insignificant, vulnerable, or unimportant, Webster describes "niche" as "a place or position particularly suitable for the person or thing in it." In other words, a niche is not necessarily something tiny. It is a place where whatever is in it is well-adapted to the place and well-suited to what it is doing in that place. That suggests the opposite of weakness; being well-suited, well-adapted, and well-adjusted reflects resilience, not weakness.

Keynote address at a conference titled Niche and Value-Added Marketing: What's in It for You? on September 18, 2001. Mary Adams, editor at the Leopold Center for Sustainable Agriculture, assisted with the research for and revision of this paper.

Other definitions of niche markets include "any marketing system (in part or in whole) that does not use the current commodity-based marketing channels."[3] Operating with the correct definition doesn't ensure success in the market. One can be right and still go out of business.

Productivity and Competition

Many of us probably think that niche markets are not competitive. I suspect that this concept derives from a history of operating in a marketing paradigm in which the concept of competitiveness is quite narrow. Going back to Henry Ford, and Frederick Taylor before him, we have relied on a single industrial model that produces everything from automobiles to Twinkies. Ford used Frederick Taylor's "scientific management" theories as the basis for his mass-production assembly line. Taylor's theory holds that the lowest-cost supplier of a mass-produced, undifferentiated commodity earns the competitive advantage.

Michael Porter has pointed out this is a rather narrow way to view competition.[4] Although a competitive advantage can be gained through efficient mass production, this sole technique does not capture the full range of competitive possibilities. Porter argues, correctly I think, that "productivity" is a better avenue for understanding competitive advantage than "competition." Porter defines productivity in terms of output produced by labor or capital. Productivity, he suggests, depends not only on the efficiency with which products are produced; it also depends on the product's quality and features. Thus, the two basic types of competitive advantage are lower cost and differentiation.[5] He states:

- Lower cost is the ability of a firm to design, produce, and market a comparable product more efficiently than its competitors.
- Differentiation is the ability to provide unique and superior value to the buyer in terms of product quality, special features, or after-sale service.
- Differentiation allows a firm to command a premium price, which leads to superior profitability provided costs are comparable to those of competitors.[6]

Finally, Porter suggests that "it is difficult, though not impossible, to be both lower-cost and differentiated relative to competitors."[7] Porter offers food-industry examples to make his point. In the chocolate industry, Hershey and M&M/Mars have decided to compete as lower-cost suppliers by mass-producing and mass-marketing standardized candy bars as cheaply as possible. Lindt and Tobler/Jacobs in Switzerland, however, decided to compete mainly by selling premium products at higher prices, through more limited and specialized distribution channels. To achieve their business objectives, Lindt and Tobler/Jacobs use only top-quality ingredients, produce numerous items, and spend more time processing their products, the opposite of Taylor's scientific-management model. Each approach is successful in its particular market.

Porter's analysis suggests that niche marketing can be successful depending on one's products, target market, and marketing strategy. An important general question, then, is whether agricultural producers have the right products to develop successful niche markets. The main goal of this essay is to address this question from the perspective of midwestern pork producers. The focus here is on pork, but these concepts can be used as models for other products marketed through value chains.

Marketing through value chains connects producers, processors, and retailers to bring differentiated products to market. Examples of such value chains already exist.[8] The specific questions I wish to address are:

- Do niche markets promise advantages to producers?
- Can they be expanded to provide opportunities for more producers?
- Are niche markets sustainable?

These questions can be explored by examining what is happening on the farm, in the marketplace, and to the infrastructure that serves the food and agriculture industry. In this way, we can evaluate whether there is a promising future for value chains to sell into niche markets.

On the Farm

What is happening on the farm? Two pictures are emerging. Using 1997 USDA data, Willard Cochrane concluded that the future of midsize farms in America is uncertain.[9] Because the majority of midwestern farms are midsize, the future of farming in the Corn Belt is called into question.

Most commodity sales (61 percent) are captured by a small number of very large farms, and those farms enter into contracts to mass-produce specialized, uniform commodities as cheaply as possible. At the other end of the scale, a much larger number of small farms capture only 9 percent of sales. Increasingly, these farms use direct marketing. Direct marketing is a niche that appears safe from entry by competing large farms, because large farms cannot easily put a human face on their commodities. Additionally, large farms appear to have little interest in cultivating those markets.

A modest number of farms in between these two groups present the greatest opportunity, and perhaps the greatest challenge, in terms of niche marketing. From a marketing perspective, the farms in the middle increasingly find themselves falling through the cracks between today's undifferentiated, contract markets and the small, highly differentiated direct markets. For the most part, these farms are too small to access the contract markets. Large processing firms that issue the contracts only want to do business with large producers, to reduce their transaction costs. Midsize farms cannot readily access direct markets because those markets tend to be too small and the farms too bound to commodity production. Midsize farms, however, can access both direct markets and differentiated value chains.

However, midsize farms are not the only vulnerable enterprises. As the food industry consolidates in manufacturing and retail sectors, midsize processors and midsize retailers are also threatened. Entrepreneurs in this midsize category are sometimes called the "tweenies" because they fall in between the two thriving markets.

Can we conclude from this analysis that midsize entrepreneurs (farmers, manufacturers, and retailers) are doomed to economic extinction? Or do they have an unprecedented opportunity to differentiate themselves, develop new value chains that connect them, and bring unique products that appeal to sophisticated consumers into the marketplace? Remember, Porter argues that it is difficult, though not impossible, for the same firm to be *both* a lowest-cost supplier of an undifferentiated commodity *and* a supplier of a higher-priced, differentiated product.

If we do not create new, differentiated markets that work for midsize farmers, they may disappear from the landscape, which highlights a broader range of concerns. Small and midsize farmers still manage more than 80 percent of the nation's farmland.[10] They are the farmers in the best position to take good care of the land, because most have lived on their land long enough and intimately enough to know how to care for it wisely. If they have sufficient information and market incentives, they will take care of it well. So if midsize farms are unable to access markets and they disappear, who will step in to provide this public good to our society?

A second picture of what is happening on the farm comes from Stewart Smith, agricultural economist at the University of Maine.[11] Smith suggests that the agricultural economy comprises three sectors. He has analyzed the rate of economic activity in each of those sectors during the eighty-year period from 1910 to 1990. According to Smith, farm sector share of income has shrunk dramatically (from 41 percent to 9 percent) during that time. Simultaneously, economic activity in the market and input sectors almost doubled. Smith argues that "technology is the linchpin" that accounts for this farm sector contraction, because most of the technologies adopted by farmers "result in a shift of activity from the farm to the nonfarm sectors." For our purposes it is not important to understand why this occurred; we need to focus on what it means for the future of farm income.

A common prescription for improving farm income is to increase farm size and invest in more purchased inputs. This will increase yield and spread costs over a larger production unit. But that plan ties up the farmer's capital and management to produce more undifferentiated commodities, depriving him or her of the opportunity to use those resources to engage in activities with lower costs or that produce more income. Moreover, scant evidence exists that the expansion/yield-increase strategy has worked to improve farmers' net income.[12]

Small farmers can most easily enter direct-marketing relationships. Large farmers may not want or be able to enter niche markets because their farms are designed to produce mass quantities of undifferentiated commodities. A midsize farm may not be large enough to access large markets, but in cooperation with other farmers, processors, and retailers, they may be able to produce and market differentiated products with unique qualities that command higher prices. Given the right marketing relationships, farmers may be in a position to capture part of that higher value and retain it on the farm.

In the Market

Producers also need to explore the marketplace as they consider whether niche markets are appropriate. What signals are food markets giving us? Are there real, solid opportunities in the marketplace to develop and supply differentiated products with unique qualities? Rick Levine (cofounder of Sun Microsystems) and his colleagues suggest that the successful business strategies of the twentieth century will not work in the twenty-first century. The twentieth-century marketplace was dominated by mass marketers who attracted buyers by broadcasting information to them. Consumers made their buying decisions based on the attractiveness of the message.

Rick Levine and his colleagues argue that this era is ending because of the Internet.[13] Consumers have developed the habit of having a conversation about everything that affects their lives, about whatever they want, any time they wish. Markets of the future will be conversations.

The end of the broadcast era suggests opportunities for niche markets. A recent British news article explains how some of these new "conversation" markets are already surfacing.[14] A group of entrepreneurs developed a value chain connecting small and midsize farmers (who had differentiated their livestock in ways that made them attractive to consumers) with processors, distributors, and retailers to maintain the identity of the meat product through the food chain. The value chain provided customers with the opportunity to consider all the information about the meat they buy—who raised the animal, how it was raised, how it was fed, what its medical history was. Consumers can access this information from the Internet, including a picture of the farmer who produced the animal and of the landscape on the farm where the animal was raised.

Another example of creative marketing niches can be found in Waukon, Iowa, where Yosef Abrams developed a niche for kosher dairy products. Abrams plans to set up a kosher cheese factory there, supplied by cooperating dairy farmers. He noted, "It's not hard to sell something that is very good."

Niche markets supplied by small and midsize farmers and connected to value chains can bring products with a human face into the marketplace. By providing opportunities for conversation, they can gain a competitive advantage. Mass markets cannot realistically create meaningful opportunities for real conversations about their products because they are neither segregated nor differentiated.

A second market challenge is the heterogeneity of consumers. Michael Adams, a Canadian marketing expert, contends that mass marketing is challenged by the demand for diverse products. We are "pre-boomers" and "boomers" and "generation Xers." Within these groupings, especially among the Xers, there are "tribes" whose tastes are based on different lifestyles.[15] Adams suggests that consumers increasingly want to do business with humane and ethical organizations and to eschew organizations that are paternalistic or that promote institutional authority. This reinforces the notion that food producers that genuinely invite consumers to have a conversation about their product will be successful. Trying to "convince" consumers that they should buy products, regardless of production practices or relationship linkages, is a losing strategy. Trying to convince consumers that a product is safe simply because regulatory agencies have said so probably will also be ineffective. Such strategies appear paternalistic and appeal to institutional authority.

A third social phenomenon emerging in the marketplace was revealed by Harvey Hartman of the Hartman Group. Hartman indicated that food consumers seek "trust and authenticity," characteristics that cannot be fabricated or "broadcast."[16] Niche markets utilizing intimate value chains have a distinct comparative advantage marketing trust and authenticity. Trust has to be earned. One of the quickest ways to earn trust is to provide full transparency of all aspects of the product's life cycle. Buying from such sources "restores integrity to the retail market."

New opportunities are emerging to market food as a *story,* with farmers as an integral part of the story. In today's market, the pig's tale may become at least as important as the pig's tail.

Infrastructure

Is the current food and agriculture sector infrastructure receptive to value chain niche markets? The manufacturing and retail/broker sectors of the food and agriculture industry have consolidated dramatically, reducing consumer choice in the marketplace.

Bill Heffernan, rural sociologist at the University of Missouri, and his colleagues have been tracking food manufacturing and agricultural input consolidation.[17] During the last three years, retail food sales of the five top food retailers jumped from 24 percent of the total to 42 percent.[18] Over the next few years, fewer than six global food retailers will dominate the entire global retail sector, and only one, Wal-Mart, is a U.S.-based corporation. As the balance of power shifts to retailers, they will increasingly "dictate terms to food manufacturers who then force changes back through the system to the farm level."[19] Farmers will have to meet the needs of consolidated (mostly foreign) retail corporate entities.

We already know how this works. For several decades, food processors have increasingly dictated on-farm management practices. Indeed, many leading mainstream farm magazines began telling farmers that the processor, not the consumer, was their customer. Both farmers and manufacturers will now begin to manage their operations to meet the business objectives of the consolidated retailer, rather than the needs of the consumer. This has enormous implications for niche markets and the farmers who might want to become part of the value chains that supply those markets. How can small value chains of farmers, processors, and distributors meet consumer demand for a range of differentiated products when shelf space is controlled by a tiny number of mass-marketing giants?

Slotting allowances are another problem. According to Heffernan's report, it takes $50,000 to place "one jar size of specialty pickles on the shelves of four major grocery chains in Tampa, Florida."[20]

Consolidation of food brokers poses yet another challenge. A recent article in the *New York Times* pointed out that placement of products on store shelves is determined increasingly by a very few consolidated food brokers who charge enormous fees to represent your product.[21] Food brokers not only determine which products get placed on supermarket shelves, they also largely manage the shelves. The services of a food broker are, consequently, often essential to the successful sale of food products. Even popular products that have won taste awards don't make it onto store shelves simply because their manufacturers cannot find or afford brokers to represent them.

Nevertheless, consumer demand still has enormous influence in the marketplace. Mary Swalla-Holmes, project coordinator for Iowa State University's Value-Added Agriculture program, reported (based on field research) that "if as few as fifteen consumers ask for a specific product at the same store during the same week, the store manager will usually find a way to get the product into the store."[22] Despite the dismal picture painted in the *New York Times* article about food brokers, June Holley, president of the Appalachian Center for Economic Networks, asserted that "it is still possible to get unique food products into regional stores with imaginative promotion."[23]

Theresa Marquez, marketing specialist with Organic Valley Foods, described "guerrilla marketing" techniques that can help promote unique products. For example, she said the Stoneyfield Company increased sales by hiring teenagers to give away containers of Stoneyfield yogurt to subway riders in New York City to thank them for using public transportation.[24] Niche marketing may be limited only by our imagination.

The Role of the Land-Grant University

Land-grant universities, with their network of extension services, are in a perfect position to create an alliance of producer associations, processors, retailers, consumer associations, investors, conservation organizations, and community leaders. They can foster conversations about opportunities that enable farmers to retain more value on the farm, communities to recycle more local wealth, and citizens to benefit from cleaner water, healthier soil, and more robust landscapes. Creating healthy local communities can be both ecologically sound and economically lucrative. The environmental benefits of such business ventures are part of the marketing story, which in turn can make the products more attractive in the market.

The university community needs to play the role of catalyst and servant in this scenario, not the role of parent or overseer. Today's sophisticated customer will not respond well to institutional authority or paternalism. The land-grant university can reassert its traditional role of public service and public-interest science by:

- Serving as a catalyst to help foster conversation among the various parties
- Providing access to research that can help solve problems along the way
- Responding to educational needs to supply information vital to the success of these new marketing ventures

Facing the Future

So where does this leave producers? If we become part of a unique food story that differentiates the food we produce in a way that is attractive to consumers, and if we want to become part of a value chain to bring that product into the marketplace, can we capture more value on the farm? The possibility looks pretty attractive, especially when the alternative—producing more for less—is so bleak. Still, value-chain niche marketing seems scary.

Three final thoughts come to mind. First, if we become immobilized by fear in the face of food-industry consolidation or the many other economic forces at work in the current global economy, market success is less likely. Trends always look most foreboding while they are in place, but the thing about trends is that they always change. Most market-driven successes have hinged on an entrepreneur's intuitive capacity to anticipate new opportunities. Once a new market trend becomes well-established, most of the opportunity to benefit from it will have vanished. The time to take advantage of a trend is just before it becomes established. We need to develop our intuitive capacity for spotting niche-marketing opportunities on the horizon.

Second, no group of producers, conglomeration of processors, or network of distributors will make niche marketing successful simply by developing powerful marketing strategies. On-the-street observations and intuitive capacity will make niche marketing successful, not boardroom schemes.

In *The Tipping Point,* Malcolm Gladwell suggests that new markets, like most other significant social changes, arise through "contagious behavior" rather than organized activities.[25] New markets take on their own life and develop as a result of circumstances that are largely beyond our control. New markets happen because someone starts to do something different that captures the imagination of others, and the public takes notice. Gladwell likens it to an epidemic: it begins with the infection of a few people; then it spreads; and after a while the phenomenon reaches a "tipping point" and becomes a trend.

Gladwell uses the example of the comeback of Hush Puppies in 1994–1995 to illustrate his theory. The manufacturer was about to phase them out because of sluggish sales. Then demand suddenly exploded without the benefit of advertising. A group of kids in the East Village of New York City simply started wearing them. The time and place were right, and Hush Puppies became cool to wear. Soon everyone wanted to wear them.[26] If we think we only have to develop clever alpha-male strategies to be successful, we will probably fail. We need to listen, observe, anticipate serendipitous events, pay attention to context, and be modest.

Third, we need to pay attention to core values. Campaigns to sell food products in niche markets must have integrity and be authentic. The food story with potential for success has to provide actual rewards for farmers who are part of the story, practice good environmental stewardship, treat laborers fairly and animals humanely, and feature real people who truly care that good, healthy, delicious food gets onto the table of the customer.

"Spin" was a part of the broadcast era. It will not serve us well in the conversation era. Remember that niche market customers will be having conversations with whomever they choose, whenever they wish.[27] This doesn't mean that only small and midsize companies can play. The SYSCO Corporation is pursuing niche-marketing value chains to connect producers of unique food products with restaurant chefs. Organic Valley Foods, owned by farmers, has now grown into a $100 million business and is selling its unique dairy products in mainstream supermarkets. Niman Ranch sells its products in some of the most upscale restaurants in the country. Size is ultimately not the determining factor; what matters is preserving authenticity, listening to the customer, keeping the conversation alive, and building trust.

Technologies may facilitate telling food stories effectively and authentically. In Danish supermarkets, scanners enable customers to trace meat products to an animal on the farm. They can bring up the entire food story of a product on a computer screen right in the store. Some market analysts doubt American shoppers will spend the time to access food stories in this manner. However, while shoppers are often rushed, at other times they want to have personally rich and meaningful experiences. In Denmark, consumers initially scanned their products in the stores enthusiastically. Then interest dropped off and the stores took them out. But consumers demanded their return because they wanted the *option* to scan products and read the stories.

Other possibilities for telling our food stories with full transparency exist. Reid Harward envisions the use of handheld scanners to determine, at a glance, the entire food history of each product. Did the company use questionable labor practices in producing the product? Was the energy used to produce the product exceptionally polluting? Were the animals raised in conditions that allowed them to freely perform their normal functions? The scanner will tell them.[28]

In a few years, the food market may look a lot different from the way it looks today. And farmers may be much more closely connected to customers, even if they don't manage a community-supported agriculture endeavor or sell in a farmer's market.

A Bright Future for "Farmers of the Middle"

One of [Benjamin] Franklin's goals in life was to provide useful advice for aspiring middle-class shopkeepers and tradesmen. He was America's godfather of self-help business books. By creating what he called a strong "middling class," he hoped to lay the foundation for his vision of a stable civic society in America. . . . The "middling people" should be the proud sinews of the new land.[1]
—Walter Isaacson

The notion that the middle class is somehow the bedrock of American civic society has deep roots in our culture. In 1774, Benjamin Franklin wrote that the very survival of the Province of Pennsylvania depended on "the middling people"—the "farmers, shopkeepers and tradesmen of this city and country." Franklin argued that "mistaken principles of religion" combined with "a love of worldly power," exercised by a few elite in positions of authority, threatened to undo the good life envisioned by the majority in the middle.[2] America's modern-day middling people, especially the farmers of the middle, are once again under siege.

According to the data from the 2002 agriculture census, in just five years (1997–2002), the United States lost 14.5 percent of its midsize farms, those with gross sales between $50,000 and $500,000. In many midwest states, where farming anchors the state's economy, midsize operator losses were even higher: Iowa, 18.5 percent; Michigan, 18 percent; and Illinois, 16.5 percent.[3]

There are many reasons for these dismal statistics. Ever-increasing con-

---

This is an edited version of a paper that first appeared in Holly George-Warren, ed., *Farm Aid: A Song for America* (Emmaus, Pa.: Rodale Books, 2005).

centration in the industrial food sector forces farmers to expand their operations to maintain access to markets. Large firms prefer doing business with large farms because it reduces their transaction costs. Increased fossil-fuel costs (the basis of almost all industrial farm inputs) puts undercapitalized farmers at a competitive disadvantage. The predominant business culture in our society insists that in a market-based economy, efficiency is the *only* important social and economic "good"; thus, the loss of the midsize farms is simply an "inevitable" outcome of free-market forces at work. Furthermore, current federal farm policies have tended to favor large farms.

During this same five-year period when farms of the middle have been disappearing, the number of megafarms (those with more than $500,000 in gross sales) has been increasing. At the same time, the number of the very small farms (farms with less than $5,000 in gross sales) has also been increasing. These trends reflect growth in direct-market sales (mainly by small farms) and highly concentrated, bulk commodity farm sales (mostly by megafarms, which produce a few commodities under contract to highly concentrated firms).

What emerges is a bipolar food system that offers consumers only two food choices: buying directly from small farmers through farmers' markets, Internet sales, and other direct-marketing arrangements; or buying mass-produced (usually highly processed) foods that arrive through supply chains dominated by megafood firms offering virtually no traceability or differentiated characteristics.

These circumstances place America's independent family farm in a vulnerable position. Pushed out of the mass-production commodity market by economies of scale and prevented from direct marketing due to the lack of adequate infrastructure to accommodate their productive capacity, midsize farms are disappearing. Most Americans seemed unconcerned about these trends. As long as branded products continued to show up in local supermarkets at reasonable prices, customers seemed satisfied. *Fast, convenient,* and *cheap* has become the siren call of the marketplace.

Fortunately, this situation is changing. While these grim farm statistics have been playing out, an unprecedented new market, uniquely suited to the farms in the middle, has emerged. Demand is increasing for high-quality, differentiated foods that include compelling food stories and that are marketed by new supply-chain relationships. *Fast, convenient,* and *cheap* is being challenged by *memory, romance,* and *trust.* A new business culture is needed to meet the growing demands of this new market.

Restaurant chefs are no longer satisfied with the usual humdrum fare. They still wish to provide their customers with great-tasting food, but they also want to be able to tell diners where the food came from. They want to know what kind of environmental stewardship was practiced in producing it and bringing it to their tables, how the animals that provide the meat on their plates were treated, and how the farmers and farm workers who produced the food were compensated. In addition, health care providers have taken a new interest in the kind of food being fed to patients in hospitals. Should they really be serving meat from animals that have been fed subtherapeutic antibiotics when antibiotic resistance is a mounting health care problem?

The dramatic increase in obesity and diabetes among children is motivating school boards to examine the food served in school-lunch programs. University students are pressuring administrators to provide better-tasting, locally grown, more nutritious food in university cafeterias. Nursing homes and long-term care facilities are exploring investments in healthy foods that could decrease long-term care costs for their clients.

These emerging markets place new demands on food-service providers for highly differentiated food products. It is always difficult to change an entrenched business culture. Most farmers have been conditioned to believe that the only way to be competitive in today's global economy is to be the lowest-cost supplier of a mass-produced commodity. The economic pressures of the past half century have left us with an aging farm population. There are almost five times as many farmers over age sixty-five as under age thirty-five. Food firms that have operated on the principle of competition with other players in the chain will have a hard time operating as partners in a system that offers products with unique values.

Inadequate infrastructure poses additional challenges, but developing these enterprises offers many opportunities for rural economic development. Constructing moderate-sized, efficient, multispecies meat-processing facilities similar to some of the new-generation abattoirs in Europe might generate and retain wealth within rural communities throughout the United States.

These efforts will require investment capital. Although investors have traditionally been less attracted to food-related enterprises than to new technologies, venture capitalists may still wish to support enterprises that address the health and well-being of their own communities. There is a small but growing group of socially conscious investors who are now more open to unique, environmentally friendly food enterprises as targets for investment.

Farmers and their partners in values-based value chains need reliable information as they enter this new business world. The land-grant universities need to take a fresh look at their research and extension activities. For example, if farmers are to be compensated adequately for their role in the value chain, data are needed on the cost of production for the many new, differentiated food products. Food customers who want to buy particular food products because such purchases "support local family farmers" will need assurances that this claim is authentic. Farmers may also require unique seeds to produce plants with specific qualities of taste and nutrition. The research community may need to work with farmers to develop new varieties.

To bring these new products into the marketplace in an efficient manner, farmers will need marketing networks. Each network could feature its own branded, unique, differentiated product, and all the networks could be united in a national program. This program would guarantee that common environmental and social standards were met, verified through a third-party certification system, and identified by a common seal. Already, such networks are evolving in various regions of the country, and systems are in place that adhere to organic and crop improvement standards. Such certification programs will identify all of the value-chain partners, in effect creating a third tier in the food system: besides direct markets and mass-commodity markets, we would have highly differentiated values-based value-chain markets.[4]

We need new government policy options so that the farmers who produce these unique products are not discriminated against by policies that were designed primarily to meet the needs of farmers producing undifferentiated commodity products. Fortunately, a national Agriculture of the Middle program has begun to address many of these issues. The program includes leaders from farms, universities, industry, government agencies, and nonprofit organizations. There is reasonable optimism that these challenges can be addressed successfully.

Market demand is a powerful economic driver, and as long as the public continues to demand unique products, entrepreneurs will find a way to meet that demand. It is my hope that our "middling" farmers will benefit from this emerging market trend.

Revitalizing Rural Communities

How Churches Can Help

The groups that had most completely shaken off the old symbolisms were those that were most ready for the American adventure: they turned themselves easily to the mastery of the external environment. To them matter alone mattered.[1]
—Lewis Mumford

There is a popular perception in America that rural communities are places of failure, a perception apparently shared by rural communities themselves. By the late 1980s, most rural citizens in the Midwest harbored the notion that their communities were dying. The metaphor that dominated the thinking of rural community residents was the "corpse." Rural citizens believed that the death of their communities was inevitable, and their only reason for staying around was to prepare the corpse for burial. Still, some believed that a new industry might yet come to town and revive the corpse.[2]

By the early 1990s, the media had come to similar conclusions. Dismissing the relevance of rural communities in the American economy, Margaret Usdansky suggested that small rural towns in the United States had "a lot of history, little else." Usdansky claimed that small rural towns began with the railroads, but the arrival of the Model T began to "wipe out the need for small commercial centers as surely as if Ford had driven through their storefronts."[3]

This perception of rural places as failed communities seems to pervade our culture. Reflecting on his own experience as a youngster growing up in

A modified form of this speech was given at the forty-third annual meeting of the Northern Plains Conference of the United Church of Christ, Bismarck, North Dakota, June 10, 2006.

a small community, author and poet Bill Holm wrote: "At fifteen, I could define failure fast: to die in Minneota, Minnesota."[4] If you can't escape the rural community in which you are unfortunate enough to grow up, then by definition you are a failure.

I came face to face with this culture of failure in 1976 when I decided to leave an academic career in Boston to return to our family farm in North Dakota. My colleagues at the university and my neighbors in North Dakota were equally perplexed about my decision. And clearly at the heart of their bewilderment was a curiosity: why would *anyone* deliberately choose to go from success to failure?

What's Wrong with Rural America?

Are rural communities no longer relevant? Is rural America populated with failed communities? Are rural people inferior? Do they lack the inherent assets to be successful?

Of course, the answer to those questions is "no." There is a reason that industries routinely set up shop in rural communities to obtain labor for their enterprises. They know that rural communities still produce the social capital that they desperately need: a strong sense of purpose, ingenuity, and dependability. Rural communities also seem to be successful at producing leadership. Gregory Page, CEO of Cargill; Rick Schnieders, CEO of SYSCO; Tom Brokaw, longtime news anchor for NBC; and Norman Borlaug, credited with inaugurating the green revolution, all grew up and were educated in small rural communities in the Midwest. We can all name similar stars who grew up in our presumably "failed" rural communities. Why then have we written off our rural communities?

The answer to that question is complex. To partially answer it and to illuminate how the faith community can play a pivotal role in revitalizing our rural communities, it may be well to recall a bit of history. Five hundred years ago, European immigrants began imposing a unique kind of culture on the North American landscape that has affected our rural communities. Lewis Mumford, one of the top scholars of the history of American culture, reminds us that European immigrants emerged from a cultural vacuum. By the seventeenth century, the culture of the Middle Ages had broken down, and old symbols were no longer meaningful. In the wake of this cultural transformation, Europeans began to migrate to North America; the most eager were the most disenchanted with the old values and were looking for a fresh start, in a new environment, based on a new way of being in the world. They were ready to master the external environment. "To them matter alone mattered."

The Puritans were prime examples of immigrants who shook off the old symbols and developed a new ethic that has since dominated American culture. Puritans came here intent on creating a "new kingdom of God on Earth." Exploiting the natural resources of the wilderness for economic gain was in large measure consonant with creating the kingdom of God. For them, success in this venture was clear evidence that they were fulfilling God's will. They believed that exploiting this "wasteland" and turning it into a shining example of economic productivity was their "manifest destiny."

In fact, as the European immigrants saw it, the "failure" of Native Americans to exercise their god-given duty to properly make use of this wasteland was sufficient justification to take the land away from the Indians who had lived here for fifteen thousand years.[5] Because they hadn't made proper use of the land they gave up their right to it. "Matter alone mattered."

This spiritual vacuum also disposed European immigrants to decimate native culture. European immigrants saw no value in the rich indigenous myths that were attuned to the ecological and cultural fabric of this "new" world, according to Frederick Turner.[6] Had they arrived with the ability to appreciate the value of what was already here rather than with an inclination toward taking inventory, they might have developed a different life that would have included a richer appreciation of, and a different role for, rural communities.

This spiritual vacuum—the notion that God had brought them here to exploit the raw materials of nature, to build a human-dominated kingdom of God—was the basis for developing an economy of resource exploitation. Their predisposition to master the external environment and maximize short-term returns shaped the economic role that rural communities were expected to play: an economy in which "matter alone mattered."

Karl Stauber, president of the Northwest Area Foundation, is a thoughtful investigator of the roots of rural poverty and the requirements for revitalizing our rural communities. He contends that rural communities have gone through several phases in a social contract that always relegated them to the role of raw-material suppliers. Rural communities have never been regarded as valuable in themselves; they were valued only insofar as they provided raw materials for the larger economy.

According to Stauber, the first phase of rural America was the *frontier,* which lasted from the end of the Revolutionary War to the late 1800s. During this phase, rural America was expected to provide the raw materials to support trade. Our young nation initially had very little manufacturing capacity, so it imported most of its manufactured goods, creating a huge trade deficit. Exporting raw materials, especially cotton, tobacco, and timber, helped to balance that trade deficit. Because rural communities provided essential raw materials from the frontier, the public supported rural communities through "government-sponsored exploration, military protection, [and] government-sponsored displacement of the existing cultures and people."[7] Once again, "matter alone mattered."

The second phase Stauber calls the *storehouse* phase. The frontier had disappeared by the 1890s, and the Industrial Revolution gripped urban America. To service the industrial economy, the population shifted to urban areas. Rural America was expected to provide the commodities to feed the "urban machine." When Thomas Jefferson was president, more than 90 percent of Americans were farmers; by 1920, half of the U.S. population lived in rural communities; and by the end of the storehouse period in the early 1970s, only a little more than a quarter of Americans still lived in rural areas.

The industrialization of America demanded a more labor-efficient agriculture to "free" people from the "drudgery" of agriculture so that they could work in industry to improve our common quality of life. In response to this new social demand, our land-grant universities devoted significant research to developing a constant stream of new technologies that required less labor on the farm, reducing the need for people in our rural communities. In addition to supporting the work done by land-grant universities, the American people supported exploitation of rural communities through the opening of public lands for mining and logging and through subsidies to rail and water transportation, irrigation projects, rural electrification, telephone systems, and crops.[8]

As the storehouse period came to a close in the 1970s, economies of scale became the new strategy for maximizing wealth. The deregulation of the airline industry and numerous other enterprises signaled that the new economy would be determined solely by market power. Consolidation became the principal strategy for domination in the food and agriculture system.[9] Once again, "matter alone mattered."

Capital accumulated primarily in the marketing and input sectors of the agricultural economy during most of the industrial period, and rural communities were expected to provide cheap labor and cheap raw materials to feed the industrial machine. Farmers and rural communities were left undercapitalized and at a distinct disadvantage in a world of economies of scale and winner-take-all capitalism.

While a few public subsidies to rural communities have been kept in place, the tolerance for such subsidies on the part of urban and suburban taxpayers is clearly waning. The majority of citizens now live in suburbs, and they see little connection between the welfare of rural communities and their own suburban communities. Rural communities are still only a source of cheap labor and raw materials for the purpose of adding value elsewhere. Their inability to compete with lower-priced raw materials from other parts of the world is interpreted as a market signal that they are not competitive and are therefore failed communities. "Matter alone matters" continues to be the theology that defines our rural communities.

Powerful forces that are deeply entrenched in our culture and infrastructure seem poised to rape the few remaining resources from rural communities. So we might be forgiven if the "corpse" is the metaphor that comes to mind when we think about the long-term future of our rural communities. Even thoughtful visions for alternative futures for rural America would actually *eliminate* many of our rural communities. The Poppers' famous proposal suggested that there is little reason to hope that we can maintain viable human communities in the rural landscape, especially in the western plains. They proposed converting the Plains to a wildlife preserve, a "buffalo commons."[10]

Is there hope for a different future for rural America?

Willard Cochran, one of the most imaginative agricultural policy researchers of our time, has suggested we restructure the entire farm belt by identifying those lands that best lend themselves to sustainable crop production. Crop production would be limited to those lands that have rich topsoil and that are not dependent on large quantities of irrigation or susceptible to soil erosion. Land not suitable for crop production would be converted to grass and domestic livestock production.[11] Cochran argues that the plan would reduce the surplus production of commodity crops, the "curse" of American agriculture. By reducing surplus supply, farmers would be in a better competitive position to capture more value from the marketplace, garner more income for rural communities, and encourage a more sustainable agriculture.

Such proposals, however, fail to get to the heart of the problem: the cultural and spiritual vacuum that has plagued our rural communities from the beginning. I think if we are to revitalize our rural communities, we have to face the fact that there is a spiritual dimension to community health. We have to acknowledge the fact that matter is not all that matters.

When we ask whether there is any hope for rural communities, I think we have to clarify what we mean by "hope." A cultural heritage that has taught us that matter alone matters has deprived us of a true meaning of hope; consequently, we are easily prone to pessimism. In our materialistic culture, hope means that there has to be something out in the world that gives us reasons to be optimistic. A few contemporary visionaries have demonstrated that hope, at least as interpreted from the perspective of faith, is *not* based on what we see out in the world but on what we value inside ourselves. Václav Havel, Paulo Freire, Wendell Berry, and Martin Luther King Jr. have all reminded us that hope is not confidence that things will turn out fine; hope is a commitment to justice even when there appears to be little to be gained by making that commitment. Wendell Berry refers to such hope as "difficult hope."[12] Three years before Václav Havel became president of Czechoslovakia, when the country was still a dictatorship, he was asked if there was any hope for his homeland. "Hope is a state of mind, not of the world," he replied. Hope is not a belief that things will go well, he said, but a willingness to work for something because it is right.

Rosa Parks stands as one of the great symbols of hope in our time. From a perspective of things turning out well, Rosa Parks had no reason to be optimistic when she refused to go to the back of the bus on that fateful day in Montgomery, Alabama. Given the culture and power structures of the time, the likely outcome from such a brash act was arrest and jail time, but at a deep level she knew it was the right thing to do.

And then, as sometimes happens, a convergence of events took place that caused that simple act of courage and hope to change the world. As we would say in our faith community, God used that simple act to bring salvation to the human family by revealing to us that we are *all* God's children. Discrimination of any kind is inconsistent with the kingdom of God. God indeed is "still speaking," as we like to remind ourselves in our United Church of Christ communion. In our faith, hope is *always* characterized this way. In almost every biblical story, there is very little to be optimistic about, but people still find a way to hope.

Would we have been hopeful had we been a slave and led out of Egypt to make a treacherous journey across the desert to a strange and distant land? As the prophet Isaiah reminds us, that little band of slaves had been in slavery for so long they had lost most of their humanity. Who would have believed that anything of significance could have come of them; and yet, they became the "people of God." Would we have been hopeful on that first Christmas Eve had we been in that cold, smelly barn where a couple of teenagers gave birth to their first child, without so much as a pail of warm water, as Martin Luther described the scene? And yet it was an event that forever changed the world.

Are we hopeful that the kingdom of God can come into our lives from a simple act of kindness toward a stranger, indeed toward an enemy, beaten by robbers and left in a ditch on the roadside to die? In the Good Samaritan parable, Jesus implies that this is the *only* way to enter the fullness of life. Do *we* hope that the fullness of life, the kingdom of God, can come into our lives by interrupting *our* business journeys to attend to the needs of one of the least of these? Do we have hope that the kingdom of God can come into our lives by being present to the least of these in our rural communities?

Hopeful changes don't occur because we engineer them or wield power; they come because we respond in faith in our communities and take the time to be neighbors to each other. We also know that such changes don't always come on our watch just because we do the right thing. Of all the women who started the women's suffrage movement in the nineteenth century, only *one* lived to actually exercise the right to vote.

Grounding our hope in faith is, I believe, essential to the revitalization of our rural communities. We know it is not right for rural communities and their resources to be exploited for the sole purpose of accumulating wealth elsewhere. We know it is not right that we import all the goods we need and devote our labor to making cheap raw materials for export, thus depriving our communities of the benefits that come from producing those goods ourselves.

We know it is not right to operate by the "colonialist principle" that assumes that "it is permissible to ruin one place or culture for the sake of another," as Wendell Berry has so eloquently put it.[13] We know it's not right, so we must refuse to sit in the back of the bus. We have to choose to be neighbors to each other in our communities, welcome the love of God into our lives, and together build a future for our rural communities based on justice and love rather than dominance and exploitation. More than matter *has* to matter if we are going to revitalize our rural communities.

How Can Churches Help?

The church obviously has a role in revitalizing our rural communities. Who better than the faith community to call attention to these issues:

- Matter is *not* the only thing that matters.
- Cooperation and equity may do more to produce a healthy economy in the long run than competition and violence.
- We cannot have thriving economies without a framework of justice.
- A world in which almost half of the world's people live on less than $2 a day, while a tiny fraction controls the majority of the world's wealth, cannot produce a secure social order or a healthy global economy.

Leaders of the financial institutions in rural communities recognize that further wealth concentration is not in their best interests. While centralization of power and wealth may be seductive in the short run, they ultimately do not lead to a healthy and secure economy, because when communities disappear, banks disappear with them.[14]

Some in the scientific community are aware that extreme concentration and centralization of economic power is dysfunctional. In 1992, John Gardner (then the superintendent of the North Dakota State University Carrington Research and Extension Center) and his wife, Julie, were decrying the lack of scientific basis for the bias against family farms and rural communities. They said, "We'd like to suggest that perhaps there is an economic bias against the people who care for the land and produce the agricultural wealth. . . . The 'family farm' may prove more valuable than serving as a romantic image of yesteryear. It's beginning to appear that centralization, either by government or economic might, is not the best strategy to deal with either the natural world or our social and economic structures."[15]

A friend and colleague who teaches economics at New Mexico State University wrote recently that "all problems seem to point to the same path. There is a new vision emerging demonstrating how we can solve problems and at the same time create a better world, and it all depends on collaboration, love, respect, beauty, and fairness. The time has passed when we think we can solve problems with domination, competition, and violence. It seems the artists and spiritual leaders have been saying this forever, and maybe now the scientists are beginning to see it as well."[16]

So shouldn't our rural churches become part of this emerging economic vision, rather than being captivated by the matter-alone-matters theology? If the church does become part of this new vision of rural economies, what role is it best suited for?

If the history of our faith is still a valid guide for appropriate action, then the church's role is *not* one that joins us to the political power structure of the day. The fusion of religion and politics has almost always been disastrous for the church and the long-term welfare of communities, from Constantine to the present. In God's kingdom, a "voice crying in the wilderness" is preferable to a cozy relationship on K Street.

If so, how can we be that voice crying in the wilderness in the twenty-first century? This is where we need to become our most creative and prayerful: most *creative* because we have to entertain new and unconventional ways of being in the world, and most *prayerful* because we have to be the most attentive, the most humble, and the most open to the voice of God in our midst. If we truly believe that God still speaks today, then we have to engage in the practice of listening. As our faith reminds us, such listening is always most effective in community, "wherever two or three are gathered together."

In our faith, it appears that the reason we need to do this in community is that none of us as individuals seems to be very good at recognizing God's voice in the world. Too often as individuals we seem to confuse God's voice with our own deluded arrogance. Meeting together as community, in humility, listening to each other, seems to be an essential ingredient. The community is also essential to hearing the voice of God because God only meets us in the flesh, when we choose to be a neighbor to an enemy on the road to Jericho and engage each other in humility and love.

In our faith, the "two or three gathered together" are not limited to priests and deacons; often ordinary fishermen, sinners, farmers, and unanticipated enemies are found on the road to Jericho. God does not meet us in the sanctuaries of religion but in our everyday lives, when we least expect it, and always in moments when we choose to be a neighbor to the other, especially the other in need. To illustrate, a few true stories may serve to stimulate our imagination and prayerfulness as we seek to identify roles that churches in the northern plains may play in revitalizing rural communities.

The first story comes from Muhammad Yunus, founder of the Grameen Bank. In his wonderful book *Banker to the Poor*, Yunus explains how he came to develop microlending networks among some of the world's poorest people, enabling them to use their skills to lift themselves out of poverty. In 1974, famine spread across Bangladesh while Yunus was teaching economics at a local university. As the famine spread, people were dying of starvation near his lecture hall. Yunus questioned what good his complex economic theories were when children were dying of starvation across the street.[17]

Yunus discovered that most poor people had no access to capital, and women were often in the best position to create new microeconomies in their own communities. He began by loaning $27 of his own money to a group of forty-two women who were organized so that they became a source of inspiration and accountability for each other. Despite complete repayment of that loan and subsequent examples of poor people paying back loans faithfully, Yunus never convinced local banks that poor people were good credit risks. So, with the help of his students, he created a microlending institution.

Yunus learned the folly of viewing the world of poverty from a distance because one cannot fully understand a community from afar; one tends to become arrogant when not fully engaged with the people one seeks to serve. So he chose to study poverty at close range, engaging people to learn from them what was needed. He learned that the key was to make small loans to people so that they could use their own ingenuity to become self-sufficient.

Yunus made microloans available to small networks of people in numerous poor communities so they could become self-employed entrepreneurs. The little pockets of wealth they created supported local economies that pushed back the specter of poverty. Because all of this was done in the context of community, with people in the community supporting each other and holding each other accountable, repayment rates were high: "Indeed, more than 98 percent of our loans are repaid. The poor know that this credit is their only opportunity to break out of poverty. They do not have any cushion whatsoever to fall back on. If they run afoul of this one loan, they will have lost their one and only chance to get out of the rut."[18]

With this record of success, microcredit in the context of community has transformed development paradigms, and microcredit has spread to many parts of the world. More than 250 institutions in almost a hundred countries now operate microcredit programs. The Grameen Bank model of economic development is based on principles transcending the narrow perspective that assumes that matter alone matters. Here is an economic system that is based on collaboration, love, respect, beauty, and fairness. In this model, local wealth expands to benefit the entire community.

A second story comes from the antipoverty program launched in 1998 by the Northwest Area Foundation in Minneapolis. The foundation decided to focus its mission on reducing long-term poverty by inviting people living in poor communities in the Northwest to engage with each other. They conducted asset self-assessments to determine indigenous strengths and opportunities in their own communities. The communities were invited to imagine their own futures and identify emerging new markets, so that the foundation could provide start-up resources as part of long-term financial commitments to enable them to begin their journey out of poverty.

Numerous stories are now emerging from this process.[19] The citizens of Miner County, South Dakota, found through a self-assessment that senior citizens were a significant economic asset to their community. Almost 30 percent of the county's economic base came from pensions, social security, Medicare payments, and other senior income. They realized that "when five seniors left town it was the equivalent of losing a small business." So the county invested in a for-profit assisted-living facility. Because the facility was locally owned and marketed, seniors trusted it more, and they stayed in the community. Now the facility houses more than twenty seniors and employs sixteen people. With more people patronizing local businesses, local churches can collect more offerings, which helps revitalize community spirit.

The third story involves the pastor and governing council of the First United Methodist Church in Newton, Iowa. The pastor and council took $5,000 out of their reserve fund. The next Sunday, the pastor preached a sermon based on the parable of the talents in chapter 25 of Matthew.

After the sermon, he invited fifty volunteers to come forward. No one knew exactly what they were volunteering for.

When all fifty were lined up at the altar, the pastor handed each a $100 bill, as in the parable of the talents, and then asked them to go into the community and make the most of the money. According to the story, this simple act immeasurably enriched the lives of people in the community, often helping them through periods of temporary crisis, and it also enriched the lives of the volunteers. The $100 bill frequently leveraged hundreds of additional dollars to address problems the community had ignored for years. According to the volunteers, the responsibility to wisely invest $100 in the community's welfare, in the context of the parable of the talents, was taken so seriously that they all devoted a great deal of time in prayer and imagination to make sure they used these "talents" wisely.[20]

A final story also comes from Iowa. Even though the number of dairies in Iowa has fallen by 60 percent since 1990, ten years ago Russell Sheeder decided to quit his UPS job to buy a farm and begin dairying. He bought a small farm, put it into grass, and decided not to use growth hormones or subtherapeutic antibiotics. These management strategies allowed him to differentiate his product in the marketplace. The Sheeders bottle the milk on their own farm and sell to area restaurants and grocery stores. A growing number of customers now *wait* for the milk because it tastes so good. There are now seven such microdairies in Iowa serving as an economic stimulus in their communities because there is very little import/export activity—all of the resources used on the farms are generated by the farms—and all of the wealth generated by these farms remains in the community.

This last story is but one signal that a new market is emerging in our food system that could provide new opportunities to rejuvenate our rural communities.

Values-based marketing provides unique opportunities for farmers, local communities, and churches to work together to develop a new regional food economy based on collaboration, love, respect, beauty, and fairness. These are the values this emerging market wants to support. The food that this market wants can best be produced by family farmers, linked together in marketing networks with their own brand—food that allows customers to engage the farmers who produce the food. Collaboration and cooperation are essential to achieving these market objectives. To the extent that we still have (or can rekindle) trusting relationships in our rural communities, these new values-based markets give a distinct comparative advantage to our rural communities.

Because the farm identity of such products is essential in these new markets, these foods must be processed in local community facilities where the identity of each product can be maintained all the way from farm to table. Such local enterprises can help expand wealth in local rural communities. These new food chains can be designed to operate on values that best serve the community and the market, ensuring that farmers receive fair compensation and that more of the wealth generated will be retained in the community.

This is not an idle pipe dream. Although it is a market that is only now beginning to emerge, there are already examples of successful ventures: Organic Valley Family of Farms, Natural Country Beef, Shepherd's Grain, Heritage Acres, Niman Ranch, and Naturally Iowa. The National Farmers Union board of directors recently agreed to use their vast membership organization to help organize farmers into more of these marketing networks. We do not have to let our rural communities evolve into pockets of poverty interspersed with leisure islands occupied by the idle rich who move into our communities for lifestyle reasons.[21]

Even business leaders see a very different future for our global economies, and their projections hold much promise for our rural communities. Business design specialist John Thackara suggests that the industrial economy has reached its end. The old economy is too exploitive to survive much longer, and the new economy will be based on community networks that operate on "relationship value." He asserts that our future food and agriculture system will become decentralized into regional foodsheds, and our health care systems will be restructured to operate on social capital, defined as "networks, together with shared norms, values and understandings, that facilitate cooperation within or among groups."[22] This is a future in which more than matter matters!

This evolving future provides our rural churches with a unique opportunity to become partners in these ventures. Who better than the faith community to help design these new concepts based on a theology that more than matter matters—that long-term community health is based on collaboration, love, respect, beauty, and fairness.

With imagination and prayerfulness, we can choose to be neighbors to each other and to those around us, allow God to speak to us in new ways, and bring new life and meaning to our rural communities. Even if we aren't optimistic about the future, our faith calls upon us to do the right thing—to love God through our neighbors, wherever two or three are gathered together, to service and care for his creation, and to boldly move forward in faith.

Rethinking Food

One way or another, reruralization will be the dominant social trend of the twenty-first century. . . . More food will be produced in cities than is the case today. . . . This implies the need for a minimum of 40 to 50 million additional farmers as oil and gas availability declines. How soon will the need arise? . . . We are looking at a transition that must occur over the next twenty to thirty years, and that must begin approximately now.[1]
—Richard Heinberg

During the past 150 years, we fully incorporated our food system into the industrial economy. Accordingly, the industrial principles of specialization, simplification, and consolidation now dominate our food web—production, processing, and distribution. However, our food system will likely undergo significant changes in the decades ahead.

This industrial food system has proved incredibly successful. Yields of a few crops rose spectacularly. Milk, meat, and egg production increased exponentially. Efficiencies improved, and transaction costs were cut. The cost per unit of food decreased dramatically. And despite the recent explosion of human population and increased rate of human consumption, we still managed to produce enough food to supply the caloric requirements of every person on the planet. The continuing malnutrition of about 1 billion people at the moment is *not* due to lack of production.

We often fail to recognize that the success of this industrial food system depends on several key resources that are now in sharp decline. Nor have we fully acknowledged the ecological costs associated with our modern food miracle.

The era of cheap energy that fuels our industrial economy will be short-lived. The energy that made the industrial economy possible was derived from stored, concentrated resources—principally coal, oil, and natural gas—that had accumulated beneath the Earth's surface over several million years. Coal launched the industrial revolution, and while coal still provides part of the energy for our industrial economy, oil and natural gas have enabled the economy to thrive. The first producing oil well in the United States became operational in 1859; by 1970, the United States had already reached peak oil production. Since then we have sustained the industrial economy by relying increasingly on imported oil and natural gas.

We are now on the brink of peak global oil production, and we have nowhere to turn for new sources of stored, concentrated energy. While many forms of alternative energy are being explored and produced, it is unlikely that any of these current dispersed forms of energy will reach the energy-profit ratios we have become accustomed to with oil and natural gas. Our new energy landscape is likely to significantly alter the food system, and those changes are only a short time ahead.

One of the most significant changes that our new energy future will likely impose on us is the demand for much more human labor. A reduction in labor requirements, made possible primarily by replacing labor with cheap energy was, of course, one of the great achievements of our industrial food system.

Given this accomplishment, the suggestion that we shift to a more labor-intensive food system is tantamount to heresy. For more than a century it has been a source of pride that we have freed ourselves from the "drudgery" of farm work, we have eliminated slavery—much of which used to provide the human labor to produce our food and fiber—and we have reduced the number of farmers required to feed us from one in three to one in more than one hundred. The notion of "freeing" people from agricultural labor is now deeply embedded in our culture. It is considered one of the great achievements of modern life.

However, an alternative food culture is emerging. We now know that the industrial food system has been at least partly responsible for the deterioration of our rural communities. At the same time, there is a growing interest in moving back into rural areas and reconnecting with some aspects of that quality of life.[2,3] As energy costs spiral upward, more urban dwellers may migrate to rural communities to produce some of their own food and enjoy the quality of life that comes from being more intimately connected with nature. Richard Heinberg calls this the "reruralization" of America, which he sees as the "dominant social trend of the twenty-first century."[4]

Barbara Kingsolver experimented with such a move to a rural area. She reports that her family's quality of life improved when they decided to grow much of their food on their own farm.[5] In addition, we know that the costs of isolation from nature, as we have moved from farms to cities, amount to a "nature deficit disorder" that can have numerous health consequences, as Richard Louv reminds us.[6]

None of this suggests we will "go back" to an agriculture that we practiced in the preindustrial period, because it is never possible to go back in time. Evolution only moves forward, and the emergent properties of evolution change the entire biotic community in ways that makes it impossible to go back. But we may well retrieve some past elements of wisdom and combine them with the best science available today. We can craft new food-production systems that are less dependent on cheap energy, huge amounts of water, and unusually stable climates. In fact, some farmers have already transitioned to agriculture systems based on this new paradigm, and they appear to be very productive, using much less energy than that needed for industrial agriculture.[7]

While the end of cheap, stored, concentrated energy may prompt some people to migrate to communities that require less energy consumption and grow more of their own food or become part of community food coalitions, others may be motivated by the growing awareness that the miracle of our industrial food system comes at enormous ecological costs that threaten our capacity for food production in the future. Soil erosion, salinization, desertification, deforestation, loss of biodiversity, depletion of freshwater resources, and pollution all are unintended outcomes of our modern industrial production system that threaten the ability of future generations to produce food.

While there are many possible solutions to all of these problems, the deindustrialization of agriculture is emerging as one alternative. Farmers' markets, community-supported agriculture operations, school gardens, urban agriculture, biointensive agriculture, perennial polyculture, and other initiatives already are growing at a rapid rate and enabling many people to engage in the pleasure of producing and consuming food with superior attributes. While all of these nonindustrial approaches still amount to only a tiny part of our food system, they are creating a new food culture that may become more significant as energy and ecological costs continue to rise.

There are precedents for such transformations. During World War II, when much of our human capital was tied up in military operations, we developed the "victory gardens" concept and produced more than 40 percent of our vegetables through these gardening activities. When Cuba was faced with an energy crisis precipitated by the collapse of the Soviet Union and the U.S. trade embargo, they had to remake their food system. Their industrial farming systems, dependent on cheap energy, came to a halt. Cubans adopted local, labor-intensive, organic agriculture. Large, state-owned farms were broken up into smaller farmer-managed operations. Farmers' markets flowered, parking lots were converted to urban gardens, and rooftop gardens were developed.

When I was in Cuba eight years ago, fifty thousand tons of food per year were being produced *inside* the city of Havana. Since then, I understand that the amount has increased substantially. Research farms were experimenting with various multicropping and plant/animal combinations to determine the most energy-efficient systems. Ecological principles informed many of the novel pest-management systems that were introduced. With the exception of sugar cane, we saw almost no monocultures, because they were considered too inefficient. While Cuba is unique in its climate, culture, and the way in which its energy crisis emerged, it serves as an example of how the end of cheap energy can lead to creative alternatives grounded in modern science.

It has occurred to me that if we are to prepare for our own transition to a postindustrial agriculture and food system, we need to anticipate some of the changes and get a head start preparing for them. We will need to engage in numerous experiments. It is partly to engage in such preparations that I have decided recently to become more involved in the work of the Stone Barns Center for Food and Agriculture in Pocantico Hills, New York. The Stone Barns Center is a project initiated by David Rockefeller and members of his family, in collaboration with restaurateurs Dan and David Barber. Stone Barns operates a farm, a restaurant, and a classroom in a collaborative effort that serves as a laboratory, an exhibit, and a conservatory. Comprising eighty acres of land with European-style stone farm buildings, it is an experiment in sustainability in an urban setting that combines learning with the pleasure of good eating. This experiment uses past and current knowledge to consciously shape an urban-based food system that is grounded in natural processes and strives to become sustainable in its distinctive setting.

Stone Barns is a center for exploring sustainability in an urban setting. We believe that it is the effort, the journey, the learning as we go that is needed to prepare for our new food future. We believe that the knowledge gleaned from our explorations will help us design part of the agriculture of the future.

In this regard, Stone Barns provides several valuable services to the food and agriculture communities. Children in the New York City region visit to gain firsthand knowledge about where food comes from. Kids either arrive with their parents (usually on weekends) or by bus with school teachers (usually during the week), or they can participate in one of the Stone Barns summer camps. They see animals raised in natural settings where the animals exhibit their normal behaviors. They can see where the animals are processed into meat at the Stone Barns processing facility. They can see how vegetables are grown and even help with tending the gardens. They can eat the food they see produced on the farms in the Blue Hill Cafe or join their parents for an incredible meal at the Blue Hill Restaurant at Stone Barns. And, perhaps more important, they spend time outdoors and connect with nature in a safe environment.

The farms at Stone Barns are managed by two creative farmers, Jack Algiere on the horticulture farm and Craig Haney at the grass-based animal farm. The apprentices who work with each of the two men learn how to become farmers. Typically, the apprentices did not grow up on a farm, but they became apprentices because they want to become farmers. Volunteers help explain the farm, the composting operation, and the conserving activities to children and, in turn, learn about food and agriculture themselves. Numerous media reports have described these unique farming operations.[8–10]

Programs for all ages are ongoing at Stone Barns. Topics related to various aspects of food and agriculture sustainability are explored and discussed. Programs emphasize how our work fits into the global and environmental context in which we and future generations are likely to find ourselves.

Stone Barns is attempting, through exploration and demonstration, to suggest ways that urban communities can move toward a sustainable food and agriculture system. Our farmers are constantly exploring how to produce nutrient-rich meat and vegetables without expensive external energy inputs, to form healthy soils that produce great-tasting food served in the restaurant a few yards away. They are examining how to raise animals in natural settings, humanely, using low-energy inputs. They are demonstrating how to compost wastes from the operations and return them to the soil, which improves the health of the soil and the food produced from it. Excess compost is made available to local gardeners and sold in local stores. Our farmers are also experimenting with unique seeds and breeds that are adapted to natural farming, to ensure the availability of the biological and genetic diversity necessary for successful agroecological farming.

The relationships being established between the farmers and the chefs in the restaurant point to another set of unique and important outcomes. The farmers learn what the chefs need to be successful in the restaurant as they work to ensure the pleasure of good, healthy eating. The chefs learn what challenges and opportunities the farmers face, given their local ecology, to meet those requirements. Both groups become more effective in achieving their respective goals.

Because Stone Barns includes both for-profit operations (the restaurant and cafe) and a nonprofit arm (the program and outreach activities), we also have opportunities to explore new management techniques. It can be difficult to balance objectives that sometimes compete. Creating and maintaining team spirit and developing collaborative management systems while exploring ways to combine technical, agricultural, and food-service tasks with social-organization issues is proving to be a challenging but stimulating experience. Our circumstances often lead to creative tension and the opportunity to develop management systems that can direct such tension into productive results.

Being connected with both the Leopold Center for Sustainable Agriculture in the heart of rural Iowa and the Stone Barns Center for Food and Agriculture on the edge of New York City gives me a rare, and perhaps unprecedented, opportunity to explore the many dimensions of sustainability in both rural and urban settings as we face the challenges of developing a postindustrial food system. I am confident, based on my involvement with both centers, that we can learn much from each other.

Using What We Know to
Make a Difference

Evolution rises from the bottom up—so too does hope.[1]
—Paul Hawken

In academic circles we often explore problems in great depth but fail to come up with creative ways to solve problems. Consequently we end up knowing a lot about problems but little about how to solve them—so we often end up failing to make a difference. As I wrestled with this challenge it occurred to me that there are at least four questions that we might fruitfully address:

- What do we think we know?
- What is the narrative that informs our interpretation of the world we live in?
- What kind of difference do we want to make?
- How can we begin to make that difference?

What Do We Think We Know?

I think we know that our current agricultural, political, educational, economic, and health care systems are becoming increasingly dysfunctional. I think we know that the dominant narrative that informs those institutions is outdated and needs to be reframed.

I think it is clear that humans cannot stop evolution or arrest change

This piece was prepared for and presented at the Mountain Sky Friends of Charlie meeting, October 7–12, 2008. For almost a decade, Charles Sing of the University of Michigan has arranged for a biennial gathering of scholars from agriculture and medicine to explore issues of common concern.

at any particular stage of desired equilibrium. Social and biological systems are too dynamic and too complex for us to effectively wield such control. There are still a few Cartesian engineers in our midst who continue to think we can be the "masters and possessors" of nature, believing it may be possible to control our destiny with superior new technologies. I am far from optimistic regarding such efforts. No matter how much command and control we exercise, or how many brilliant and powerful technologies we may invent, the planet we inhabit will continue to move through adaptive cycles that are determined by complex synergies that we will never fully understand, let alone control. That seems to be the fundamental, undeniable lesson of ecology. Our focus must be on adaptation and cooperation, not command and control. Consequently, I think Wendell Berry is right when he admonishes us to adopt the Socratic "way of ignorance" rather than the way of arrogance, if we are to have any hope of finding our way.[2]

I think we know that the industrial era has shaped both our economy and our culture, which largely determines the way we collectively think and act. We also know that this industrial economy is dependent on a collection of natural resources that we have been aggressively mining for well over a century and that are now in a state of decline. Accordingly, our industrial era will predictably be relatively short-lived, forcing us to make a major transition in how we conduct our human affairs.

Anthropologist Ernest Schusky has designated this industrial period—which came into its own in the early 1900s—the "neocaloric era" because it is almost entirely dependent on "old calories" (principally fossil fuels). Because these calories are old (having been stored up for many millennia), finite, and subject to aggressive mining, they will be used up in a relatively brief period in the time line of human history.[3] As these "old calories" are used up it will become increasingly difficult for us to sustain our industrial economy.

We also know that the overriding goal of this industrial economy has been to maximize efficient production and short-term return. Given this single-minded goal, we have paid little attention to the health of our finite biosphere, or to the resources produced by that biosphere that are the foundation of any human economy. As a result, we have severely degraded the very resources on which our economy depends.

As it turns out, this natural capital is worth more than all of our human capital combined, yet our industrial economy continues to disregard the value of natural capital and the need to maintain its resilience. As natural capital erodes, we begin to experience "uneconomic growth."[4]

We also know that there are at least four natural resources, which are part of that natural capital, that have been crucial to the success of our industrial economy for more than a century. They are cheap energy, surplus freshwater, stable climates, and natural sinks. Each of these natural resources played a key role in creating and sustaining the industrial economy, and each of them is now in a state of decline, issues that have been summarized previously in this volume, particularly in the essay "Food as Relationship."

The erosion of each of these four resources, so vital to an industrial economy, strongly suggests that this economy cannot long endure. The fact that our political, educational, social, and economic institutions are designed to serve the industrial economy is a signal that our institutions will also become increasingly dysfunctional and that the narrative that continues to inform them is outdated. A significant transition to a different economy with different structure and functioning is therefore highly likely in the decades ahead. Such world-changing transitions can either lead to a "great turning" or a "great unraveling."[5] So, while the challenges are daunting, they also provide us with *unprecedented opportunities to make a difference.*

What Is the Narrative That Informs Our Interpretation of the World We Live In?

The important role that narratives play in the way we think and act is almost never acknowledged in our culture. I believe this is a serious barrier to change.

Scott Peters's enlightening analysis describes the way narratives play an important role in determining our thoughts and actions in public universities.[6] His examination of the role of narrative in public universities is instructive for understanding how narratives shape our thought and action in all of life.

According to Peters, two predominant narratives define our public universities today. He describes these narratives as the "heroic metanarrative" and the "tragic counternarrative." The heroic metanarrative presents our universities as the heroes that democratized learning and produced scientific experts who developed new knowledge and technologies to solve problems, improve agricultural productivity, and advance the material interests of everyone. The tragic counternarrative characterizes our universities as part of the problem, contributing to the consolidation of power and the demise of rural communities. It is this degradation of our environment that now puts us on the edge of planetary crisis. Peters believes that neither of these narratives serves us well, and he calls for the creation of a new narrative grounded in freedom and sustainability. I would also argue that the predominant narratives inhibit change because the heroic narrative denies the need for change, and the tragic narrative suggests that change may be impossible because the false heroic narrative is too entrenched to allow for change.

Peters's description of the dominant narratives was played out in real life recently at Iowa State University (ISU). An ISU student published an essay in the student paper questioning the university's cozy relationship with a giant industrial seed company.[7] She cogently articulated the tragic counternarrative and asked how the university could meet its own goals (putting more farmers on the land, for example) as long as it was beholden to the very companies who were promoting an agricultural system that was forcing farmers off the land. The student was hoping to stimulate debate about an issue she deeply cared about.

Three days later the dean of the College of Agriculture published a response to the student's essay, in which she expressed her disappointment in the student's "ill-informed and relentlessly negative opinion . . . toward the generosity of Monsanto."[8] The dean went on to chastise the student for identifying "an easy target" and attributed her misguided behavior to "human nature." It was somewhat ironic that a little over a week before these articles appeared in the *Iowa State Daily,* the business section of the *New York Times* featured a thoughtful front-page article that raised many of the same concerns expressed by the student.[9]

Here in stark relief are the two narratives that Scott Peters refers to in his essay. The heroic metanarrative, articulated by the dean, depicts the university and its industrial partners as the heroes that are developing new technologies that benefit farmers and society at large while providing jobs for students. The student's tragic counternarrative presents the university and its collusion with industry as an arrangement that subordinates agriculture to the interests of industry and deters the university from investing in research that will create a sustainable agriculture capable of meeting the challenges of the future.

The dean's response also reveals another feature that is characteristic of heroic metanarratives: presenting the dominant narrative as the *only* true scenario and denigrating alternative scenarios as "ill informed." It is now commonplace for the proponents of heroic metanarratives to claim that they are "science-based," while alternative narratives are discredited as "junk science" promulgated by uninformed "activists." In her article the dean goes a step further, entering theological territory when she claims that the student's ill-informed article was not the first, nor will it be the last, of such false diatribes because they are simply a part of "human nature."

Unfortunately, such claims to have superior truth (especially when made by those who hold powerful positions) over the "ill-informed" views of those who perceive a different truth (and generally are on the fringes of society) have a chilling effect on the very debate we need to examine our narratives. Consequently, we also fail to examine the harmful, unintended consequences of some of those same heroic technologies or to examine alternatives—technologies that have, at least in part, led us to the point of crossing a planetary threshold to a different structure and function. The claimed superior science-based technologies tend to close any debate about the goals of those technologies or whether they ultimately contribute to the common good.[10]

The pretension to superiority implicit in the "sound science" claims also reinforces the unfortunate culture of exceptionalism, so deeply ingrained in our society, which tends to discourage genuine diplomacy and the evolution of mutually beneficial solutions to problems, both locally and globally.

Perhaps the deepest irony in all this is that the heroic metanarrative actually discourages genuine scientific inquiry and distorts the core purpose of science. As Michael Polanyi, Gregory Bateson, and others have demonstrated, there is no such thing as "objective" truth that establishes incontrovertible facts that no longer need to be questioned. As Bateson puts it so starkly, "Science *probes*, it does not prove."[11] Science is an ongoing process, not an accumulation of facts.

Peters argues that the viability of our public institutions depends on crafting a third, prophetic narrative, grounded in the struggles for freedom and sustainability. Such a new narrative would enable us to understand the challenges we face and to engage in activities that make a difference. I would argue that we need a plurality of narratives and the freedom to choose from among them, and I would argue that such democratic narratives, offering context-dependent solutions, are essential to the task of making a difference.

The reason narratives are essential to making a difference is that it is impossible to even begin a conversation (witness the student's effort to begin a debate on corporate influence in our universities) if we fail to recognize that our dominant narrative is dictating conclusions rather than inviting genuine dialogue. Our dominant narratives are now so pervasive that we confuse them with reality.

It seems to me, therefore, that one of the significant, concrete contributions that scholars can make is to expose the fallacies in our current narratives and then, like the ISU student, invite vigorous debate. Vigorous, democratic debate that constantly challenges entrenched narratives is one of the most effective ways to allow a new narrative to emerge that reflects our evolving understanding of reality, and *that* might well be the necessary precursor to making a difference.

For example, we know from ecology and evolutionary biology that reality is always changing, replete with emergent properties, and constantly moving through adaptive cycles. Our current narratives, on the other hand, tend to remain static and have become entrenched ideologies resistant to change. Our predominant industrial narrative—with roots in the seventeenth century—still leads us to believe that nature is a collection of largely disconnected objects that serve as raw materials to be exploited solely for the benefit of the human species. All the while it has become increasingly clear that our planet consists of a highly complex, interdependent web of life of which we are an integral part.

Our dominant narrative considers it an inalienable right to exploit any object of nature that we think may benefit us. In reality, our exploitive behavior has so degraded the ecological health of the land that it now threatens to push the planet across a threshold to a different structure and function.[12] Our industrial narrative even suggests that we need not worry about depleting natural resources because we will always be able to invent synthetic substitutes to replace them.[13] In reality, given the value of the ecosystem services provided by our natural resources, such a synthetic world would be unaffordable even at today's relatively cheap energy prices and even if it were technically possible.

Our heroic metanarrative has similarly characterized the "free market" as inerrant. According to our current industrial narrative, questioning the "goodness" and infallibility of the free market is heresy. A few years ago Harvey Cox argued that infallible-free-market ideology had reached a point of appropriating much of the language of long-established theological dogma.[14] In reality, free markets are far from infallible, as we are learning, once again, from the current bitter financial crises.

This industrial narrative captures our imagination, shapes our thinking, imprisons us, and prevents us from investigating resilient and creative alternatives that might enable us to adapt more creatively to the challenges facing us. Our predominant narrative has also led institutions to invest considerable capital in infrastructure that now embraces the industrial economy. Consequently, incredibly strong short-term economic incentives create pressure to maintain the current system rather than investing in infrastructure that would facilitate transitioning to a new economy.

Accordingly, we are much more likely to continue subsidizing current infrastructure than we are to invest in alternative infrastructure. We are much more likely to continue insisting on greater specialization and efficiency than we are to invest in the kind of redundancy, decentralization, and diversity that could increase the likelihood of greater resilience and adaptability in the face of rapid changes. If we are to make a difference we will need to find ways to convey the fact that increased efficiency, subsidization, and control suppresses novelty and therefore stifles the innovation and imagination we will need to adapt to a postindustrial economy.

Part of what makes change difficult is that it is hard for people, captured by their predominant existing narratives, to imagine a different narrative that might provide them with a better quality of life than the one they are currently experiencing. For example, I think most people in America, given our dominant narrative, believe that our current quality of life is as good as it has ever been and are reluctant to change. The actual data demonstrate, however, that well-being has actually decreased significantly since the 1970s. We now experience the highest rates of depression and suicide, dependence on antidepressants, frenetic work schedules, and reduced time with family or hobbies.[15]

Creating a new narrative will require imaginative thinking to lead to a new paradigm. I believe our engagement with the arts and humanities will become critical because the arts can help us imagine a better life than the one we currently have. This can be done through movies, television shows, street theater, soap operas, and other drama venues. The humanities can expose us to literature that can help us develop better social theories that bring more meaning to our lives. And faith communities can help us better understand and develop the deeper meanings of life that help us transcend our baser instincts—which can often be self-destructive—and appropriate the true meaning of hope.

If optimism and pessimism are the only available perspectives on our future, we have little reason to act. A pessimistic view suggests there is no way to improve things, so we may as well give up. An optimistic view naively believes that things will turn out fine, so we need not take action. With hope, however, we do the right thing even when there is no realistic expectation that things will get better. It is hope, rather than pessimism or optimism, that motivates us to make a difference.

This kind of hope invites us to become involved in changes that may already be happening around us but to which we are blind because we have either become cynical or naive due to lack of engagement. Through hopeful engagement we begin to realize that more often than not we do not need to start a revolution; we just need to stop sleeping through the ones that are already happening. When conditions are such that change is required, then change in some respect is already under way. A "blessed unrest" is often already taking place beneath the surface of our awareness.

What Kind of Difference Do We Want to Make?

In a democratic society, a conception of the difference we want to make should come from a process that evolves from the bottom up and not from one that is imposed from the top down. Citizens need to engage in conversations with each other and with citizens throughout the global family through global networks.

That said, citizens will need a context for engaging in conversations creatively and productively. That means, I think, that we have to provide citizens with some sense of the changes that are coming toward us and some perspective on what we need to do to get a head start preparing for those changes. If that is a valid observation, there is a need for a philosophical/ecological/social framework that citizens can use to explore the kinds of changes they want to make in the interest of sustainability in their own communities.

We might consider providing citizens with two suggestions derived from recent ecological and social research that might lead communities into conversations that will help them determine the kind of difference they want to make.

The first of these suggestions is that we should explore ways to redesign our current biophysical and social systems to make them resilient enough to be less likely to cross a threshold into a different kind of functioning. In other words, we should invite communities to explore ways for their social and biological systems to absorb potential future shocks and disturbances without undergoing a regime shift. For example, a community might explore what kind of agriculture it should put on the landscape that would continue to produce a sufficient amount of food anticipating three shocks: oil reaching $300 a barrel, having only half the amount of freshwater currently available, and experiencing twice the number of severe weather events. Imagining a farming system that would be sustainable under those circumstances might prepare the community for some of the changes coming their way in the decades ahead. The "transition town" movement is an excellent model for practical ways to approach such daunting tasks.[16]

The second suggestion is that we should explore how to build sufficient diversity and redundancy into the social and biophysical systems in the community so that if or when a system does cross a threshold into a new regime, it still retains its adaptive and transformative capacity so that the essential goods and services necessary for survival are retained. For example, how could the new agriculture described above include sufficient redundancy and diversity so that if a threshold is crossed despite the newly designed farming system, it would still be possible to farm successfully in the changed regime? A mixture of plant and animal species with extensive genetic diversity, including a mixture that is at least half perennials, might make conversion to a new system compatible with a new and emerging ecology.

Using such ecologically informed guidelines, it might be possible for citizens to begin imagining the kinds of change they need to make in their own communities and to start taking action to implement them.

How Do We Begin to Make That Difference?

Figuring out how to make a difference is, of course, the more daunting task. Naturally, there are no easy or uniform answers. But let me offer four suggestions that may be useful in our journey toward deciding how to make a difference in our communities.

1. Openly scrutinize the narrative within which we are currently making our decisions, determining our careers, and establishing our political and social agendas. This exercise entertains the possibility of adopting an alternative narrative that is more compatible with our changing circumstances. The underlying question here is, "What do we value?" Let us acknowledge at the outset that there is no such thing as "value-free" inquiry or action. The conclusion that value-free decision-making is superior to a values-based approach is itself a value judgment. Furthermore, assuming that our decisions are value-free will likely have the additional unintended consequence of imprisoning us in a paradigm that prevents us from engaging in careful, scientific investigation of the values we adopt.

2. Recognize that we all live out of narratives we have created and that the narrative we adopt largely determines how we see the world as well as the actions we choose. None of us can objectively "know" the world we live in; we can only interpret reality from the perspective of the narrative within which we live. That narrative is determined by our personal history and culture. We cannot step outside that skin of personal history and experience. It is this "subsidiary awareness"[17] out of which we each operate that shapes our narrative. This recognition goes a long way toward encouraging the kind of humility that invites conversations with nature and reduces the likelihood of unintended negative consequences that often attend decisions made in arrogance.

3. To choose a narrative that is appropriate for meeting the challenges before us and prepare ourselves and our communities to adapt to them, it may be helpful to entertain several questions:
   (a) Which framework, industrial or ecological, can best prepare us to meet the changes ahead?
   (b) Will control management or adaptive management be the most effective for meeting the challenges we will be facing in the coming decades?

(c) Can our role as professionals be most effective as detached experts or as scholar/citizens engaged in our communities? Is it time to re-examine the scientist/activist dichotomy that has become a part of our culture?

(d) Is investing in ecological health more relevant than subsidizing our industrial economy?

(e) How do we determine well-being? Is well-being enhanced by the magnitude of our personal wealth and our independence from others, or is it linked to the degree of communal security and shared responsibility we create?

(f) Which path is most likely to lead us to real prosperity? Is it the pursuit of our own self-interest or the evolution of an ecological conscience?

(g) How can we best secure the future common good? Is it by waiting for scientific certainty or by taking precautionary action?

4. Clarify how change happens. There are numerous theories of change. Which of these can best serve our desire to make a difference?

(a) The Lone Ranger model. Some believe that change happens through heroic actions on the part of the few. Someone rides into town with superior ideas and actions, brings change to the community, and rides off into the sunset. Promises of quick technological solutions to complex problems are just one of the current iterations of the Lone Ranger model. However, this is not to dismiss the value that outside experts can play in bringing about change. Often the perspective of an outside expert can provide imaginative insights that would be missing without that outlook.

(b) The Margaret Mead model. An often-quoted idea has been attributed to Margaret Mead: "Never doubt that a small group of thoughtful, committed citizens can change the world. Indeed, it is the only thing that ever has." Although we do not know if she actually ever said this, it has emerged as a theory of change. Certainly there is some evidence pointing to the fact that change sometimes happens this way (Jesus and his twelve disciples, for example). But is it really the *only* thing that has ever brought about change?

(c) The Thomas Jefferson model. Thomas Jefferson believed that if people are given correct information and the freedom to do the right thing, they will bring about the appropriate changes in their communities. I'm sure we can all think of instances in which that has not occurred, despite the proper conditions being met.

(d) The Adam Smith model. Adam Smith believed that even if people were given the right information and had the freedom to do the right thing, they still were unlikely to do the right thing unless there was some incentive for them to do so. But incentives, even those driven by the free market, are sometimes not in the best interest of the larger community. This theory of change promotes a degree of selfishness that can inhibit change that comes from shared perspectives.

(e) The Jared Diamond model. Based on his study of past civilizations, Jared Diamond concluded that those civilizations that correctly assessed their current situations, anticipated the changes coming toward them, and got a head start on preparing for those changes thrived. Those that failed in that exercise collapsed. This historical analysis suggests that preparing for change may sometimes be more important than facilitating change.

(f) The Karl Stauber model. As president of the Northwest Area Foundation, Karl Stauber determined that change never happens at the centers of power because those in power seldom invite change. Change happens on the fringes because people on the fringes are the ones who experience the need for change. Conclusion? We must work with those in our communities who live on the fringes of society.

(g) The Milton Friedman model. In his new book *The Bridge at the Edge of the World,* Gus Speth reminds us that Milton Friedman asserted that change rarely happens without a crisis, but that when the crisis comes we need "ideas floating around" that direct the change toward the future we want.

(h) The Paul Hawken model. Based on four years of research, Paul Hawken has concluded that there are millions of grassroots organizations throughout the world that are in a state of "blessed unrest" and ready to participate in significant change. He believes that some trigger event could mobilize this unrest into a significant force for global change.

(i) The Thomas Berry model. Thomas Berry suggests that crises are "moments of grace." Crises always unsettle things, producing opportunities for great change that are not available in the more benign, settled moments.

(j) Joy's law. One of the many "Joy's laws" promulgated by Bill Joy, cofounder of Sun Microsystems, holds that in any given sphere of activity, most of the pertinent knowledge will reside outside the boundaries of any one organization. This law suggests that no matter how large or powerful any organization or institution may get, it cannot control innovation, implying that one of the impediments to change is lack of imagination and hope.

So what can we do to make a difference? Personally, I do not have much confidence in the Lone Ranger model of change. Even if it does bring about change, the community doesn't own it due to lack of involvement and therefore is not likely to embrace it. The Margaret Mead model is inspiring and in certain circumstances can certainly make a difference. The Thomas Jefferson model is appealing, and we would all like to believe that it is true, but probably it can be successful only if an active, engaged free press (like the one he envisioned) truly informs the public, instead of being captured by the industrial paradigm, which uses media outlets primarily for entertainment purposes.

The Adam Smith model certainly motivates us to act because it serves our own self-interests. But certainly we are now aware that self-interest as a primary motivation can lead to the kind of "you are on your own" economy that we are currently experiencing and is, if anything, a barrier to change. The Jared Diamond model can make us aware that our current circumstances can lead to collapse if we fail to act in advance.

I think the Karl Stauber model is instructive. It is true that people at the centers of power are reluctant to change, because as long as they can wield power from their privileged positions, they can temporarily control much of their own destinies and therefore are likely to resist change. People on the fringes of society are much more likely to be aware of the need for change and therefore more likely to become involved. So perhaps one of the things we can do is to identify the people who are on the fringes and help organize them into communities of change. Stauber's model and Paul Hawken's blessed unrest complement each other rather nicely.

I think that Milton Friedman's and Thomas Berry's models also have a great deal of merit. A barrier to becoming change agents may be our failure to recognize opportunities for change in the midst of the chaos that crises bring and which we fear. So maybe we can make a difference by anticipating the opportunities for change that crises will bring—and there will likely be no shortage of crises in the decades ahead.

I think that Joy's law is useful in that it reminds us that the citadels of power, which we often fear and which often immobilize us, need not paralyze us. Knowledge, imagination, creativity, innovation, and cooperation are all great tools of change that power cannot co-opt without our permission.

There are probably many avenues to change. Different times, places, and circumstances may call for different strategies or change models. In other words, any of the theories of change may be appropriate in specific circumstances.

I think one of the most important things that the community of scholars could do is to reconsider their roles as academics and professionals. Part of the narrative that has evolved in academic institutions is the notion that it is our responsibility to explore discrete bits of reality, informed by the strict rules of our disciplines; remain objective so as to protect the purity of our inquiries; and extend our findings to the public, absenting ourselves of any further action or involvement. While that narrative has merits, it seems woefully inadequate to prepare us for the challenges rapidly bearing down upon us. We must now become active public scholars and citizens, engage our fellow citizens in the streets and shops of our communities, and become part of the blessed unrest that is emerging.

Several examples of citizen/scholar exist, and they may be evidence that "blessed unrest" is under way. For example, Bill McKibben has demonstrated how the arts, in the form of street theater, can be an effective vehicle for change. While Bill is not an academic in the traditional sense, he is a scholar-in-residence at Middlebury College. His Step It Up campaign was the largest demonstration to date in America on climate change and made climate change real for thousands of people. His 350 campaign demonstrates how imagination and engagement can make a difference. Climatologists have now asserted that we need to reduce our greenhouse gases to 350 particles per million. Bill recognized that this cannot be accomplished without a global effort. But we don't have a global language, let alone a global culture, through which we can communicate such an urgent message. Bill decided that mathematics was the one global language at our disposal and so started a campaign to embed the number 350 into the global consciousness through various forms of street theater. While the campaign is still in its early stages, it seems to be gaining momentum.[18] The 350 campaign combines local community organization with global networking potential.

Another example is the "transition town" movement. According to an article in the *Christian Science Monitor,* transition towns began three years ago as part of a student project in Ireland. In transition towns, local groups organize to transition their communities from high energy consumption to being low-oil economies. Local citizen groups have created tool kits to "reskill" community members to dramatically reduce energy use. They also have met with city officials to engage them in projects that raise the consciousness of the political establishment.[19]

Numerous farmers around the world are now weaning themselves from energy-intensive farming and converting to polyculture operations in which biological synergies replace energy inputs. Farmers like Joel Salatin in Virginia and Takao Furuno in Japan have been leaders in designing this kind of agriculture.[20] University researchers have begun to explore polyculture designs on research farms.[21]

Different challenges, of course, require different strategies. The forgivingness of nature works to our advantage as we begin to restore the health of soils and planetary biodiversity. Restoring soil health and biodiversity will be critical to reducing water and energy consumption in food production. We may still have an opportunity to avoid crossing a threshold to a different regime with respect to ecological restoration, but we may not be so fortunate regarding climate change. Instead, we may have to focus on adapting to a planet with very different characteristics.

From an evolutionary perspective, our survival as a species probably is not the result of always carefully thinking things out and obtaining definitive scientific proof before acting to escape from life-threatening situations. It is more likely that we survived because of timely gut reactions. Thus, we may also want to reconsider our current bias toward our logical, computational minds and give more credence to our primordial, autonomic minds. The general public may respond more eagerly to a passionate call to action than to a tightly reasoned treatise.[22]

Finally, as Paul Roberts has indicated, the "real question" in our time is "not *whether* change is going to come, but whether the shift will be peaceful and orderly, or chaotic and violent, because we waited too long to begin planning for it."[23]

Afterword

4/13/09
Professor Kirschenmann:

It was a little over twenty-eight years ago that a young writer from *The Farmer/Dakota Farmer* magazine came to interview you at your farm in North Dakota. I was that writer, and I recall our visit very clearly, including the nearly completed earth-shelter home you were building on your beloved prairie. I came away very impressed with what you were doing with building a healthy cropping regime. You opened a door to new possibilities for farmers and new/old ways of doing things. It remains one of my favorite interview experiences.

Although I sent you a copy of the article for your review, it was never published. I don't recall if I ever contacted you with the outcome. While you may not recall the interview or the story, you may enjoy, to borrow an overused tag line from Paul Harvey, "the rest of the story."

You were one of two organic farmers I had interviewed. The other was Paul Burley from Blue Earth County, Minnesota. Before agreeing to the interview, Paul asked me to make the following promise: "If you can't tell the story as I have told it to you, don't do it."

This was 1980, and farm chemicals were king in the ag publishing business. Our publisher and our sales manager couldn't get enough corn and soybean stories, nor could they see why we even had a sheep editor (one of my multiple titles). When I turned in the article, it met with immediate concerns from the managing editor, who shared it with the editor, who ran it by an extension soil scientist. They all concluded that it was impossible to make a good living doing what you and Paul were doing. It would be misleading to present such information to the readers of the magazine.

My managing editor finally offered me this compromise. He would run the article, but alongside it would run a counterpoint in which the extension soil scientist would refute the points you and Paul had made. I knew that the "debate" would be one-sided and felt it would not reflect fairly on you or Paul. I chose to withhold the story.

I left the magazine later that year. The story was one of several reasons I chose to look for another job. While I have continued to write mostly within the conventional ag theater, your and Paul's efforts opened me to a new way of farming and thinking. Since then, I have watched your leadership role in agriculture expand and advance along with organic agriculture and a new appreciation for sustainability.

Congratulations and thank you for what you have given American agriculture. I will always regret that I wasn't one of the first to write about you and your views, but I did come close.

Best regards,
Jim Ruen
Lanesboro, Minnesota

Notes

Editor's Introduction

1. Paul Hawken, *Blessed Unrest: How the Largest Social Movement in History Is Restoring Grace, Justice, and Beauty to the World* (New York: Penguin, 2008).

2. E. Mendelson, "Auden and God," *New York Review of Books,* December 6, 2007.

Preface

1. Aldo Leopold, *A Sand County Almanac* (New York: Oxford University Press, 1949), 221.

2. In this regard, I have found Brian Walker and David Salt's *Resilience Thinking* (Washington, D.C.: Island Press, 2006) particularly useful.

Theological Reflections while Castrating Calves

1. Michael Polanyi, *The Tacit Dimension* (Garden City, N.Y.: Anchor Books, 1976), 18 (emphasis mine).

2. Garry Wills, *What Paul Meant* (Peabody, Mass.: Viking Press, 2006).

3. Tom Wessels, *The Myth of Progress: Toward a Sustainable Future* (Burlington, Vt.: University of Vermont Press, 2006).

4. Quoted in Mark Buchanan, *Nexus: Small Worlds and the Groundbreaking Science of Networks* (New York: W. W. Norton & Co., 2002), 152.

On Behalf of American Farmers

1. Stephen H. Schneider, *The Genesis Strategy: Climate and Global Survival* (New York: Plenum Press, 1976).

2. E. F. Schumacher, *Small Is Beautiful: Economics as if People Mattered* (New York: Harper and Row, 1973).

3. William Lockeretz, "The Lessons of the Dust Bowl," *American Scientist* 66 (1978): 560–69.

4. William A. Albrecht, *The Albrecht Papers,* ed. Charles Walters (Raytown, Mo.: Acres USA, 1975), 63.

Low-Input Farming in Practice

1. E. F. Schumacher, *A Guide for the Perplexed* (New York: Harper and Row, 1977), 105.

2. Wendell Berry, preface to *Meeting the Expectations of the Land,* ed. W. Jackson, W. Berry, and B. Coleman (Berkeley, Calif.: North Point Press, 1984), x.

3. William Lockeretz, "Open Questions in Sustainable Agriculture," *American Journal of Alternative Agriculture* 3 (1988): 174–81.

4. Stuart Hill, quoted in Carole Giangrande and Lister Sinclair, *Culture and Agriculture* (Montreal, Que.: Canadian Broadcasting Company Transcripts, 1987).

5. Jim Bender, "How to Convert to Pesticide Free Farming," *Acres U.S.A.* 19 (1989): 19, 31.

6. E. F. Schumacher, *Good Work* (New York: Harper and Row, 1979).

7. William Ball, "Crop Rotations for North Dakota," *North Dakota State University Extension Service, Extension Bulletin* 48 (1987).

8. Walter Goldstein, "Thoughts on Drought Proofing Your Farm: A Biodynamic Approach," *Michael Fields Agricultural Institute Bulletin* 1 (1989).

9. V. L. Anderson, "The Fertility Value of Livestock Manure," in *Proceedings of Beef Production Field Day, September 8–9, 1988* (Carrington, N.D.: North Dakota State University, Carrington Research Extension Center, 1988).

10. Herbert H. Koepf, Roderick Shouldice, and Walter Goldstein, *The Biodynamic Farm* (New York: Anthroposophic Press, 1989).

11. Niccolo Machiavelli, *The Prince,* trans. George Bull (London: Penguin Books, 1999), 12.

12. Ibid.

13. Ibid., 22–23.

14. Ibid., 81.

15. Ibid., 73.

A Transcendent Vision

1. Scouring is a diarrhea that calves pick up easily from one another in cold, wet conditions. It can cause them to dehydrate rather quickly, and death is not uncommon.

Expanding the Vision of Sustainable Agriculture

1. David C. Korten, *When Corporations Rule the World* (San Francisco: Berrett-Koehler Publishers, 1995).

2. Niles Eldredge, *Dominion: Can Nature and Culture Co-Exist?* (New York: Henry Holt and Co., 1995), 168.

3. Ibid., 93.

4. Ibid., 155–56.

5. Ibid.

6. Ibid., 158.

7. Ibid.

8. Miguel A. Altieri, ed., *Agroecology: The Scientific Basis of Alternative Agriculture* (Boulder, Colo.: Westview Press, 1987).

9. S. B. Hecht, "The Evolution of Agroecological Thought," in *Agroecology: The Scientific Basis of Alternative Agriculture,* ed. Miguel A. Altieri, 1–19 (Boulder, Colo.: Westview Press, 1987).

10. Eugene P. Odum, "Properties of Ecosystems," in *Agricultural Ecosystems: Unifying Concepts,* ed. Richard Lowrance, Benjamin R. Stinner, and Garfield J. House (New York: John Wiley & Sons, 1984), 9.

11. Odum, "Properties of Ecosystems," 8.

12. Paul B. Thompson, *The Spirit of the Soil: Agriculture and Environmental Ethics* (London: Routledge, 1995).

13. R. Edward Grumbine, *Ghost Bears: Exploring the Biodiversity Crisis* (Washington, D.C.: Island Press, 1992).

14. Korten, *When Corporations Rule,* 234.

15. Ervin Laszlo, *Choice: Evolution or Extinction? A Thinking Person's Guide to Global Issues* (New York: G. P. Putnam's Sons, 1994), 27.

16. Ibid.

17. Wendell Berry, *Sex, Economy, Freedom & Community* (New York: Pantheon Books, 1993), 49.

18. Adam Smith, *An Inquiry into the Nature and Causes of the Wealth of Nations* (1776; repr., New York: Random House, 1994).

19. See the work of William D. Heffernan on the evolution of consolidation in the food and agriculture system during the past twenty years, available at http://www.food circles.missouri.edu/consol.htm.

20. Rick Welsh, *The Industrial Reorganization of U.S. Agriculture: An Overview & Background Report* (Greenbelt, Md.: Henry A. Wallace Institute for Alternative Agriculture, 1996).

21. USDA Advisory Committee on Agricultural Concentration, *Concentration in Agriculture* (Washington, D.C.: U.S. Department of Agriculture, Agricultural Marketing Service, 1996).

22. William D. Heffernan, "Concentration of Agricultural Markets—1992" (unpublished paper, 1995, available from the author).

23. Ibid.

24. Richard Behar, "Arkansas Pecking Order," *Time,* October 26, 1992, 54.

25. Dennis T. Avery, *Saving the Planet with Pesticides and Plastic: The Environmental Triumph of High-Yield Farming* (Indianapolis: Hudson Institute, Inc., 1995).

26. Laszlo, 39.

27. Laszlo, 37–38.

28. Laszlo, 39.

29. Korten, *When Corporations Rule,* 171.

30. Tracy I. Hewitt and Katie R. Smith, *Intensive Agriculture and Environmental Quality: Examining the Newest Agricultural Myth* (Greenbelt, Md.: Henry A. Wallace Institute for Alterative Agriculture, 1995).

31. Helena Norberg-Hodge, *Ancient Futures: Learning from Ladakh* (San Francisco: Sierra Club Books, 1991).

32. Ibid., 56–57.

33. Erich Fromm, *To Have or to Be?* (New York: Harper and Row, 1976).

34. Ibid., 2.

35. Ibid.

36. John B. Cobb, *Sustaining the Common Good: A Christian Perspective on the Global Economy* (Cleveland, Ohio: Pilgrim Press, 1994).

37. Alice Waters, "A Letter to President Clinton and Vice President Gore," quoted in *The Cultivar,* Spring 1996, 7.

The Role of Independent Beef Producers in Rural Development

1. Will Lathrop, *Future of the Beef Industry* (Poteau, Okla.: Kerr Center for Sustainable Agriculture, 1997), available at http://kerrcenter.com.

2. Richard Behar, "Arkansas Pecking Order," *Time,* October 26, 1992, 52–54.

Foreword to *Farming with the Wild*

1. Cotton Mather, *Magnolia Christi Americana* (Hartford, Conn.: Siles Andres and Son, 1855).

2. Aldo Leopold, *A Sand County Almanac* (New York: Oxford University Press, 1949), 204.

3. Ibid., 221.

4. Richard C. Lewontin, *The Triple Helix: Gene, Organism, and Environment* (Cambridge, Mass.: Harvard University Press, 2000).

5. David Abram, *The Spell of the Sensuous: Perception and Language in a More-Than-Human World* (New York: Vintage Books, 1996).

On Being an "Objective" Farmer

1. Barry Lopez, "The Naturalist," *Orion,* Autumn 2001, 39–43.

2. Ibid.

3. Ibid.

4. Ibid.

5. Ibid.

6. Ibid.

7. National Research Council, *Frontiers in Agricultural Research: Food, Health, Environment, and Communities* (Washington, D.C.: National Academies Press, 2003), 169.

Being at Home

1. René Descartes, *Discourse on Method,* 1637, quoted in Morris Berman, *The Reenchantment of the World* (Ithaca, N.Y.: Cornell University Press, 1981), 25.

2. Lynn Margulis and Dorion Sagan, *Microcosmos: Four Billion Years of Microbial Evolution* (New York: Summit Books, 1986), 35.

3. Stephen H. Buhner, *The Lost Language of Plants: The Ecological Importance of Plant Medicines to Life on Earth* (White River Junction, Vt.: Chelsea Green Publishing, 2002), 6–7.

4. Larry L. Rasmussen, *Earth Community, Earth Ethics* (Maryknoll, N.Y.: Orbis Books, 1996), 90.

5. David Abram, "The Eclipse of the Sensuous," *Tikkun,* September/October 2003, 33–37, 65–69.

6. Margulis and Sagan, *Microcosmos.*

7. Richard C. Lewontin, *The Triple Helix: Gene, Organism, and Environment* (Cambridge, Mass.: Harvard University Press, 2000).

8. For a delightful and informative account of the role of microbes in our evolution, see Margulis and Sagan, *Microcosmos.*

9. Rasmussen, *Earth Community,* 90.

10. Brian Swimme, *The Hidden Heart of the Cosmos: Humanity and the New Story* (Maryknoll, N.Y.: Orbis Books, 1996), 111.

11. Michael Jackson, *At Home in the World* (Durham, N.C.: Duke University Press, 1995)

12. Aldo Leopold, *A Sand County Almanac* (New York: Oxford University Press, 1949), 204.

13. Swimme, *Hidden Heart,* 111.

14. Ibid., 100.

15. David Abram, *The Spell of the Sensuous: Perception and Language in a More-Than-Human World* (New York: Vintage Books, 1996), 268.

16. Warner Heisenberg, *Physics and Philosophy: The Revolution in Modern Science* (New York: Harper and Row, 1958).

17. Lance Gunderson, C. S. Holling, and Steve Light, *Barriers and Bridges to the Renewal of Ecosystems and Institutions* (New York: Columbia University Press, 1995).

18. Leopold, *Sand County,* 204 (emphasis added).

19. Mark Buchanan, *Nexus: Small Worlds and the Groundbreaking Science of Networks* (New York: W. W. Norton & Co., 2002), 141.

20. Buchanan, *Nexus,* 152.

21. Rasmussen, *Earth Community,* 97.

22. Berman, *Reenchantment,* 158.

23. L. Shannon Jung, *Food for Life: The Spirituality and Ethics of Eating* (Minneapolis: Fortress Press, 2004).

24. Amartya K. Sen, *On Ethics and Economics* (Oxford: Blackwell, 1987), 18.

25. Harvey Cox, "The Market as God: Living in the New Dispensation," *Atlantic Monthly,* March 1999, 18–23.

26. John R. Saul, "The Collapse of Globalism: And the Rebirth of Nationalism," *Harper's,* March 2004, 33–43.

27. Homer, *The Odyssey,* book 11, trans. Richmond A. Lattimore (New York: Harper and Row, 1967).

28. Brian Swimme and Thomas M. Berry, *The Universe Story: From the Primordial Flaring Forth to the Ecozoic Era—A Celebration of the Unfolding of the Cosmos* (San Francisco: Harper San Francisco, 1992).

29. Buhner, *Lost Language of Plants,* 6–7.

30. Ibid., 289.

The Pleasure of Good Eating

1. Martin Rogoff and Stephen Rawlins, "Food Security: A Technological Alternative," *Bioscience* 37 (1987): 805–7.

2. William D. Heffernan, personal communication.

3. John R. Saul, "The Collapse of Globalism: And the Rebirth of Nationalism," *Harper's,* March 2004, 33–43.

4. John Thackara, *In the Bubble: Designing in a Complex World* (Cambridge, Mass.: MIT Press, 2005).

Is Sustainability in Our Energy Future?

1. Martin K. Hubbert, "Energy from Fossil Fuels," *Science* 109 (1949): 103–9.

2. Red Cavaney, "Global Oil Production About to Peak? A Recurring Myth," *World Watch,* January/February 2006, 13–15.

3. Masae Shiyomi and Hiroshi Koizumi, eds., *Structure and Function in Agroecosystem Design and Management* (Boca Raton, Fla.: CRC Press, 2001).

4. Ibid.

5. Takao Furuno, *The Power of Duck: Integrated Rice and Duck Farming* (Sisters Creek, Australia: Tagari Publications, 2001).

6. Joel F. Salatin, *You Can Farm: The Entrepreneur's Guide to Start and Succeed in a Farm Enterprise* (Swoope, Va.: Polyface, 1998).

7. Jeff Kuntz, personal communication.

8. Francis Thicke, personal communication.

9. Dick Thompson, personal communication.

10. Dana Houghton, "The Enemy of My Enemy," *The Furrow,* January 2006, 7–8. Available at http://www.deere.com/en_US/ag/furrow/index.html.

A Journey toward Sustainability

1. Bryan G. Norton, *Sustainability: A Philosophy of Adaptive Ecosystem Management* (Chicago: University of Chicago Press, 2005).

2. Joseph Fiksel, "A Philosophy of Adaptive Ecosystem Management," *Sustainability: Science, Practice and Policy* 2 (2006): 14–21. http://www.resilience.osu.edu/CFR-site/pdf/0608-028.fiksel.pdf.

3. Aldo Leopold, *A Sand County Almanac* (New York: Oxford University Press, 1949).

4. Wendell Berry, *What Are People For? Essays* (San Francisco: North Point Press, 1990).

5. Takao Furuno, *The Power of Duck: Integrated Rice and Duck Farming* (Sisters Creek, Australia: Tagari Publications, 2001).

6. For a concise overview of these agriculturalists, see Philip Conford, *The Origins of the Organic Movement* (Edinburgh: Floris Books, 2001).

7. Sir Albert Howard, *The Soil and Health: A Study of Organic Agriculture* (Lexington: University Press of Kentucky, 2006), 193.

8. Sir Albert Howard, *An Agricultural Testament* (New York: Oxford University Press, 1943), 4.

9. Leopold, *Sand County,* 221.

10. Howard, *Soil and Health,* 66.

11. Ibid., 66–67.

12. Bill Hincher and Sonny Dominguez, *July, August, and Winter: A Cartoon Look at North Dakota* (Minot, N.D.: Pex Publishing, 1965).

13. C. S. Holling, "What Barriers? What Bridges?" in *Barriers and Bridges to the*

Renewal of Ecosystems and Institutions, ed. Lance Gunderson, C. S. Holling, and Stephen S. Light, 3–34 (New York: Columbia University Press, 1995).

14. Gary Larson, *There's a Hair in My Dirt! A Worm's Story* (New York: HarperCollins, 1998).

15. Rattan Lal, "There Is No Such Thing as a Free Biofuel from Crop Residues," *CSA News* 52 (2007): 12–13.

16. Berry, *What Are People For?*

17. John P. Reganold, Lloyd F. Elliott, and Yvonne L. Unger, "Long-Term Effects of Organic and Conventional Farming on Soil Erosion," *Nature* 330 (1987): 370–72.

18. John P. Reganold et al., "Sustainability of Three Apple Production Systems," *Nature* 410 (2001): 926–30.

19. John Thackara, *In the Bubble: Designing in a Complex World* (Cambridge, Mass.: MIT Press, 2005).

On Learning to Farm Ecologically on the Prairie

1. David B. Danborn, *Our Purpose Is to Serve* (Fargo, N.D.: North Dakota State University, Institute for Regional Studies, 1990), 113.

2. Herbert C. Hanson, "Ecology in Agriculture," *Ecology* 20 (1939): 111–17.

3. Ibid.

4. Ibid.

5. Ibid.

6. Ibid.

7. Ibid.

8. Quoted in Wendell Berry, *What Are People For? Essays* (San Francisco: North Point Press, 1990), 103.

9. Heinz R. Pagels, *The Cosmic Code: Quantum Physics as the Language of Nature* (New York: Bantam Books, 1982), 49.

10. A. C. Rola and P. L. Pingali, *Pesticides, Rice Productivity and Farmers' Health: An Economic Assessment* (Manila: IRRI Publications, 1993).

11. Ibid.

12. Ibid.

13. Hanson, "Ecology in Agriculture."

14. David Pimentel et al., "Environmental and Economic Costs of Pesticide Use," *BioScience* 42 (1992): 750.

15. Donella H. Meadows, Dennis L. Meadows, and Jorgen Randers, *Beyond the Limits: Confronting Global Collapse, Envisioning a Sustainable Future* (White River Junction, Vt.: Chelsea Green Publishing, 1992), 53–54.

16. David Ehrenfeld, "Ecosystem Health," *Orion,* Winter 1993, 13.

17. R. Edward Grumbine, *Ghost Bears: Exploring the Biodiversity Crisis* (Washington, D.C.: Island Press, 1992).

18. Stewart Smith, "Farming Activities and Family Farms: Getting the Concepts Right" (presentation at U.S. congressional Joint Economic Committee symposium, Agricultural Industrialization and Family Farms: The Role of Federal Policy, Washington, D.C., October 21, 1992).

19. Ibid.

20. Frederick H. Buttel, "Ideology and Agricultural Technology in the Late Twentieth Century: Biotechnology as Symbol and Substance," *Agriculture and Human Values* 10 (1993): 6–7.

21. Eric T. Freyfogle, *Justice and the Earth: Images for our Planetary Survival* (New York: Free Press, 1993), 6–7.

22. Ibid.

23. Carolyn E. Grygiel, personal communication.

24. Juan Izquierdo, "New Varieties for Sustainable Agriculture: Genetic Improvements Assisted by Biotechnology" (unpublished paper, part of study/action packet for World Food Day teleconference, 1993).

25. Meadows et al., *Beyond the Limits*, 53.

26. John Ikerd, "The Question of Good Science," *American Journal of Alternative Agriculture* 8 (1993): 91.

27. Jack Kloppenburg Jr. and Neva Hassanein, "As You Know . . . Farmers' Knowledge and Sustainable Agriculture," *As You Sow—Social Issues in Agriculture,* April 1993, 1.

28. Ibid., 3.

29. For a comprehensive treatment of this subject, see Herman E. Daly, John B. Cobb, and Clifford W. Cobb, *For the Common Good: Redirecting the Economy toward Community, the Environment, and a Sustainable Future* (Boston: Beacon Press, 1989).

30. Patrick Madden, "Beyond Conventional Economics—An Examination of the Values Implicit in the Neoclassical Economic Paradigm as Applied to the Evaluation of Agricultural Research," in *New Directions for Agriculture and Agriculture Research: Neglected Dimensions and Emerging Alternatives,* ed. Kenneth A. Dahlberg (Totowa, N.J.: Rowman & Allanheld, 1986), 254.

31. Willard W. Cochrane, *The Development of American Agriculture: A Historical Analysis* (Minneapolis: University of Minnesota Press, 1979), 387–95.

32. Paul Gruchow, "Despite Payments, Rural Areas Get Short End of Stick," *Star Tribune,* November 28, 1992.

33. David and Marcia Pimentel, *Food, Energy, and Society* (New York: John Wiley, 1979).

34. Paul Faeth, *Paying the Farm Bill: U.S. Agricultural Policy and the Transition to Sustainable Agriculture* (Washington, D.C.: World Resources Institute, 1991).

35. John Ikerd, "Impacts of Policy on the Economics of Sustainable Agriculture" (unpublished paper, December 2, 1992), 10.

36. *Fall River Review,* Ashton, Idaho, August 15, 1991.

37. William D. Heffernan and Douglas H. Constance, "Concentration of Agricultural Markets" (unpublished paper, 1990). Heffernan and Constance's analysis of concentration ratios in various commodity groups shows that in most agricultural markets, the concentration ratio ranged from 40 to 60 percent ownership by four or fewer corporations by the end of 1990. Further concentration has taken place since then. The paper is available from the author.

38. Ken Taylor, personal communication.

Can Organic Agriculture Feed the World?
And Is That the Right Question?

1. T. R. Malthus, *An Essay on the Principle of Population: Text, Sources and Background, Criticism,* ed. Philip Appleman (New York: W. W. Norton & Co., 1976).

2. G. Easterbrook, "Forgotten Benefactor of Humanity," *Atlantic Monthly,* January 1997, 75–82.

3. Niles Eldredge, *Dominion: Can Nature and Culture Co-Exist?* (New York: Henry Holt & Co., 1995).

4. Ibid., 162.

5. Ibid., 163.

6. Derrick Jensen, "Hush of the Hives," *New York Times Magazine,* October 13, 1996.

7. Lester R. Brown, *Tough Choices: Facing the Challenge of Food Scarcity* (New York: W. W. Norton & Co., 1996).

8. Stephen H. Schneider, *The Genesis Strategy: Climate and Global Survival* (New York: Plenum Press, 1976).

9. Wendell Berry, "Prayers and Sayings of the Mad Farmer," in *Collected Poems, 1957–1982* (San Francisco: North Point Press, 1984), 131.

10. Christopher Flavin, "Climate Change and Storm Damage: The Insurance Costs Keep Rising," *World Watch,* January–February 1997, 10–11.

11. Berry, *Collected Poems,* 131.

12. Tracy I. Hewitt and Katie R. Smith, *Intensive Agriculture and Environmental Quality: Examining the Newest Agricultural Myth* (Greenbelt, Md.: Henry A. Wallace Institute for Alternative Agriculture, 1995).

13. A. A. Spindler and J. D. Schultz, "Comparison of Dietary Variety and Ethnic Food Consumption among Chinese, Chinese-American and White American Women," *Agriculture and Human Values* 13 (1996): 65.

14. Easterbrook, "Forgotten Benefactor."

15. *All Things Considered,* National Public Radio, July 31 and August 7, 1994.

16. Ibid.

17. Vandana Shiva, *The Violence of the Green Revolution: Third World Agriculture, Ecology, and Politics* (London: Zed Books Ltd., 1991).

18. Jeremy Rifkin, *Beyond Beef: The Rise and Fall of the Cattle Culture* (New York: Dutton, 1992).

19. D. A. Wedin and D. Tilman, "Influence of Nitrogen Loading and Species Composition on Carbon Balance of Grasslands," *Science* 274 (1996): 1721.

20. P. Bagla and J. Kaiser, "India's Spreading Health Crisis Draws Global Arsenic Experts," *Science* 274 (1996): 174–75.

21. Yvonne Baskin, "Curbing Undesirable Invaders," *BioScience* 46 (1996): 732–36.

22. Judy Soule, Danielle Carré, and Wes Jackson, "Ecological Impact of Modern Agriculture," in *Agroecology,* ed. C. Ronald Carroll, John H. Vandermeer, and Peter Rosset, 165–88 (New York: McGraw-Hill, 1990).

23. National Research Council, *Lost Crops of Africa*, vol. 1, *Grains* (Washington, D.C.: National Academies Press, 1996).

24. Baskin, "Curbing Undesirable Invaders."

25. Jane Rissler and Margaret G. Mellon, *The Ecological Risks of Engineered Crops* (Cambridge, Mass.: MIT Press, 1996).

26. A. A. Snow and P. M. Palma, "Commercialization of Transgenic Plants: Potential Ecological Risks," *BioScience* 47 (1997): 86–96.

27. Advisory Panel on Food Security, Agriculture, Forestry, and Environment to the World Commission on Environment and Development, *Food 2000: Global Policies for Sustainable Agriculture* (London: Zed Books, 1987).

28. Daniel Quinn, *The Story of B* (New York: Bantam Books, 1996).

29. S. A. Clancy, *Farming Practices for a Sustainable Agriculture in North Dakota* (Carrington, N.D.: North Dakota State University, Carrington Research Extension Office, 1993).

30. Helena Norberg-Hodge, *Ancient Futures: Learning from Ladakh* (San Francisco: Sierra Club Books, 1991).

31. Frances Moore Lappé and Joseph Collins, *World Hunger: Twelve Myths* (New York: Grove Press, 1986).

32. Cornelia Butler Flora, *The Sustainable Agriculturist and the New Economy* (St. Paul, Minn.: Minnesota Department of Agriculture, Energy, and Sustainable Agriculture Program, 1996).

33. Berry, *Collected Poems*, 131.

Biotechnology on the Ground

1. Willard W. Cochrane, *Farm Prices: Myth and Reality* (Minneapolis: University of Minnesota Press, 1958).

2. Amartya K. Sen, *Poverty and Famines: An Essay on Entitlement and Deprivation* (Oxford: Clarendon Press, 1981).

3. Amartya K. Sen, "Food, Economics and Entitlements," *WIDER Working Papers*, February 1986.

4. W. J. Lewis et al., "A Total System Approach to Sustainable Pest Management," *Proceedings of the National Academy of Sciences of the United States of America* 94 (1997): 12243–48.

5. Peter M. Senge, *The Fifth Discipline: The Art and Practice of the Learning Organization* (New York: Doubleday & Co., 1990).

6. Ibid., 61.

7. Robert Van den Bosch, *The Pesticide Conspiracy* (Garden City, N.Y.: Doubleday & Co., 1978).

8. Lewis et al., "Total System Approach."

9. F. Huang et al., "Inheritance of Resistance to *Bacillus thuringiensis* Toxin (Dipel ES) in the European Corn Borer," *Science* 284 (1999): 966–67.

10. Mike Holmberg, "Business," *Successful Farming* 97 (1999): 33.

11. Stewart Smith, "Farming Activities and Family Farms: Getting the Concepts Right" (presentation at U.S. congressional Joint Economic Committee symposium, Ag-

ricultural Industrialization and Family Farms: The Role of Federal Policy, Washington, D.C., October 21, 1992).

12. Paul Thompson, *The Spirit of the Soil: Agriculture and Environmental Ethics* (London: Routledge Publishing Co., 1995).

13. Smith, "Farming Activities."

14. "Farmer Sells Unmodified Crops in Europe," *Jamestown (N.D.) Sun,* May 25, 1999.

Questioning Biotechnology's Claims and Imagining Alternatives

1. Aldo Leopold, *A Sand County Almanac* (New York: Oxford University Press, 1949).

2. Richard C. Lewontin, *Biology as Ideology: The Doctrine of DNA* (New York: Harper Perennial, 1993), 13.

3. Ibid., 87–91.

4. Ibid., 26.

5. Ibid., 27.

6. Amartya K. Sen, *Poverty and Famines: An Essay on Entitlement and Deprivation* (Oxford: Clarendon Press, 1981).

7. Amartya K. Sen, *Resources, Values and Development* (Cambridge, Mass.: Harvard University Press, 1984).

8. Klaus M. Leisinger, "The 'Political Economy' of Agricultural Biotechnology for the Developing World" (unpublished paper, 2000). Available from the author.

9. Yvonne Baskin, *The Work of Nature* (Washington, D.C.: Island Press, 1997).

10. Ibid., 41.

11. Ibid., 42.

12. Robert F. Service, "Microbiologists Explore Life's Rich, Hidden Kingdoms," *Science* 275 (1997): 1740.

13. Evelyn Fox Keller, *The Century of the Gene* (Cambridge, Mass.: Harvard University Press, 2000).

14. Richard C. Lewontin, quoted in Michael Pollan, "Playing God in the Garden," *New York Times Magazine,* October 25, 1998, 49.

15. Mario Giampietro, "Sustainability and Technological Development in Agriculture: A Critical Appraisal of Genetic Engineering," *BioScience* 44 (1994): 677–90.

16. Frederick Kirschenmann and Carolyn Raffensperger, "Genetic Engineering and Sustainability: Rethinking the Environmental and Agricultural Issues" (unpublished paper, 1995), 6. Available from the author.

17. Bill Joy, "Why the Future Doesn't Need Us," *Wired,* April 2000, 240–42.

18. Ibid., 242.

19. Mary-Howell Martens, "Strategies to Reduce GMO Contamination on Organic Farms," *Acres USA,* March 2001. Available at http://www.acresusa.com/toolbox/articles .htm.

20. David Vetter, personal communication, 2000.

21. Leisinger, "'Political Economy,'" 2.

22. Willis L. Peterson, "Are Large Farms More Efficient?" (staff paper P97–2, Department of Applied Economics, University of Minnesota, Minneapolis, 1997).

23. Marty Strange, *Family Farming: A New Economic Vision* (Lincoln, Neb.: University of Nebraska Press, 1988).

24. Leisinger, "'Political Economy,'" 2–3.

25. National Research Council, *Soil and Water Quality: An Agenda for Agriculture* (Washington, D.C.: National Academies Press, 1993).

26. David C. Korten, *When Corporations Rule the World* (West Hartford, Conn.: Kumarian Press, 1995), 48.

27. Leisinger, "'Political Economy,'" 11.

28. Ibid.

29. Ibid., 12.

30. Ibid., 17.

31. Heinz R. Pagels, *The Cosmic Code: Quantum Physics as the Language of Nature* (New York: Bantam Books, 1982).

32. John Pesek, "Research Findings on Alternative Methods: Based on the NRC Report on Alternative Agriculture" (paper presented at Northwest Farm Managers Association meeting, February 26, 1990). Available from the author.

33. Barb Baylor Anderson, "21st Century Model T: Council Jumps into Biotech Revolution Driver's Seat," *Agri-Marketing,* July/August 2000, 74–76.

34. Leisinger, "'Political Economy.'"

35. Stephen H. Schneider, *The Genesis Strategy: Climate and Global Survival* (New York: Plenum Press, 1976), 14.

36. Leopold, *Sand County*, 220.

37. Leisinger, "'Political Economy,'" 15.

38. Gretchen C. Daily et al., "The Value of Nature and the Nature of Value," *Science* 289 (2000): 395–96.

39. Michael Gray, "Proscriptive Use of Transgenic Hybrids for Corn Rootworms: An Ominous Cloud on the Horizon?" in *Proceedings of the Illinois Crop Protection Technology Conference* (Urbana: University of Illinois, Cooperative Extension Service, 2000).

40. Dan Ferber, "New Corn Plant Draws Fire From GM Food Opponents," *Science* 287 (2000): 1390–91.

41. Jim Ritchie, "Corn Hybrids with Non-GMO Resistance . . . Zap Rootworms the Natural Way," *Soybean Digest* 60 (2000): 14.

42. "Variety Spices up Chinese Rice Yields," *Science* 289 (2000): 1122–23.

43. Mae-Wan Ho, "One Bird—Ten Thousand Treasures," *The Ecologist* 29 (1999): 339.

44. Brian Halweil, "Biotech, African Corn, and the Vampire Weed," *World Watch,* September/October 2001, 26–31.

45. Land Institute, *Land Report No. 67* (Salina, Kan.: Land Institute, 2000).

46. J. Patrick Madden and Scott G. Chaplowe, eds., *For All Generations: Making World Agriculture More Sustainable* (Glendale, Calif.: OM Publishing, 1996).

47. Richard Manning, *Food's Frontier: The Next Green Revolution* (New York: North Point Press, 2000).

48. Ibid., 218.

49. Ellen Goodman, "Cloning of Endangered Species Isn't a Parlor Trick," *Des Moines Register,* October 18, 2000.

50. John Kaufmann (comment made during a panel presentation at the Wisconsin Academy of Sciences conference, Madison, Wis., November 3–4, 2000).

51. Stuart Newman, "Epigenetics vs. Genetic Determinism," in *Made Not Born: The Troubling World of Biotechnology,* ed. Casey Walker (San Francisco: Sierra Club, 2000), 27.

52. Carol Kaesuk Yoon, "Scientists Find a Plant That Dupes Birds into Spreading Its Seeds," *New York Times,* July 12, 1994.

53. Joy, "Why the Future Doesn't Need Us," 243.

Why American Agriculture Is Not Sustainable

1. Aldo Leopold, *A Sand County Almanac* (New York: Oxford University Press, 1949).

2. Paul Hawken, *The Ecology of Commerce: A Declaration of Sustainability* (New York: Harper Business, 1993).

3. Philip Conford, *The Origins of the Organic Movement* (Edinburgh: Floris Books, 2001).

4. Hawken, *Ecology of Commerce.*

5. World Commission on Environment and Development, *Our Common Future* (Oxford: Oxford University Press, 1987), 8.

6. National Research Council, *Soil and Water Quality: An Agenda for Agriculture* (Washington, D.C.: National Academies Press, 1993).

7. Ibid.

8. Paul Maedor et al., "Soil Fertility and Biodiversity in Organic Farming," *Science* 296 (2002): 1694–97.

9. Tom Horton and Heather Dewar, "Cycle of Growth and Devastation," *Baltimore Sun,* September 25, 2000.

10. National Research Council, *Soil and Water Quality,* 44–45.

11. Masae Shiyomi and Hiroshi Koizumi, eds., *Structure and Function in Agroecosystem Design and Management* (Boca Raton, Fla.: CRC Press, 2001).

12. Alison G. Power, "Linking Ecological Sustainability and World Food Needs," *Environment, Development and Sustainability* 1 (1999): 185–96.

13. David Tilman and J. A. Downing, "Biodiversity and Stability in Grasslands," *Nature* 367 (1994): 363–64.

14. David Tilman et al., "Forecasting Agriculturally Driven Global Environmental Change," *Science* 292 (2001): 281–84.

15. David Tilman et al., "Diversity and Productivity in a Long-Term Grassland Experiment," *Science* 294 (2001): 843–45.

16. Takao Furuno, *The Power of Duck: Integrated Rice and Duck Farming* (Sisters Creek, Australia: Tagari Publications, 2001).

17. Joel F. Salatin, *Salad Bar Beef* (Swoope, Va.: Polyface, 1995).

18. Jules Pretty and Rachel Hine's "Portraits of Sustainable Agriculture Projects and Initiatives" are good examples, available at http://www.essex.ac.uk/ces/research/susag/SAFEW47casessusag.shtm.

19. Shiyomi and Koizumi, *Structure and Function,* 2.

20. Mathis Wackernagel et al., "Tracking the Ecological Overshoot of the Human Economy," *Proceedings of the National Academy of Sciences of the United States of America* 99 (2002): 9266–71.

21. Suzanne W. Simard et al., "Net Transfer of Carbon between Ectomycorrhizal Tree Species in the Field," *Nature* 388 (1997): 579–82.

22. T. Helgasson et al., "Ploughing Up the Wood-Wide Web?" *Nature* 394 (1998): 431.

23. Amartya K. Sen, *On Ethics and Economics* (Oxford: Blackwell, 1987).

24. Herbert C. Hanson, "Ecology in Agriculture," *Ecology* 20 (1939): 111–17.

25. Leopold, *Sand County.*

26. Ibid.

27. Ibid.

28. Hawken, *Ecology of Commerce*, 210.

29. Richard C. Lewontin, *The Triple Helix: Gene, Organism, and Environment* (Cambridge, Mass.: Harvard University Press, 2000).

30. Ibid., 68.

31. Leopold, *Sand County*, 214–15.

32. Hawken, *Ecology of Commerce*, 211.

33. Leopold, *Sand County*, 221.

34. Ibid., 209.

What Constitutes Sound Science?

1. Alfred North Whitehead, *Science and the Modern World* (New York: MacMillan Co., 1925), 163.

2. Michael Polanyi, *Science, Faith and Society* (Chicago: University of Chicago Press, 1946), 24.

3. Marion Nestle, *Food Politics: How the Food Industry Influences Nutrition and Health* (Berkeley: University of California Press, 2002).

4. Barry Commoner, "Unraveling the DNA Myth: The Spurious Foundation of Genetic Engineering," *Harper's*, February 2002, 39–47.

5. Evelyn Fox Keller, *The Century of the Gene* (Cambridge, Mass.: Harvard University Press, 2000), 69.

6. Ibid., 139.

7. Ibid., 7.

8. Norman E. Borlaug, "Ending World Hunger: The Promise of Biotechnology and the Threat of Antiscience Zealotry," *Transactions of the Wisconsin Academy of Sciences, Arts and Letters* 89 (2001): 25–34.

9. This trend was criticized at least as far back as 1971. See Jerome R. Ravetz, *Scientific Knowledge and Its Social Problems* (New York: Oxford University Press, 1971).

10. Vannevar Bush, *Science, the Endless Frontier: A Report to the President* (Washington, D.C.: United States Government Printing Office, 1945).

11. Carolyn Raffensperger, "The Precautionary Principle as Guide to a Public Interest Research Agenda" (unpublished paper, 2002). Available from the author.

12. Lance Gunderson, C. S. Holling, and Steve Light, eds., *Barriers and Bridges to the Renewal of Ecosystems and Institutions* (New York: Columbia University Press, 1995).

13. Jennifer L. Wilkins et al., "Moving from Debate to Dialogue about Genetically Engineered Foods and Crops: Insights from a Land Grant University," *Journal of Sustainable Agriculture* 18 (2001): 167–201.

14. Ibid.

15. Jane Lubchenco, "Entering the Century of the Environment: A New Social Contract for Science," *Science* 279 (1998): 491–97.

16. Ibid.

17. Ibid.

18. Ibid.

19. Quoted in Carolyn Merchant, *The Death of Nature: Women, Ecology, and the Scientific Revolution* (San Francisco: Harper and Row, 1983), 249.

20. Ibid., 250.

21. Richard Strohman, "Maneuvering in the Complex Path from Genotype to Phenotype," *Science* 296 (2002): 701–3.

22. David Abram, *The Spell of the Sensuous: Perception and Language in a More-Than-Human World* (New York: Vintage Books, 1996), 264.

23. Michael Polanyi, *Personal Knowledge: Toward a Post-critical Philosophy* (Chicago: University of Chicago Press, 1958).

24. Michael Polanyi, *The Tacit Dimension* (Garden City, N.Y.: Doubleday & Co., 1967).

25. Polanyi, *Science, Faith and Society.*

26. Michael Polanyi, *Knowing and Being: Essays by Michael Polanyi,* ed. Marjorie Grene (Chicago: University of Chicago Press, 1969).

27. Harold L. Davis, "Objectivity in Science—A Dangerous Illusion?" *Scientific Research* 4 (1969): 25.

28. Polanyi, *Tacit Dimension,* 9.

29. Richard C. Lewontin, *The Triple Helix: Gene, Organism, and Environment* (Cambridge, Mass.: Harvard University Press, 2000).

30. Stephen L. Talbott, "Ecological Conversations: Wildness, Anthropocentrism, and Deep Ecology," *Netfuture,* January 10, 2002. Available at http://www.netfuture.org.

31. Aldo Leopold, *A Sand County Almanac* (New York: Oxford University Press, 1949).

32. Abram, *Spell of the Sensuous,* 268.

And Then What? Attending to the Context of Our Innovations

1. Harold J. Morowitz, *The Emergence of Everything: How the World Became Complex* (New York: Oxford University Press, 2002), 20, 14.

2. G. David Hurd, personal communication.

3. Jack Hokikian, *The Science of Disorder: Understanding the Complexity, Uncertainty, and Pollution in Our World* (Los Angeles: Los Feliz Publishing, 2002).

4. Ibid., 227.

5. Morowitz, *Emergence of Everything.*

6. Bill Joy, "Why the Future Doesn't Need Us," *Wired,* April 2000, 240–42.

7. Nancy Willard, *The Sorcerer's Apprentice* (New York: Blue Sky Press, 1993).

8. Ibid.

9. Barry Commoner, "Summary of the Conference: On the Meaning of Ecological Failures in International Development," in *The Careless Technology: Ecology and International Development,* ed. M. Taghi Farvar and John P. Milton, xxi–xxix (Garden City, N.Y.: Natural History Press, 1972).

10. Lester R. Brown, *Eco-Economy: Building an Economy for the Earth* (New York: W. W. Norton & Co., 2001).

11. Cynthia Pollock, quoted in Carolyn Raffensperger, "Waste Disposal and Decommissioning," in *Governing the Atom: The Politics of Risk,* ed. John Byrne and Steven M. Hoffman (New Brunswick, N.J.: Transaction Publishers, 1996), 177.

12. Commoner, "Summary of the Conference," xxii.

13. Ibid.

14. Ibid., xxv.

15. Richard Levins and Cynthia Lopez, "Toward an Ecosocial View of Health," *International Journal of Health Services* 29 (1999): 261–93.

16. Niles Eldredge, *Dominion: Can Nature and Culture Co-Exist?* (New York: Henry Holt & Co., 1995).

17. W. J. Lewis et al., "A Total System Approach to Sustainable Pest Management," *Proceedings of the National Academy of Sciences of the United States of America* 94 (1997): 12243–48.

18. Ibid.

19. Martyn Poliakoff et al., "Green Chemistry: Science and Politics of Change," *Science* 297 (2002): 807–10.

20. Janine M. Benyus, *Biomimicry: Innovation Inspired by Nature* (New York: William Morrow & Co., 1997).

21. Morowitz, *Emergence of Everything*, 14.

22. Wendell Berry, *What Are People For? Essays* (San Francisco: North Point Press, 1990), 208–9.

23. Poliakoff, "Green Chemistry."

24. Frederick Kirschenmann, "Can We Say 'Yes' to Agriculture Using the Precautionary Principle: A Farmer's Perspective," in *Protecting Public Health and the Environment: Implementing the Precautionary Principle,* ed. Carolyn Raffensperger and Joel Tickner, 279–88 (Washington, D.C.: Island Press, 1999).

Food as Relationship

1. Michael Pollan, "Unhappy Meals," *New York Times Magazine,* January 28, 2007. Available at www.michaelpollan.com/article.php?id=87.

2. Sir Albert Howard, *An Agricultural Testament* (New York: Oxford University Press; 1940), 28.

3. Fred Magdoff and Harold van Es, *Building Soils for Better Crops* (Washington, D.C.: Sustainable Agriculture Network, 2000), 10.

4. Sir Albert Howard, *The Soil and Health: A Study of Organic Agriculture* (Lexington: University Press of Kentucky, 2006), 59, 63.

5. Ibid., 260–61.

6. Ibid. (all emphases are Howard's).

7. Ibid., 189.

8. The percentage spent on food is provided by the USDA's Economic Research Service, available at http://www.cnpp.usda.gov/Publications/FoodPlans/MiscPubs/AmericanFood-01-30-08.pdf. The percentage spent on health care was provided by Gary Swartz, MD, Mayo Clinic, Rochester, Minnesota, personal communication. The national average

health care insurance policy premium for a family of four is now between $10,000 and $12,000 per year; when Medicare payroll taxes (1.45 percent if employed, 2.9 percent if self-employed) and the parts of federal and state taxes that go to support health spending are added, a person with an annual income of $60,000 pays 18 percent.

9. Herman E. Daly, *Ecological Economics and the Ecology of Economics: Essays in Criticism* (Northampton, Mass.: Edward Elgar, 1999).

10. Richard Manning, "The Oil We Eat: Following the Food Chain Back to Iraq," *Harper's,* February 2004, 37–45.

11. Ernest L. Schusky, *Culture and Agriculture: An Ecological Introduction to Traditional and Modern Farming Systems* (New York: Bergin & Garvey Publishers, 1989).

12. Ibid., xii–xiii.

13. Richard Heinberg, *Power Down: Options and Actions for a Post-Carbon World* (Gabriola Island, B.C., Canada: New Society Publishers, 2004).

14. Paul Roberts, *The End of Oil: On the Edge of a Perilous New World* (Boston: Houghton Mifflin Co., 2004).

15. National Academy of Sciences, Panel on Climate Variations, *Understanding Climate Change* (Washington, D.C.: National Academy of Sciences, 1975).

16. Cynthia Rosenzweig and Daniel Hillel, "Potential Impacts of Climate Change on Agriculture and Food Supply," *Consequences,* Summer 1995. Available at http://www.gcrio.org/CONSEQUENCES/summer95/agriculture.html.

17. Cynthia Rosenzweig et al., "Climate Change and Extreme Weather Events: Implications for Food Production, Plant Diseases and Pests," *Global Change and Human Health* 2 (2001): 90–104.

18. Lester R. Brown, *Plan B 2.0: Rescuing a Planet under Stress and a Civilization in Trouble* (New York: W. W. Norton & Co., 2006), 42–44.

19. BBC News, "World Water Crisis," available at http://news.bbc.co.uk/hi/english/static/in_depth/world/2000/world_water_crisis/default.stm.

20. Judith D. Soule and Jon K. Piper, *Farming in Nature's Image: An Ecological Approach to Agriculture* (Washington, D.C.: Island Press, 1992).

21. P. E. V. Charman and B. W. Murphy, *Soils: Their Properties and Management* (South Melbourne, Australia: Oxford University Press, 2000), 14–15.

22. W. C. Lowdermilk, "Conquest of the Land through 7,000 Years," *Agricultural Information Bulletin of the U.S. Soil Conservation Service* 99 (1953): 1–24. Available at http://www.nrcs.usda.gov/technical/ecs/agecol/conquest.html.

23. Natural Resources Conservation Service, "Soil Erosion," *Conservation Resource Brief* 602 (2006): 1–9. Available at www.nrcs.usda.gov/feature/outlook/Soil%20Erosion.pdf.

24. Howard, *Soil and Health*, 59.

25. Michael P. Russelle, Martin H. Entz, and Alan J. Franzluebbers, "Reconsidering Integrated Crop-Livestock Systems in North America," *Agronomy Journal* 99 (2007): 325–34.

26. John R. Teasdale, Charles B. Coffman, and Ruth W. Mangum, "Potential Long-term Benefits of No-tillage and Organic Cropping Systems for Grain Production and Soil Improvement," *Agronomy Journal* 99 (2007): 1297–1305.

27. William Bryant Logan, *Dirt: The Ecstatic Skin of the Earth* (New York: Riverhead Books, 1995), 63. Logan reflects what Hans Jenny has been saying about soil his "whole life."

28. Hans Jenny, *Factors of Soil Formation: A System of Quantitative Pedology* (New York: McGraw-Hill Book Company, 1941), 8, 198.

29. Paul Maedor et al., "Soil Fertility and Biodiversity in Organic Farming," *Science* 296 (2002): 1694–97.

30. W. J. Lewis et al., "A Total System Approach to Sustainable Pest Management," *Proceedings of the National Academy of Sciences of the United States of America* 94 (1997): 12243–48.

31. John P. Reganold, Lloyd F. Elliott, and Yvonne L. Unger, "Long-Term Effects of Organic and Conventional Farming on Soil Erosion," *Nature* 330 (1987): 370–72.

32. Frederick L. Kirschenmann, "Potential for a New Generation of Biodiversity in Agroecosystems of the Future," *Agronomy Journal* 99 (2007): 373–76.

33. Russelle et al., "Reconsidering Integrated Crop-Livestock Systems."

34. Organic Valley Family of Farms home page, available at http://www.organicvalley.coop.

35. Wendell Berry, James P. Herman, and Christopher B. Michael, with reply by Freeman Dyson, "'Our Biotech Future': An Exchange," *New York Review of Books,* September 27, 2007.

36. Bill McKibben, *Deep Economy: The Wealth of Communities and the Durable Future* (New York: Henry Holt and Co., 2007).

37. Richard Heinberg, "Fifty Million Farmers" (lecture, twenty-sixth Annual E. F. Schumacher Lectures, Stockbridge, Mass., 2006). Available at http://www.smallisbeautiful.org/publications/heinberg_06.html.

38. This information is available from Chuck Benbrook at Benbrook Consulting Enterprise (e-mail: cbenbrook@organic-center.org).

39. Erin M. Tegtmeier and Michael D. Duffy, "External Costs of Agricultural Production in the United States," *International Journal of Agricultural Sustainability* 2 (2004): 1–20.

40. J. N. Pretty et al., "An Assessment of the Total External Costs of UK Agriculture," *Agricultural Systems* 65 (2000): 113–36.

41. Ken Meter at Crossroads Research Center. Available at http://www.crcworks.org/rural.html.

42. Jack Kloppenburg Jr., John Hendrickson, and G. W. Stevenson, "Coming into the Foodshed," *Agriculture and Human Values* 13 (1996): 33–42.

43. Heinberg, "Fifty Million Farmers," 20.

Redefining Sustainability

1. C. S. Holling, "Resilience and Stability of Ecological Systems," *Annual Review of Ecology and Systematics* 4 (1973): 1–23.

2. Brian Walker and David Salt, *Resilience Thinking* (Washington, D.C.: Island Press, 2006), xi, x.

3. Associated Press, "Floods Strip Midwest of Tons of Valuable Topsoil," MSNBC, July 27, 2008, http://www.msnbc.msn.com/id/25874549.

4. Aldo Leopold, *A Sand County Almanac* (New York: Oxford University Press, 1949), 210.

5. Ibid., 221.

What's an Education For?

1. E. F. Schumacher, *Small Is Beautiful: Economics as if People Mattered* (New York: Harper and Row, 1973).

2. Stephen H. Schneider, *The Genesis Strategy: Climate and Global Survival* (New York: Plenum Press, 1976).

3. Studs Terkel, *Working: People Talk about What They Do All Day and How They Feel about What They Do* (New York, Pantheon Books, 1974).

4. Jack N. Arbolino, personal communication.

Resolving Conflicts in American Land-Use Values

1. Sidney E. Mead, *The Lively Experiment: The Shaping of Christianity in America* (New York: Harper and Row, 1963).

2. For a compelling study on this subject, see William Cronon, *Changes in the Land: Indians, Colonists, and the Ecology of New England* (New York: Hill and Wang, 1983).

3. Wendell Berry, *The Unsettling of America: Culture & Agriculture* (San Francisco: Sierra Club Books, 1977), 47.

4. John Seymour and Herbert Girardet, *Far From Paradise: The Story of Man's Impact on the Environment* (London: British Broadcasting Corporation, 1986).

What About the Next Twenty Years? Or "It's Turtles All the Way Down"

1. Stephen W. Hawking, *A Brief History of Time: From the Big Bang to Black Holes* (Toronto: Bantam Books, 1988), 1.

2. Heinz R. Pagels, *The Cosmic Code: Quantum Physics as the Language of Nature* (New York: Bantam Books, 1982), xiii.

3. Ibid., 48.

4. Ibid., 46.

5. Paul M. Kennedy, *Preparing for the Twenty-first Century* (New York: Random House, 1993), 74–80.

6. Lois Phillips Hudson, *The Bones of Plenty* (St. Paul: Minnesota Historical Society Press, 1984), viii.

7. Brian Swimme and Thomas M. Berry, *The Universe Story: From the Primordial Flaring Forth to the Ecozoic Era—A Celebration of the Unfolding of the Cosmos* (San Francisco: Harper San Francisco, 1992), 3.

8. Wendell Berry, "Decolonizing Rural America," *Audubon,* March–April 1993, 100–105.

9. Ibid., 100.

10. Center for Rural Affairs, *Annual Report 1992–1993* (Lyons, Neb.: Center for Rural Affairs, 1993).

11. Kennedy, *Preparing for the Twenty-first Century,* 94.

12. William Greider, *Who Will Tell the People: The Betrayal of American Democracy* (New York: Simon and Schuster, 1992), 407–8.

13. Swimme and Berry, *The Universe Story*, 1.

14. Ibid., 243–44.

Rediscovering American Agriculture

1. William Cronon, *Changes in the Land: Indians, Colonists, and the Ecology of New England* (New York: Hill and Wang, 1983), 127–28.

2. Ibid., 128, 126.

3. Frederick Turner, *Beyond Geography: The Western Spirit against the Wilderness* (New Brunswick, N.J.: Rutgers University Press, 1990), 256.

4. Cronon, *Changes in the Land*, 126.

5. Presentation given in Bismarck, N.D., January 1991.

6. Paul Faeth, *Paying the Farm Bill: U.S. Agricultural Policy and the Transition to Sustainable Agriculture* (Washington, D.C.: World Resources Institute, 1991), 32–33.

7. David and Marcia Pimentel, *Food, Energy, and Society* (New York: John Wiley, 1979), 164–65.

8. Alvin Toffler, *Powershift: Knowledge, Wealth, and Violence at the Edge of the 21st Century* (New York: Bantam, 1990).

9. Wendell Berry, *The Unsettling of America: Culture & Agriculture* (San Francisco: Sierra Club Books, 1977), 147.

10. Lewis Mumford, *The Golden Day: A Study in American Experience and Culture* (New York: Boni and Liveright, 1926), 30–31.

11. Ibid., 203.

Spirituality and Cooperatives

1. Lauren Artress, *Walking a Sacred Path: Rediscovering the Labyrinth as a Spiritual Tool* (New York: Riverhead Books, 1995).

2. Thomas Moore, *Care of the Soul: A Guide for Cultivating Depth and Sacredness in Everyday Life* (New York: HarperCollins, 1992), 232.

3. John B. Cobb, *Sustaining the Common Good: A Christian Perspective on the Global Economy* (Cleveland, Ohio: Pilgrim Press, 1994), 33.

4. Curtis W. Stofferahn, *The North Dakota Centennial Rural Life Poll* (Grand Forks, N.D.: Social Science Research Institute, University of North Dakota, 1991).

5. Cobb, *Sustaining the Common Good*, 35.

6. Alvin Toffler, *Powershift: Knowledge, Wealth, and Violence at the Edge of the 21st Century* (New York: Bantam, 1990).

7. Tova Green, Peter Woodward, and Fran Peavey, *Insight and Action: How to Discover and Support a Life of Integrity and Commitment to Change* (Philadelphia: New Society Publishers, 1994).

8. William Greider, *Who Will Tell the People: The Betrayal of American Democracy* (New York: Simon & Schuster, 1992), 406–8.

In Search of Objectivity, or How to
Create a Credible Certification Program

1. Werner Heisenberg, *Physics and Philosophy: The Revolution in Modern Science* (New York: Harper and Row, 1958), 81.

On Becoming Lovers of the Soil

1. Hans Jenny, "My Friend, the Soil," interview with Kevin Stuart, *Whole Earth*, Spring 1999. Available at http://findarticles.com/p/articles/mi_m0GER/is_1999_Spring/ai_54321347.

2. Sigmar Groeneveld, Lee Hoinacki, and Ivan Illich, "The Earthy Virtue of Place," *New Perspectives Quarterly*, Winter 1991.

3. Ibid.

4. Earl Butz, "Our Greatest Risk," *The World and I*, December 1992.

5. Clarissa Pinkola Estes, *How to Love a Woman* (Boulder, Colo.: Sounds True Recordings, 1993).

6. Wendell Berry, *What Are People For? Essays* (San Francisco: North Point Press, 1990), 143–52.

7. Wesley Granberg-Michaelson, ed., *Tending the Garden: Essays on the Gospel and the Earth* (Grand Rapids, Mich.: Eerdmans, 1987).

Challenges Facing Philosophy as We Enter the Twenty-first Century

1. Wendell Berry, *Sex, Economy, Freedom & Community* (New York: Pantheon Books, 1993), 125.

2. Sidney E. Mead, *The Lively Experiment: The Shaping of Christianity in America* (New York: Harper and Row, 1963), 151.

3. Yvonne Baskin, *The Work of Nature* (Washington, D.C.: Island Press, 1997).

4. William Rees and M. Wackernagel, "Ecological Footprints and Appropriated Economy," in *Investing in Natural Capital: The Ecological Economics Approach to Sustainability*, ed. A. M. Janson, M. Hammer, C. Folke, and R. Costanza (Washington, D.C.: Island Press, 1994).

5. Calvin L. Beale, "Salient Features of the Demography of American Agriculture," in David L. Brown, Donald Field, and James Zuiches, eds. *The Demography of Rural Life* (University Park, Pa.: Northeast Regional Center for Rural Development, University of Pennsylvania, 1993), publication NE-64.

6. Willard W. Cochrane, "A Food and Agriculture Policy for the 21st Century" (unpublished manuscript, 1999). Available from the author.

7. Steven C. Blank, *The End of Agriculture in the American Portfolio* (Westport, Conn.: Quorum Books, 1998).

8. Niles Eldredge, *Dominion: Can Nature and Culture Co-exist?* (New York: Henry Holt & Co., 1995).

9. Lance Gunderson, C. S. Holling, and Steve Light, eds., *Barriers and Bridges to the Renewal of Ecosystems and Institutions* (New York: Columbia University Press, 1995).

10. Herman E. Daly, *Beyond Growth: The Economics of Sustainable Development* (Boston: Beacon Press, 1996).

11. Aldo Leopold, *A Sand County Almanac* (New York: Oxford University Press, 1949).

12. Dennis Normile, "Variety Spices Up Chinese Rice Yields," *Science* 289 (2000): 1122–23.

13. Reg Morrison, *The Spirit in the Gene: Humanity's Proud Illusion and the Laws of Nature* (Ithaca, N.Y.: Cornell University Press, 1999).

14. Ibid., 190.

15. Ibid., 191.

16. Ibid.

17. David Abram, *The Spell of the Sensuous: Perception and Language in a More-Than-Human World* (New York: Vintage Books, 1996).

18. Maurice Merleau-Ponty, *The Primacy of Perception, and Other Essays on Phenomenological Psychology, the Philosophy of Art, History, and Politics* (Evanston, Ill.: Northwestern University Press, 1964).

19. Abram, *Spell of the Sensuous*, 27.

20. Ibid., 185.

21. Ibid., 183.

22. Ibid., 270.

23. Jane Lubchenco, "Entering the Century of the Environment: A New Social Contract for Science," *Science* 279 (1998): 491–97.

24. William Lockeretz, ed., *Visions of American Agriculture* (Ames, Iowa: Iowa State University Press, 1997).

25. Paula Hirschboeck, "Sophia: Ensouling Scholarship," *Network* 167, no. 1 (1999).

26. Herman E. Daly, John B. Cobb, and Clifford W. Cobb, *For the Common Good: Redirecting the Economy toward Community, the Environment, and a Sustainable Future* (Boston: Beacon Press, 1989).

27. Abram, *Spell of the Sensuous*, 274.

28. William E. Rees, "Scale, Complexity and the Conundrum of Sustainability," in *Planning Sustainability,* ed. Michael Kenny and James Meadowcroft (New York: Routledge, 1999).

A Pig's Tale: Marketing Stories for New Value Chains

1. Henry Ford, *My Life and Work* (New York: Garden City Publishing Co., 1922), 72.

2. Rick Levine, ed., *The Cluetrain Manifesto: The End of Business as Usual* (Cambridge, Mass.: Perseus Publishing, 2000), 151.

3. Mark Storlie, *Comparing Swine Niche Market Opportunities* (Ames, Iowa: Iowa State University Extension, 2001). Available at http://www.ipic.iastate.edu/information/IowaPorkNiche.pdf.

4. Michael E. Porter, *The Competitive Advantage of Nations* (New York: Free Press, 1990).

5. Ibid., 36.

6. Ibid., 37.

7. Ibid., 38.

8. Niman Ranch, Organic Valley, and America Fresh are a few of the niche market value chains already in operation, linking farmers, processors, and retailers to bring unique products into the marketplace.

9. Willard W. Cochrane, "A Food and Agriculture Policy for the 21st Century" (unpublished paper, 1999). Available from the author.

10. Michael Duffy, associate director of the Leopold Center, calculated that 81 per-

cent of today's farmland is still managed by small and midsize farmers, using Cochrane's categories, while 19 percent is being managed by large farms.

11. Stewart Smith, "Farming Activities and Family Farms: Getting the Concepts Right" (presentation at U.S. congressional Joint Economic Committee symposium, Agricultural Industrialization and Family Farms: The Role of Federal Policy, Washington, D.C., October 21, 1992).

12. Michael Duffy found that from 1950 to 1998, net farm income for Iowa farmers remained essentially flat, despite a thirteenfold increase in gross income.

13. Levine, ed., *Cluetrain*.

14. Jo Knowsley, "You Saw the Cow, Now Eat Its Meat," *The Mail on Sunday,* September 2, 2001, 37. (I am indebted to Iowa State student Matt Miller for this information.)

15. Michael Adams, *Better Happy Than Rich? Canadians, Money, and the Meaning of Life* (Toronto: Viking Press, 2001). For more information, see http://www.environics.ca.

16. Harvey Hartman, Hartman Group. Conference presentation, April 2000.

17. William D. Heffernan, Mary Hendrickson, and Robert Gronski, *Consolidation in the Food and Agriculture System* (Washington, D.C.: National Farmers Union, 1999). Available at http://home.hiwaay.net/-becraft/NFUFarmCrisis.htm.

18. Mary Hendrickson et al., *Consolidation in Food Retailing and Dairy: Implications for Farmers and Consumers in a Global Food System* (Washington, D.C.: National Farmers Union, 2001). Available from the author.

19. Ibid., 1.

20. Heffernan et al., *Consolidation*.

21. Kate Murphy, "Food Brokers Are Bigger, So Shelves Look Smaller," *New York Times,* September 2, 2001, 4.

22. Mary Swalla-Holmes, personal communication.

23. June Holley, personal communication, in reference to Murphy, "Food Brokers."

24. Theresa Marquez, personal communication.

25. Malcolm Gladwell, *The Tipping Point: How Little Things Can Make a Big Difference* (Boston: Little, Brown and Co., 2000).

26. Ibid.

27. For a great example of a set of core values designed for niche markets, see the "business principles" adopted by America Fresh, Inc., a California-based company that has developed a niche market value chain linking vegetable growers and restaurants through a Web-based farmer's market.

28. Reid Harward, "The Viridian Product Scanner," *Whole Earth,* Summer 2001, 71.

A Bright Future for "Farmers of the Middle"

1. Walter Isaacson, *A Benjamin Franklin Reader* (New York: Simon & Schuster, 2003), 146.

2. Ibid., 135.

3. U.S. Department of Agriculture, *2002 Census of Agriculture,* vol. 1, part 51, *Geographic Area Series: United States Summary and State Data* (Washington, D.C.: National Agricultural Statistics Service, 2004).

4. Thomas A. Lyson, G. W. Stevenson, and Rick Welsh, eds., *Food and the Mid-Level Farm: Renewing an Agriculture of the Middle* (Cambridge, Mass.: MIT Press, 2008).

Revitalizing Rural Communities: How Churches Can Help

1. Lewis Mumford, *The Golden Day: A Study in American Experience and Culture* (New York: Boni and Liveright, 1926), 30–31.

2. Curtis W. Stofferahn et al., "Growth Fundamentalism in Dying Rural Towns: Implications for Rural Development Practitioners," *Agriculture and Human Values* 8 (1991): 25–34.

3. Margaret L. Usdansky, "Need for Little Places Disappeared," *USA Today,* January 6, 1992.

4. Bill Holm, *The Music of Failure* (Marshall, Minn.: Plains Press, 1985), 56.

5. William Cronon, *Changes in the Land: Indians, Colonists, and the Ecology of New England* (New York: Hill and Wang, 1983), 127–28.

6. Frederick Turner, *Beyond Geography: The Western Spirit against the Wilderness* (New Brunswick, N.J.: Rutgers University Press, 1990), 256.

7. Karl N. Stauber, "Why Invest in Rural America—and How? A Critical Public Policy Question for the Twenty-first Century" (speech delivered for the Center for the Study of Rural America, Federal Reserve Bank of Kansas City, Mo., April 30, 2001). A version of this speech was published in *Economic Review,* second quarter 2001, 33–63. Available at http://www.kc.frb.org/PUBLICAT/ECONREV/PDF/2q01stau.pdf.

8. Stauber, "Why Invest."

9. See the work of William D. Heffernan and Mary Hendrickson on the evolution of consolidation in the food and agriculture system during the past 20 years: http://www.foodcircles.missouri.edu/consol.htm.

10. Frank Popper and Deborah Popper, *The Buffalo Commons Thesis of Land Use in the Great Plains Region*, sound recording of lecture presented during the University Lecture Series, Iowa State University, Ames, Iowa, 1993.

11. Willard W. Cochrane, "American Agricultural Abundance: Curse or Opportunity?" (unpublished paper, 2001). Available from the author.

12. Wendell Berry, *What Are People For? Essays* (San Francisco: North Point Press, 1990), 57.

13. Wendell Berry, *Sex, Economy, Freedom & Community* (New York: Pantheon Books, 1993), 128.

14. In conversations with numerous bankers in rural communities, almost without exception they agreed that further wealth concentration will not work for them; wealth expansion is needed instead.

15. John and Julie Gardner, "Dakotans Rarely Question Social, Economic Destiny," *Farm and Ranch Guide,* December 1992, 4.

16. Constance L. Falk, personal communication.

17. Muhammad Yunus, with Alan Jolis, *Banker to the Poor: Micro-Lending and the Battle against World Poverty* (New York: Public Affairs, 1999).

18. Ibid., 58.

19. See, for example, the Northwest Area Foundation's 2005 Annual Update, "Can

Communities Reduce Poverty?" Available from the Foundation, 60 Plato Boulevard East, Suite 400, St. Paul, MN 55107.

20. Gary Marzolf, "What Would You Do If Your Pastor Gave You $100?" *ABC Evening News,* March 3, 2006.

21. Jededia Purdy, "The New Culture of Rural America," *American Prospect,* December 20, 1999. Available at http://www.prospect.org/cs/articles?article=the_new_culture_of_rural_america.

22. John Thackara, *In the Bubble: Designing in a Complex World* (Cambridge, Mass.: MIT Press, 2005), 113.

Rethinking Food

1. Richard Heinberg, *Peak Everything: Waking Up to the Century of Declines* (Gabriola Island, B.C., Canada: New Society Publishers, 2007), 60.

2. Sarah Dewees, Linda Labao, and Louis E. Swanson, "Local Economic Development in an Age of Devolution: The Question of Rural Localities," *Rural Sociology* 68 (2003): 182–206.

3. Sonya Salamon, "From Hometown to Nontown: Rural Community Effects of Suburbanization," *Rural Sociology* 68 (2003): 1–24.

4. Heinberg, *Peak Everything,* 60.

5. Barbara Kingsolver, Steven L. Hopp, and Camille Kingsolver, *Animal, Vegetable, Miracle: A Year of Food Life* (New York: HarperCollins, 2007).

6. Richard Louv, *Last Child in the Woods: Saving Our Children from Nature Deficit Disorder* (Chapel Hill, N.C.: Algonquin Books, 2005).

7. See, for example, Takao Furuno, *The Power of Duck: Integrated Rice and Duck Farming* (Sisters Creek, Australia: Tagari Publications, 2001).

8. Peter Kaminsky, "In Season: Bearing Fruit . . . and Vegetables," *House and Garden,* November 2006, 74.

9. Anthony B. Freund, "Stone Barns: Farm Fresh," *Town and Country,* January 2005, 148–53.

10. Rene Ebersole, "Happy Meals," *Audubon,* March–April 2007, 84–91.

Using What We Know to Make a Difference

1. Paul Hawken, *Blessed Unrest: How the Largest Social Movement in History Is Restoring Grace, Justice, and Beauty to the World* (New York: Penguin, 2008), 25.

2. Wendell Berry, *The Way of Ignorance* (Emeryville, Calif.: Shoemaker & Hoard, 2005).

3. Ernest L. Schusky, *Culture and Agriculture: An Ecological Introduction to Traditional and Modern Farming Systems* (New York: Bergin & Garvey Publishers, 1989).

4. Herman Daly, "Economics in a Full World," *Scientific American,* September 2005, 100–107.

5. David C. Korten, *The Great Turning: From Empire to Earth Community* (Bloomfield, Conn.: Kumarian Press, 2006).

6. Scott Peters, "Changing the Story about Higher Education's Public Purposes and Work: Land-Grants, Liberty, and the Little Country Theater," Foreseeable Futures 6 (Syracuse, N.Y.: Imagining America, 2006).

7. Ellen Walsh, "Motivation for Grant from 'Soulless Entity' Should Be Examined," *Iowa State Daily,* September 17, 2008. Available at http://www.iowastatedaily.com/ar ticles/2008/09/17/opinion/doc48d1b57a4d0a0384527252.prt.

8. Wendy Wintersteen, "Feedback: Monsanto's Generous Gift Will Benefit Students," *Iowa State Daily,* September 9, 2008.

9. Janet Roe-Dupree, "When Academia Puts Profit ahead of Wonder," *New York Times,* September 7, 2008.

10. For an excellent essay on these deeper issues, see Inmaculada de Mel-Martin, "Biotechnologies Tweaking Here, Tuning There, Is That All We Need," *Philosophy Now,* July/August 2006, 35–37.

11. On this issue, two books are recommended: Gregory Bateson, *Mind and Nature: A Necessary Unity* (Cresskill, N.J.: Hampton Press, 2002), and Michael Polanyi, *The Tacit Dimension* (Garden City, N.Y.: Anchor Books, 1967).

12. See the UN report, *Millennium Ecosystem Assessment Synthesis,* available at http://www.millenniumassessment.org/en/index.aspx.

13. Julian Simon, for example, was a relentless proponent of this view.

14. Harvey Cox, "The Market as God," *Atlantic Monthly,* March 1999, 18–23.

15. Tim Kasser, *The High Price of Materialism* (Cambridge, Mass.: MIT Press, 2002).

16. Rob Hopkins, *The Transition Handbook: From Oil Dependency to Local Resilience* (White River Junction, Vt.: Chelsea Green Publishing, 2008).

17. "Subsidiary awareness" is the term Michael Polanyi uses to describe this personal knowledge phenomenon that we cannot escape. Subsidiary awareness is the reason why communal discourse among scientists is so important to the establishment of scientific knowledge.

18. See http://www.350.org/.

19. Judith D. Schwartz, "Communities Plan for a Low-Energy Future," *Christian Science Monitor,* September 11, 2008.

20. Frederick Kirschenmann, "Potential for a New Generation of Biodiversity in Agroecosystems of the Future," *Agronomy Journal* 99 (2007): 2.

21. Vicki Johnson, "Ohio Polyculturist Shares His Secrets of Biodiversity," *Farm World,* September 4, 2008.

22. Richard H. Thalere and Cass R. Sunstein, *Nudge: Improving Decisions about Health, Wealth and Happiness* (New York: Penguin Books, 2009).

23. Paul Roberts, *The End of Oil: On the Edge of a Perilous New World* (Boston: Houghton Mifflin Co., 2008), 14.

Selected Bibliography

Abram, David. *The Spell of the Sensuous: Perception and Language in a More-Than-Human World*. New York: Vintage Books, 1996.

Adams, Michael. *Better Happy Than Rich? Canadians, Money, and the Meaning of Life*. Toronto: Viking Press, 2001.

Advisory Panel on Food Security, Agriculture, Forestry, and Environment to the World Commission on Environment and Development. *Food 2000—Global Policies for Sustainable Agriculture*. London: Zed Books, 1987.

Altieri, Miguel A., ed. *Agroecology: The Scientific Basis of Alternative Agriculture*. Boulder, Colo.: Westview Press, 1987.

Artress, Lauren. *Walking a Sacred Path: Rediscovering the Labyrinth as a Spiritual Tool*. New York: Riverhead Books, 1995.

Avery, Dennis T. *Saving the Planet with Pesticides and Plastic: The Environmental Triumph of High-Yield Farming*. Indianapolis: Hudson Institute, 1995.

Baskin, Yvonne. *The Work of Nature*. Washington, D.C.: Island Press, 1997.

Bateson, Gregory. *Mind and Nature: A Necessary Unity*. Cresskill, N.J.: Hampton Press, 2002.

Benyus, Janine M. *Biomimicry: Innovation Inspired by Nature*. New York: William Morrow & Co., 1997.

Berman, Morris. *The Reenchantment of the World*. Ithaca, N.Y.: Cornell University Press, 1981.

Berry, Wendell. *Collected Poems, 1957–1982*. San Francisco: North Point Press, 1984.

———. *Sex, Economy, Freedom & Community*. New York: Pantheon Books, 1993.

———. *The Unsettling of America: Culture & Agriculture*. San Francisco: Sierra Club Books, 1977.

———. *The Way of Ignorance*. Emeryville, Calif.: Shoemaker & Hoard, 2005.

———. *What Are People For? Essays*. San Francisco: North Point Press, 1990.

Blank, Steven C. *The End of Agriculture in the American Portfolio*. Westport, Conn.: Quorum Books, 1998.

Brown, David L., Donald Field, and James Zuiches. *The Demography of Rural Life*. University Park, Pa.: Northeast Regional Center for Rural Development, University of Pennsylvania, 1993. Publication NE-64.

Brown, Lester R. *Eco-Economy: Building an Economy for the Earth*. New York: W. W. Norton & Co., 2001.

———. *Plan B 2.0: Rescuing a Planet under Stress and a Civilization in Trouble.* New York: W. W. Norton & Co., 2006.

———. *Tough Choices: Facing the Challenge of Food Scarcity.* New York: W. W. Norton & Co., 1996.

Buchanan, Mark. *Nexus: Small Worlds and the Groundbreaking Science of Networks.* New York: W. W. Norton & Co., 2002.

Buhner, Stephen H. *The Lost Language of Plants: The Ecological Importance of Plant Medicines to Life on Earth.* White River Junction, Vt.: Chelsea Green Publishing, 2002.

Bush, Vannevar. *Science, the Endless Frontier: A Report to the President.* Washington, D.C.: United States Government Printing Office, 1945.

Buttle, Frederick H., and Robert M. Goodman, ed. *Of Frankenfoods and Golden Rice: Risks, Rewards, and Realities of Genetically Modified Foods.* Madison, Wis.: Wisconsin Academy of Sciences, 2001.

Byrne, John, and Steven M. Hoffman, ed. *Governing the Atom: The Politics of Risk.* New Brunswick: Transaction Publishers, 1996.

Carroll, C. Ronald, John H. Vandermeer, and Peter Rosset, eds. *Agroecology.* New York: McGraw-Hill, 1990.

Charman, P. E. V., and B. W. Murphy. *Soils: Their Properties and Management.* South Melbourne, Australia: Oxford University Press, 2000.

Clancy, S. A. *Farming Practices for a Sustainable Agriculture in North Dakota.* Carrington, N.D.: North Dakota State University, Carrington Research Extension Office, 1993.

Cobb, John B. *Sustaining the Common Good: A Christian Perspective on the Global Economy.* Cleveland, Ohio: Pilgrim Press, 1994.

Cochrane, Willard W. *The Development of American Agriculture: A Historical Analysis.* Minneapolis: University of Minnesota Press, 1979.

———. *Farm Prices: Myth and Reality.* Minneapolis: University of Minnesota Press, 1958.

Conford, Philip. *The Origins of the Organic Movement.* Edinburgh: Floris Books, 2001.

Cronon, William. *Changes in the Land: Indians, Colonists, and the Ecology of New England.* New York: Hill and Wang, 1983.

Dahlberg, Kenneth A., ed. *New Directions for Agriculture and Agriculture Research: Neglected Dimensions and Emerging Alternatives.* Totowa, N.J.: Rowman & Allanheld, 1986.

Daly, Herman E. *Beyond Growth: The Economics of Sustainable Development.* Boston: Beacon Press, 1996.

———. *Ecological Economics and the Ecology of Economics: Essays in Criticism.* Northampton, Mass.: Edward Elgar, 1999.

Daly, Herman E., John B. Cobb, and Clifford W. Cobb. *For the Common Good: Redirecting the Economy toward Community, the Environment, and a Sustainable Future.* Boston: Beacon Press, 1989.

Danborn, David B. *Our Purpose Is to Serve.* Fargo, N.D.: North Dakota State University, Institute for Regional Studies, 1990.

Eldredge, Niles. *Dominion: Can Nature and Culture Co-Exist?* New York: Henry Holt & Co., 1995.

Estes, Clarissa Pinkola. *How to Love a Woman.* Boulder, Colo.: Sounds True Recordings, 1993.

Selected Bibliography

Faeth, Paul. *Paying the Farm Bill: U.S. Agricultural Policy and the Transition to Sustainable Agriculture.* Washington, D.C.: World Resources Institute, 1991.

Farvar, M. Taghi, and John P. Milton, ed. *The Careless Technology: Ecology and International Development.* Garden City, N.Y.: Natural History Press, 1972.

Flora, Cornelia Butler. *The Sustainable Agriculturist and the New Economy.* St. Paul, Minn.: Minnesota Department of Agriculture, Energy and Sustainable Agriculture Program, 1996.

Ford, Henry. *My Life and Work.* New York: Garden City Publishing Co., 1922.

Freyfogle, Eric T. *Justice and the Earth: Images for our Planetary Survival.* New York: Free Press, 1993.

Fromm, Erich. *To Have or to Be?* New York: Harper and Row, 1976.

Furuno, Takao. *The Power of Duck: Integrated Rice and Duck Farming.* Sisters Creek, Australia: Tagari Publications, 2001.

George-Warren, Holly, ed. *Farm Aid: A Song for America.* Emmaus, Pa.: Rodale Books, 2005.

Gladwell, Malcolm. *The Tipping Point: How Little Things Can Make a Big Difference.* Boston: Little, Brown and Company, 2000.

Grandberg-Michaelson, Wesley, ed. *Tending the Garden.* Grand Rapids, Mich.: Wm. B. Eerdmans Publishing Co., 1987.

Green, Tova, Peter Woodward, and Fran Peavey. *Insight and Action: How to Discover and Support a Life of Integrity and Commitment to Change.* Philadelphia: New Society Publishers, 1994.

Greider, William. *Who Will Tell the People: The Betrayal of American Democracy.* New York: Simon & Schuster, 1992.

Grumbine, R. Edward. *Ghost Bears: Exploring the Biodiversity Crisis.* Washington, D.C.: Island Press, 1992.

Gunderson, Lance, C. S. Holling, and Steve Light, eds. *Barriers and Bridges to the Renewal of Ecosystems and Institutions.* New York: Columbia University Press, 1995.

Hawken, Paul. *Blessed Unrest: How the Largest Social Movement in History Is Restoring Grace, Justice, and Beauty to the World.* New York: Penguin, 2008.

———. *The Ecology of Commerce: A Declaration of Sustainability.* New York: Harper Business, 1993.

Hawking, Stephen W. *A Brief History of Time: From the Big Bang to Black Holes.* Toronto: Bantam Books, 1988.

Heffernan, William D., Mary Hendrickson, and Robert Gronski. *Consolidation in the Food and Agriculture System.* Washington, D.C.: National Farmers Union, 1999. Available at http://home.hiwaay.net/~becraft/NFUFarmCrisis.htm.

Heinberg, Richard. *Peak Everything: Waking Up to the Century of Declines.* Gabriola Island, B.C., Canada: New Society Publishers, 2007.

———. *Power Down: Options and Actions for a Post-Carbon World.* Gabriola Island, B.C., Canada: New Society Publishers, 2004.

Heisenberg, Warner. *Physics and Philosophy: The Revolution in Modern Science.* New York: Harper and Row, 1958.

Hewitt, Tracy I., and Katie R. Smith. *Intensive Agriculture and Environmental Quality: Examining the Newest Agricultural Myth.* Greenbelt, Md.: Henry A. Wallace Institute for Alternative Agriculture, 1995.

Selected Bibliography

Hokikian, Jack. *The Science of Disorder: Understanding the Complexity, Uncertainty, and Pollution in Our World.* Los Angeles: Los Feliz Publishing, 2002.

Holm, Bill. *The Music of Failure.* Marshall, Minn.: Plains Press, 1985.

Hopkins, Rob. The *Transition Handbook: From Oil Dependency to Local Resilience.* White River Junction, Vt.: Chelsea Green Publishing, 2008.

Howard, Sir Albert. *An Agricultural Testament.* New York: Oxford University Press, 1943.

———. *The Soil and Health: A Study of Organic Agriculture.* Lexington: University Press of Kentucky, 2006.

Hudson, Lois Phillips. *The Bones of Plenty.* St. Paul: Minnesota Historical Society Press, 1984. Reprint of Boston: Little, Brown, 1962.

Imhoff, Daniel. *Farming with the Wild: Enhancing Biodiversity on Farms and Ranches.* San Francisco: Sierra Club Books, 2003.

Isaacson, Walter. *A Benjamin Franklin Reader.* New York: Simon & Schuster, 2003.

Jack, Zachary, M., ed. *Black Earth and Ivory Tower: New American Essays from Farm and Classroom.* Columbia, S.C.: University of South Carolina Press, 2005.

Jackson, Michael. *At Home in the World.* Durham, N.C.: Duke University Press, 1995.

Jackson, W., W. Berry, and B. Coleman, eds. *Meeting the Expectations of the Land.* Berkeley, Calif.: North Point Press, 1984.

Janson, A. M., M. Hammer, C. Folke, and R. Costanza, eds. *Investing in Natural Capital: The Ecological Economics Approach to Sustainability.* Washington, D.C.: Island Press, 1994.

Jenny, Hans. *Factors of Soil Formation: A System of Quantitative Pedology.* New York: McGraw-Hill Book Company, 1941.

Jung, L. Shannon. *Food for Life: The Spirituality and Ethics of Eating.* Minneapolis: Fortress Press, 2004.

Kasser, Tim. *The High Price of Materialism.* Cambridge, Mass.: MIT Press, 2002.

Keller, Evelyn Fox. *The Century of the Gene.* Cambridge, Mass.: Harvard University Press, 2000.

Kennedy, Paul M. *Preparing for the Twenty-first Century.* New York: Random House, 1993.

Kenny, Michael, and James Meadowcroft, ed. *Planning Sustainability.* New York: Routledge, 1999.

Kingsolver, Barbara, Steven L. Hopp, and Camille Kingsolver. *Animal, Vegetable, Miracle: A Year of Food Life.* New York: HarperCollins, 2007.

Koepf, Herbert H., Roderick Shouldice, and Walter Goldstein. *The Biodynamic Farm.* New York: Anthroposophic Press, 1989.

Korten, David C. *The Great Turning: From Empire to Earth Community.* Bloomfield, Conn.: Kumarian Press, Inc., 2006.

———. *When Corporations Rule the World.* West Hartford, Conn.: Kumarian Press, 1995.

Land Institute. *Land Report No. 67.* Salina, Kans.: Land Institute, 2000.

Lappé, Frances Moore, and Joseph Collins. *World Hunger: Twelve Myths.* New York: Grove Press, 1986.

Larson, Gary. *There's a Hair in My Dirt! A Worm's Story.* New York: HarperCollins, 1998.

Laszlo, Ervin. *Choice: Evolution or Extinction? A Thinking Person's Guide to Global Issues.* New York: G. P. Putnam's Sons, 1994.

Leopold, Aldo. *A Sand County Almanac.* New York: Oxford University Press, 1949.

Levine, Rick, ed. *The Cluetrain Manifesto: The End of Business as Usual.* Cambridge, Mass.: Perseus Publishing, 2000.

Lewontin, Richard C. *Biology as Ideology: The Doctrine of DNA.* New York: HarperPerennial, 1993.

———. *The Triple Helix: Gene, Organism, and Environment.* Cambridge, Mass.: Harvard University Press, 2000.

Lockeretz, William, ed. *Visions of American Agriculture.* Ames, Iowa: Iowa State University Press, 1997.

Logan, William Bryant. *Dirt: The Ecstatic Skin of the Earth.* New York: Riverhead Books, 1995.

Louv, Richard. *Last Child in the Woods: Saving Our Children from Nature Deficit Disorder.* Chapel Hill, N.C.: Algonquin Books, 2005.

Lowrance, Richard, Benjamin R. Stinner, and Garfield J. House, ed. *Agricultural Ecosystems: Unifying Concepts.* New York: John Wiley & Sons, 1984.

Lyson, Thomas A., G. W. Stevenson, and Rick Welsh, eds. *Food and the Mid-Level Farm: Renewing an Agriculture of the Middle.* Cambridge, Mass.: MIT Press, 2008.

Machiavelli, Niccolo. *The Prince.* Translated by George Bull. London: Penguin Books, 1999.

Madden, J. Patrick, and Scott G. Chaplowe, eds. *For All Generations: Making World Agriculture More Sustainable.* Glendale, Calif.: OM Publishing, 1996.

Magdoff, Fred, and Harold van Es. *Building Soils for Better Crops.* Washington, D.C.: Sustainable Agriculture Network, 2000.

Malthus, T. R. *An Essay on the Principle of Population: Text, Sources and Background, Criticism.* Edited by Philip Appleman. New York: W. W. Norton & Co., 1976.

Manning, Richard. *Food's Frontier: The Next Green Revolution.* New York: North Point Press, 2000.

Margulis, Lynn, and Dorion Sagan. *Microcosmos: Four Billion Years of Microbial Evolution.* New York: Summit Books, 1986.

McKibben, Bill. *Deep Economy: The Wealth of Communities and the Durable Future.* New York: Henry Holt and Co., 2007.

Mead, Sidney E. *The Lively Experiment: The Shaping of Christianity in America.* New York: Harper and Row, 1963.

Meadows, Donella H., Dennis L. Meadows, and Jorgen Randers. *Beyond the Limits: Confronting Global Collapse, Envisioning a Sustainable Future.* White River Junction, Vt.: Chelsea Green Publishing, 1992.

Merchant, Carolyn. *The Death of Nature: Women, Ecology, and the Scientific Revolution.* San Francisco: Harper and Row, 1983.

Merleau-Ponty, Maurice. *The Primacy of Perception, and Other Essays on Phenomenological Psychology, the Philosophy of Art, History, and Politics.* Evanston, Ill.: Northwestern University Press, 1964.

Moore, Thomas. *Care of the Soul: A Guide for Cultivating Depth and Sacredness in Everyday Life.* New York: HarperCollins, 1992.

Morowitz, Harold J. *The Emergence of Everything: How the World Became Complex*. New York: Oxford University Press, 2002.

Morrison, Reg. *The Spirit in the Gene: Humanity's Proud Illusion and the Laws of Nature*. Ithaca, N.Y.: Cornell University Press, 1999.

Mumford, Lewis. *The Golden Day: A Study in American Experience and Culture*. New York: Boni and Liveright, 1926.

National Academy of Sciences, Panel on Climate Variations. *Understanding Climate Change*. Washington, D.C.: National Academy of Sciences, 1975.

National Research Council. *Frontiers in Agricultural Research: Food, Health, Environment, and Communities*. Washington, D.C.: National Academies Press, 2003.

————. *Lost Crops of Africa*. Vol. 1, *Grains*. Washington, D.C.: National Academy Press, 1996.

————. *Soil and Water Quality: An Agenda for Agriculture*. Washington, D.C.: National Academies Press, 1993.

Nestle, Marion. *Food Politics: How the Food Industry Influences Nutrition and Health*. Berkeley: University of California Press, 2002.

Norberg-Hodge, Helena. *Ancient Futures: Learning from Ladakh*. San Francisco: Sierra Club Books, 1991.

Norton, Bryan G. *Sustainability: A Philosophy of Adaptive Ecosystem Management*. Chicago: University of Chicago Press, 2005.

Pagels, Heinz R. *The Cosmic Code: Quantum Physics as the Language of Nature*. New York: Bantam Books, 1982.

Peters, Scott. "Changing the Story about Higher Education's Public Purposes and Work: Land-Grants, Liberty, and the Little Country Theater." Foreseeable Futures 6. Syracuse, N.Y.: Imagining America, 2006.

Pimentel, David, and Marcia Pimentel. *Food, Energy, and Society*. New York: John Wiley, 1979.

Polanyi, Michael. *Knowing and Being: Essays by Michael Polanyi*. Edited by Marjorie Grene. Chicago: University of Chicago Press, 1969.

————. *Personal Knowledge: Toward a Post-Critical Philosophy*. Chicago: University of Chicago Press, 1958.

————. *Science, Faith and Society*. Chicago: University of Chicago Press, 1946.

————. *The Tacit Dimension*. Gloucester, Mass.: Doubleday & Co.,1983.

Pollan, Michael. The *Omnivore's Dilemma: A Natural History of Four Meals*. New York: Penguin Press, 2006.

Porter, Michael E. *The Competitive Advantage of Nations*. New York: Free Press, 1998.

Quinn, Daniel. *The Story of B*. New York: Bantam Books, 1996.

Raffensperger, Carolyn, and Joel Tickner, eds. *Protecting Public Health and the Environment: Implementing the Precautionary Principle*. Washington, D.C.: Island Press, 1999.

Rasmussen, Larry L. *Earth Community, Earth Ethics*. Maryknoll, N.Y.: Orbis Books, 1996.

Ravetz, Jerome R. *Scientific Knowledge and Its Social Problems*. New York: Oxford University Press, 1971.

Rifkin, Jeremy. *Beyond Beef: The Rise and Fall of the Cattle Culture*. New York: Dutton, 1992.

Rissler, Jane, and Margaret G. Mellon. *The Ecological Risks of Engineered Crops*. Cambridge, Mass.: MIT Press, 1996.

Roberts, Paul. *The End of Oil: On the Edge of a Perilous New World*. Boston: Houghton Mifflin Co., 2004.

Salatin, Joel F. *Salad Bar Beef*. Swoope, Va.: Polyface, Inc., 1995.

———. *You Can Farm: the Entrepreneur's Guide to Start and Succeed in a Farm Enterprise*. Swoope, Va.: Polyface, 1998.

Schneider, Stephen H. *The Genesis Strategy: Climate and Global Survival*. New York: Plenum Press, 1976.

Schumacher, E. F. *Good Work*. New York: Harper and Row, 1979.

———. *A Guide for the Perplexed*. New York: Harper and Row, 1977.

———. *Small Is Beautiful: Economics as if People Mattered*. New York: Harper and Row, 1973.

Schusky, Ernest L. *Culture and Agriculture: An Ecological Introduction to Traditional and Modern Farming Systems*. New York: Bergin & Garvey Publishers, 1989.

Sen, Amartya K. *On Ethics and Economics*. Oxford: Blackwell, 1987.

———. *Poverty and Famines: An Essay on Entitlement and Deprivation*. Oxford: Clarendon Press, 1981.

———. *Resources, Values and Development*. Cambridge, Mass.: Harvard University Press, 1984.

Senge, Peter M. *The Fifth Discipline: The Art and Practice of the Learning Organization*. New York: Doubleday & Co., 1990.

Seymour, John, and Herbert Girardet. *Far From Paradise: The Story of Man's Impact on the Environment*. London: British Broadcasting Corporation, 1986.

Shiva, Vandana. *The Violence of the Green Revolution: Third World Agriculture, Ecology, and Politics*. London: Zed Books Ltd., 1991.

Shiyomi, Masae, and Hiroshi Koizumi, eds. *Structure and Function in Agroecosystem Design and Management*. Boca Raton, Fla.: CRC Press, 2001.

Smith, Adam. *An Inquiry into the Nature and Causes of the Wealth of Nations*. 1776. Reprint, New York: Random House, 1994.

Soule, Judith D., and Jon K. Piper. *Farming in Nature's Image: An Ecological Approach to Agriculture*. Washington, D.C.: Island Press, 1992.

Stofferahn, Curtis W. *The North Dakota Centennial Rural Life Poll*. Grand Forks, N.D.: Social Science Research Institute, University of North Dakota, 1991.

Strange, Marty. *Family Farming: A New Economic Vision*. Lincoln, Neb.: University of Nebraska Press, 1988.

Swimme, Brian. *The Hidden Heart of the Cosmos: Humanity and the New Story*. Maryknoll, N.Y.: Orbis Books, 1996.

Swimme, Brian, and Thomas M. Berry. *The Universe Story: From the Primordial Flaring Forth to the Ecozoic Era—A Celebration of the Unfolding of the Cosmos*. San Francisco: Harper San Francisco, 1992.

Terkel, Studs. *Working: People Talk about What They Do All Day and How They Feel about What They Do*. New York: Pantheon Books, 1974.

Selected Bibliography

Thackara, John. *In the Bubble: Designing in a Complex World*. Cambridge, Mass.: MIT Press, 2005.

Thalere, Richard H., and Cass R. Sunstein. *Nudge: Improving Decisions about Health, Wealth and Happiness*. New York: Penguin Books, 2009.

Thompson, Paul. *The Spirit of the Soil: Agriculture and Environmental Ethics*. London: Routledge Publishing Co., 1995.

Toffler, Alvin. *Powershift: Knowledge, Wealth, and Violence at the Edge of the 21st Century*. New York: Bantam, 1990.

Turner, Frederick. *Beyond Geography: The Western Spirit against the Wilderness*. New Brunswick, N.J.: Rutgers University Press, 1990.

Van den Bosch, Robert. *The Pesticide Conspiracy*. Garden City, N.Y.: Doubleday & Co., 1978.

Walker, Brian, and David Salt. *Resilience Thinking*. Washington, D.C.: Island Press, 2006.

Walker, Casey, ed. *Made Not Born: The Troubling World of Biotechnology*. San Francisco: Sierra Club, 2000.

Welsh, Rick. *The Industrial Reorganization of U.S. Agriculture: An Overview & Background Report*. Greenbelt, Md.: Henry A. Wallace Institute for Alternative Agriculture, 1996.

Wessels, Tom. *The Myth of Progress: Toward a Sustainable Future*. Burlington, Vt.: University of Vermont Press, 2006.

Whitehead, Alfred North. *Science and the Modern World*. New York: The MacMillan Co., 1925.

Willard, Nancy. *The Sorcerer's Apprentice*. New York: Blue Sky Press, 1993.

Wills, Garry. *What Paul Meant*. Peabody, Mass.: Viking Press, 2006.

Woodruff, Paul. *Reverence: Renewing a Forgotten Virtue*. New York: Oxford University Press, 2002.

World Commission on Environment and Development. *Our Common Future*. Oxford, UK: Oxford University Press, 1987.

Yunus, Muhammad, with Alan Jolis. *Banker to the Poor: Micro-Lending and the Battle against World Poverty*. New York: Public Affairs, 1999.

Index

Index

Printed in the United States
by Baker & Taylor Publisher Services